LIVING RUINS

LIVING RUINS

NATIVE ENGAGEMENTS WITH PAST MATERIALITIES IN CONTEMPORARY MESOAMERICA, AMAZONIA, AND THE ANDES

Edited by
Philippe Erikson and
Valentina Vapnarsky

UNIVERSITY PRESS OF COLORADO
Louisville

© 2022 by University Press of Colorado

Published by University Press of Colorado
245 Century Circle, Suite 202
Louisville, Colorado 80027

All rights reserved
Manufactured in the United States of America.

 The University Press of Colorado is a proud member of the Association of University Presses.

The University Press of Colorado is a cooperative publishing enterprise supported, in part, by Adams State University, Colorado State University, Fort Lewis College, Metropolitan State University of Denver, University of Alaska Fairbanks, University of Colorado, University of Denver, University of Northern Colorado, University of Wyoming, Utah State University, and Western Colorado University.

∞ This paper meets the requirements of the ANSI/NISO Z39.48–1992 (Permanence of Paper).

ISBN: 978-1-64642-285-2 (hardcover)
ISBN: 978-1-64642-286-9 (ebook)
https://doi.org/10.5876/9781646422869

Library of Congress Cataloging-in-Publication Data

Names: Erikson, Philippe, editor. | Vapnarsky, Valentina, editor.
Title: Living ruins : native engagements with past materialities in contemporary Mesoamerica, Amazonia, and the Andes / edited by Philippe Erikson and Valentina Vapnarsky.
Description: Louisville : University Press of Colorado, [2022] | Includes bibliographical references and index.
Identifiers: LCCN 2022017997 (print) | LCCN 2022017998 (ebook) | ISBN 9781646422852 (hardcover) | ISBN 9781646422869 (ebook)
Subjects: LCSH: Indians of Central America—Antiquities. | Indians of Mexico—Antiquities. | Indians of South America—Antiquities. | Excavations (Archaeology)—Central America. | Excavations (Archaeology)—Mexico. | Excavations (Archaeology)—South America. | Indians of Central America—Material culture. | Indians of Mexico—Material culture. | Indians of South America—Material culture.
Classification: LCC F1219.7 .L57 2022 (print) | LCC F1219.7 (ebook) | DDC 972.8/01—dc23/eng/20220504
LC record available at https://lccn.loc.gov/2022017997
LC ebook record available at https://lccn.loc.gov/2022017998

The University Press of Colorado gratefully acknowledges the support of the Université Paris Nanterre toward this publication.

Cover photograph © Rafael Dorantes. Cover design by lendroit.com.

Contents

Acknowledgments vii

Introduction: Living Ruins and Vertiginous Vestiges: Amerindian Engagements with Remnants of the Past
   Philippe Erikson and Valentina Vapnarsky   3

1. Patrimonialization, Defilement, and the Zombification of Yanesha Cultural Heritage (Peruvian Amazonia)
   Fernando Santos-Granero   39

2. Maya Living Ruins: The Hidden Places of Interlocking Temporalities
   Valentina Vapnarsky   74

3. Deserted Ruins? Maya Tseltal and Ch'ol Engagement with Salient Spaces
   Cédric Becquey and Marie Chosson   104

4. Where Past and Future Meet... Abandoned Village Sites as Cruxes of Political, Historical, and Eschatological Narratives among the Chácobo of Bolivian Amazonia
   Philippe Erikson   124

5. Grounds for Political Claims: Earthworks and Anthropogenic Soils as Cultural Heritage and Sources of Territorial Legitimation in Brazilian Amazonia
    Pirjo Kristiina Virtanen and Emilie Stoll   147

6. Inca Vestiges: From Prehumans to New Agers
    Antoinette Molinié   172

7. The Topography of Time: Pre-Hispanic Ruins, Topographical Vestiges, and the Controversial Andean New Year (North Potosí, Bolivian Andes)
    Laurence Charlier Zeineddine   202

8. Disparate Ancestors: Convergent Pasts and the Dynamics of Heritage in the Southern Andean Altiplano (Uyuni, Bolivia)
    Pablo Cruz   232

Index   257
List of Contributors   271

Acknowledgments

This volume is an outcome of the project Fabriq'am: The Making of "Heritages": Memory, Knowledge, and Politics in Amerindia Today (ANR-12-CULT-005; 2013–2016) and the symposium "De l'évanescence et de la pérennité des choses" that was organized as part of the project's final international conference, "Culture: Modes d'emploi—La patrimonialisation à l'épreuve du terrain" (Paris, May 30–June 1, 2016). Over the years of the project and the days of the conference, we benefited from numerous discussions with the project members, and the new perspectives that emerged have greatly contributed to give shape to the book.

We are particularly grateful to the two anonymous reviewers for their stimulating suggestions as well as to our colleagues who generously commented on our introduction: Chloé Andrieu, Anath Ariel de Vidas, Margaret Buckner, Beth Conklin, Jacques Galinier, Vincent Hirtzel, and Fernando Santos-Granero. We are specially indebted to Rachel Fudge for her meticulous editing of the manuscript.

LIVING RUINS

INTRODUCTION

Living Ruins and Vertiginous Vestiges

Amerindian Engagements with Remnants of the Past

PHILIPPE ERIKSON AND
VALENTINA VAPNARSKY

Tikal in Guatemala, Machu Picchu in Peru, Marajó in Brazil, broken pots or stone axes in grandma's kitchen hut, most anywhere in Native South American or Mesoamerican villages . . . Many if not most contemporary Amerindian peoples live surrounded by ruins, relics, and other vestiges of the past. Some, such as pyramids, fortresses, or petroglyphs, are tokens of bygone splendor. Others are mere heaps of stone or modest pottery sherds half buried in backyards, swidden gardens, or the garbage piles of abandoned villages. Some are major tourist attractions, well-maintained or even revered; others are simply ignored, by locals and foreigners alike, or even feared, strictly avoided or kept secret. Such places are subject to elaborate narratives, surrounded by sophisticated beliefs, and loci of ritual activity, all of which have heretofore received insufficient attention. This volume aims to fill that gap by exploring Native South American and Mesoamerican peoples' perceptions and conceptions of ruins and other highly significant traces of the past. Our title, *Living Ruins*, emphasizes the fact that many Amerindians live in close proximity to such places and traces. It also alludes to these places' intrinsic "aliveness," antiquities (including ruins) often being endowed with agency of their own or secondhand animacy brought about by spirits entrapped in them. For better or for worse, vestiges are therefore both something you live with or near and also something with a life of their own.

https://doi.org/10.5876/9781646422869.c000

In recent years, the study of cultural heritage has become a major issue (Stefano and Davis 2016), and conservation or management of the so-called "sacred" sites and landscapes of the Americas has attracted increasing scholarly interest (Bassie-Sweet 2008; Liljeblad and Verschuuren 2019). In the aftermath of the Native American Graves Protection and Repatriation Act (NAGPRA) of 1990, the issue of cultural affiliation in relation to Native peoples' engagement with sites has triggered lively debates in the United States (Liebmann 2008). An important body of work has probed the extent to which procedures leading to cultural heritage are enmeshed with ethnic demands and Indigenous revival movements, ruins playing an essential role in this process (Sarmiento and Hitchner 2017). Community-based archaeology—along with its variants known as collaborative, intercultural, or multicultural archaeology—has also been booming, even deep in the Amazon rainforest (Cabral 2015; Schaan 2012). As a result, interaction between archaeologists and Native communities has been closely scrutinized, highlighting the ambivalence and multiplicity of these relationships, as well as the extent to which archaeological work has sometimes transformed the way Indigenous people envision their landscape, ethnicity, and history (Castañeda 1996; Gnecco and Ayala 2016; McAnany 2016; Smith and Wobst 2005). Several books explore the issue of past conceptions of ruins, especially in Mesoamerica (Kristan-Graham and Amrhein 2015; Stanton and Magnoni 2008). Ours is therefore not the first edited volume to examine Indigenous perceptions of ruins—or vestiges, as we prefer to call them to acknowledge the well-known fact that "authentic ruins" exist only as a product of modernity (Hell and Schönle 2009). However, such topics have been tackled mostly by archaeologists, with more weight placed on bygone rather than contemporary societies. Other contributions have generally come from scholars whose interests lie in geography, environmental studies, history, political science, sociology, or cultural studies (DeSilvey and Edensor 2013; Kaltmeier and Rufer 2016; Lazzara and Unruh 2009). Very little research has concentrated specifically on emic perspectives on vestiges, and most studies have focused on ethical and methodological matters rather than Indigenous narratives and perspectives. Insights from social and cultural anthropologists, with long-term commitment to deep ethnography, are still too rare and much in need.

This volume emerged from a major research program devoted to heritage and patrimonialization (or cultural heritagization) in Amerindian societies, with a strong emphasis on emic perspectives.[1] An international array of anthropologists, all experienced fieldworkers with strong command of vernacular languages, spent several years exchanging ideas about Amazonian, Andean, and Central American regimes of historicity. Particular attention was paid to how recently imported Western concepts such as folklore, heritage, and culture were incorporated into Native narratives and traditional ways of reconstructing and relating to the past (Ariel de Vidas and Hirtzel, forthcoming; Charlier and Vapnarsky 2017). The underlying conceptions of space and various theories of knowledge and materiality were also closely scrutinized. Along the way, an increasingly complex picture of ruins, vestiges, and other salient loci of remembrance gradually emerged from our collective endeavor. That led to this book, which aims to decenter and decolonize—and thereby recenter and revernacularize—the study of relationships between Indigenous people and the vestiges they live among. Our main goal is to draw a more meaningful portrait of Amerindian peoples' practices, discourses, and ideologies in relation to ruins, relics, and other vestiges, as envisioned from their own perspectives.

None of the authors are themselves members of Indigenous communities but all have spent decades learning Amerindian languages and gaining in-depth, intimate knowledge of the people they have lived with and learned from. Even though research conducted by Indigenous people is a welcome step on the road toward decolonizing imperial Western knowledge (Chilisa 2012; Fabian 2006; Rivera Cusicanqui 2012), anthropology is certainly not about *being* or *becoming* Other (Brown 2003; Kuper 2003). Even when practiced by Native anthropologists, its endeavor is rather to *understand* alterity and, through cultural translation, to make such understanding cross-culturally accessible. This is not cultural extractivism or appropriation but, we hope, a way to preclude narcissistic solipsism and pave the way to comparative analysis. In other words, anthropology is about getting to know people well enough to grasp *their* point of view and empathetically explain social phenomena from *their* perspective. It is an exercise in reflexive open-mindedness and ideational cross-fertilization. In this respect, the use of academic metalanguage to rephrase Indigenous concepts stands out as the best way to make the "exotic" "intelligible." However cumbersome, it is not meant to impose symbolic domination or a Western lens on Indigenous narratives but, on the contrary, to rid such narratives of what, inspired by Edward Said (1978), we might call the "orientalist" strings with which they come attached and acknowledge their sophistication. Ever since Boas, no better way has yet been found to celebrate cultural diversity and honor its complexity.

Another advantage of a methodology based on long-term commitment to extensive fieldwork is that it also wards off the predicament of what could be labeled "indigenized stereotype," that is, the mere repetition of cultural clichés that bilingual consultants have learned to flatter their "gringo" interlocutors, feeding them what they know they want to hear and/or are able to understand.

What Alcida Ramos (1998) aptly labeled "the hyperreal Indian" (the idealized simulacrum of an "Indian" created in the image of the NGOs' ethically perfect hologram) actually does exist . . . at least as a posture adopted for tourists or during superficial interviews. The contrast between what people tell each other in their native tongues and what they routinely tell outsiders when asked about the same topic is often enormous. This is particularly true when it comes to discussing foreign concepts such as cultural heritage and other interculturally sensitive issues.

REVISITING A FEW COMMON NOTIONS

Amerindian peoples maintain a vast array of attitudes and feelings with regard to vestiges, instantiated by ritual and nonritual acts as well as by explicit and implicit narratives. Yet, we often fail to perceive these because of false or stereotyped impressions brought about by our own conceptual toolkit. This invites us to question some of the pivotal terms of heritage studies. Specifically, we will concentrate on "ruins/vestiges," "sacredness," and "continuity."

Ruins/Vestiges

To start with, let us rehabilitate the concept of "vestiges," which we suggest using on par with, if not in preference to, "ruins." Most research on material traces of the past tends to concentrate on architectonic monuments. Yet such structures—usually abandoned, destroyed, or diverted from their original function, and often eroded and damaged by the passage of time—are far from being the only ones worthy of remembrance or invested with commemorative value. Natural elements such as mountains, boulders, waterfalls, lakes, and large trees are just as liable to emerge as pointers to past events. As one of our authors once phrased it, history can also be written in the landscape (Santos-Granero 1998), even if some of the markers are sometimes barely perceptible, covered by forest regrowth or layers of topsoil. Geoglyphs and mounds, palm groves, layers of pottery sherds, and even anthropogenic dark soils are some of the many other remnants or traces just as worthy of study as temples, pyramids, or palaces (Virtanen and Stoll, chapter 5). Even the seemingly spontaneous emergence of cultivars in Amazonian swidden gardens elicits numerous comments, being (correctly) assumed by Amerindians, such as the Makushi or the Matis, to be the product of past agricultural activity (Rival and McKey 2008). Plants can also be remainders, and thereby reminders, of the past.[2]

To take into account such variety, the term *vestiges* is often more adequate than *ruins*. *Vestiges* comes from the Latin *vestigium*, "a step's imprint," "a human or animal footprint," and this etymology points to the more general notion of "trace." In more recent times, in the wake of Romanticism, the term *vestiges* has taken on the meaning of what remains of something that has disappeared or been destroyed (Stoler 2008). This places emphasis on what no longer is, to the detriment of an indexical relation to a living presence, obscuring the fact that this indexical function is precisely what often makes vestiges so salient in Amerindian cultures. Throughout this volume, wherever Amerindian engagement with historicity is at stake, the term *vestiges* should be read with this etymology in mind, all romanticism aside.

Sacredness/Sacrality

Many writings on Amerindian conceptions of remnants of the past, especially pertaining to North America, highlight their so-called "sacredness" and the ensuing defilement that any form of trespassing on the part of outsiders might lead to (Sarmiento and Hitchner 2017). Yet, terms such as *sacred* or *sacredness* usually refer to very poorly defined notions used as catchall phrases by many scholars (as well as Amerindian stakeholders) when dealing with ruins or symbolically significant sites and landscapes. These notions, despite their long life in anthropology (Dehouve 2018), are not only fuzzy but have also been imbued with semantic and pragmatic thickness by colonial missionary conversions and recent evangelization processes. They have also been promoted on the world heritage scene by the UNESCO label "sacred site," which offers official recognition and protection, and has worked its way into Indigenous self-presentation narratives. It has also been influential in important constitutional changes. In Guatemala, the 1996 peace agreements after the civil war, which acknowledged human rights violations and violence against the Indigenous Maya population and enacted resettlement laws, also included an agreement on the right to access and perform ceremonies in "sacred sites" (*lugares sacrados*), including those in protected archaeological sites (Cojtí Cuxil 1994; Estrada Peña 2012).[3]

These side effects of colonial or modern proselytism often remain opaque to inside and outside viewers. Yet "holy" lurks behind the sacred, and the notion clearly points to Old World values. As shown by the essays in this volume, what is often lumped together under the umbrella label "sacred places" amounts to a ragtag collection of behaviors, attitudes, beliefs, and other ways of relating to such places (ritual activity, avoidance, intentional oblivion, narrative shifting, etc.), which beg for better understanding. Defining a place as "sacred" is just another way of saying it has some kind of importance but diverts us from trying to find out why. In an astute comment on this topic, Keith Basso encourages us to consider "that the Western Apache language contains three distinct words for marking *kinds* of 'sacredness,' that at least three Apache terms could be translated (all of them imprecisely) as meaning 'spiritual' or 'holy,' and that no Apache word comes even close to our own understanding of 'nature'" (1996, 156).

Aware of this predicament, and to bypass the term *sacredness*, some analysts of archaeological remains have mustered alternative notions such as *animacy* or *ensoulment* (Joyce and Barber 2015; Stross 1998). However, these concepts also have been prone to overgeneralization. Such is the case, for instance, for *ensoulment*, particularly in vogue with Mayanist archaeologists, which has been adopted from specific ethnographies and sometimes uncritically extended to other temporal and cultural contexts (Begel, Chosson, and Becquey 2022). We are still in need of more in-depth reflection on the different conceptions of places and the ontological or relational properties these new labels might be hiding. A distinction should be made between animating in the sense of "giving a soul" vs. "giving life to" vs. "allowing to be a living space," each implying quite distinct entities and sets of relationships (Pitrou 2015). The notion of "salient places," with salience precisely defined from a memorial, historical, experiential, sensorial, or praxis-oriented perspective—or any combination of the above—would certainly provide a better operational framework.

Atavistic Continuity

Finally, heritage stakeholders and sometimes even researchers frequently consider a given population's relationship with vestiges to be based on "continuity," in other words, as grounded in historical connections and ongoing long-term (continuous or occasional) occupation. In some countries, Native people are now asked, if not forced, to resort to DNA tests with increased frequency to prove the supposed "authenticity" of their "natural patrimonial rights" (Canghiari 2015, 8). Unless they are backed up by solid arguments attesting to "continuity," claims filed by contemporary occupants or would-be stewards of vestiges, however legitimate, face rejection. In a similar vein, plundering of antiques by Indigenous tomb raiders is often deemed to result from a break in the genealogical link between them and the original occupants of the looted sites. And, indeed, at first sight, opening ruins up for the taking would seem to require a lack of emotional attachment to them. Closer scrutiny, however, shows that ruptures in time, in Amerindian cultures, do not necessarily imply severance of links. Nor does breaking, throwing away, or selling something necessarily imply indifference (see note 10). The chapters in this volume demonstrate that people can be attached to vestiges precisely because of local conceptions of the historical, memorial, or ontological ruptures that are seen as having founded their attachment. Furthermore, the chapters show that commitment to vestiges often follows dashed lines. It comes and goes, which greatly helps create a sense of abandonment, whether seasonal, episodic, or permanent. As we shall see below, most Amerindians traditionally pay little attention to direct links of ancestry, and they are unlikely to spontaneously highlight continuous occupancy from initial construction to the present day as grounds for legitimizing their rights (Virtanen and Stoll, chapter 5; Vapnarsky, chapter 2). Consequently, even where human remains are involved, such considerations should certainly not appear as a sine qua non condition to back their claims and justify Indigenous rights in such matters. The Lenape, despite being the original occupants of the land (Banner 2005), have no chance to reclaim Manhattan on genealogic grounds alone, but that does not preclude legitimate attachment to their new homelands in Oklahoma, Ontario, Wisconsin, or elsewhere.

CONFLICTING CONCEPTIONS OF RUINS, VESTIGES, AND "CULTURAL HERITAGE"

Most tourists—as well as many scholars—tend to believe ruins are places to which Amerindians are emotionally and historically attached, insofar as they are crucial elements of their cultural heritage and reminders of their forebears' past magnificence. Yet, given how prone we Westerners are to automatically ascribing "cultural" value to just about any old heap of stones, isn't this a mere reflection of our own ethnocentrism? We celebrate and value hallmarks of cultural heritage and spend fortunes to restore, highlight, and catalog remembrance sites, significant landmarks, and just about any place esteemed for its symbolic, nostalgic, or spiritual qualities. We are fond of memorials and love to place commemorative plaques, headstones, and markers of all kinds to remind passersby that, for better or for worse, something noteworthy happened here or there. As tourists or citizens, we are attracted to such places, hoping we might find some kind of connection with the past just by being there, that we might somehow be able to "feel" historical meaning by our mere physical presence. But why should Amerindian peoples be governed by the same obsessions?

Admittedly, Western reasoning being highly contagious, this sometimes happens. In Mexico, near the Maya ruins of Palenque and Bonampak, for instance, Tseltal immigrants clearly adhere to patrimonial ideals: they explicitly object to ruins being systematically associated with Lacandon, the official, state-sponsored gatekeepers of the ruins, arguing that they, too, are equally heirs of Maya past splendor and are therefore wrongly being despoiled of their heritage (Balsanelli 2018). Actually, from an archaeological perspective, the Tseltal and the Lacandon are equally right, since they are indeed both of Maya descent, even though the ruins were built by the ancestors of yet other Maya groups, of the Cholan branch (Palka 2014, 31). Nearby, in Tikal (Guatemala), lowland Itza Maya ritual specialists—who consider themselves descendants of the pyramid builders—make a living as *guías espirituales*, spiritual guides, entertaining visitors with generic Maya ceremonies and esoteric calendrical lore they have recently learned from highland K'iche' teachers sponsored by the Academia de Lenguas Mayas (Estrada Peña 2012). Here, again, ruins can indeed appear as something to be proud of and identify with, specific ethnic affiliation notwithstanding. If direct genealogical links are critical for political claims, they are much less indispensable when it comes to spiritual matters.

The strategy of claiming rights derived from some generic Native birthright is more and more widespread. The Paresi (Mato Grosso, Brazil) have recently integrated local petroglyph designs into their repertoire of body-art motifs to stress alleged continuity and justify land claims (Prado Moi and Fagundes Morales 2016).[4] Likewise, much to the Wayana's dismay, the Teko in French Guiana are now making (and selling) painted wooden carvings resembling those of their Wayana neighbors, but they take great care to use "generic Indian" petroglyph motifs rather than traditional "specifically Wayana" designs, so as to legitimize their sharing in this valuable heritage (Kulijaman and Camargo 2012). Similar examples of neopatrimonial enthusiasm are found all across the Americas, sometimes even reaching religious proportions, especially in the wake of New Age movements (Galinier and Molinié 2013).

These newer examples reflect a clash between the younger generation's point of view and that of their elders. Lacandon youngsters, for instance, associate the ruins in their surroundings with their direct ancestors, whereas older people attribute them to the gods or to extinct, previous forms of humanity (Balsanelli 2018, 236–37). Referring to the Yucatec Maya, who also live near massively popular archaeological sites, Robert Redfield clearly stated, nearly a century ago, that "it is the archaeologist, not the Indian, who sees the grandson living in the broken shell of the grandfather's mansion; certainly the Indian attributes to the situation no quality of pathos. The ruins are not, for him, a heritage" (1932, 300). Their descendants now listen to Maya rap songs promoting essentialist views of their culture (Cru 2015) and collect (if only to sell) the ancient clay figurines that their ancestors systematically smashed for fear they might be housing harmful entities (Armstrong-Fumero 2001I, 73; 2014, 766). Likewise, around the Uyuni Salt Flat, Andean people have recently created new links to idealized ancestors attached to the ruins. As a result, weddings and other community celebrations are now held in places that once were feared and avoided (Cruz, chapter 8). Many Amazonian peoples, especially in Brazil, now cherish ritual objects they traditionally would have discarded once the ceremony was over (Brown 2003), and many have introduced indigenized reflexes of the word *cultura* into their lexicon (Carneiro da Cunha 2006; Vapnarsky, Yvinec and Becquey 2022). Deforestation transforms the memorial value of geoglyphs, and new laws on Indigenous territorial rights induce narrative shifts toward "ancestral land" and "sacred sites," in total contrast with the attitudes and beliefs of previous generations (Virtanen and Stoll, chapter 5). Radical changes, indeed, bringing about important consequences.

Increased acceptance of the Western notion of "cultural heritage" obviously results from contemporary contact with mainstream Western ideology. It also is frequently enhanced by financial incentives from the tourism industry, national funding programs, preservation NGOs, or a longing for autochthony driven by political agendas or territorial claims. "Cultural heritage" and stances of ancestrality are also critical in Indigenous environmental struggles against the encroachment of extractive industries (e.g., mines and pipelines) and, more basically, in support of land claims. In an age of neoliberal multiculturalism and contested indigeneities (Muehlmann 2009), what Molinié (2016) aptly labels "the globalization of tradition" has become a trend in most parts of the Americas. Yet, the chapters in this volume clearly show that "cultural heritage" is a foreign concept for most Amerindian peoples, who relate to vestiges in their own distinct ways. They might consider ruins to be theirs when they endorse a generic Pan-Amerindian status but adopt a different stance away from interactions with tourists and other outsiders. Village life and more intimate settings allow for the expression of distinct sets of ideas based on the Indigenous logics and emic perspectives this book intends to elucidate.

To state it slightly differently: in public discourse, archaeological sites are increasingly becoming "sacred" and promoted as tokens of "ancestral links with mother earth," emerging places of *sumak kawsay* (*buen vivir*, good life), and so on. Paradoxically, however, this often happens in cultural environments in which such notions previously had little if any relevance and sometimes even clashed with traditional ways of relating to the land and to the past. The incongruity of "sacredness" has already been discussed, and the numerous misunderstandings engendered by the artificial notion of *sumak kawsay* are well known (Alonso

González and Vásquez 2015; Quick and Spartz 2018; Whitten and Whitten 2015). Let us now turn to ancestrality, a pivotal concept with respect to *Living Ruins*.

WHERE HAVE ALL THE ANCESTORS GONE?

Diverging conceptions of generational succession and its ultimate meaning is certainly one of the main reasons why the notion of "cultural heritage" fails to account for Amerindian peoples' relations to vestiges. Ever since Manuela Carneiro da Cunha's groundbreaking work on this topic, the Americanist literature, especially that pertaining to Amazonia, has been replete with considerations about the clear-cut desire to sever links with the world of the dead (Carneiro da Cunha 1978; Fausto and Heckenberger 2007). This leads to what is commonly known as genealogical amnesia, which drives people to "remember to forget," to use a phrase coined by Taylor (1993). The Amazonian Matis, whose autonym is *deshan mikitbo* ("upstream people"), have a fitting metaphor to express their version of this script (Erikson 2007). They consider life to be a constant struggle to flow upstream, fighting against the current. Facing downstream, while bathing or even just lying in a hammock, is deemed to have detrimental effects on one's longevity and prospective progeny. Downstream is the realm of the deceased, of dangerous spirits, and, incidentally, of white men. The past is therefore literally what you turn your back to, certainly not what you celebrate and strive for. Such views—reflections of which are found among numerous other groups—have strong implications for how people relate to ruins, remnants, or relics of any kind.

Admittedly, Andean and Mesoamerican peoples are clearly less averse to the idea of continuity and the linear succession of generations (Fitzsimmons and Shimada 2011; Salas Carreño 2019). Centuries of missionary attempts to disconnect would-be converts from their "pagan" ancestors have not entirely succeeded. Ironically, destruction of the material basis of their "idolatry" often resulted in the emergence of ritually significant vestiges. But even in those Christianized parts of the Americas, identification with the primeval builders of surrounding ruins is far from systematic, and other cultural constraints can hinder strong connections with them or even emphasize ruptures. After all, acknowledging ancestrality does not necessarily imply your ancestors were the ones who built the surrounding structures. Many groups ascribe the origin of what are now ruins to entities of entirely different ontological status: monsters, giants, spirits, or protohumans from mythological times. In other cases, ruins might simply be neglected despite the acknowledgment of a direct link with the initial builders. The ruins are then left in the custody of whoever took over, such as "White Men" or any other type of malevolent being (Santos-Granero, chapter 1; Becquey and Chosson, chapter 3). People can also value "foreign" vestiges, such as those encountered during journeys or pilgrimages through other ethnic territories. When it comes to relating with ruins, acknowledgment of direct descent is therefore a secondary issue: links with the predecessors are sometimes explicitly rejected, or implicitly reframed, rupture being favored instead, as shown by several chapters in this volume (Charlier Zeineddine, chapter 7; Cruz, chapter 8; Vapnarsky, chapter 2; Virtanen and Stoll, chapter 5). This comes as no surprise, given the nature of Amerindian regimes of memory and the fact that the status of owner or master (even for kinship) is more often achieved than ascribed (Fausto 2012).

In Native South America, what is considered to be truly yours is that which you have produced with your hands, body, or thoughts, or which comes from the outside and which you have conquered in one way or another, rather than something you have inherited and that is passed down from one generation to the next. In fact, "appropriation" is often what makes "property" legitimate; in some instances, even proper names, far from being passed down through the family, are systematically acquired from the outside world of animals or enemies. This accounts for the fact that, even in the absence of genealogical connections, it is always possible to create links with whoever controls the vestiges, be they gods, spirits, guardians, or other entities. Seducing, appeasing, summoning, or taming them can suffice, and, in some cases, it is even possible to retrospectively "adopt" ancestors, as happens among the Quechua and those they call *awlanchis* (Salas Carreño 2019, 207). In other words, connections with vestiges do indeed occur, but they are based on very different grounds than those usually stressed when cultural heritage is at stake. Legacy is certainly not a key concept in Native America.

As an increasing volume of scholarly writing demonstrates, Amazonian "property rights," particularly with regard to land tenure, derive less from inheritance, transmission, and permanence than from appropriation, that is, the ability to gain control over a plot and temporarily become its custodian and master (Brightman, Fausto, and Grotti 2016; Santos-Granero 2015). Once the human owners/masters are gone, fallow fields, ancient households, and ruins are "up for grabs" by a vast array of ghosts, spirits, and malevolent entities, turning them into dangerous rather than attractive places. Even in areas of greater sedentism, such as the Andes and Mesoamerica, "taming" the land remains an issue (Vapnarsky, chapter 2). Moreover, in these regions, as Byron Hamann noted in a discussion of pre-Hispanic Aztec, Mixtec, and Yucatec conceptions of the physical remains of their past, "Ancient artefacts are repeatedly interpreted as relics from a previous age of creation, a flawed era subsequently destroyed to make way for the properly ordered 'present'" (2002, 352; see also López Luján 2019). The picture is very much the same for the Andes, as shown by the chapters by Charlier Zeineddine, Molinié, and Cruz in the present volume.

In such a context, Amerindians' seeming lack of interest in vestiges comes as less of a surprise. It reflects the low value they might place on past human production in general. As a man from Aguacatenango once told Marie Chosson (chapter 3): "[Archaeologists] found some old knives. Those are our ancestors' knives, but why would anyone want to keep them? I don't think they still cut, and we have our own knives. If I throw away my machete because it's broken, do you think my grandchildren want to keep it?" Charlier Zeineddine (chapter 7) also mentions antique Andean artifacts and pottery being discarded because of their uselessness. By contrast, other remnants receive a good deal of ritual attention, especially when they are linked to other-than-human creators (see below). Coin-sized pottery sherds found on the Andean altiplano are usually ignored, but sometimes they are used as currency for ritual payments to ancestral spirits. Antique half-moon-shaped stone axes figure prominently in one of the major Krahô rituals, to the extent that the Museu Paulista solemnly agreed to return one such axe from their collection in 1986. Yet: "an intriguing aspect of the entire episode was that *this axe was nothing like the ordinary archaeological ones that villagers found so easily in the ground*, which they repaired by replacing the handles, ornaments, and designs. Rather, this was their supreme axe, the one that used to sing in the distant past, the axe that, according to another narrative, their ancestors used to kill the chief of a mythical people known as the Cokãmkiere" (Melatti 1999, emphasis added). A fondness for the accumulation of ancient things has also been observed among the Trio, but as a token of one's own past achievements rather than as heirlooms (Grotti 2011). In Mesoamerica, it is not rare to find ancient half-broken clay figurines and even potsherds on the altar of ritual specialists, where they may act as therapeutic instruments, spiritual attractors, as well as connectors between distinct intersecting temporalities (Armstrong-Fumero 2011; Galinier 1990, 549; Hanks 2000). Whether artifacts are disregarded or not, Amerindian attitudes toward vestiges and remainders are essentially ambivalent, oscillating between fascination and fear and, in modern settings, between patrimonial pride and (meta-)physical discomfort. With regard to ruins, stakeholder communities seem stuck between the rock of strong incentives for preservation and the hard place of what McAnany (2016) aptly labels the "haunting question" of their eerie animacy.

RELUCTANT HEIRS, AMBIVALENT HERITAGE

Most of the case studies collected in this volume eloquently emphasize the very ambivalent nature of ruins for Amerindian peoples, and lead to the conclusion that, despite intensive exogenous efforts to turn vestiges into "precious heirlooms," "valued legacies," or "cultural heritage," many groups would rather relegate them to oblivion. Santos-Granero's contribution to this volume neatly makes this point (chapter 1). He argues that the Yanesha of Central Peru are strikingly averse to the current patrimonial frenzy, to the point of considering it a form of defilement or even "zombification," as he phrases it. In spite of their crucial role in Yanesha cosmology and mythology, places such as the Palmazú shrine, the Cerro de la Sal, and Juan Santos Atahuallpa's tomb are, to use the author's words, systematically "disremembered." Why glorify the past if it was anything but glorious and attracts the attention of frightful foreigners?

Becquey and Chosson (chapter 3), in their comparison of Tseltal and Ch'ol apprehension of vestiges, stress local disbelief that the impressive pre-Hispanic monuments that tourists flock to could ever have been built by ordinary humans. Their very imposing dimensions rule out the possibility that they could have been built solely through traditional construction techniques. Only spirits and chthonian entities could have erected them, just as stone churches—the real locus of village identity—could never have been built without the divine intervention of the Virgin Mary and her possum helpers. This translates into a lack of interest in ruins, which sometimes leads to the deterioration or even plundering of the structures.

Vapnarsky (chapter 2) argues that, despite their proximity to prominent tourist destinations like Tulum and Coba, few local Yucatec Maya have ever bothered to visit these ancient sites, in part because they have been dispossessed of their ownership and even custody. The ruins nonetheless play a crucial part in their history of past humanities and future expectations since, according to a well-known prophecy, the petrified beings who are entrapped in the stelae erected in those sites will someday arise and help the contemporary Maya recover their political autonomy. On the other hand, Yucatec Maya relate in more interactional and complex ways with discrete pre-Hispanic mounds and ancient—but comparatively modest—structures found closer to their homes. Although hidden in the forest, these locales, where rituals are held, have ambivalent properties that make them more significant than the major sites advertised by flashy road signs and on soft drink cans all around the so-called Riviera Maya.

Turning to Amazonia, Virtanen and Stoll (chapter 5) describe how the Apurinã and Manchineri people of the upper Purus River region tends to avoid the spectacular geometric precolonial earthworks that abound in their environment, considering them to be crucial sites of transformation, both dangerous and powerful. They are strictly avoided for the fear of the presences of nonhuman beings of the past. In his discussion of the Chácobo of the Bolivian lowlands, Erikson (chapter 4) shows how contemporary narratives about an abandoned village site in which an inordinate number of people died a couple of generations ago figure significantly in their eschatology. Recently deceased people are said to be systematically drawn there, even if they had never been there during their lifetimes. This provides yet another example of vestiges no one has any real reason to be attracted to, being places associated with malevolent spirits, to be avoided at all costs.

The last three chapters show that, albeit with some variation, Andean peoples display comparable attitudes toward ruins, relics, burial grounds, and other ancient remains. Bolivian and Peruvian peasants of Aymara or Quechua descent see such vestiges as traces of the *ch'ullpa*, the "people of before," who are considered predecessors rather than ancestors and whose ontological status differs from that of contemporary humans. Rather than initial creation followed by gradual evolution, Andean cosmology envisions the timeline as a succession of eras (called *pachakuti*), each ending in a major collapse that gives way to a new creation and new forms of life. Mummies, in that respect, are considered to be the charred remains of presolar beings who were burned to death when the current age, and its gruesomely radiant sun, came to be. Consequently, Charlier Zeineddine's interlocutors were rather appalled by former Bolivian president Evo Morales's attempts to glorify the past by celebrating a so-called "Andean New Year" in salient places like Tiwanaku. The government and contemporary activists[5] saw this celebration as an attempt to abolish the deleterious impact of European colonization by bridging the gap between contemporary society and the pre-Hispanic period when such structures were built. Ordinary peasants, on the other hand, expressed their fear of the calamities likely to result from such imprudent redemption of bygone times characterized by chaos and monstrosity.

Molinié's chapter 6 also addresses the perils ascribed to ruins by the Quechan-speaking inhabitants of Yucay, in Cuzco's Sacred Valley of the Andes, in Peru. As the author learned at her own expense when attempting to visit the monumental Inca stone terraces in the vicinity, contact with such places, especially burial sites, is particularly fearsome. They expose one to the daunting *ch'ullpa* disease, which causes the skin to burst at the joints to let the remnants of prehuman ancestors flow out in the form of yellowish burned bones. Cruz (chapter 8) describes how other Quechan speakers living much farther south, in the Salar de Uyuni region, resort to elaborate strategies to avoid similar perils. They take turns staffing the reception desks at local museums to minimize exposure time to the dangerous relics housed within. Human remains are shuffled around and elaborately staged to attract tourists, or to create new links with the past, but not without great anxiety and extreme caution. In the absence of high-tech solutions, such as the glass frames used by major museums to protect humans from too-intimate contact with the dangerous emanations from mummies and skeletons, sophisticated and exhausting prophylactic mental tricks are required. To avoid highly hazardous interactions with *ch'ullpas*, one must constantly endeavor to refrain from thinking about them (a strategy also noted by Charlier Zeineddine).

Most of the case studies in this book stress discontinuity between contemporary Amerindians and the "ancestors" deemed responsible for building ancient structures. All assert the ambivalence, complexity, and indirectness of the relations with the entities lurking in the ruins. Admittedly, especially nowadays, vestiges are increasingly becoming tokens, if not totems, of people's identity: they have been promoted to the status of relics of a glorious past, and they have become welcome (or unwelcome) sources of income, turning local people into willing (or unwilling) stakeholders in the tourism industry or partners in archaeological projects. Modern cults have also turned ruins and vestiges into places of worship, where capitalism, ecology, decolonization, and/or New Age values are celebrated from high noon to full moon, regardless of Amerindian conceptions of ritual time and cyclicity.[6] But, as we have seen, vestiges are just as often considered mere heaps of useless, even sinister, stones. Spirits often lurk nearby, and local Amerindians, unlike New Agers, refuse to consider them as a limitless source of positive energy or "good vibrations" (Molinié, chapter 6). In fact, it is precisely because of their connections with death and the past that ruins, fallow plots (their Amazonian counterparts), and other derelict spaces are as likely to be feared and avoided as placed in the spotlight. Yet, this is not to say that vestiges play a secondary role in Amerindian lives. On the contrary, they strongly impact Native people's daily routines and eventually work their way into their cosmology and value systems.

LIVING (WITH) VESTIGES

It should be clear by now that the title we chose for this book, *Living Ruins*, is not meant to promote the "lively," attractive, or positively valued properties of vestiges. Rather, it points toward our main interests: first, the way Native South and Mesoamerican peoples live in the vicinity of ruins and other remnants of the past; and, second, the way these places are brought to life, endowed as they are with moral and supernatural agency. The contributors to this collection are as interested in the connections to vestiges forged through daily habitation as in the elaborate metanarratives about them. So before turning to the more cosmological dimension of ruins, let us first concentrate on what actually happens there, on what people do and feel, in practical terms, during ordinary interactions, as well as on the tactile, sensorial, and emotional levels involved.

Obviously, people's intimate feelings and complex sensory experiences when they are near vestiges are far from easily observable. Yet, there are many hints that local inhabitants, when in the immediate vicinity of ruins, are likely to experience a certain sense of "otherness," or even a feeling of "otherworldliness," as though confronted with a different kind of reality. This could be due in part to physical characteristics such as thermal shocks, or the pleasant yet eerie sensation produced by cooler air blowing in and around ruins. Vapnarsky (chapter 2) describes how such breezes—produced by the presence of underground cavities—are deemed particularly dangerous. Anyone who chances to find a treasure near an ancient mound is encouraged to leave it untouched, for fear of the airborne diseases that likely surround the mounds. Pathogenic winds associated with ruins are also a recurring topic in the Andean and Amazonian regions, and are discussed in several chapters in this volume (Charlier Zeineddine, chapter 7; Erikson, chapter 4; Molinié, chapter 6; Santos-Granero, chapter 1).

Sounds produce another kind of connection with vestiges. The specific acoustics of ruins, in particular, elicit revealing comments. Echoing a foundational paper by Stobart (2006), Charlier Zeineddine (chapter 7) speaks of the "animated soundscape" and the intriguing "inner sounds" of Andean ruins, emphasizing the sound-based inferences they produce for the people who live near or approach them. Vapnarsky (chapter 2) makes similar observations for the Yucatec Maya, who also consider the sounds of conversations or domesticated animals sometimes heard in the midst of ruins a clear indexical sign—if not irrefutable proof—of the presence of invisible but perceptible entities living within them and within earshot of passersby. This phenomenon is widespread throughout Mesoamerica (López Austin 2015, 184). Much has been said about shape-shifting and the versatility of body forms in Amerindian ontologies, but the aural is often perceived as more difficult to alter, thus providing a more fundamental exposé of the true nature of beings (Civrieux 1980, 2–3).

In addition to such sensorial experiences of vestiges, there are other forms of everyday engagement with remnant spaces that stem from their economic potential and the opportunity they afford to collect useful products. Stones can easily be recycled as simple construction elements, for decorative purposes, or as raw material for ritual accessories. Even stelae can have what archaeologists and art historians call "reuse value" (Brilliant and Kenney 2011), just as bones from pre-Hispanic skeletons can be shuffled around, circulated, or reprocessed for prophylactic, commemorative, or ritual purposes (Cruz, chapter 8). Furthermore, the sale of antique artifacts has become an economically significant activity for many Amerindians. These practices can lead to conflict between Indigenous peoples—seen as a threat to the sites—and the official heritage wardens or scholars who are ethically obliged and legally empowered to protect them (Armstrong-Fumero 2014). Even more significantly, perhaps, the lands surrounding ruins are, as we shall see, noteworthy for the subsistence activities they allow.

It is now well-known that Amerindians have greatly altered the layout of their lands, modifying the distribution of plants and animals and the quality of soils in ways favorable to human occupation. Protásio Frikel (1978), for trees, and Olga Linares (1976), for animals,[7] were among the first scholars to raise these groundbreaking ideas, which were systematically explored and popularized in the late 1980s by the innovative work of Bill Balée, followed by a whole generation of academics (Balée 2013; Balée and Erickson 2006; Posey and Balée 1989). Unsurprisingly, prehistoric occupancy and contemporary fertility are closely associated in both subsistence practices and symbolism, as was neatly summarized by Descola's concept of "domesticated nature" (Descola [1986] 1996). Ancient sites, in the most down-to-earth manner, are bountiful places, lush with natural (and supernatural) resources.

Throughout the Americas, dark soil is considered the most fertile, and black earth is systematically associated with past human (or superhuman) occupation (Virtanen and Stoll, chapter 5). In Brazil, black soil is known as "*terra preta do Indio*," or "black earth of the *Indian*" (emphasis ours). In Maya lowlands, ancient occupation is seen as a criterion of soil fertility (Teran and Rasmussen 1994, 139), and the Otomi go so far as to collect soil from graveyards to fertilize their fields (Galinier 1990, 544–45).[8] Ancient dwelling sites are also places where products are plentiful, some of them not found elsewhere. In the Andes, where potatoes are commonly considered akin to human beings (and dehydrated ones, known as *chuño*, akin to mummies), wild varieties known as *atuq papa* are found in abundance near ruins, where they are collected for their medicinal properties (Hall 2018). Corrals are built close to the ruins so that llamas and other animals may profit from the energy emanating from them (Salas Carreño 2019). In Amazonia, people such as the Matis can name a wide range of semiferal edible plants found in abandoned gardens, which grow nowhere else. More significantly, the peach palms (*Bactris gasipaes*) planted in their swiddens—a major seasonal foodstuff—give fruit only several years after the gardens have been abandoned. This important resource is thus closely associated with the past, previous generations, and estranged ancestral spirits (Erikson 1996). A comparable situation holds for the *ramon* (breadfruit tree, *Brosimum alicastrum*) in the Maya lowlands of Mesoamerica. Indigenous populations as well as archaeologists acknowledge that this tree, which is especially valued for its fruit, abunds near ruins.[9]

RUINS AND VESTIGES AS LIVING ENTITIES

Another facet of vestiges is precisely their aliveness, that is, their qualification as "living" entities. Hence, "living vestiges" means living amid them but not just in a topological sense. Ruins provide more than a picturesque setting for daily lives: they can also be considered partners in their own right, imbued with what Santos-Granero (2008) aptly calls an "occult life." Ruins are neighbors as much as they are material background. They are far from inert, but the difficulty lies in understanding precisely what makes these places alive and what distinguishes them from other living materials, places, or landscapes. As shown by a growing body of recent work, the "living" properties of things may be related to distinct types of processes and causalities, from being alive to giving life (Hall 2012 for the Andes; Pitrou 2015 for Mesoamerica; Praet 2013 for lowland South America). Regarding vestiges, this aliveness may be provided by the nature of the materials they are made of, by the acts involved in their transformation into artifacts and structures, by the presence of nonhuman (spiritual, divine, prehuman, or other) inhabitants of the "abandoned" places, or by their multitemporal liminal status. In fact, these different aspects are usually found in various combinations that uphold the aliveness of vestiges.

In the Andes and Mesoamerica, most salient vestiges are made of stone, and stones themselves are imbued with their own life and agency. From an Andean perspective: "every wrinkle in the Earth's physiognomy—every hill, knoll, plain, ridge, rock outcrop, or lake—possesses a name and a personality" (Allen [1988] 2002, 41). In this animated rocky landscape, mountains, ghost-haunted ruins, but also lithomorphs and other "sacred" lithic entities, as well as many other stones (*waqa, illa,* "compassion stones"), have "vital energy" (*sami*) and agency in their own way (Allen 2016; Charlier Zeineddine, chapter 7). The compact hardness of stones, which makes them—like certain skeletal remains—powerful agents and the most potent sources of energy, does not imply "a lack of animation, but a different state of animation–life crystallized, as it were" (Allen [1988] 2002, 63). This force is intimately connected with lightning and sunlight, whose power they absorb and condense.

In Mesoamerica, the Lacandon paradigmatically illustrate a situation in which stones are endowed with life. Much like the Yucatec Maya (chapter 2), they believe that all minerals live and die, and that their power or vital energy can be increased by their relation to ancient places and the fact that they have been manufactured. The Lacandon consider that all stones are alive and have a soul called "*pixan*" (for this reason, some are placed near houses to protect them), but those found in ruins—as well as lithic figurines, especially those in jade and obsidian—are imbued with a specific power. Thus, until recently small effigies or simple stones collected in ruins were put in each of the incense burners that represented their gods, in the ritual process of giving them life. The incense burners' renovation ritual consisted of extracting the stone from the previous incense burner (which amounted to "killing" it) and inserting it into the new one (Balsanelli 2018, 448; Tozzer 1907, 109–10).[10] The lithic objects collected in the ruins—terrestrial home of the gods—carry with them some sort of divine essence or potentiality and a vital energy or force, which derive from their origin and are transmissible.

While today's Lacandon have abandoned these religious practices, beliefs related to the living properties of stones found in ancient places still thrive. We experienced this recently during a stroll in the forested surroundings of a Lacandon village, in Chiapas. A young boy showed us the way to *la tumba de los dioses* ("the tomb of the gods"), guiding us along a steep, narrow path to an overhanging boulder about four or five meters high, at the foot of which a score of burners were scattered around, in rather poor condition, even broken. These living burners had been discarded by the last of the traditional Lacandon leaders to still possess them, their sons refusing to worship them any longer. The site had been desecrated by outsiders, and most of the stones had been stolen. The burners were therefore solemnly pronounced dead. However, our young guide was eager to direct our attention to the boulder that covered the "tomb," which he described as a "meteorite." The first time his father had taken him to visit the site, two years earlier, it was much smaller, but, he insisted, it had since grown several meters taller and was bound to keep on growing in the coming years. The burners had been "killed" by the theft of the stones they contained, but we were later told that in this process, their vital energy and the force imbued by ancestral gods had been transferred to the bigger rock, as shown by the dazzling speed with which it grew. In other words, the burners had been traditionally brought to life by powers given by the living stones found in ruins, but now their mere presence had turned the place itself into a powerful ruin. The depiction of the boulder as a "meteorite" was but a modern and sidereal version of the belief that ruins are the terrestrial abode of gods who came down from the skies.

Such examples show that although ruins can be seen as the products and traces of temporal ruptures, they nonetheless find their way into a continuous flow of animated, personified, living, and powerful materialities and places that make for a complex cultural landscape. This may come as no surprise given the generalized Amerindian proclivity toward animism, brought to light by recent research in the era of the "ontological turn" (Holbraad and Pedersen 2017). This also accounts for the fact that, sometimes, ruins are not even the most prominent item of the series: in chapter 3, Becquey and Chosson show that in Chiapas the ruins of temples and pyramids seem to contain far less agency than mountains or churches, and therefore attract far less attention. In an animist environment, ghosts are but one example of a vast array of spirits, and ruins are but one of the many salient places of the ontological landscape.

In addition to minerals, other materials, such as ceramics, textiles, or bare bones, may also act as powerful living indexes of the past. In the Andes, skeletal remains are reputably liable to bleed (Charlier Zeineddine, chapter 7), and they are sometimes kept to "protect" places (Allen [1988] 2002, 59). As previously mentioned, Molinié (chapter 6) explains how she discovered that approaching a prehuman tomb causes one's joints to snap open and release the small bones of *machu* ancestors. Like other similar illnesses of the underworld, this widely diffused Andean affliction (called *ch'ullpasqa*, "of the *ch'ullpa*") is a progressive possession that culminates in the affected person's transformation into a *ch'ullpa*, a thing from the ancient times (Cruz, chapter 8). Because of their potential to reactivate the past, and despite the danger this entails, human remains are typically manipulated to reanimate (if not recreate) vestiges. This ranges from the tradition of keeping and carrying along your forebears' bones, found in some nomadic groups of lowland South America (Erikson, chapter 4), to the possible rearrangement of bones into new bodies and settings. One of the most striking examples of the latter is provided by Cruz in chapter 8, with his description of the baroque and composite scenography that the Quechua people around the Uyuni Salt Flat in Bolivia create with mummies and pre-Hispanic bones (and even Christian ones when there are not enough of the former), ornamented with old and new paraphernalia, such as dogtags, hats, and textiles. These recreations are motivated by Native people's desire to attract tourists to local "handmade" museums, but the fact that they eventually become new places for community rituals shows that there are more than economic reasons behind such reshuffling of bones. Foreigners are sometimes accused of robbing and manipulating bones for their own selfish purposes. Santos-Granero (chapter 1) reports how, according to a Yanesha myth, white men once defiled the tomb of Yompor Santo', one of their heroes, and used the bones to make an effigy in his exact likeness. They did such a good job that the figure could never be disassembled and became a church effigy, an object of adoration by the white people.

This dismembering, reshuffling, and reassembling of human remains is similar to the way stones from ruins may be regularly combined with artifacts to create new ritual objects. However, rocks and stones found in ruins probably receive extra attention for having been manipulated in ancient times. They differ from other minerals in that they were cut, polished, piled up, and arranged in architectonic structures that are quite distinct from those built by contemporary humans. Some took the form of spectacular terraces, stunning pyramids, and other impressive monuments. Amerindians willingly offer comments on the unimaginable, perhaps even supernatural, techniques that must have been employed to produce them. Tales are told of stones that were lightened, lifted by giants, made to float by magic whistling, or modeled like clay in days when they were astonishingly more malleable than the unbreakable stones of our times (see Cruz, chapter 8; Charlier Zeineddine, chapter 7; Vapnarsky, chapter 2). Such amazing manufacturing techniques are evidence of the builders of these places and contribute to the energy they are deemed to hold. This energy results from activity itself, as work in its Mesoamerican sense produces more than mere materiality: it more basically generates life, cosmic movements, and social relations (Ariel de Vidas 2020). An extreme form of manufacturing transformation can be found in the process of petrification, or lithomorphosis, which is sometimes seen as the origin of vestiges in the Andes (Charlier Zeineddine, chapter 7), Mesoamerica (Vapnarsky, chapter 2) and, to a lesser degree, Amazonia (Santos-Granero, chapter 1; Daillant 1997; Renard-Casevitz 1993).[11]

This etiology of the ruins accounts for the continuing presence, in contemporary spaces, of beings from bygone times congealed in stones or stelae. The petrified beings eventually appear as much more than mere memorial indexes. In the present day, at recurrent moments (e.g., certain phases of the moon's cycle in the Andes) or at expected times announced by prophecies (in Mesoamerica), the beings are resuscitated, or rather they regain their dormant mobility. Lithomorphosis is but a temporary state, epitomizing the petrified beings' potential to reunify disconnected temporalities, in a convincing demonstration of the temporal coalescence that vestiges seem to stand for.

The "aliveness" of vestiges may therefore also be largely attributable to their inhabitants, either those whose residual presence is cast in stones, stelae, drawings, or bones or spirits attracted to them at a later time. Ruins can be considered the proper homes of guardian spirits (Vapnarsky, chapter 2) or the dwellings of inadvertently perspectivist gods for whom the remnants of stone buildings look just like the thatched-roof houses in which humans live (Boremanse 1998, 202; McGee 1983, 107). In cases such as these, vestiges appear as mirror images of human dwellings, brought to life by their spirit or godlike occupants whose ontological statuses might be totally different but whose lifestyles mimic those of ordinary humans living in quasi-ordinary villages. Temporal ruptures and ontological disconnections notwithstanding, parallel yet contemporary worlds are thereby established. Ruins can thus be seen as putative extensions of the domestic space in the forest or nonurban space or, conversely, as metaphoric mountains or marks of wilderness in the urban landscape (Halperin 2014.) This leads to hybrid ambivalent forms, beyond nature and culture (Descola [2005] 2013), deemed extremely powerful because of their very liminality and hence considered to be highly significant features of the surroundings.

CONCLUSION

The chapters in this volume present case studies of Amerindian societies ranging from the Uyuni Salt Flat in southern Bolivia to the highlands of Chiapas in Mexico. Despite such broad geographical spread, the chapters show striking similarities in the conception of vestiges, one of the most obvious being that they are systematically imbued with liminal and ambivalent properties. Loci, or even agents, of complex interactions rather than objects of memorial veneration, vestiges act as multitemporal shifters par excellence. In Halperin's synthesis, vestiges "materialize a distant past and they contribute to a constantly shifting present . . . both stable and unstable, exerting an enduring presence while continuously reconstituted by those who live amongst them" (2014, 339).

Vestiges are not just a time capsule but an ontological space shuttle. In disruptive—yet alluring—ways, they connect the living with the dead, people with spirits, and present-day humans with long-gone prehumans. They make the past merge with the ongoing present and other parallel times but link them with much more complex, albeit tenuous, threads than those that string together the continuous lines presupposed by the Western model of cultural heritage, based on ancestry and inheritance. Vestiges are also thought of as places that link seemingly opposite spaces, for example, high and low territories, mountains and caves, the celestial world and the underworld, urban and forest realms. Usually simultaneously dangerous and beneficial, they are either avoided or are approached with great precautions, despite their appealing fertility and active powers. They may be diverse in nature and be integrated into complexes of animated places, of which they may not be the most salient. They are sometimes ignored, until patrimonialization rears its ugly head and places them in the spotlight.

In this introduction, we have mainly focused on the similarities found across the continent, more patent between the Andes and Mesoamerica, but sometimes shared with Amazonian societies as well. However, the chapters also show some contrasts, both clear-cut and subtle, expressing internal and sociohistorical conditions, that should be further explored. In particular, the chapters show differing regimes of historicity and the role of forgetfulness in the construction of the collective self, and with conceptions of personhood and nonhuman agencies. Such contrasts involve colonial history and Catholicism's influence on eschatology and the properties of ritual objects and places. They also may stem in part from the affordances of the surroundings and their topography, the presence (or absence) of stones, and environmental factors in the durability of architectural structures, for example, the high, freezing, rocky plateau of the Andes, where everything remains, as opposed to the tropical forest of Amazonia, where everything seems to quickly disintegrate.

Another factor to consider is the influence of postcolonial politics, which led to the implementation, in the 1940s, of national institutes dedicated to the conservation and promotion of "culture heritage" and officially recognized "archaeological sites."[12] Imbued with the Western ethics of preservation at all costs, these government agencies have usually dispossessed autochthonous populations of access to ruins or, at the very least, distanced stakeholder communities from stewardship of their ancestral landscape. Initially driven by similar ideologies in all countries, these politics have subsequently diverged, evolving over the years in different directions. In Guatemala, for instance, the Maya gained the official right to practice (nontouristic) ritual ceremonies on archaeological sites in the 1990s, whereas Mexico still forbids—or only barely tolerates—them.

Over the years, and increasingly so in recent times, Amerindian peoples' territorial, cosmological, and eschatological conceptions have undergone rapid transformations. Relationships with ruins are no exception, however counterintuitive this notion might seem due to our preconceived idea that, because of their antiquity, ruins would serve as the cornerstone of continuity. The chapters in this volume show that vestiges are indeed a moving field, where notions have been rapidly altered in the wake of historical transformation. Among the numerous factors involved, the influence of colonial and Christian values are of prime importance, as they have radically transformed ritual life and relationships with (dead) souls and ancestors. This has sometimes brought about the rejection of the "pagan" past associated with vestiges. Sometimes, to the contrary, vestiges have been promoted to main protagonists of millenarian scenarios. Moreover, the systematic employment of local Native people as workforce in archaeological excavations was certainly influential. It left them with the challenge of reconciling their traditional views of ruins with the academic narratives and sometimes-transgressive routines regulating the manipulation of ancient artifacts. Modern nationalism has at times led to the expropriation of the Indigenous past by the state, resulting in a rather complex situation, often exacerbated by NGOs and other patrimonial stakeholders. The promotion of cultural heritage has led to identity crises and conflicts surrounding issues of cultural legitimacy and ownership of the past. Living vestiges are increasingly subject to litigation. Consequently, as the loci of political and symbolical antagonism, they have acquired cultural hybridity of sorts, in a no-man's land halfway between zombification and glorification.

On a more theoretical level, in articulation with more ethnographically oriented perspectives, the chapters in this volume engage with recently debated issues, such as regimes of historicity and regimes of knowledge, cultural landscapes, conceptions of personhood, artifacts, and materiality. They also add to the lively body of work on the invention of tradition, neo-Indianism, and what we might call "retrospective ethnogenesis." Beyond nourishing these crucial topics in anthropology, our in-depth case studies, we hope, facilitate a greater self-expression of Indigenous views and provide new insights for a better understanding of the various types of reactions to and involvement with cultural heritage programs among Native communities, with implications for project management.

The chapters reveal a plurality of ways of perceiving and interacting with vestiges across the Americas. Many shared principles have emerged, as well as significant variations between different groups, resulting from different historical and sociocultural backgrounds. Clearly, ruins and remnants are highly salient for Amerindian peoples, but in subtle ways, whose complexity is only reinforced by the strings attached to their rephrasing in the idiom of cultural heritage. Illustrating and deciphering such complexity is the task we have taken on in this ethnographic survey of traces of the past in Native Amazonia, Mesoamerica, and the Andes.

OVERVIEW OF THE VOLUME

In chapter 1, Fernando Santos-Granero studies how Yanesha people have been particularly reluctant in the face of past attempts at patrimonialization. Through an analysis of the historical trajectories of three ancient landmarks, he explores the reasons for such reticence, arguing that it might stem from the association of these sites with the notions of *a'tsepeñets*, a failure in the completion of ritual undertakings, which leads to defilement, and *a'mchecheñets*, the desoulment or loss of the power/vitality contained in ritual objects, places, and specialists as a consequence of defilement. Patrimonialization efforts, in this context, are perceived as a "zombification" of cultural heritage, that is, a futile attempt to bestow a semblance of life on something long dead and deprived of mystical power. Santos-Granero proposes that Western proclivity for patrimonialization, on the one hand, and Yanesha reticence, on the other, express not only contrasting regimes of historicity but, above all, opposing cultural strategies for building collective identities—one based on an "omnivorous memory," the other on "selective amnesia." A greater openness to patrimonialization in recent years could be a sign, however, of a shift in Yanesha modes of conceiving and dealing with the past.

Maya conceptions of history are structured by beliefs in a series of successive humankinds that have left their imprint on today's landscape. As revealed by the chapters in the book, however, different Maya groups instantiate this articulation between history and cultural space in contrasting ways. In chapter 2, Valentina Vapnarsky shows that the Lowland Yucatec Maya conceive of vestiges as living, generative and demanding places, which interlace different temporalities, either as dwellings of the guardian spirits—creating a memory of ritual practice, habituation, and regeneration—or as remnants of petrified dormant cultures, instantiating a state of latency and constitutive of cyclical history. They act as sorts of hotspots that materialize the tenuous and essential link between humans of previous eras, spirits, and the deceased. Their significance is based on different kinds of ruptures: historical, ontological, and interactional. The need to maintain these constitutive ruptures also accounts for the eagerness of some Maya communities to protect ruins from being explored, studied, rebuilt, or turned into touristic attractions.

In contrast, in chapter 3 Cédric Becquey and Marie Chosson illustrate how some of the Maya people from Chiapas—the Chol and the Tseltal in particular—consider nearby monumental sites only as remains of past corrals in which previous forms of humanity herded monstrous jaguars. Ordinary Maya humans, they believe, could not possibly have erected such imposing, oversized, roofless, and collapsed structures. The true chosen homes of spirits, souls, saints, and other celestial entities worthy of worship are mountains, volcanoes, ravines, and churches—not ruins. These constitute their "salient spaces," objects of collective interest, because their physical and/or symbolic characteristics make them distinctive on the community landscape. The authors highlight the diversity of places where community memories are anchored, places where spirits, souls, and other entities are thought to be present. They also show how the dynamic and mobile nature of these entities, and the constant nurturing of relations with them, facilitates the possibility for new sites to emerge, often in connection with a desire to regain control of previously neglected places. These salient sites include archaeological ruins, due to their contemporary significance gained thanks to new discourses circulated by state-induced patrimonialization.

In chapter 4, Philippe Erikson argues that, in the Bolivian Amazon, Chácobo eschatological narratives have paradoxically turned a place of past suffering into one of future bliss. He explains how the remains of Xabaya, an abandoned village site where innumerable people suffered and died in the late 1960s, have retrospectively been ascribed positive valency: the spirits of recently deceased people, instead of being scattered in the forest as they used to be, now allegedly converge there for lavish postmortem feasts. He argues that this paradoxical turn of events probably results from the fact that Xabaya is also remembered as the locus of emerging ethnicity, being the place where the battered remaining members of previously dispersed groups, each bearing a different name, regrouped and collectively became the unified people now known as Chácobo. The ruins of Xabaya, far from vestiges of unspeakable past suffering, became a marker of collective identity, converting remainders of a past tragedy into hopes for a bright future.

In chapter 5, Pirjo Kristiina Virtanen and Emilie Stoll's study shows that for the Amazonian Apurinã and Manchineri, the massive geometric ditched enclosures of their landscape are places to avoid rather than to celebrate. They perceive them as homes to master spirits and other monstrous beings, unfit for human occupation. However, in their attempts to communicate their territorial and political claims to national authorities and administrative agents, they now describe them as precolonial ceremonial sites and also use them to advocate Indigenous politics and advance their territorial demands. Local riverside (*caboclo*) populations in Brazilian Amazonia make similar uses of dark soils, which, being associated with precolonial Indigenous settlements and practices, are apt indicators of their ancestors' presence, thus backing their claims of continuous occupancy. This chapter offers a fine-grained analysis of these contextually variable "shifting narratives."

Antoinette Molinié's chapter 6, on the Andes, concentrates on various properties and new functions ascribed to Inca vestiges. She first shows how, in the Yucay region, Inca vestiges occupy a liminal zone that turns them into powerful instruments for structuring the space and time of Quechua communities. For this very reason, locals also see them as places replete with malevolent energy, affecting boundary body parts such as skin and joints. Next, concentrating on vestiges that cater to tourists, such as the ruins of Pisac, she explores the contrast between Western tourists' and local inhabitants' conceptions of these places. The former see them as sources of positive energy, which they come to capture, while the latter fear the malevolent energy emanating from these ruins, which might ravish them in a much more threatening way and must therefore be pacified by offerings and sacrifices. In sum, the high-tech pilgrims visit the ruins hoping to enhance their well-being by absorbing the very forces Quechua people would rather placate.

In her study of Native conceptions of geological formations in North Potosí (Bolivia), Laurence Charlier Zeineddine (chapter 7) shows the intimate and complex relationship between the Quechua-speaking people and these stone formations, believed to have been built by presolar people who were then petrified. These remnants of past generations are considered to be still active today and liable to prey on humans. Indigenous communities therefore were shocked by President Evo Morales's attempts to glorify Native tradition by reinstating the so-called "Andean New Year" and "solar time." For Indigenous communities, the major archaeological sites where the Andean New Year ceremonies take place are not historical landmarks but rather anchors in a complex multitemporal landscape. They seek rupture rather than continuity with past periods, and consider it safer to willingly avoid thinking about stony remains of the past rather than to celebrate them in the name of decolonization. Nowadays, Catholics and Pentecostals display diverging discursive and interactional commemorative practices, but as far as vestiges of the past are concerned, they all prefer to obliterate or forget them altogether, rather than integrate and highlight them.

The last chapter, by Pablo Cruz, explores a paradigmatic case that neatly weaves together the different threads of this book. He observes how the booming tourist industry that has recently emerged in the Uyuni Salt Flat and surrounding region has brought about an intense process of patrimonialization of both the natural landscape and the local culture. Incentivized by tourist agencies, the state, international aid agencies, NGOs, and some academics, campesino Indigenous communities have begun to produce their own tourist attractions. Many of these center on archaeological ruins that have consequently gained the previously nonexistent local status of "material and tangible heritage," "archaeological site," or "patrimonial artifact." Over the course of just a few years, mummified human remains and ancient objects began to appear in caves, organized into elaborate scenes, many of them idealized reconstructions, and so did different types of museums, sometimes involving the ransacking of other caves and reshuffling of the objects and mummies (*ch'ullpas*) they contained. In a cultural context where Inca burial sites are full of supernatural dangers, this dynamic has led local inhabitants to critically reconsider conflicting narratives about the past. It has provoked redefinitions of the past and of material vestiges that articulate what, to Western eyes, might appear to be incompatible realities.

NOTES

1. Fabriq'Am: The Making of "Heritages": Memory, Knowledge, and Politics in Amerindia Today, ANR-12-CULT-005 (2013–2016). See: http://fabriqam.hypotheses.org/.

2. Conklin (2020) has recently discussed the association of Native Amazonian death rituals with the animacy of social-ecological life processes.

3. In this context, Maya intellectuals actively engaged in the struggle for the official recognition of the concept of "sacred sites" (*lugares sagrados*), which they saw as an alternative to Western notions such as ruins or archaeological sites. In 2012, they lost their fight for the creation of a Congreso Nacional de Lugares Sagrados (National Conference of Sacred Sites) in which representatives of the Indigenous groups of Guatemala would have participated in decision-making about the management, preservation, and use of archaeological sites, as well as research. For practical and legal information about Guatemalan sacred sites, see the official site: http://mcd.gob.gt/unidad-de-lugares-sagrados-y-practica-de-la-espiritualidad-maya/.

4. This is reminiscent of the stylistic changes in the Amazonian Yawanawa's body paint after the filming of the 2009 blockbuster *Avatar*, for which one of their most charismatic leaders had served as consultant. In need of a model for the aliens, the film's director drew inspiration from the face paintings of people he had been introduced to by his consultant (a man known as Tashka). This resulted in simplified, grossly enlarged, and rather kitsch motifs that ultimately became trendy among the Yawanawa, who started copying these copies of their former selves. A fine example of how overplaying one's own traditions can retrospectively result in their literal alienation!

5. Including scholars of Aymara descent such as Fernández-Osco (2016).

6. New Agers sunbathing at noon to benefit from the sun's energetic rays is seen as dangerous, if not ludicrous, by local people (Molinié, chapter 6).

7. Olga Linares's innovative concept of "garden hunting" could be extended to

account for "fallow hunting" as well, considering the propensity of fallows to attract game. Someone might also relate this to the belief, commonly held in Amazonia, that ancestors return from the land of the dead and offer their bodies, transformed into peccaries, to feed their descendants.

8. Bernardino de Sahagún, in the famous sixteenth-century Florentine Codex, documented conceptions of Central Mexican Nahuas, stating: "*Ay otra manera de tierra fértil, que se llama Callali, quiere decir, tierra donde a estado edificada alguna casa, y después que se cava y siembra es fértil* [There is another kind of fertile soil, which is called Callali, meaning soil on which a house had been built, and afterwards it is dug out, planted and fertile]" (our translation, Libro undecimo, folio 227 verso). (Thanks to Dominique Michelet for pointing out this reference.)

9. Until recently, breadfruit was used as a maize substitute in periods of famine, and it is known to attract animals who feed on its leaves and fruits (Atran, Lois, and Ucan Ek' 2004; Dussol et al. 2017; Ford and Nigh 2016; Lambert and Arnason 1982).

10. That many artifacts found in ruins are broken might be seen as a clear indication that they are "dead." In the Andes, textiles are thought to be alive, which is why cutting them (to make handicrafts, for instance) is a rather dubious act (Desrosiers 2000). Yet, caution is always required. For example, Fernández-Osco (2016, 341) reports a case in an Aymara community where ancient weavings, deemed harmless, had been sold; but the purchasers were asked to return them after an epidemic outbreak, which was assumed to have been caused by this offense to the community's ancestors.

11. Following Daillant (1997), a process of "salification" akin to "petrification" accounts for the mythological origin of the major source of salt in Chimane territory: a salt mountain said to result from the transformation of a goddesses and her newborn child into salt, the life-giving product people now avidly collect there. Petroglyphs and other markings in the rocks in the vicinity are allegedly the footprints left by the goddess's demiurge husband to let people know where to find salt, while the nearby river is allegedly the amniotic liquid of the divine parturient: a living, watery ruin of sorts.

12. The Brazilian Instituto do Patrimônio Histórico e Artístico Nacional (IPHAN) was originally created as the Serviço do Patrimônio Histórico e Artístico Nacional (SPHAN) in 1937. The Mexican Instituto Nacional de Antropología e Historia (INAH) was created in 1939, and the Guatemalan Instituto de Antropología e Historia de Guatemala (IDAEH) in 1946. In Colombia, the ICANH (Instituto Nacional de Antropologia e Historia) was formed by the fusion of the Servicio Arqueológico Nacional (founded in 1938) and the Instituto Etnológico (founded in 1941). In Peru, the Museo Nacional de Antropología y Arqueología gained autonomy from the Museo Nacional in 1945, whereas in Bolivia, the Instituto Nacional de Arqueología (INAR) was founded in 1975 as an offshoot of the Instituto Indigenista Boliviano of which Carlos Ponce Sangines became head in 1952.

REFERENCES

Allen, Catherine. (1988) 2002. *The Hold Life Has: Coca and Cultural Identity in an Andean Community*. 2nd ed. Washington, DC: Smithsonian Institution.

Allen, Catherine. 2016. "Stones Who Love Me: Dimensionality, Enclosure and Petrification in Andean Culture." *Archives des Sciences Sociales des Religions* 174: 327–46.

Alonso González, Pablo, and Alfredo Macías Vázquez. 2015. "An Ontological Turn in the Debate on *Buen Vivir–Sumak Kawsay* in Ecuador: Ideology, Knowledge, and the Common." *Latin American and Caribbean Ethnic Studies* 10 (3): 315–34.

Ariel de Vidas, Anath. 2020. "Collaborative Anthropology, Work, and Textual Reception in a Mexican Nahua Village." *American Ethnologist* 47 (3): 289–302.

Ariel de Vidas, Anath, and Vincent Hirtzel, eds. Forthcoming. "The Terms of Culture: Idioms of Reflexivity among Indigenous Peoples in Latin America." Special issue, *Anthropological Quarterly* 95(3).

Armstrong-Fumero, Fernando. 2011. "Words and Things in Yucatán: Post-Structuralism and the Everyday Life of Mayan Multiculturalism." *The Journal of the Royal Anthropological Institute* 17 (1): 63–81.

Armstrong-Fumero, Fernando. 2014. "A Tale of Two Mayan Babels: Vernacular Histories of the Maya and the Limits of Inclusion." *Ethnohistory* 61 (4): 761–84.

Atran, Scott, Ximena Lois, and Edilberto Ucan Ek'. 2004. *Plants of the Petén Itza' Maya*. Ann Arbor: Museum of Anthropology, University of Michigan.

Balée, William. 2013. *Cultural Forests of the Amazon: A Historical Ecology of People and Their Landscapes*. Tuscaloosa: University of Alabama Press.

Balée, William, and Clark Erickson. 2006. *Time and Complexity in Historical Ecology: Studies in the Neotropical Lowlands*. New York: Columbia University Press.

Balsanelli, Alice. 2018. "Jach Winik y winik: La construcción de la identidad y de la alteridad entre los lacandones de la selva chiapaneca." PhD diss., Escuela Nacional de Antropología e Historia (ENAH), México.

Banner, Stuart. 2005. *How the Indians Lost Their Land: Law and Power on the Frontier*. Cambridge, MA: Harvard University Press.

Bassie-Sweet, Karen. 2008. *Maya Sacred Geography and the Creator Deities*. Norman: University of Oklahoma Press.

Basso, Keith. 1996. *Wisdom Sits in Places: Landscape and Language Among the Western Apache*. Albuquerque: University of New Mexico Press.

Begel, Johann, Marie Chosson, and Cédric Becquey. 2022. "Materiality and Agentivity of Structure Building Rituals: An Ethno-Archaeological Approach." In *Materiality in Rituals: A Deep History of Ritual Practice*, edited by Lisa Johnson and Rosemary Joyce. Louisville: University Press of Colorado.

Boremanse, Didier. 1998. "Representaciones metafóricas de los antiguos mayas en mitos y ritos religiosos lacandones." *Journal de la Société des Américanistes* 84 (1): 201–9.

Brightman, Marc, Carlos Fausto, and Vanessa Grotti, eds. 2016. *Ownership and Nurture: Studies in Native Amazonian Property Relations*. London: Berghahn Books.

Brilliant, Richard, and Dale Kinney, eds. 2011. *Reuse Value: Spolia and Appropriation in Art and Architecture from Constantine to Sherrie Levine*. Surrey/Burlington: Ashgate.

Brown, Michael. 2003. *Who Owns Native Culture?* Cambridge, MA: Harvard University Press.

Cabral, Mariana Petry. 2015. "Traces of Past Subjects: Experiencing Indigenous Thought as an Archaeological Mode of Knowledge." *Journal of Contemporary Archaeology* 2 (2): S4–7.

Canghiari, Emanuela. 2015. "Se réapproprier le passé: Patrimonialisation des vestiges archéologiques et inclusion sociale en Lambayeque (Pérou)." *Cahiers des Amériques latines* 78: 115–31.

Carneiro da Cunha, Manuela. 1978. *Os mortos e os outros: Uma análise do sistema funerário e da noção de pessoa entre os índios Krahó*. São Paulo: Editora Hucitec.

Carneiro da Cunha, Manuela. 2006. *"Culture" and Culture: Traditional Knowledge and Intellectual Rights*. Chicago: Prickly Paradigm Press.

Castañeda, Quetsil. 1996. *In the Museum of Maya Culture*. Minneapolis: University of Minnesota Press.

Charlier, Laurence, and Valentina Vapnarsky. 2017. "De l'évanescence et de la pérennité des choses (dans les sociétés amérindiennes)." *Nuevo Mundo Mundos Nuevos*. Accessed August 2019. https://doi.org/10.4000/nuevomundo.70174.

Chilisa, Bagele. 2012. *Indigenous Research Methodologies*. Thousand Oaks, CA: Sage.

Civrieux, Marc de. 1980. *Watunna: An Orinoco Creation Cycle*. Edited and translated by David M. Guss. San Francisco: North Point Press.

Cojtí Cuxil, Demetrio. 1994. *Políticas para la reivindicación de los mayas de hoy (Fundamento de los Derechos Específicos del Pueblo Maya)*. Guatemala: Cholsamaj.

Conklin, Beth. 2020. "Burning Sorrow: Engaging the Animacy of Social-Ecological Life Processes in Native Amazonian Death Rituals." In *Sacred Matter: Animacy and Authority in the Americas*, ed. Steve Kosiba, John Wayne Janusek, and Thomas B.F. Cummins, 105–29. Washington, DC: Dumbarton Oaks.

Cru, Josep. 2015. "Bilingual Rapping in Yucatán, Mexico: Strategic Choices for Maya Language Legitimation and Revitalization." *International Journal of Bilingual Education and Bilingualism* 20 (5): 481–96.

Daillant, Isabelle. 1997. "'Porque ahí parió la mujer de Dios': La salina de los Chimanes y la destrucción de sus petroglifos." *Boletín SIARB (Sociedad de Investigación del Arte Rupestre de Bolivia)* 11: 53–67.

Dehouve, Danièle. 2018. "*Sacer* et sacré, notion *emic* et catégorie anthropologique." In *Autour de la notion de sacer*, edited by Thibaud Lanfranchi, 17–37. Rome: École française de Rome.

Descola, Philippe. (1986) 1996. *In the Society of Nature: A Native Ecology in Amazonia*. Cambridge: Cambridge University Press.

Descola, Philippe. (2005) 2013. *Beyond Nature and Culture*. Chicago: University of Chicago Press.

DeSilvey, Caitlin, and Tim Edensor. 2013. "Reckoning with Ruins." *Progress in Human Geography* 37(4): 465–85.

Desrosiers, Sophie. 2000. "Le tissu comme un être vivant? À propos du tissage à quatre lisières dans les Andes." In *Lisières et bordures: Actes des premières journées d'étude de l'association française pour l'étude du textile (Paris, 13–14 juin 1996)*, edited by Françoise Cousin, Sophie Desrosiers, Danielle Geirnaert, and Nicole Pellegrin, 117–25. Bonnes: Les Gorgones.

Dussol Lydie, Michelle Elliott, Dominique Michelet, and Philippe Nondédéo. 2017. "Ancient Maya Sylviculture of Breadnut (*Brosimum alicastrum* Sw.) and Sapodilla (*Manilkara zapota* [L.] P. Royen) at Naachtun (Guatemala): A Reconstruction Based on Charcoal Analysis." *Quaternary International* 457: 29–42.

Erikson, Philippe. 1996. *La griffe des aïeux: marquage du corps et démarquages ethniques chez les Matis d'Amazonie*. Paris/Louvain: Peeters.

Erikson, Philippe. 2007. "Faces from the Past. Just How 'Ancestral' Are Matis 'Ancestor Spirit' Masks?" In *Time Matters: History, Memory and Identity in Amazonia*, edited by Carlos Fausto and Michael Heckenberger, 219–42. Gainesville: University of Florida Press.

Estrada Peña, Canek. 2012. "Lugares sagrados de los mayas de Guatemala: otra manera de pensar el patrimonio cultural." *KinKaban Revista digital del Centro de Estudios Interdisciplinarios de las Culturas Mesoamericanas* 2: 52–58.

Fabian, Johannes. 2006. "The Other Revisited: Critical Afterthoughts." *Anthropological Theory* 6 (2): 139–52.

Fausto, Carlos. 2012. "Too Many Owners: Mastery and Ownership in Amazonia." In *Animism in Rainforest and Tundra: Personhood, Animals, Plants and Things in Amazonia and Siberia*, edited by Marc Brightman, Vanessa Elisa Grotti, and Olga Ulturgasheva, 29–47. New York: Berghahn.

Fausto, Carlos, and Michael Heckenberger, eds. 2007. *Time and Memory in Indigenous Amazonia*. Gainesville: University Press of Florida.

Fernández-Osco, Marcelo. 2016. "Bolivian Archaeology: Another Link in the Chain of Coloniality?" In *Indigenous Peoples and Archaeology in Latin America*, edited by Cristóbal Gnecco and Patricia Ayala, 333–44. London/New York: Routledge.

Fitzsimmons, James, and Izumi Shimada, eds. 2011. *Living with the Dead: Mortuary Ritual in Mesoamerica*. Tucson: University of Arizona Press.

Ford, Anabel, and Ronald Nigh. 2016. *The Maya Forest Garden: Eight Millennia of Sustainable Cultivation of the Tropical Woodlands*. New York: Routledge.

Frikel, Protásio. 1978. "Áreas de arboricultura pré-agrícola na amazônia: Notas preliminares." *Revista de Antropologia* 21 (1): 45–52.

Galinier, Jacques. 1990. *La Mitad del Mundo—Cuerpo y cosmos en los rituales otomíes*. Mexico: Universidad Nacional Autónoma de México, Centro de Estudios Mexicanos y Centroamericanos, Instituto Nacional Indigenista. UNAM-CEMCA-INI.

Galinier, Jacques, and Antoinette Molinié. (2006) 2013. *The Neo-Indians: A Religion for the Third Millenium*. Boulder: University Press of Colorado.

Gnecco, Cristóbal, and Patricia Ayala, eds. 2016. *Indigenous Peoples and Archaeology in Latin America*. London/New York: Routledge.

Grotti, Vanessa. 2011. "Like Scars on the Body's Skin: The Display of Ancient Things in Trio Houses (Northeast Amazonia)." In *The Archaeological Encounter: Anthropological Perspectives*, edited by Paulo Fortis and Istvan Praet, 236–62. St. Andrews: Centre for Amerindian, Latin American and Caribbean Studies, University of St. Andrews (Occasional publication 33).

Halperin, Christina. 2014. "Ruins in Pre-Columbian Maya Urban Landscapes." *Cambridge Archaelogical Journal* 24: 321–44.

Hall, Ingrid. 2012. "Labourer la terre, tisser la vie. Éclats d'analogies dans les Andes Sud-péruviennes." *Journal de la société des américanistes* 98 (1): 101–31.

Hall, Ingrid. 2018. "Les ancêtres au prisme des pommes de terre non domestiquées: Une perspective andine." *Frontières* 29 (2). https://doi.org/10.7202/1044161ar.

Hamann, Byron. 2002. "The Social Life of Pre-Sunrise Things: Indigenous Mesoamerican Archaeology." *Current Anthropology* 43 (3): 351–69.

Hanks, William F. 2000. "Copresence and Alterity in Maya Ritual Practice." In *Intertexts: Writings and Language, Utterance and Context*, 221–48. Lanham, MD: Rowman and Littlefield.

Hell, Julia, and Andreas Schönle, eds. 2009. *Ruins of Modernity*. Durham, NC: Duke University Press.

Holbraad, Martin, and Morten Axel Pedersen. 2017. *The Ontological Turn: An Anthropological Exposition*. Cambridge: Cambridge University Press.

Joyce, Arthur A., and Sarah B. Barber. 2015. "Ensoulment, Entrapment, and Political Centralization." *Current Anthropology* 56 (6): 819–47.

Kaltmeier, Olaf, and Mario Rufer, eds. 2016. *Entangled Heritages: Postcolonial Perspectives on the Uses of the Past in Latin America*. London: Routledge.

Kristan-Graham, Cynthia, and Laura Amrhein, eds. 2015. *Memory Traces: Analyzing Sacred Space at Five Mesoamerican Sites*. Boulder: University Press of Colorado.

Kulijaman, Mataliwa, and Eliane Camargo. 2012. "*Maluwana*. Discurso a favor del reconcimiento de un patrimonio inmaterial apalaï y wayana." In *Tradición, escritura y patrimonialización*, edited by Anne-Gaël Bilhaut and Silvia Macedo, 23–42. Quito: Abya Yala.

Kuper, Adam. 2003. "The Return of the Native." *Current Anthropology* 44 (3): 389–402.

Lambert, J. D. H., and J. T. Arnason. 1982. "Ramón and Maya Ruins: An Ecological, Not an Economic, Relation." *Science* 216 (4543): 298–99.

Lazzara, Michael, and Vicky Unruh, eds. 2009. *Telling Ruins in Latin America*. New York: Palgrave Macmillan.

Liebmann, Matthew. 2008. "Postcolonial Cultural Affiliation: Essentialism, Hybridity, and Nagpra." In *Archaeology and the Postcolonial Critique*, edited by Matthew Liebmann and Uzma Z. Rivzi, 73–90. Lanham, MD: AltaMira Press.

Liljeblad, Jonathan, and Bas Verschuuren, eds. 2019. *Indigenous Perspectives on Sacred Natural Sites: Culture, Governance and Conservation*. London: Routledge.

Linares, Olga. 1976. "'Garden Hunting' in the American Tropics." *Human Ecology* 4 (4): 331–49.

López Austin, Alfredo. 2015. "Los gigantes que viven dentro de las piedras." *Reflexiones metodológicas: Estudios de cultura náhuatl* 49: 161–97.

López Luján, Leonardo. 2019. *Pretérito pluscuamperfecto: Visiones mesoaméricanas de los vestigios arqueológicos*. Lección inaugural, El Colegio Nacional, México.

McAnany, Patricia. 2016. *Maya Cultural Heritage: How Archaeologists and Indigenous Communities Engage the Past*. Lanham, MD: Rowman and Littlefield.

McGee, R. Jon. 1983. "Sacrifice and Cannibalism: An Analysis of Myth and Ritual among the Lacandon Maya of Chiapas, México." PhD diss., Rice University.

Melatti, Julio Cezar. 1999. *Krahô*, December 1999. https://pib.socioambiental.org/en/Povo:Krah%C3%B4.

Molinié, Antoinette. (2013) 2016. "The Invention of Andean New Age: The Globalization of Tradition." In *New Age in Latin America: Popular Variations and Ethnic Appropriations*, edited by Angela Renée de la Torre Castellanos, María Cristina del Refugio Gutiérrez, and Nahayeilli Juárez-Hue, 291–315. Leiden: Brill.

Muehlmann, Shaylih. 2009. "How Do Real Indians Fish? Neoliberal Multiculturalism and Contested Indigeneities in the Colorado Delta." *American Anthropologist* (n.s.) 111 (4): 468–79.

Palka, Joel. 2014. *Maya Pilgrimage to Ritual Landscapes: Insights from Archaeology, History, and Ethnography*. Albuquerque: University of New Mexico Press.

Pitrou, Perig. 2015. "Life as a Process of Making in the Mixe Highlands (Oaxaca, Mexico): Towards a 'General Pragmatics' of Life." *Journal of the Royal Anthropological Institute* (n.s.) 21: 86–105.

Posey, Darrell Addison, and William L. Balée. 1989. *Resource Management in Amazonia: Indigenous and Folk Strategies*. Bronx: New York Botanical Garden.

Prado Moi, Flavia, and Walter Fagundes Morales. 2016. "Paresi Cultural Heritage." In *Indigenous Peoples and Archaeology in Latin America*, edited by Cristóbal Gnecco and Patricia Ayala, 315–31. London: Routledge.

Praet, Istvan. 2013. *Animism and the Question of Life*. London: Routledge.

Quick, Joe, and James T. Spartz. 2018. "On the Pursuit of Good Living in Highland Ecuador: Critical Indigenous Discourses of Sumak Kawsay." *Latin American Research Review* 53 (4): 757–69.

Ramos, Alcida Rita. 1994. "The Hyperreal Indian." *Critique of Anthropology* 14 (2): 153–71.

Redfield, Robert. 1932. "Maya Archaeology as the Mayas See It." *Sociologus* 8: 299–309.

Renard-Casevitz, France-Marie. 1993. "Guerriers du sel, sauniers de la paix." *L'Homme* 33 (2–4): 25–43.

Rival, Laura, and Doyle McKey. 2008. "Domestication and Diversity in Manioc (*Manihot esculenta* Crantz ssp. *esculenta*, Euphorbiaceae)." *Current Anthropology* 49 (6): 1119–28.

Rivera Andía, Juan Javier, ed. 2019. *Non-Humans in Amerindian South America: Ethnographies of Indigenous Cosmologies, Rituals and Songs*. London: Berghahn Books.

Rivera Cusicanqui, Silvia. 2012. "*Ch'ixinakax utxiwa*: A Reflection on the Practices and Discourses of Decolonization." *South Atlantic Quarterly* 111 (1): 95–109.

Saïd, Edward W. 1978. *Orientalism*. New York: Pantheon.

Salas Carreño, Guillermo. 2019. "On Quechua Relatedness to Contemporary and Ancient Dead." In *Non-Humans in Amerindian South America: Ethnographies of Indigenous Cosmologies, Rituals and Songs*, edited by Juan Javier Rivera Andía, 197–223. London: Berghahn Books.

Santos-Granero, Fernando. 1998. "Writing History into the Landscape: Space, Myth, and Ritual in Contemporary Amazonia." *American Ethnologist* 25 (2): 128–48.

Santos-Granero, Fernando, ed. 2008. *The Occult Life of Things: Native Amazonian Theories of Materiality and Personhood*. Tucson: University of Arizona Press.

Santos-Granero, Fernando, ed. 2015. *Images of Public Wealth or the Anatomy of Well-Being in Indigenous Amazonia*. Tucson: University of Arizona Press.

Sarmiento, Fausto, and Sarah Hitchner, eds. 2017. *Indigeneity and the Sacred: Indigenous Revival and the Conservation of Sacred Natural Sites in the Americas*. London: Berghahn Books.

Schaan, Denise, ed. 2012. *Sacred Geographies of Ancient Amazonia: Historical Ecology of Social Complexity* (New Frontiers in Historical Ecology 3). Walnut Creek, CA: Left Coast Press.

Smith, Claire, and H. Martin Wobst, eds. 2005. *Indigenous Archaeologies: Decolonising Theory and Practice*. London: Routledge.

Stanton, Travis, and Aline Magnoni, eds. 2008. *Ruins of the Past: The Use and Perception of Abandoned Structures in the Maya Lowlands*. Boulder: University Press of Colorado.

Stefano, Michelle L., and Peter Davis, eds. 2016. *The Routledge Companion to Intangible Cultural Heritage*. London: Routledge.

Stobart, Henry. 2006. "The Animated Soundscape and the Mountain's Bones." In *Kay Pacha: Cultivating Earth and Water in the Andes*, edited by Penelope Dransart, 99–106. Oxford: British Archaeological Reports.

Stoler, Ann Laura. 2008. "Imperial Debris: Reflections on Ruins and Ruination." *Cultural Anthropology* 23 (2): 191–219.

Stross, Brian. 1998. "Seven Ingredients in Mesoamerican Ensoulment." In *The Sowing and the Dawning: Termination, Dedication, and Transformation in the Archaeological and Ethnographic Record of Mesoamerica*, edited by Shirley B. Mock, 31–39. Albuquerque: University of New Mexico Press.

Taylor, Anne Christine. 1993. "Remembering to Forget: Identity, Mourning and Memory Among the Jivaro." *Man* 28 (4): 653–78.

Teran, Silvia, and Christian Rasmussen. 1994. *La milpa de los mayas*. Yucatán: DANIDA.

Tozzer, Alfred Marston. 1907. *A Comparative Study in the Mayas and the Lacandones*. New York: Archaeological Institute of America/McMillan.

Vapnarsky, Valentina, Cédric Yvinec, and Cédric Becquey. 2022. "'Culture': Say It with Grammar! The Expression of Notions Related to 'Culture' in Amerindian Languages." *Anthropological Quarterly* 95(3).

Whitten, Norman, and Dorothea Whitten. 2015. "Clashing Concepts of the 'Good Life': Beauty, Knowledge and Vision versus National Wealth in Amazonian Ecuador." In *Images of Public Wealth or the Anatomy of Well-Being in Indigenous Amazonia*, edited by Fernando Santos-Granero, 191–215. Tucson: University of Arizona Press.

1

Patrimonialization, Defilement, and the Zombification of Yanesha Cultural Heritage (Peruvian Amazonia)

Fernando Santos-Granero

In a world in which patrimonialization—along with its evil twin depatrimonialization—has become an industry, a political statement, and a key instrument for the construction of all kinds of national and regional identities, the Yanesha of Peru's Selva Central region have remained strangely unaffected by this powerful trend.[1] In spite of the abundance, in their territory, of culturally significant ruins and landmarks that still loom large in their oral tradition, they have shown no interest in reclaiming these as their cultural heritage. This chapter aims to understand why this is and what—if anything—it might tell us about Native Amazonian societies and patrimonialization efforts in general. There is no doubt, as many have argued, that patrimonialization—here understood as the preservation of cultural heritage elevated to the status of deliberate policy or strategy—is a product of Western cultural history, a form of conceiving and handling key cultural assets that has developed organically alongside the process of formation of modern nation-states (Arantes 2013, 39). Patrimonialization is thus a relatively new phenomenon, originating in Europe in the late seventeenth century with the beginning of the so-called Age of Reason (Bevan 2006, 21).

Despite its relative novelty, this way of relating to cultural heritage is sustained by views of the world, social life, and temporality that are much older. As the coordinators of the Fabriq'Am (2016) project have noted, such Western understandings are not only alien

https://doi.org/10.5876/9781646422869.c001

but often antithetical to Native Amazonian ontologies and worldviews. This radical opposition explains why in some academic circles the notion of patrimonialization, as well as official efforts at patrimonializing, are regarded with suspicion, especially when the cultural dynamic of heritage-holder communities may be affected (Arantes 2013, 39).

I confess upfront that I count myself among those who feel a certain unease with regards to the *mise en patrimoine* of Indigenous cultural heritage. My reservations derive not so much from the view that patrimonialization is a form of "mercantilization of the authentic," as some have argued (Frigolé 2011), but because, following Yanesha people's understandings, I perceive patrimonialization as a form of "zombification" of cultural heritage; that is, a rather dreary attempt to bring back to life something long dead or deprived of vitality. This chapter, however, is not a diatribe against patrimonialization, which under certain circumstances can be a powerful political instrument for the defense and promotion of Indigenous rights. Rather, I seek to understand why Yanesha people have opted to relegate to oblivion certain elements of their cultural heritage—which were important components of their ancient public wealth—and why they have been so reticent in the face of exogenous attempts to bring these cultural elements back to the forefront of their historical memory.

In the first part of this chapter, I address the Yanesha tendency to disremember certain elements of their cultural heritage by focusing on three important landmarks that many non-Yanesha people consider to be key elements of Yanesha patrimony: the Palmazú shrine, home of the stone gods Yompor Yompere and Yachor Mamas; the Cerro de la Sal, where Queñtoʼ, the ancient Salt Person, transformed into a salt mountain; and the tomb of Juan Santos Atahuallpa, the millenarian eighteenth-century Andean leader, known in Yanesha oral tradition as Yompor Santoʼ or Our Father Santoʼ. I then examine Yanesha restraint with regards to patrimonialization by focusing on an early attempt to restore the Palmazú shrine. In the third section I explore the Yanesha conceptions that explain their reluctance to patrimonialize, placing emphasis on the notions of failure/defilement (*aʼtsepeñets*) and appeasement/desoulment (*aʼmchecheñets*), and their resistance toward what they regard—although not in these words—as a zombification of their cultural heritage. I conclude by proposing that Western proclivity and Yanesha reticence toward patrimonialization express not only contrasting regimes of historicity but, above all, opposing cultural strategies for building of collective identities: one based on an omnivorous memory, the other on selective amnesia. Finally, I discuss Yanesha people's increasing receptivity to patrimonialization projects in recent years, which might indicate an important shift in Yanesha modes of conceiving and preserving/expunging the past.

DISREMEMBERING THE CULTURAL HERITAGE

The Palmazú shrine, the Cerro de la Sal, and Juan Santos Atahuallpa's tomb occupy central places in Yanesha cosmology and mythology. All of them have been lost to Yanesha people for over a century and are now located on private lands. For many years, I wondered why Yanesha leaders made no attempt to recover these important landmarks, which are still mentioned in myths, songs, and oral tradition. This lack of interest was all the more intriguing since the Yanesha are among the first Native Amazonian peoples in Peru to have founded their own pan-ethnic organization (in 1969) and to have fought for their territorial rights. How to explain why, after more than fifty years of systematic and quite successful collective struggle to secure land titles, personal documents, schools, and health services, none of the successive leaders of the Yanesha organization has turned the reclamation of these landmarks into a political banner to mobilize their followers and obtain additional concessions from the Peruvian government? There are several possible explanations. I argue, however, that the main reason for this indifference is a resolute determination to disremember certain elements of Yanesha cultural heritage that are no longer socially or culturally meaningful despite their past relevance. Before examining the importance of forgetfulness or selective amnesia in Yanesha regimes of historicity, it is first necessary to discuss the complex processes of making and unmaking of each of these mythically relevant sites. This, I hope, will help to elucidate the paradoxical situation of these landmarks, which have an outstanding place in Yanesha mythology but generate so little interest among contemporary Yanesha people.

The Palmazú Shrine

According to Yanesha time reckoning, the Palmazú shrine is the oldest of the landmarks considered here. Its origin is related to the mythical ascension of Yompor Ror, the present-day sun, to the sky world, an event that is said to have inaugurated the third, present era of Yanesha history.[2] Yanesha elders assert that the earth was illuminated by Yompor Rret, an evil sun deity who enjoyed tormenting the Yanesha people with all kinds of catastrophes. When, out of compassion for the Yanesha, Yompor Ror decided to dethrone Rret, he summoned his three brothers and their sisters/wives to go to the sky world

FIGURE 1.1. *Palmaso stone gods. Source: Oxapampa.biz 2020.*

with him. Instead of waiting for Ror, his siblings ran ahead, eager to reach Cheporepen, the mountain from which they were supposed to climb to the sky world. This angered Yompor Ror, triggering his transformative powers. When he encountered his brother Yompor Yompere, Yompere's wife Yachor Mamas, and their followers, he turned them into stone, leaving them behind to support the earth (see figure 1.1).

Given that Yompor Yompere and his wife were considered to be among the few high-ranking gods that remained on the earth, their home at Palmazú became an important ceremonial center and pilgrimage site that attracted not only Yanesha people but also Ashaninka devotees from the Upper Perené River valley and even Conibo believers from the distant Pachitea and Ucayali Rivers (Navarro 1924, 390; Rojas Zolezzi 1987, 113; Santos-Granero 1991, 285; Weiss 1975, 272). We do not know when exactly Palmazú began to function as a shrine, but given the similarities between the Yanesha stone gods and the Andean *huacas*, it is more than possible that it was already functioning in pre-Columbian times. According to Yanesha oral history, the stone divinities were attended by a *cornesha'*, or Yanesha priestly leader. The last acting priest of the Palmazú shrine was Santos Ortiz, better known as Tsachopeñ, who is still remembered as one of the wisest Yanesha leaders (Santos-Granero 2015, 96–99).³ Tsachopeñ presided over a large temple or worship house (*puerahua*) consisting of a rectangular thatched building surrounded by a round ceremonial plaza. The stone divinities were kept within the worship house.

According to oral tradition, the attending *cornesha'* prayed in the early morning and before dusk, asking the stone gods to grant health and strength to his followers, make cultivated plants grow strong, and guarantee the abundance of game animals. In addition, he made daily offerings of coca leaves and strongly brewed manioc beer to the stone divinities in a small wooden structure located in an enclosure within the temple. The Palmazú shrine also housed a god-sent fire, known as *cañtell* or *yompor poyoroc̈hen*, Our Father's portent, which Tsachopeñ claimed had appeared to him miraculously in the middle of the forest as a material manifestation of Yompor Ror, the sun deity. Permanently kept alight, the divine fire of Palmazú was considered to be so powerful that other Yanesha and Ashaninka shaman-priests obtained permission from Tsachopeñ to carry the fire and worship it in their own ceremonial centers. These offshoots of the divine fire of Palmazú acted as a constant reminder of the shrine, extending its fame throughout the region.

The Palmazú shrine was also the site of large collective ceremonies, which Tsachopeñ organized periodically to honor the stone divinities. These ritual gatherings lasted several days, attracting pilgrims from all over the Yanesha territory. Some arrived several days in advance to help harvest the shrine's gardens, procure game meat and fish, and brew manioc beer. They brought offerings of coca leaves, salted fish, and smoked meat to the stone gods, asking them for vitality and abundance. While in the shrine they were asked to behave in a moral way and comply with a series of prescriptions and interdictions. Pilgrims worshipped the gods by singing and dancing to the rhythm of diverse styles of *coshamñats*, worship music. The mixed sounds of panpipes, drums, and human voices were believed to ascend to the sky world and please the gods. Particularly important was the performance of various worship songs whose main protagonists were Yompor Yompere and Yachor Mamas. Through these songs, and the recounting of their origin myth, the stone divinities were commemorated, celebrated, and metaphorically brought back to life. Above all, these shared activities—both secular and ritual—generated a sense of moral community and helped to develop strong emotional ties to the enshrined place.

The first documentary reference to the Palmazú shrine comes from an 1897 cadastral map of the colonies of Oxapampa and Pozuzo, where it appears under the name *Idolos de los infieles* ("infidels' idols") within a twenty-five-hectare lot

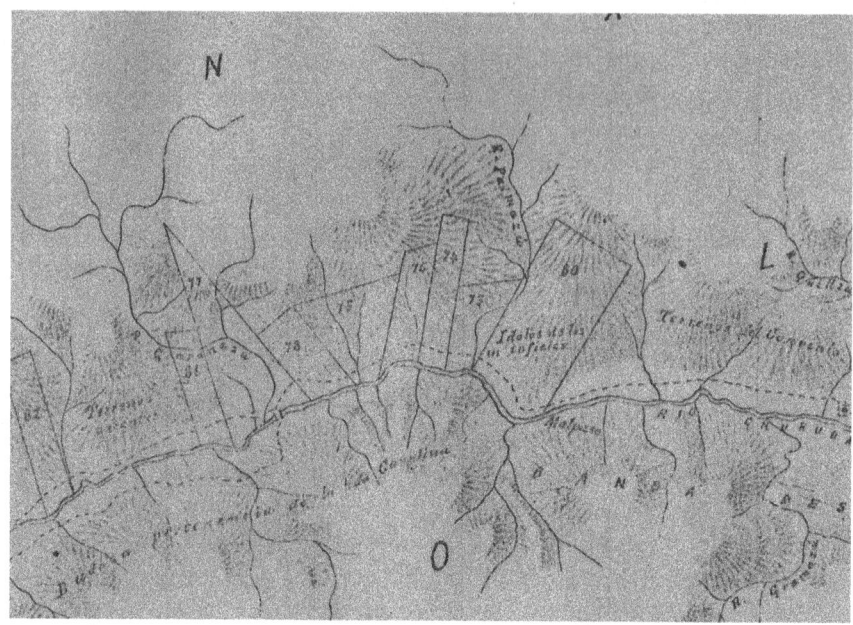

FIGURE 1.2. "Idolos de los infieles" *(infidels' idols) shown in cadastral map by the Ministry of Public Works, 1897. Source: Plano (1897).*

belonging to colonist Gaspar Cárdenas (Plano 1897) (see figure 1.2). Five years later, when engineer Augusto Tamayo (1904, 18) inspected the area, the lot had been incorporated into a larger hacienda owned by a José M. de la Torre. In his field report Tamayo mentions that in Hacienda Palmazú there were "some historical monoliths which natives worshipped reverently in the old days" (18). This suggests that by 1902 the shrine was no longer active. That same year, however, Swiss navy officer Luis Bailly-Maitre (1908, 622–23) left a description of the ceremonies held at the *capilla de los chunchos* ("Indians' chapel"), as he called it, that confirms oral tradition and leaves no doubt that in 1902 Palmazú was still fully functioning as a ceremonial center. "In this place the Amuesha worship three large upright stones; they come from afar to make offerings to them. They mutter long prayers and they retreat dancing, without turning their backs on the idols. In this place, they keep alight, day and night, a sacred fire formed by three logs that touch on their ends; worshipping and the preparation of manioc beer is in charge of some sorcerers [*brujos*]" (Bailly Maitre 1908, 623).

By 1910, when Fr. Bernardino Izaguirre visited the area, the situation had changed substantially. The Franciscan missionary points out that the land in

FIGURE 1.3. *Cerro de la Sal in a seventeenth-century map. Source: Archivo General de Indias: MP-Perú-Chile, 194.*

which the large stones sat had been recently farmed. He noted that the stone divinities were still "superstitiously worshipped" by the local Indians but added, quite happily, that the hut the Yanesha had built to shelter them had disappeared (Izaguirre quoted in Ortiz 1967: I, 426). This indicates that sometime before 1910 the Palmazú worship house had been razed or allowed to decay. It is possible, however, that the stone gods continued to attract pilgrims for some time. In any case, it was not long before the site was totally abandoned, since in the early 1920s, Fr. Manuel Navarro (1924, 390) reported that "until recently" Natives had worshipped the stone gods under the guidance of an elderly *brujo*, suggesting that by then not only had the worship house disappeared but, more important, that ceremonies were no longer held at the shrine.

THE CERRO DE LA SAL

The second site, the Cerro de la Sal or Salt Mountain, was an important landmark not only in Yanesha but also in Ashaninka and Matsigenka mythology. Located in the confluence of De la Sal and Entaz Rivers, shortly before the latter flows into the Paucartambo River, the Cerro rises on the boundaries between the Yanesha and Ashaninka territories (see figure 1.3). According to

FIGURE 1.4. *Cerro de la Sal's red salt vein washed by Posopno, the Río de la Sal.* Photo: Fernando Santos-Granero.

Yanesha mythology, this landmark originated after Yompor Ror's ascension to heaven, which makes it younger than the Palmazú shrine. Known as Posapno by Yanesha people and Pareni by the Ashaninka, the Cerro de la Sal is actually composed of three hills: a larger one traversed from top to bottom by a long vein of reddish salt, and two smaller ones containing veins of whiter crystalline salt (Memorial [1663] 1986, 153). At the feet of the larger hill runs a small stream, known as Posopno, or Río de la Sal, whose waters are permanently salty from the slow erosion of the hill's salt vein (see figure 1.4).

Yanesha elders assert that the Cerro de la Sal is the transformed body of Yato Queñṯoṯ or Posona', the primordial Salt Man, who was sent to earth by the sun god so that his human creatures would have something to season their food with.[4] Queñṯoṯ was always covered with sweat bees and had a rotten smell, so people rejected him. Only an old priestly leader who lived on the Paucartambo River guessed his real identity and invited Queñṯoṯ to stay with his family. After a while, Queñṯoṯ revealed his godly origin and asked his hosts to kill him so that he could turn into salt. When they did so, all the different kinds of salt that exist today appeared: some of them edible, others harmful to human beings.

Sitting at the crossroads of the Amazon and the Andes, the Cerro de la Sal attracted a multitude of highland and lowland peoples who came every year to extract salt or obtain it through trade (Amich 1975, 43). Although the first documentary evidence on the Cerro de la Sal dates to 1637, it is more than probable that Indigenous peoples exploited its salt veins in pre-Columbian times (Amich 1975, 45). According to early colonial documents, visitors in search of salt arrived en masse at the Cerro during the dry season, which extends from June to August (Tibesar 1950, 104). They came on foot or paddled in rafts or canoes up the Perené River. The environs of the salt mine were inhabited by Yanesha and Ashaninka people, who were the only ones entitled to boil the raw blocks of red salt, clean the evaporated salt, and mold it into the cakes of pure salt that were used as a kind of currency throughout the region (Renard-Casevitz 2002, 131–32). Yanesha visitors made offerings of coca leaves, lime, and *chamairo*[5] to Yato Queñṯoṯ since they believed that extracting salt required cutting up the body of the ancient deity. In addition, the salt-making specialists performed various rituals, including fasting, vigils, and sexual abstinence, to ensure the production of the finest salt cakes. Visitors settled in temporary lean-tos on the stone beaches that appear along the Paucartambo and Perené Rivers during the dry season and spent part of the time fishing and salting the catch for their return trip.

Early colonial documents indicate that the Cerro de la Sal was also an important ceremonial center. In a 1663 report to the Spanish king, Capt. Pedro Bohórques asserted that the inhabitants of the Cerro de la Sal extracted salt from the larger hill but held ritual gatherings on the two smaller ones (Memorial 1663, 153). Bohórques used the term *idolatrar*, "to worship," to describe these ceremonies. Given the absence of priestly leaders differentiated from shamans among the Ashaninka, it is likely that these ceremonies were officiated by Yanesha specialists in honor of Yato Queñṯoṯ. The Franciscan missionaries who, since the early seventeenth century, attempted to convert the Yanesha and Ashaninka were so aware of the economic and ritual importance of the Cerro de la Sal that they constantly requested the authorities to occupy the site by force so as to better control the Native populations (Biedma 1981, 172; San Antonio 1750, 5r; San Joseph 1750, 14v).

The importance of the Cerro de la Sal increased after the Spaniards were expelled from the region in 1742. By then, Yanesha worship houses began to be associated with ironworks, a technology that the Yanesha and Ashaninka had learned from the Spaniards during the first half of the eighteenth century and developed during the second half (Santos-Granero 1988, 9). In 1876, when the Peruvian military invaded the region after more than one hundred years of isolation, Col. La Rosa found a large worship house—fifteen by twelve meters—at the foot of the Cerro de la Sal (cited in Raimondi 1874–1902: III, 560). In this house he found large jars of manioc beer, abundant food, and numerous painted masks, suggesting that the local people were about to hold a large gathering. Ten years later, a smaller temple—twelve by ten meters—was reported on the Cerro's summit by Fr. Gabriel Sala (quoted by Ortiz 1967: I, 394). Both worship houses were associated with ironworks. According to oral tradition, these were attended by priest/blacksmiths or by blacksmiths associated with priestly leaders (Santos-Granero 1988, 15). Iron was obtained from surface ore found in several places along the Paucartambo River, close to the Cerro de la Sal, and was extracted by heating the ore in large brick furnaces (Raimondi 1879: III, 560–61) (see figure 1.5). Yanesha elders claim that iron is the transformed body of Aserr, the primordial Iron Person, who was made to appear by Yompor Santo' to benefit Yanesha people.[6] The production of metal tools further increased the economic and ceremonial relevance of the Cerro de la Sal among Yanesha people and their neighbors.

Despite the gradual reoccupation of their lands beginning in 1847, the Yanesha and Ashaninka continued to visit the Cerro de la Sal to extract salt, obtain iron tools, and attend ceremonies held at its temple/ironworks until well into the nineteenth century. In 1891, however, the government granted the Peruvian Corporation Ltd., a company that grouped the country's British bondholders, half a million hectares along both banks of the Perené River (Barclay 1989, 44). The concession comprised not only large portions of the Yanesha and Ashaninka territories but also the renowned Cerro de la Sal. With the aim of growing high-quality coffee for the international market, the Peruvian Corporation turned these lands into the Perené Colony. To force the Yanesha and Ashaninka people living within the colony to work for them, in 1897 its administrators forbade them to extract salt from the Cerro (Varese 1973, 255–56). This generated great animosity among Native people and led to

FIGURE 1.5. *Ashaninka ironworks showing iron melting furnace, 1883.* Source: Ordinaire (1988, 193).

a general Yanesha-Ashaninka revolt against the British colony and its white-mestizo colonists. Once the rebellion was put down, the government sent an inspector to evaluate the situation. As a result of the latter's report, in 1898, the government placed the Cerro de la Sal under the administration of the Estanco de la Sal, the national salt agency. From then on, extraction of salt from the Cerro became a state monopoly, and Indigenous people were not allowed to enter the grounds.

Juan Santos Atahuallpa's Tomb

Juan Santos was an Andean highland mestizo trained by Jesuit priests who, in 1742, persuaded the Yanesha and their neighbors, the Ashaninka (Campa), Yine (Piro), and Conibo, to join forces to expel the Spaniards from their territories (Santos-Granero 1993). After a surprise appearance among the Ashaninka of the Gran Pajonal, Juan Santos established his headquarters in Metraro, an upland site in the Upper Perené valley, in the interface of Yanesha and Ashaninka territories (see figure 1.6). La Purísima Concepción de Metraro

FIGURE 1.6. *Juan Santos Atahuallpa in painting by Fr. Gabriel Sala. Source: Biblioteca del Convento de Santa Rosa de Ocopa.*

had become an important mission after its founding by the Franciscans in 1715 (Santos-Granero 2004, 191). From this strategically located place, Juan Santos Atahuallpa and his allies systematically attacked mission posts, cattle haciendas, sugarcane plantations, textile mills, and Andean frontier towns. By the end of 1742, the rebels had expelled all Spaniards from the region. In later years, the lands they occupied appeared in Spanish maps as "Amajes and villages tyrannized by the rebel" or "Villages of the Campas nation tyrannized by the rebel Juan Santos Atahualpa" (Cano y Olmedilla 1775).

Juan Santos persuaded his different constituencies—namely, highland and lowland Indigenous peoples, African slaves, mestizos, and impoverished Spaniards—to join him through a discourse that mixed anticolonial demands with millenarian promises (Santos-Granero 1993). The name he chose for himself, Juan Santos Atahuallpa Apuinga Guainacapac Jesús Sacramentado, expresses the hybrid nature of his politico-religious discourse, which combined elements from Andean, Christian, and Amazonian cultural traditions (Zarzar 1989). To attract Native Amazonians, he played on widespread world-shifting expectations indicating that a savior would one day restore humankind's lost immortality (Santos-Granero 2018). He succeeded in creating a following and is now remembered as a divine emissary called Yompor Santo',

Our Father Santo', in Yanesha mythology (Santos-Granero 1991, 80), and Apinka or Sacaramentaro in Ashaninka tradition (Mihas 2014, 34–50; Rojas Zolezzi 1994, 58–61).

Yanesha elders claim that Yompor Santo' was a white man with blond hair who was sent by the creator god at a time when Yanesha people were losing their identity and becoming like white people.[7] He settled in the house of a devoted priestly leader in Metraro, which Yanesha people consider as an *axis mundi* connecting heaven to earth. There, he made Yanesha people multiply miraculously. His new followers built him a large worship house, from which he taught them new ideas and practices and, above all, how to lead a correct life. This blissful period ended when Shellmem, Yompor Santo's evil classificatory brother killed him out of envy and jealousy. Before dying, however, Santo' promised his followers that he would resurrect five days after his death to make them immortal. According to Yanesha myths, the color came back to Yompor Santo's face several times, but he finally died for good. The hero's followers placed his body in a silver coffin, together with his silver cross and scepter. They then positioned the coffin in the center of Yompor Santo's worship house, where it was guarded by his disciples.

Yanesha mythology is partly confirmed by documentary evidence. Col. Ernesto La Combe (1905: VII, 493), a French explorer who visited Juan Santos's tomb in 1891, described it as a large house, eighteen meters long by eight meters wide, supported by eight wooden pillars and covered by a thatched gable roof. At the center of the house, which was oriented toward the east, there was a mound a meter and a half high made of thick jacaranda wood planks. Albino Carranza (1894, 23), who visited the tomb with La Combe, reported that "Indian" people assembled every year in Metraro to commemorate Juan Santos's accomplishments. J. F. Pazos Varela (quoted in Loayza 1942, xiv), who also visited the tomb, was more precise, writing in 1940 that the site was the object of periodical pilgrimages by Yanesha and Ashaninka people. Both authors assert that every year pilgrims took turns providing the dead hero with a new white cotton tunic—the Yanesha and Ashaninka traditional dress—which was laid on top of his funeral mound. This is confirmed by Yanesha oral sources asserting that pilgrims also brought the dead leader new shoulder bags, seed chest bands, feather headdresses, and a new bow and arrows. According to Yanesha elders, there were at least four temple/ironworks in the environs of Metraro (Santos-Granero 1988, 13–14), and one was close to Juan Santos Atahuallpa's tomb (Remy 1898, 9–10). The ceremonies held annually in honor of Juan Santos were probably led by the Yanesha priestly leader in charge of this latter temple/ironworks.

Celebrations at Juan Santos's tomb continued for a century and a half, until 1891, when the government started construction of the Pichis Trail, a dirt road that was meant to connect Lima with a navigable Amazonian river. The proposed road passed close to Juan Santos's tomb, which until then had been off-limits to white people. The first frictions between the people of Metraro and the road builders with regards to Juan Santos's tomb began when the government commission sent to break ground for the new road occupied the mausoleum (Parró 1892, 44). According to La Combe (1892, 419), on that occasion Joaquín Capelo, the engineer in charge of supervising the road building, took one of the planks that covered Juan Santos's tomb to use as a distance post. The next morning the removed plank—on which Capelo had painted a number—had been mysteriously moved back to its original position. Out of respect for the Yanesha and Ashaninka, Capelo left the removed plank where it was. Unfortunately, other visitors were not as respectful. In late 1891, when British planters Arthur Sinclair and Alexander Ross camped at the tomb while inspecting the Perené Colony, the grave had already been dug up and Juan Santos's bones, which they were told belonged to Atahuallpa, the last Inca, were scattered on the ground (Sinclair 1895, 25–26). Shortly after, having heard of the importance that the Yanesha and Ashaninka accorded to Juan Santos's tomb and fearing, perhaps, that the figure of the ancient hero could be used to rally Indigenous people against the government forces occupying their lands, the Prefect of Junín ordered his remains to be removed to the highland city of Tarma (Carranza 1894, 23). According to one source, Juan Santos's remains were buried in Tarma's cemetery (Pazos Varela, quoted in Loayza 1942, xv). But by 1894 nobody really knew where the hero's remains had been deposited (Carranza 1894, 23).

There is no doubt that the three landmarks discussed here loom large in Yanesha oral tradition. They are not merely instances of "history written into the landscape," that is, geographical marks that, read on their own or in association with others, evoke in the informed reader a variety of narratives about the mythical or historical past (Santos-Granero 1998). These were rather "lived landmarks," insofar as the powerful divinities that they embodied were evoked and brought back to life periodically through the performativity of ritual action. The collective offerings, prayers, and feasts performed in situ allowed people not only to keep the past alive in the collective memory but to actually infuse it with renewed life during each collective gathering. More important, these three landmarks were considered to be important components of Yanesha environmental public wealth,[8] a type of wealth consisting of all the things and beings produced by the divinities for the benefit and sustenance of the Yanesha as a whole (Santos-Granero 2015, 90).

The ceremonies performed at these landmarks were aimed at raising up/ resurrecting (*tantateñets*) the memory of the powerful beings embodied in them and of the events in which they had a leading role. The purpose of such commemorative acts was to summon these powerful gods and ask them to share their divine power (*parets*) with Yanesha people, thus ensuring the latter's vitality and reproduction. In other words, these three sites were important constituents of what I have called the Yanesha "political economy of life," crucial sources of vitality in a cosmos characterized by rife interspecific competition over life forces that ensured both Yanesha reproduction and the prospect of future immortality (Santos-Granero 2015, 92–95).

RETICENCE TOWARD PATRIMONIALIZATION

As we have seen, these three landmarks are remembered in myths and oral history, but they have been disremembered as ritual sites, obliterated, as it were, from Yanesha ceremonial life. They excite old memories but seem to have lost their capability to engage present-day Yanesha people and, thus, produce new memories. It is surprising that in the more than one hundred years since the Yanesha were forced to abandon these landmarks they have shown little interest in recovering them or demanding their return. Not only have Yanesha people shown little inclination toward recovering these sites, but they have been quite reticent in the face of the one and only attempt at patrimonialization that I am aware of.

The story of this attempt, concerning the Palmazú shrine, has been recounted by anthropologist Richard Chase Smith (1977, 1981, 2011) with more or less detail in at least three of his works. In his doctoral dissertation, Smith noted in passing that "in 1973, a cooperative effort was made to restore the site of the sacred stones in the Chorobamba valley which had been severely damaged by vandalism, and to re-institute the rites there which had been neglected for several decades" (Smith 1977, 229). This experience allowed him to gain a better understanding of Yanesha ceremonial life.

In another work, based on large excerpts from his field diaries, Smith (1981) presents a much more detailed account of the attempt to restore the Palmazú shrine. He says that on February 17, 1973, he and a dozen Yanesha men and women from the neighboring community of Miraflores—known today as Tsachopen—went to Palmazú to visit the stone gods. The group was headed by grandfather Santiago and consisted mostly of his family and close relatives. When they arrived, the women embraced Yompor Yompere and talked to Yachor Mamas. Then the leader intoned a lengthy prayer. The attendants brought out plates of roasted manioc and gourds of manioc beer, which grandfather Santiago placed as offerings at the head of Our Father Yompere. After doing this, they sat down to rest under the shade, the men behind Yompor Yompere and the women behind Yachor Mamas. While resting, grandfather Santiago recounted the origin story of the stone deities. When he finished, Pedro, one of the attendants, expressed his sadness at seeing the stone gods lying on their backs, overgrown with weeds and shrubs. It was then, according to Smith (1981, 123), that "Pedro excitedly told [them] of his dream of getting people together to lift the stones back on their feet, to clean up the area, and to rebuild a religious house there." To which Smith added: "I secretly shared his dream." The visit ended with people sharing a cupful of the blessed manioc beer and singing *coshamñats* songs in praise of the stone deities. Smith ends his account by asserting, "I was deeply moved by the experience as was, I think, everyone else."

Seven months later, on September 5, 1973, Smith (1981, 127) wrote in his diary: "It has happened! It has actually happened! For years I've been dreaming of raising Our Father Yompere' back on his feet. And yesterday we did it." He goes on to describe how, together with forty men, women, and children from Miraflores and other neighboring communities, they had managed to lift Yompor Yompere. They began shortly after dawn with a long prayer in honor of the stone gods intoned by grandfather Santiago. Then manioc beer and coca leaves were passed around. When all the attendants, including the youngest children, had shared a cupful of beer and a handful of coca leaves, the elder men sat together to consult their coca for a sign that it was an appropriate time to lift the stones. After determining that the time was right, all the attendants set out to lift Yompor Yompere. Despite their efforts, however, the stone god would not budge. People became discouraged. Finally, some people cut down poles to use as levers, and they were able to lift the stone god inch by inch. It took all morning, but by noon Our Father Yompere was back on his feet. "The excitement was tremendous: the grandfather chanted a lengthy prayer, the women sang their songs of praise and happiness, and the grandmother cried" (Smith 1981, 128). Afterward, they went back to Miraflores, where the devotees spent the night drinking manioc beer, singing traditional music, and evoking Yompor Yompere.

The effort to reestablish the Palmazú shrine was, however, short-lived. Despite Pedro's dream, Yanesha people never rebuilt the worship house, and ceremonies were never fully restored. In fact, in the following decades Yanesha people made no attempt to rescue the shrine from foreign hands. The people of Miraflores fought long and hard to regain the lands that the Franciscans of the neighboring Quillazú mission had obtained in their name in 1884 but had kept as their private property (Smith 1974). They persisted until the government gave them back most of the occupied lands. In contrast, they never demanded the devolution of the lands in which the stone gods sat, which are still—as far as I know—in private hands.

THE ZOMBIFICATION OF PUBLIC WEALTH

How to understand such indifference to the fate of these landmarks? It could be argued that Yanesha disinterest results from an unjust property system that privileges and defends the powerful and literate while despoiling and marginalizing the illiterate. Dispossessed of these sites and lacking the kind of knowledge that only formal schooling provides, Yanesha people would not have had the necessary tools to defend their rights. While not entirely wrong, such argument omits the fact that literacy among Yanesha people, which began in the late 1940s, accelerated in the 1950s and 1960s (Smith 1981, 122). As a result, by 1975, around 55 percent of Yanesha people were literate (Chirif et al. 1975, 239), and by the end of the twentieth century the number had increased to 78 percent (Mora and Zarzar 1997). Today, Yanesha are among the most literate Indigenous peoples in Peruvian Amazonia.

It could also be argued that during this long period the Yanesha had neither the power nor the organizational capabilities to challenge the state or the private individuals who owned these sites. But, as we have seen, the Yanesha were among the first Native Amazonian peoples in Peru to create their own ethnopolitical organization: the Congreso de Comunidades Nativas Amuesha, created in 1969 and replaced in 1981 by the Federación de Comunidades Nativas Yanesha (FECONAYA). They have been extremely successful at fighting for their lands, having acquired title to close to 80,000 hectares of land, as well as having secured the creation of national parks, communal reserves, protection forests, and biosphere reserves (Santos-Granero 2004, 169, 219). This suggests that Yanesha reticence toward patrimonialization does not derive from lack of knowledge, organizational abilities, or the will to fight.

I suggest that the answer lies not in structural economic or political factors but in Native conceptions about the success or failure of ritual undertakings, as well as the making and unmaking of mystical power. Yanesha people consider training to become a shaman or priestly leader, preparing oneself to become a good hunter, or embarking on a worship song quest as activities that are fraught with supernatural dangers and, thus, require intensive ritual preparation. Numerous factors may condemn any such enterprise to failure. Yanesha people use the term *a'tsepeñets* to describe the act of failing to attain a desired objective.[9] In ritual contexts, such failure is always attributed to intentional or unintentional ritual infractions leading to the defilement and deprivation of the supernatural force contained in ritual objects, places, and specialists. In such contexts, any immoral action, improper behavior, or breach of taboo can result in the irreversible failure of the entire mystical enterprise.

Examining how Yanesha people use this term will help clarify its scope and meaning, showing its relevance to the present analysis. In reference to quests for divine revelation, Yanesha elders assert that the ancient *cornesha'* often attributed their failure to make Yompor Ror reappear to their followers' conduct.[10] Bad intentions or negative emotions, such as hatred or wrath, were judged to be offensive to the higher gods. Foul language, arguments, and fights were also thought to displease them. Having sexual relations at the ceremonial center, and even more so at the worship house, was forbidden and for this reason pilgrims were not allowed to sleep in the *puerahua*.[11] Menstruating women could not touch the offerings brought by visitors lest they contaminate them and anger the gods. And only priestly leaders and prepubescent boys were allowed to enter the area where the beer offerings were kept to prevent their contamination by sexually active people.[12]

These ritual prescriptions and proscriptions were thought to be an integral component of the compact between the gods and humans. Yanesha people regard quests for divine revelations, as well as other ritual undertakings, as activities in which participants engage in a reciprocal, albeit asymmetrical, relation with the divinities, higher spirits, and owners/masters of animals and plants, by which they abide by certain ritual rules in exchange for the goodwill and favor of their mystically powerful counterparts. In the case of ceremonial centers, the breach of any of the above taboos was thought to make the *cornesha'* and his worship house "lose contact" with Yompor Ror.[13] Ritual infractions in such contexts compromised the quest's main goal, namely, to excite the love/compassion of the higher gods to ensure that they would continue sharing their divine breath/strength with Yanesha people, as well as comply with their ancient promise of making Yanesha people immortal once again. Immoral attitudes or behavior could not only jeopardize communication with the divinities but also cause terrible calamities. An elderly Yanesha woman recounted that when her brother, a renowned *cornesha'*, engaged in sexual acts while embarked in a ritual song quest, the gods caused a great upheaval. As she told anthropologist Richard Smith (1981, 152), "Suddenly there was a great wind, a tornado; and then loud thunderclaps nearby. The temple was torn apart and the pieces scattered at great distances. The powerful divinities were very angry."

According to Yanesha elders, when such moral transgressions occurred, the offended deities made themselves unavailable to humans. There was no solution but to abandon the ceremonial center and build a new one, since "there was no possibility of changing the motive of the ritual failure."[14] This suggests that in ritual contexts, *a'tsepeñets* refers not only to the failure resulting from moral infractions but also to the result of those actions, namely, the violation of the godly character of an object or place. In other words, in ritual contexts *a'tsepeñets* also connotes the notion of "defilement" in its sense of "to make unclean or unfit for ceremonial use" (Webster's II 1984). In effect, according to Yanesha elders, once a ceremonial center had been compromised by immoral acts, it was "no longer of use" (*ama sherbo*).[15] The offended gods left the site and, as a result, the latter became deprived of *parets* or divine power.

Yanesha people describe such a situation through the idiom *a'mchecheñets*. In mythical contexts, this refers to the act by which a supernatural being deprives of power/vitality or renders ineffective the power/vitality of another supernatural being and is often translated as "to appease" or "to subjugate" (Duff-Tripp 1998, 67). In ceremonial contexts, it refers to the action by which divinities mystically consume the strength/vitality contained in the manioc beer offered to them. In both cases, however, the term denotes the act of depriving something or someone of their power/vitality. Since in Yanesha thought the power/vitality of a being or thing is equivalent to its "soul," *a'mchecheñets* could also be translated as "to desoul." Ritual failure not only leads to the defilement of the places, objects, or persons affected by ritual infractions but also results in the loss of their power/vitality, that is, in their desoulment. According to Yanesha oral tradition, the Palmazú shrine, the Cerro de la Sal, and Yompor Santo's tomb experienced this kind of defilement but on a more serious scale, since the transgressors were not Yanesha people but *ocanesha'*, white people, whom the Yanesha regard as demonic beings that emerged from the world below when Enc (Inca) ruled.[16]

As we have seen, ceremonial gatherings at the Palmazú shrine were discontinued in the early 1920s. In the following decades, according to Yanesha oral sources, the stone gods were severely damaged by white-mestizo colonists (Smith 1977, 229). Around 1966 "colonists violated the site . . . overturning the stones, smashing some of them, and dragging others out of the site in their search for buried gold" (Smith 1981, 123). As a result, when Smith (2011, 3) visited the Palmazú shrine in 1973, he found the two larger stone gods and half a dozen small and medium-size lesser divinities overturned and lying on their backs. Ashaninka people provide a variation on the Yanesha account, saying that sometime in the 1940s white people attempted to destroy the stone gods with dynamite (Weiss 1975, 272). The dynamite failed to detonate three times. On the fourth attempt, the 1947 earthquake occurred, causing great damage throughout the Selva Central region. Afterward, according to this version, white people built a house to shelter the stones. Natives were allowed to visit the house but not to conduct rituals there.

In a similar Ashaninka narrative collected twenty years later, it is said that when mestizo colonists discovered Yompor Yompiri, they tried first to drill a hole through him, presumably to destroy him (Rojas Zolezzi 1987, 113).[17] When that failed, they tried to remove the stone god from the site to build him a house and adore him themselves. But each time they tried to carry the god away, the earth trembled. Afraid of the god's power, the colonists tried to dynamite it, but when they did so the stone god began to bleed. This led the intruders to quit their efforts. In all these accounts, the abandonment of the Palmazú shrine is attributed to the presence of white-mestizo foreigners who either occupied the site, displacing the Yanesha, tried to co-opt the stone divinities, or attempted to destroy them so that they would not continue favoring Indigenous people. Although unsuccessful, their actions defiled the shrine, compromising the Yanesha's long-standing relationship with the stone gods.

The Cerro de la Sal was similarly defiled. Between 1898, when the Cerro was placed under the administration of the national salt agency, and the early 1920s, when the introduction of industrial salt led the state to abandon the site, Yanesha people were not allowed to visit the Cerro to extract salt or celebrate their ceremonies in honor of Yato Queñtoʼ. Around that same time, the Perené Colony decided to partition and sell the area around the Cerro de la Sal to a new wave of colonists. Twenty years later, in the 1940s, the area began to be settled by mestizo colonists of Andean origin, who dynamited the Cerro's salt veins to extract salt blocks for their own consumption and to feed their cattle (Aco 2013). Yanesha people, who took all kinds of ritual precautions when extracting salt in the understanding that they were cutting the body of the generous salt god, saw the dynamiting of the Cerro de la Sal as a gross desecration of Yato Queñtoʼ's body. To avoid a similar fate, Aserr, the primordial Iron Person, had promised that if white people invaded Yanesha territory he would hide forever, for he had been created for the sole benefit of Yanesha people.[18] The brutal violation of the Cerro de la Sal by white-mestizo colonists not only defiled the place but caused the estrangement of the salt and iron gods.

The fate of Juan Santos's burial site was even bleaker. Yanesha myth tellers assert that when white people heard that Yompor Santo' had died, they came from Tarma to take his remains.[19] They waited until his corpse was reduced to bones, and then they took all of his bones, even the tiniest, with them. Some say that they used the bones to make an effigy in the exact likeness of Yompor Santo'. They did such a good job that the figure cannot be disassembled. Now, according to this tradition, white people worship Yompor Santo's effigy in a church in Tarma, presumably Saint Anne's Cathedral. The removal of the hero's remains in 1891 put an immediate end to the multiethnic ceremonies held at his tomb. Only a year later, Juan del Monte (1894, 55) reported that Juan Santos's "chapel" was falling in disrepair and that the neighboring houses had been deserted. By 1898, only a few remains of the tomb could still be seen (Remy 1898, 9–10). And when Fr. Bernardino Izaguirre (1923: II, 184) visited the tomb in 1910, he only saw "some fallen wood pillars and the hole corresponding to the tomb's location." The sequestration of Yompor Santo's remains by white people was regarded as having deprived the site of its power. Without it, the site was no longer of interest and was rapidly deserted by both Yanesha and Ashaninka people.

It is clear that, when seen from a Yanesha perspective, the abandonment of these three landmarks as a result of the colonial process owed not only to the fact that they were occupied and wrested from their hands but to a much more serious concern, namely, that they had been irremediably defiled by white people. White people's attempts to co-opt the mystical powers contained in these landmarks and the violent defilement to which they subjected them throughout the process—or after realizing they could not achieve their goal—broke the connection between the sites and the gods embodied in them. This, in turn, deprived their home places of mystical power, rendering them unfit for ceremonial use.

I contend that if Yanesha people have made little effort to reclaim these sites, it is because they feel that there is nothing to recover. From their point of view, the patrimonialization of these landmarks would not resurrect the memory of these places or infuse them with new life; it would not restore their ancient *parets*, or divine power. Patrimonialization efforts in such situations, especially if inspired and implemented by exogenous agents, can only result, from a Yanesha perspective, in the creation of zombie places. Although the term "zombie" is not part of Yanesha people's traditional vocabulary, they do have the notion of "living dead." This corresponds to people who have lost their souls for a variety of reasons: children whose souls have gone astray while following their parents into the forest; adults who have lost their soul through deep grief for the death of a loved one; or shamans who have lost their souls after being killed while wandering in jaguar guise. Such soul-less individuals continue to live for a while but are doomed to lead a half life that can only end in permanent death. In accordance with these Yanesha notions, zombie places would be dead sites given a semblance of life but actually deprived of energy or vitality; desouled places that can only survive in a half-dead state, compelled to do the bidding of the revivers rather than respond to the needs or expectations of the collectives to which they once belonged.

OMNIVOROUS MEMORY VS. SELECTIVE AMNESIA

Yanesha people's attitudes about these ancient landmarks and their reticence about past attempts at patrimonializing, then, seem to respond to a regime of historicity that is drastically different from that prevailing in Western societies.[20] Whereas patrimonialization is a long-standing cultural practice that has been key in Western ways of dealing with the past and building collective identities, it is virtually absent in Yanesha society. In effect, although patrimonialization as we know it may have originated with the Enlightenment, the Western notion that certain cultural items constitute the patrimony of a given people and are thus inextricably linked to their identity goes back to at least 586 BC, when the Oracle of Delphi came to be acknowledged as the most important Panhellenic shrine. The same is true of the notion that certain cultural artifacts form part of the "patrimony of humanity," which is already present in embryonic form in the list of the Seven Wonders of the Ancient World compiled by Herodotus in the fifth century BC.

Here I would like to underline certain general traits of Yanesha and Western regimes of historicity, not with the intention of essentializing the differences between "us" and "them" (Layton 1994, 4) but to attain a deeper understanding of Yanesha disinterest for patrimonialization. Western forms of "experiencing and being in time" (Hartog 2005, 8) are characterized by an obsession with roots, descent, genealogical interest, continuity, and remembrance. We want to know where we come from and who our ancestors were, an inclination that explains the great popularity that genealogy websites have nowadays. But we also want to know—or are made to want to know—how deep the historical roots of our collectivities are and the chain of historical events that have shaped our communities, whether the latter are real or imagined (Anderson 1983). More interestingly, despite our acceptance of change as the substance of history, we Westerners are permanently concerned with demonstrating the continuity between our past and our present. We thrive on remembrance, and our memory is both comprehensive and undiscriminating—except perhaps in those cases in which memory of the past affects national sentiment or pride. We commit almost everything to memory through a broad range of institutions or technical means: museums, libraries, archives, mausoleums and memorials, and now servers, data centers, and the cloud. Ours is an omnivorous memory that has found one of its main instruments in patrimonialization.

We enshrine those places, objects, and cultural practices that are linked to the foundations of our nations: the French Declaration of the Rights of Man and of the Citizen, Scotland's Coronation Stone (Stone of Scone), or the United States Liberty Bell. We commemorate the events that contributed to the consolidation of our communities: Spain's completion of the Reconquista in 1492, Italy's unification in 1861, or Mexico's 1917 revolution. We celebrate the individuals whose actions paved the way for the rise of new nations: Jeanne d'Arc, George Washington, or Simón Bolívar. And we memorialize and celebrate our victories against external and internal enemies: London's Trafalgar Square, Berlin's Victory Column, or Spain's Valle de los Caídos. But most strange of all, at least from a Yanesha perspective, is that we also patrimonialize places that have been defiled by extreme forms of violence, discrimination and hatred: Anne Frank's hideaway in Amsterdam, Nelson Mandela's Robben Island Prison, Lima's Museum of the Inquisition, or New York's 9/11 Memorial and Museum. Dark tourism is a flourishing industry. Our omnivorous memory accumulates and patrimonializes both victories and defeats, noble and infamous acts, saints and bandits, as well as sacred and ordinary objects. In brief, it hoards both the sublime and the grotesque, the transcendent and the trivial.

Yanesha people are much more discerning when it comes to historical memory, the result of a regime of historicity that, as I have written elsewhere (Santos-Granero 2007), is driven by millenarian expectations and characterized by a constant struggle against temporality and its multiple evils: death, disease, and oblivion. According to Yanesha people's view, the present is a time-riddled period between a timeless past and an equally timeless future: an era that began with the loss of immortality and the introduction of differences between primordial people and is now characterized by death, alterity, hierarchy, and inequality. Thus, rather than being interested in historical roots, Yanesha people disregard the events that gave rise to the present era as the cause of all their evils and look forward to the future, impelled by the hope of putting an end to history and regaining their lost immortality. Instead of privileging descent, genealogies, and focal ancestors, they favor alliance, affinity, and forgetting the dead. Rather than preserving the illusion of historical continuity, they seem to accept the convulsive nature of historical transformations, especially with regards to the appearance of new, and often violent, social agents. Last, rather than promoting remembrance, they favor disremembering as a means of expunging historical memory not from references to the crude realities of power and alterity but from indications that such realities have in any way modified their identity as Yanesha, whose literal meaning is "we, the (true) people."

This explains why Yanesha leaders have shown so little interest in recovering the abovementioned landmarks. Defiled by white invaders and abandoned by the gods that gave origin to them, these failed/defiled places are a reminder not only of the violence, inequality, and distress brought about by white-mestizos but also of the Yanesha people's inability to protect them from the invaders. More important, these defiled landmarks are a tangible expression of the many changes the Yanesha have experienced since white people reinvaded their territory in the mid-nineteenth century. Whereas Westerners embrace change and reinforce their identities by means of an omnivorous memory permanently engaged in the hoarding of all kinds of events, peoples, places, and objects, Yanesha people expunge historical memory from certain changes through selective amnesia to preserve the notion that despite the multiple transformations they have experienced, they have not changed; they have always been the same. This explains not only why they have shown little interest in repossessing their landmarks but also why they have erased them from their historical memory.

This is exactly what has happened with Yompor Santo's tomb. In the two versions of the myth of Yompor Santo' that I collected in 1983–1984, it is said that after being hit by an ensorcelled slingshot, Yompor Santo' died and was buried in Metraro, after which his tomb became an important pilgrimage site. In a video titled *Yompor Santo': A Yanesha Ancestor* (IBC 2008), Yanesha intellectual Espíritu Bautista recounts a new version of this myth, asserting that Yompor Santo' neither died nor was buried: he went straight back to the sky world of Our Grandfather Yos. The video shows a group of Yanesha people visiting Metraro, but instead of representing the site as Yompor Santo's burial place, it refers to it as the place where Yompor Santo's temple stood. Since we know from oral and documentary sources that Yompor Santo' was buried in his worship house, it becomes clear that what is being erased from Yanesha historical consciousness is neither the memory of Yompor Santo' nor that of his temple, but the recollection of his tomb and its defilement by white people.

The origin myth of the Palmazú shrine has been similarly revised. According to this new version, narrated by Juan José Espíritu Soto, chief of the community of Tsachopen, in ancient times there were two powerful brothers, Yompor Yompere, and his evil brother Yompor Ror (Astuhuaman Agüero 2008). When Yompor Yompere was going back to the Pichis valley, his evil brother transformed him and his family into stone. In this contemporary version, there is no mention that this transformation took place in the context of the gods' ascension to the sky world; that the brothers were on their way to the mountain from which they would fly to the sky world; or that the sun god Yompor Ror had explicitly asked his brothers to wait for him before they ascended. As a result of these omissions, in this version the sun god appears as a "bad brother," instead of a brother justly offended by Yompor Yompere's refusal to wait for him. Not only that, but through these erasures contemporary Yanesha have diminished the mystical power and ritual significance attributed to the Palmazú shrine and with it all traces of the memory that the place was abandoned because it was defiled by white people.

In the Yanesha case, selective amnesia is not so much an instance of passive forgetting but one of active disremembering, a practice that seems to be intrinsic to the Yanesha mode of historical consciousness, and which also holds true for the neighboring Quechua (see Charlier Zeineddine, chapter 7). By disremembering certain aspects of history, Yanesha people refuse to acknowledge the significant transformations they have undergone as the result of the white man's occupation of their lands and prolonged interaction with the national society. At the same time, they refuse to admit that white people may be in any way superior to them or have the power to change them and their history. Through selective amnesia, Yanesha people seek to keep intact their historical agency, waiting for a better time to engage once more in the pursuit of their world-transforming hopes.

EPILOGUE

Having said this, it is fair to recognize that in the past fifteen years, things may have started to change. In March 2009, when conflicts between the state and Native Amazonian peoples were running high due to the concession of oil and gas exploration permits in Indigenous lands, Peruvian President Alan García signed a supreme decree creating the Mesa de Diálogo Permanente entre el Estado y los Pueblos Indígenas Amazónicos (Table of Permanent Dialogue between the State and Amazonian Indigenous Peoples) to seek "consensual solutions" to these disagreements (Servindi 2009). FECONAYA, the Yanesha federation, had an important role in the Mesa since it was one of the founding members of CONAP, the Confederación de Nacionalidades Amazónicas del Perú (Confederation of Amazonian Nationalities of Peru), which at the time was the government's main Native Amazonian interlocutor.[21] In its first progress report, published in the official newspaper *El Peruano*, on June 30, 2009, the Indigenous members of the Mesa de Diálogo set forth their most salient demands. Among the many actions required from the state, they listed: "To declare of national interest and provide the norms and mechanisms to recognize the intangibility and protection of the monuments, sanctuaries, and natural formations that have spiritual and historical value for Indigenous Peoples" (Mesa 2009, Acción E 3.4).

The report also proposed that the regional governments and the federal Office of Protected Natural Areas[22] should implement, in coordination with the Indigenous organizations, regional projects to identify areas to be reserved and protected. Among the sites listed as having the potential to become reserved areas are the Cerro de la Sal and the Cerro [*sic*] Yompor Yompere (Mesa 2009, Acción E 5.7). Interestingly, there was no mention of Juan Santos Atahuallpa's tomb. In addition, the report proposes that the Indigenous monuments, sanctuaries, or natural formations on public lands should be delimited and given in property to the community to which they belong, which from then on would be responsible for "using, administering and preserving them" (Mesa 2009, Acción E 3.6). Were the identified landmarks located on private lands, a law should be passed providing Indigenous peoples free access to those sites (Mesa 2009, Acción E 3.5).

As far as I know, this was the first time that Peru's Native Amazonian peoples included the preservation of sites of spiritual or historical significance among their demands. That the report describes the shrine of Yompor Yompere as a *cerro*, or mountain, when it is located on a valley bottom, suggests that the person who included it in the final text did not have direct knowledge of the site. It also suggests that the idea of introducing this demand in the Mesa's report may have been proposed by non-Indigenous advisers inspired by the global patrimonialization trend promoted and endorsed by UNESCO. Be that as it may, this demand forced the government to take a stance on the issue.

A year later, in April 2010, through OEFA, the Organismo de Evaluación y Fiscalización Ambiental (Office of Environmental Evaluation and Supervision), the government presented a report addressing the demands of the Mesa's Indigenous members. In response to the request to protect Indigenous landmarks of spiritual or historical value, it instructs regional governments and the Office of Protected Natural Areas to start identifying landmarks that could be turned into reserved areas. In addition, it recommends that, of the various landmarks mentioned in the Mesa's report, the Cerro de la Sal should be granted priority as a "historical sanctuary since it was one of the sites of Juan Santos Atahuallpa's uprising" (OEFA 2010, Respuesta de Acción E 5.7). The government's backing of this Indigenous initiative seems to have renewed Yanesha people's interest about their ancient landmarks. This was reinforced when, that same year, the government, in coordination with UNESCO, decided to create

FIGURE 1.7. *Yanesha people celebrating Yompor Yompere at the Palmazú shrine, 2010. Source: Tsachopen 2010b.*

the Oxapampa-Ashaninka-Yanesha Biosphere Reserve (Tuesta 2012). Among its cultural assets is the Palmazú shrine (UNESCO 2011, 8).

In response to these patrimonialization actions, in April 2010 the people of Tsachopen organized a first visit to the stone gods of Palmazú. We do not know much about this visit. However, judging from the pictures of the event posted online, this was a memorable visit that attracted many people and included prayers, offerings, singing, and dancing (see figure 1.7).[23] Later that year, Tsachopen marked the thirty-third anniversary of its legal creation as a "Native community" with a weeklong celebration that included a visit to the "Yanesha Sanctuary of Yompor Yompere" (Tsachopen 2010a). In the following years, visiting the Palmazú shrine became a regular event. Some say that annual meetings are held on the first full moon of May (SERNANP 2012); others claim that they are held on June 24, coinciding with the Inca festivity of Inti Raimi (Municipalidad 2012). One of these visits, made on June 11, 2015, to celebrate the fifth anniversary of the creation of the Oxapampa-Ashaninka-Yanesha Biosphere Reserve, included anthropologist Richard Chase Smith and members of the Ministry of Culture's Cultural Landscape Office (IBC 2015).

Does this renewed interest in their ancient landmarks mean that Yanesha people are intent on resurrecting the memory of the gods and heroes embodied in them? Do the increasing number of visits to the Palmazú shrine mean that they wish to bring the ancient stone gods back to life? It is too soon to give a proper answer to these questions. There are signs, however, that this is not the case. To start with, it seems clear that the renewed interest in these sites has not arisen from internal concerns but has been encouraged by external agents. This would not be a problem. Often, exogenous initiatives are assumed so wholeheartedly by Native Amazonian peoples that they become as if they were their own. If this were the case, one would expect Yanesha people to show equal interest in recovering the three landmarks. But all efforts thus far have focused on the Palmazú shrine, while the other two sites languish unattended.

The renewed interest in the Palmazú shrine does not derive from a resurgence of the "ancient people's religion," as some Yanesha refer to their ancestors' beliefs. Rather, it seems to be closely associated with a tourist initiative promoted by municipal authorities, local business owners, tourist agencies, and members of the neighboring community of Tsachopen.[24] In fact, in the 2010 celebration of Tsachopen's anniversary, which lasted a full week, the visit to the stone gods of Palmazú was outshone by the mass and procession in honor of the Miraculous Virgin that took place several days later as part of the closing ceremonies (Tsachopen 2010a). This suggests that the new interest in Palmazú does not indicate a change of perception regarding its failed/defiled nature. Rather, it seems to be an instance of the instrumentalization of cultural heritage for economic advancement and the reaffirmation of new senses of ethnic identity, very much like Stonehenge, Mexico's Templo Mayor, or the Greek Parthenon. Whether this may change in the future, it is too early to say. In the meantime, the patrimonialization-cum-zombification of the Palmazú shrine has forced Yanesha people to confront the violence and changes brought about by their colonial past, putting into question the notion that they have "always been the same." Whether this will be a good or bad thing for them is also too early to determine.

NOTES

1. In the older ethnographic literature and in most historical documents, the Yanesha are known as Amuesha, Amueixa, or Amages.

2. Myth of Yompor Yompere, narrated by Pedro Ortiz, Centro Esperanza, October 26, 1983.

3. Interview with Pedro Ortiz, Centro Esperanza, October 24, 1983. Pedro Ortiz

was one of Tsachopeñ's grandsons. Since he was born around 1904, he must have been a teenager by the time the ceremonial center was abandoned between 1910 and 1920.

4. Myth of Yato Queñȋoȋ, narrated by Espíritu Francisco, San Francisco, June 25, 1983; Myth of Posona', the Salt Person, narrated by Domingo Huayol, Azuliz, December 10, 1983. See Santos-Granero (2004, 345–48) for full version of the myth of Yato Queñȋoȋ.

5. *Chamairo* (*Mussatia* sp.) is a liana that is dried and then chewed, with coca leaves and lime to sweeten the mix.

6. Myth of Aserr, the Iron Person, narrated by Domingo Huayol, Azuliz, December 10, 1983. The name Aserr derives from the Spanish *acero*, confirming that Yanesha people obtained the knowledge of iron tool production during colonial times. Other Yanesha myth tellers claim that iron originated through the self-transformation of Yachor Aserr, Our Mother Iron.

7. Myth of Yompor Santo', narrated by Amador Quinchuya, Cacazú, May 19, 1984; Myth of Yompor Santo', narrated by Pedro Ortiz, Centro Esperanza, October 21, 1983. See Santos-Granero (1991, 80–83) for full version of the myth of Yompor Santo' as recounted by Amador Quinchuya.

8. By public wealth I mean "the totality of valued things—whether material or not—over which a collectivity claims to have rights of usufruct" (Santos-Granero 2015, 90).

9. The SIL Yanesha dictionary translates this as "to dispel a desired effect" (Duff-Tripp 1998, 118).

10. Interview with Amador Quinchuya, Cacazú, May 21, 1984.

11. Interview with Margarita López, Yuncullmaz, June 20, 1983.

12. Interview with Domingo Huayol, Azuliz, June 20, 1983.

13. Interview with Amador Quinchuya, Cacazú, May 21, 1984.

14. Interview with Amador Quinchuya, Cacazú, May 21, 1984.

15. Interview with Margarita López, Yuncullmaz, June 20, 1983.

16. Myth of Enc, narrated by Pedro Ortiz, Centro Esperanza, October 24, 1983.

17. Ashaninka people pronounce the name of the Yanesha divinity Yompor Yompere as Yompor Yompiri or Yompi.

18. Myth of Aserr, the Iron Person, narrated by Domingo Huayol.

19. Myth of Yompor Santo', narrated by Amador Quinchuya.

20. I understand the notion of "regime of historicity" in Hartog's (2005, 8) restricted sense of "the way in which a society considers its past and deals with it."

21. Later on, AIDESEP, the Asociación Interétnica de Desarrollo de la Amazonía Peruana (Interethnic Association for the Development of Peruvian Amazonia) was also incorporated into the Mesa de Diálogo.

22. Servicio Nacional de Áreas Naturales Protegidas (SERNANP).

23. For more pictures of this celebration see also: http://tsachopen.blogspot.pe/2010_05_01_archive.html, and https://picasaweb.google.com/113271326314145069206/SantuarioYomporYompere?gsessionid=wZpuxJRkbVsMfXXMEMlIrg (accessed April 2016).

24. See www.facebook.com/munihuancabamba, www.oxapampa.biz, and tsachopen.blogspot.com.

REFERENCES

Aco, Pablo. 2013. *Cerro de la Sal: Reseña histórica del Cerro de la Sal: nativos, misioneros y colonos* (blog). Accessed March 2016. https://cerrolasal.wordpress.com/reconquista-quista-republicana/.

Amich, José. 1975. *Historia de las Misiones del Convento de Santa Rosa de Ocopa*. Lima: Editorial Milla Batres.

Anderson, Benedict. 1983. *Imagined Communities: Reflections on the Origin and Spread of Nationalism*. London: New Left Books.

Arantes, Antonio A. 2013. "Beyond Traditional: Cultural Mediation in the Safeguarding of Intangible Cultural Heritage." In *Anthropological Perspectives on Intangible Cultural Heritage*, edited by Lourdes Arizpe and Cristina Amescua, 39–56. New York: Springer.

Astuhuaman Agüero, Fredy Jaime. 2008. "Encuentro cultural-turístico: 2506 años de resistencia histórica cultural del pueblo indígena yanesha." *Revista Creser*, December 1, 2008. https://issuu.com/creser/docs/creser_edicion_diciembre.

Bailly-Maitre, Luis. 1908. "Viaje de estudios del Estado mayor general del ejército entre Huánuco y el Mairo." In *Colección de leyes, decretos, resoluciones y otros documentos oficiales referentes al departamento de Loreto*, vol. 14, edited by Carlos Larraburre i Correa, 593–635. Lima: Oficina Tipográfica de La Opinión Nacional.

Barclay, Frederica. 1989. *La Colonia del Perené: Capital inglés y economía cafetalera en la configuración de la región de Chanchamayo*. Iquitos: Centro de Estudios Teológicos de la Amazonía.

Bevan, Robert. 2006. *The Destruction of Memory: Architecture at War*. London: Reaktion Books.

Biedma, Manuel. 1981. *La conquista franciscana del alto Ucayali*. Lima: Editorial Milla Batres.

Cano y Olmedilla, Juan de la Cruz. 1775. *Mapa geográfico de América Meridional*. Madrid: Editor Juan de la Cruz Cano y Olmedilla y Hippolytus Ricarte.

Carranza, Albino. 1894. "Geografía descriptiva y estadística industrial de Chanchamayo." *Boletín de la Sociedad Geográfica de Lima* 4 (1–3): 1–32.

Chirif Tirado, Alberto, Carlos Mora Bernasconi, Carlos Yáñez Boluarte, and Tulio Mora Gago. 1975. *Comunidades Nativas Selva Central-Diagnóstico socio-económico*. Lima: Sistema Nacional de Apoyo a la Movilización Social.

del Monte, Juan. 1894. *Recuerdos de la montaña: episodios de un viaje de Lima-Iquitos por los ríos Azupizú, Pichis, Pachitea, Ucayali y Amazonas*. Lima: Imp. Masias.

Duff-Tripp, Martha. 1998. *Diccionario Yanesha' (Amuesha)-Castellano*. Lima: Instituto Lingüístico de Verano.

Fabriq'am. 2016. La fabrique des "patrimoines": mémoires, savoirs et politiques en Amérique indienne aujourd'hui. Accessed February 2016. https://fabriqam.hypotheses.org/.

Frigolé, Joan. 2011. "Patrimonialization and Mercantilization of the Authentic: Two Fundamental Strategies in a Tertiary Economy." In *Constructing Cultural and Natural Heritage: Parks, Museums and Rural Heritage*, ed ited by Xavier Roigé and Joan Frigolé, 13–24. Girona: Documenta Universitaria (Publicacions de l'ICRPC, 4).

Hartog, François. 2005. "Time and Heritage." *Museum International* 57 (3): 7–18.

IBC (Instituto del Bien Común). 2008. *Yompor Santo': A Yanesha Ancestor*. Video directed by Wilton Martínez, Espíritu Bautista, and Richard Chase Smith. Lima: Instituto del Bien Común. Accessed March 2016. https://www.youtube.com/watch?v=M6BLVnxrwx8.

IBC (Instituto del Bien Común). 2015. Archivo Digital de la Memoria Yanesha. Facebook post, June 11, 2015. Accessed February 2016. https://es-es.facebook.com/Archivo.Digital.Yanesha/posts/850070645069225.

Izaguirre, Bernardino (comp.). 1923. *Historia de las misiones franciscanas y narración de los progresos de la geografía en el oriente del Perú*, vol. II. Lima: Talleres Tipográficos de la Penitenciaría.

La Combe, Ernesto. 1892. "Informe que presenta el Coronel Don Ernesto de La Combe a la Sociedad Geográfica, dándole cuenta de su expedición al río Azupizú y del camino que a él conduce." *Boletín de la Sociedad Geográfica de Lima* 1 (10–12): 414–36.

La Combe, Ernesto. 1905. "Informe presentado por el Coronel Don Ernesto de La Combe a la Sociedad Geográfica de Lima, dándole cuenta de su viaje al Pichis con motivo de la inauguración del camino que conduce a ese río." In *Colección de leyes, decretos, resoluciones y otros documentos oficiales referentes al Departamento de Loreto*, vol. 7, edited by Carlos Larrabure i Correa, 486–511. Lima: Imprenta La Opinión Nacional.

Layton, Robert. 1994. *Who Needs the Past? Indigenous Values and Archaeology*. London: Routledge.

Loayza, Francisco A. 1942. *Juan Santos, el Invencible: Manuscritos del año de 1742 al año de 1755.* Lima: Editorial D. Miranda.

Memorial. (1663) 1986. "Véase en el Consejo de Indias el Memorial adjunto que se me ha dado en nombre del capitán Don Andrés Salgado de Araujo y sobre la conquista que propone se me consultara lo que se ofreze y parezieze; transcribed and with an Introduction by Fernando Santos-Granero." *Amazonía Peruana* 7 (13): 135–59; 8 (14): 131–49.

Mesa. 2009. Mesa de Diálogo entre el Estado y los Pueblos Indígenas: Avance en la Revisión y Actualización del Plan de Acción para los Asuntos Prioritarios de la Comisión Especial Multisectorial de Comunidades Nativas—Comisión Especial Multisectorial para las Comunidades Nativas (D.S. 15–2001-PCM). *Diario Oficial El Peruano*, June 30.

Mihas, Elena (with Gregorio Santos Pérez and Delia Rosas Rodríguez). 2014. *Upper Perené Arawak Narratives of History, Landscape, and Ritual.* Lincoln: University of Nebraska Press.

Mora, Carlos, and Alonso Zarzar. 1997. "Comunidades nativas en la amazonía peruana." In *Amazonía peruana, comunidades indígenas, conocimientos y tierras tituladas: Atlas y base de datos*, edited by Antonio Brack Egg and Carlos Yáñez, 1–27. Lima: GEF, PNUD, UNOPS.

Municipalidad. 2012. Atractivos y circuitos turísticos. Municipalidad Distrital de Huancabamba. Accessed February 2016. http://www.peru.gob.pe/Nuevo_Portal_Municipal/portales/Municipalidades/1553/entidad/PM_MUNICIPALIDAD_DETALLE.asp?pk_id_tema=94685&pk_id_sub_tema=12252.

Navarro, Manuel. 1924. *La Tribu Amuesha.* Lima: Escuela Tipográfica Salesiana.

OEFA. 2010. Respuestas por Acciones al Plan de Acción para los Asuntos Prioritarios de la Comisión Especial Multisectorial de Comunidades Nativas. Lima: Organismo de Evaluación y Fiscalización Ambiental (8 de abril de 2010). Accessed February 2016. http://minagri.gob.pe/portal/download/pdf/especiales/ley forestalydefaunasilvestre/comentarios-oefa-gncppii-8abr-2–8abr1o.pdf.

Ordinaire, Olivier. 1988. "Una excursión al país de los Campas." In *Del Pacífico al Atlántico y otros escritos*, edited by Olivier Ordinaire, 167–99. Iquitos: CETA/IFEA [coll. Monumenta Amazónica D1].

Ortiz, Dionisio. 1967. *Oxapampa: Visión histórica y desarrollo de la provincia de Oxapampa, en el departamento de Pasco.* 2 vols. Lima: Imprenta Editorial San Antonio.

Oxapampa.biz. 2020. Círculo de piedras Yompor Yompire. Accessed December 2020. https://oxapampa.biz/index.php?id=105.

Parró, G. 1892. "Informe del Director de Obras Públicas y presidente de la comisión inauguradora del camino de San Luis de Shuaro al Pichis." In *La Vía Central del Perú*, ed ited by Joaquín Capelo, 40–48. Lima: Imprenta Masías.

Plano. 1897. *Plano General de las Montañas del Pozuzo, Huancabamba y Oxapampa levantado por orden de la Dirección de Fomento en 1897.* Lima: Litografía San Cristóval.

Raimondi, Antonio. 1874–1902. *El Perú: Historia de la geografía del Perú.* 4 vols. Lima: Imprenta del Estado.

Remy, Federico E. 1898. *Apuntes sobre el clima y flora de la región del Pichis.* Lima: Imprenta del Monitor Popular.

Renard-Casevitz, France-Marie. 2002. "Social Forms and Regressive History: From the Campa Cluster to the Mojos and from the Mojos to the Landscaping Terrace-Builders of the Bolivian Savanna." In *Comparative Arawakan Histories: Rethinking Language Family and Culture Area in Amazonia,* edited by Jonathan D. Hill and Fernando Santos-Granero, 123–46. Urbana: University of Illinois Press.

Rojas Zolezzi, Enrique. 1987. "La percepción en el discurso mítico de los Campa Ashaninka del Perené de las relaciones de dominación política y subordinación económica surgidas del proceso de colonización." Bachelor's dissertation, Pontificia Universidad Católica del Perú.

Rojas Zolezzi, Enrique. 1994. *Los Ashaninka: Un pueblo tras el bosque.* Lima: Pontificia Universidad Católica del Perú.

San Antonio, Joseph. 1750. *Colección de informes sobre las missiones del Colegio de Santa Rosa de Ocopa.* Madrid.

San Joseph, Francisco de. (1716) 1750. "Copia de un informe hecho por el V. Padre Fr. Francisco de San Joseph, comisario de missiones del Cerro de la Sal . . . al Rmo. P. Fr. Joseph de San Antonio." In *Colección de informes sobre las missiones del Colegio de Santa Rosa de Ocopa,* edited by Joseph de San Antonio. Madrid.

Santos-Granero, Fernando. 1988. "Templos y herrerías: Utopía y re-creación cultural en la amazonía peruana, siglo XVIII." *Bulletin de l'Institut Français d'Etudes Andines* 17 (3–4): 1–22.

Santos-Granero, Fernando. 1991. *The Power of Love: The Moral Use of Knowledge Amongst the Amuesha of Central Peru.* London: Athlone Press.

Santos-Granero, Fernando. 1993. "Anticolonialismo, mesianismo y utopía en la sublevación de Juan Santos Atahuallpa, siglo XVIII." *Data, Revista del Instituto de Estudios Andinos y Amazónicos* (La Paz) 4: 133–52.

Santos-Granero, Fernando. 1998. "Writing History into the Landscape: Space, Myth and Ritual in Contemporary Amazonia." *American Ethnologist* 25 (2): 128–48.

Santos-Granero, Fernando. 2004. "Los Yanesha." In *Guía etnográfica de la alta Amazonía, Volumen IV: Matsigenka, Yánesha,* edited by Fernando Santos and Frederica Barclay, 159–359. Lima: Smithsonian Tropical Research Institute/Instituto Francés de Estudios Andinos.

Santos-Granero, Fernando. 2007. "Time Is Disease, Suffering and Oblivion: The Struggle against Temporality among the Yanesha." In *Time and Memory in Indigenous Amazonia: Anthropological Perspectives*, edited by Carlos Fausto and Michael Heckenberger, 47–73. Gainesville: University Press of Florida.

Santos-Granero, Fernando. 2015. "Public Wealth and the Yanesha Struggle for Vitality." In *Images of Public Wealth or the Anatomy of Well-being in Native Amazonia*, edited by Fernando Santos-Granero, 89–113. Tucson: University of Arizona Press.

Santos-Granero, Fernando. 2018. *Slavery and Utopia: The Wars and Dreams of an Amazonian Worldtransformer*. Austin: University of Texas Press.

SERNANP. 2012. Reserva Comunal Yanesha–Plan Maestro 2011–2016. Lima: Servicio Nacional de Áreas Naturales Protegidas por el Estado. Accessed February 2016. http://old.sernanp.gob.pe/sernanp/archivos/biblioteca/planes_maestros_2012/PM%20RCY%202011-2016.pdf.

Servindi. 2009. "Perú: gobierno crea mesa de diálogo permanente con pueblos indígenas." March 23, 2009. Accessed March 2016. https://www.servindi.org/actualidad/9471.

Sinclair, Arthur. 1895. *Tropical Lands: Recent Travels to the Sources of the Amazon, the West Indian Islands, and Ceylon*. Aberdeen: D. Wyllie & Son.

Smith, Richard Chase. 1974. "Los Amuesha: Una minoría amenazada." *Participación* 3 (5): 54–62.

Smith, Richard Chase. 1977. "Deliverance from Chaos for a Song: A Social and Religious Interpretation of the Ritual Performance of Amuesha Music." PhD dissertation, Cornell University.

Smith, Richard Chase. 1981. "The Summer Institute of Linguistics: Ethnocide Disguised as a Blessing." In *"Is God an American"? An Anthropological Perspective on the Missionary Work of the Summer Institute of Linguistics*, edited by Soren Hvalkof and Peter Aaby, 121–32. Copenhagen: IWGIA & Survival International.

Smith, Richard Chase. 2011. "¿Un sustrato Arawak en los Andes centrales? La historia oral y el espacio histórico cultural Yánesha." In *Por donde hay soplo*, edited by Jean-Pierre Chaumeil, Oscar Espinoza de Rivero, and Manuel Cornejo de Chaparro. Lima: IFEA/PUCP/CAAAP/EREA.

Tamayo, Augusto E. 1904. *Informe sobre las colonias de Oxapampa y Pozuzo y los ríos Palcazu y Pichis*. Lima: Imp. Liberal Unión.

Tibesar, Antonine S. 1950. "The Salt Trade among the Montana Indians of the Tarma Area of Eastern Peru." *Primitive Man* 23: 103–8.

Tsachopen. 2010a. Comunidad Nativa Tsachopen: Feliz 2518 aniversario. Accessed February 2016. http://tsachopen.galeon.com/.

Tsachopen. 2010b. "Programas para fines de semana." *Comunidad Nativa de Tsachopen* (blog), April 23, 2010. http://tsachopen.blogspot.com/2010/04/programas-para-fines-de-semana.html.

Tuesta, Sonaly. 2012. "En la reserva de la biósfera (aprendiendo de los yáneshas)." *Diario 16*, September 17, 2012. https://issuu.com/diario16peru/docs/17-09-2012.dg.

UNESCO. 2011. "Cuarenta años de laboratorios del desarrollo sostenible al aire libre." *Boletín trimestral de información sobre las ciencias exactas y naturales* 9 (4): 2–11. http://unesdoc.unesco.org/images/0021/002122/212222S.pdf.

Varese, Stéfano. 1973. *La sal de los cerros: una aproximación al mundo campa*. Lima: Retablo de Papel.

Webster's II. 1984. *Webster's II New Riverside University Dictionary*. Boston: Riverside Publishing Company.

Weiss, Gerald. 1975. *Campa Cosmology: The World of a Forest Tribe in South America*. New York: The American Museum of Natural History.

Zarzar, Alonso. 1989. *"Apo Capac Huayna, Jesús Sacramentado": Mito, utopía y milenarismo en el pensamiento de Juan Santos Atahualpa*. Lima: Centro Amazónico de Antropología y Aplicación Práctica.

2

Maya Living Ruins

The Hidden Places of Interlocking Temporalities

Valentina Vapnarsky

Surprising as it may sound, today's Yucatec Maya tend to be rather unfamiliar with the most spectacular remnants of their forebears' architecture. Indeed, while minor ruins—sometimes little more than heaps of stones—play a prominent role in their daily spiritual lives, this is not the case when it comes to pyramids, temples, palaces, and other majestic ruins.[1] This became clear to me while I was filming a documentary on the concept of vestiges, and I invited a group of Maya *comadres*, *compadres*, and friends from the villages I have been visiting for almost twenty-five years to explore the Coba and Tulum ruins. None of them had ever seen the ruins, now restored and open to the public, though two had previously been to Tulum, one as a child to hunt with his father, when the ruins were still covered by the surrounding forest and only accessible by walking many hours along a narrow path. Our group inspected the stones closely while listening to the tour guide, who, for the first time, was giving the tour in Maya. A few months later, one of our group, Delio, told me how he had thought long and hard and finally understood what he had seen there. Coba, he believed, featured two types of construction. The first, that of the early men, was characterized by carved, polished, and rounded stones and was similar to an ancient structure near his village known as the Tampak', where rituals are frequently held; the same characteristics were found among more discreet burial mounds in his field. The second type of construction was marked by the use of

FIGURE 2.1. *Delio Chan Chi visiting the ruins of Coba. Photo: Valentina Vapnarsky, 2015.*

resin to hold the stones together, a secret known only to ancient builders. The structures had been built by kings using their people as slaves, in the same way, he added, that contemporary hotel owners have exploited the Maya for decades as the cheapest form of labor. This comparison between monument ruins and the hotel industry, including the forced servitude of workers during these two distinct periods, was quite common among the Maya of the region.

In his comments about the stones, Delio had established connections between older ruins like Coba and Tulum, the Tampak', and his field and connections between kings and hoteliers. Each connection involved some type of rupture. Whether architectural, historical, political, or, as we will see, ritual or ontological, these ruptures ensure that these different types of structures—from majestic pyramids to small mounds in the milpas (cornfields)—retain significance in the present. And although they are all designated under the same term, *múul*, and are all considered to be living (*kuxa'an*), these structures support and reveal distinct regimes of memory and coexisting temporalities, which I aim to demonstrate in this chapter.

The role played by vestiges as active indicators of the past—or rather pasts—is well-known in Mesoamerica, where we find centuries' worth of ancient structures being repurposed in the context of political and/or religious legitimization, whether through architectural or ritual acts (López Luján 2019 and references therein) or as part of eschatological belief systems (Balsanelli 2018, 273–74; Boremanse 1998, 103). Vestiges have sometimes served as the foundations of new edifices, punctuating urban spaces with signs of a bygone age or as symbols of wilderness. They can also be used as remote sites of worship or be considered the destination of souls of the dead. In all cases, these ruins have been at the heart of political and religious life in Mesoamerican societies for many centuries, long before the conquest (Halperin 2014; Hamann 2002; Stanton and Magnoni 2008). However, closer attention should be paid to the precise modalities by which these material traces continue to shape different regimes of temporality and historicity for those Maya who have long since become detached from pre-Hispanic elites. Three main topics deserve further investigation.

The first concerns the specific and sometimes contrasting properties attributed to vestiges by the diverse Indigenous groups of Mesoamerica, properties related to the vestiges' material and cognitive memorial potential and also to the vital force and spiritual entities attached to them. These properties have not yet been sufficiently explored through the lens of local conceptions of animacy, agency, and life (see Erikson and Vapnarsky, introduction). In Maya studies, Evon Vogt's (1969, 85–90) famous ethnographical account of house ensoulment ceremonies in the Tsotsil community of Zinacantán has influenced generations of scholars, particularly archaeologists, who have used it to interpret a variety of rituals linked to manmade structures. However, the notion of ensoulment may well have been overextended, with few, if any, authors critically examining what "ensouling" and "having a soul" actually mean, as Begel, Chosson, and Becquey (2022) argue. Mesoamerican ethnographies tend to mention the *living* nature of buildings, but this notion may encompass less, or more, than having a soul. The living nature might, for instance, derive primarily from the materials used for construction, from the environment from which the materials were extracted, or from the "masters" of the materials or of the places themselves, as argued in the introduction to this volume. We need to better understand local conceptions of the internal processes, external forces, and agencies that cause vestiges to be considered *living* (see also Pitrou 2015). In the same vein, ruins are reported to have an "energy" of sorts. This notion also begs to be critically scrutinized, especially given how ubiquitous it has become in a variety of New Age and institutional narratives that endow it with meanings far removed from the original Indigenous conceptions that they allegedly stem from, and which they may in turn help to reshape (see also Erikson and Vapnarsky, introduction; Molinié, chapter 6).

Second, a deeper understanding of what vestiges mean to those living near them leads us to confront the range of relationships people have with the past, even within a single society, and to appreciate the discursive, material, experiential, and interactional forms that relating to the past may take (Armstrong-Fumero 2011; Bloch 1998; Vapnarsky 2017). Other studies have highlighted the various techniques—in particular, specific discursive genres—that Amerindian societies use to shape elaborations of biographical and historical events (see, for instance, regarding the Amazon, Basso 1995; Fausto and Heckenberger 2007; Franchetto 1993; Oakdale 2005). Furthering this perspective, our analysis of local connections to vestiges aims to shed light on the role played by forms of materiality and spatial anchoring in the shaping of regimes of temporality, which involve not only discourse and actions but also a universe of multifaceted artifacts and beings. This implies considering "the intimate tactile contact" of people who encounter remnants of the past in their quotidian life-world (Armstrong-Fumero 2011, 65) and the diverse gestures, emotions, and restrictions attached to them—in other words, how people live with ruins.

Finally, an in-depth study of local conceptions of vestiges is all the more necessary now that remains of the past are increasingly the object of heritage programs, in which Amerindians themselves are involved. Yet, while Western-style heritage actors and Maya may find consensus in ascribing value and salience to ruins, the underlying conceptions that govern these attitudes are in fact quite opposed, sometimes to the point of conflict. Such disagreements are usually confined to the realm of museums and national reserves, but they can also occur in the remote outskirts of villages, where few ever venture. That is precisely where we will transport ourselves, far from famous ruins. Whereas there has been a series of works on the relations of modern Maya with ruins in the plaza and in the outskirts of Chichen Itza' (Armstrong-Fumero 2011, 2014; Castañeda 1996; Redfield 1932), to our knowledge no such accounts exist for more remote and isolated places like those of our study.

Building on these themes, this chapter explores how present-day Yucatec Maya people relate to vestiges and how vestiges function as loci of parallel and sometimes interwoven temporalities. Moving from narratives of the past and the future to ordinary references to past and future events, and from the said to the unsaid, I will show how vestiges act as spatial and material catalysts for Maya historicity and distinguish different domains of temporality. Specific attention is paid to the role played by the spiritual or ancient entities linked to these places in various ways, whether through interaction or narrative. Vestiges appear to support an earthly cosmology that, under the guise of permanence, allows different temporal processes, in particular, regeneration and latency, to co-occur.

After an overview of the different stone arrangements that are commonly recognized by Yucatec Maya, I analyze the two main types of vestiges that index the different temporal processes that this chapter seeks to bring to light. Understanding these temporal relations requires scrutinizing local conceptualizations of the spiritual inhabitants of these places as well as Maya eschatology, and observing discreet practices and elliptic speech rather than eliciting formal, focused explanations. The final section presents an intermediary case between the two main types of vestiges, in which temporal processes accumulate and are condensed, thus intensifying somewhat the memorial and living properties of the place. The conclusion returns to the relationship between cultural heritage and regimes of temporality anchored in Maya vestiges.

HILLS AND MOUNDS, PYRAMIDS, OLD VILLAGES, AND GRAVES

The Yucatan Peninsula is a flat, karstic region, a vast expanse of forest lying at sea level, where the slightest changes in topography are conspicuous.[2] While these may be no more than hills, they often also conceal *múul*, stone mounds partially covered by vegetation and dating from times long gone for the inhabitants of the region. These sites are all the more striking in our specific study area, in the eastern part of the peninsula. For centuries, the area remained far removed from colonial powers and was sparsely inhabited until the Macehual Maya arrived here in the aftermath of the so-called Caste War in the nineteenth century. Whereas the Maya of the northern and western regions occupied urban centers relatively continuously for centuries before the Spanish conquest and their towns were marked by colonial architecture, the Macehual Maya, being relative newcomers to this eastern region, can trace the founding and history of their villages just a few generations back. This is particularly true of those living just south of Felipe Carrillo Puerto, where I have been conducting fieldwork since 1994.

During my years in the field, I came to notice how my Maya hosts would make observations about stones and their arrangement, both in the forest and the fields. First, almost swallowed up by the surrounding vegetation, are the *xla'kaaj*, old abandoned villages, the organization of which can be deduced from their similarity to contemporary settlements: low-walled yards around which paths can still be made out, the foundations of houses, and even signs of an old well. On the outskirts of inhabited villages, there are also "cemeteries," areas of overlapping stone circles set around graves (*muknal*), sometimes quite recent, though deliberately left to the mercy of the forest: clearing these places would only serve to create more space for the dead, thus inviting more death. These kinds of circles, or more modern graves, can also be found in people's backyards, where some still prefer to bury their dead, so long as the local authorities tolerate it.[3]

FIGURE 2.2. Xla' kaaj, *or abandoned villages (top left);* muknal *burial in a village cemetery (top right);* Maya house and koot *wall in an inhabited village (bottom left); man weeding near a* bu'tun *mound in his milpa (bottom right). Photos: Valentina Vapnarsky, 2015.*

In fields, the underlying layer of limestone can crop out anywhere; there are so many rocks scattered about that often the land has to be sown in an improvised, staggered pattern.[4] Rocky slopes rise out of these clearings, though rarely more than a few meters. These may be simple *bu'tun*, small, inconspicuous mounds of rocks without any discernable arrangement, believed to have simply accumulated and to continue to grow on their own. According to local beliefs, stones grow naturally. But then there are also the *múul*, "piles" or "stacks" of rocks, where one can see, or at least infer, some sort of organization (e.g., angles, flat surfaces, or alignments) and the conspicuous use of polished or carved stones.

The majority of *múul* are quite subtle, blending in with the landscape of everyday life, movement, and work, while still the object of precautions and pronouncements. Other *múul* in the area are distinguished for their large size, as well as for their architecture, such as the Tich' Muul pyramid, which only a few people have ever ascended. Closer to the village that is the focus of our study lies the palatial Tampak' *múul*, where rituals and offerings are still regularly carried out, as we will see later. And, finally, there are the *múul* that stand out most

FIGURE 2.3. Múul *left uncleared in a field. Photo: Valentina Vapnarsky, 2015.*

exceptionally, such as the pyramids and structures of faraway Kob Ha' (Coba) and Chi'ch'e'en Itza' (Chichen Itza'), which Maya speak of but never visit, and to which a number of narratives surrounding past human eras are attached.

LIVING RUINS AND FAMILIAR SPIRITS: REGENERATION

Let us start with the most ordinary type of *múul*, those that Maya come across by chance, often while hunting or clearing the forest to make room for their crops. These mounds, a few meters tall, are considered to be "living" (*kuxa'an*), inhabited by the *yuuntsilo'ob*, which roughly translates as "masters" or "lords" (*yum* "father," *-tsil* absolutive marker for kinship terms, *-o'ob* third-person plural). *Yuuntsilo'ob* is a generic term referring to the guardian spirits of a surrounding area, both earthly and celestial. These beings are also called *nukuch báalamo'ob* (etymologically: "great jaguars") or, more commonly *nukuch máako'ob*, a polysemous term that can be used to designate people (*máak*) belonging to former humans, the ancestors, the predecessors, or present-day elders (Vapnarsky and Le Guen 2011). In addition to the bond with the ancient

FIGURE 2.4. *Delio Chan Chi showing polished stones found in his milpa and attributed to previous generations. Photo: Valentina Vapnarsky, 2015.*

generations that *nukuch máako'ob* suggests, the term also functions as a sort of euphemism. In fact, only during ritual discourse can these spirits be invoked by their more specific names (Vapnarsky 2013), such as *aj kanan-k'aaxo'ob, aj kanan-moontanyailo'o, aj kanan-muulucho'ob*, "guardians of the forests, guardians of the high forest, guardians of the low mounds." Some of these ritual appellations, including the last one (*muulu'uch* is a dialectal variant of *múul*), clearly demonstrate the connection between these guardian spirits and vestiges. *Múul* are explicitly described as the houses (*naj*), or indeed homes (*otoch*), of the *yuuntsilo'ob* spirits, who are considered their *uyuumil* (third-person possessive form of *yuum*), a term commonly used in reference to the inhabitants of a house or village. Like human homes, *múul* are believed to be "living" (*kuxa'an*) as soon as they are lived in, after which they are said to have vital energy (*óol*) derived from those who reside within them. It is often said that this is why an uninhabited house will quickly fall into disrepair: without its inhabitants, its *óol* is gone.

The land surrounding a *múul* is known to be especially fertile.[5] But the spirits who—as guardians of these places—allow you to cultivate or hunt near the *múul* must first be fed (*tséent*), one of the offerings that Maya regularly make as *bo'ol-meyaj*, "labor payment." These offerings constitute a contribution for the right to use these spaces and also a reward for the services that these guardian spirits are said to provide (protecting against danger, providing rainfall, keeping the harvest safe from pests, etc.). Those who forgo these offerings incur all sorts of affliction, such as being bitten by a snake, crushed by a falling tree, blinded by thorns, or plagued by disease. These unfortunate events, together with the cries of domestic animals or the sounds of conversation heard at night or on certain days (Tuesdays and Fridays, especially around Easter), are in fact the principal signs used to infer the presence of the *yuuntsilo'ob* and thus the living (*kuxa'an*) nature of any given *múul*.[6] And though the *yuuntsilo'ob* may be connected to other places in the area, particularly the *xla'kaaj*, abandoned villages, as we will explore later, *múul* represent focal points where their presence is expressly considered to be more palpable and intense.

Some people may seek to enter *múul*, which are said to contain ancient objects—fragments of old ceramics and stone tools are commonly found across the region—and hidden treasures. But to enter a *múul*, its residents must first be appeased with the offer of a cool maize drink. Otherwise, as soon as the first stone is lifted, a cold wind will blow, of the dangerous *tankas íik'* variety, a wind that can cause headaches or fever and lead to death. In fact, an offering may not suffice, for these *yuuntsilo'ob* spirits are known to each have their own character: while the better-natured may allow you to enter their home, others may keep you out, despite your best ritual efforts.

Múul, like caves, are thought of as entrances not so much to the underworld (incidentally, a notion frequently misunderstood in ethnographies on contemporary Maya) but rather to a parallel world inhabited by spiritual beings, one not easy for humans to access. This parallel world is not necessarily underground; indeed, the *yuuntsilo'ob* are spirits that belong to the *yóok'ol kab*, "above ground," the terrestrial space where humans and animals also reside. This vast surface layer lies between the underworld (*yaanal lu'um*, "below ground")—an aquatic realm at the bottom of which lies the *metnal*, the deepest underworld layer, today associated with hellfire—and the celestial layers (*uyaal ka'an*), at the top of which reside the higher deities (see also

Hanks 1990, 304–6). Within this cosmogony, the *yuuntsilo'ob* are the entities closest to humankind in the spiritual and divine hierarchy presided over by *Ki'ichkelem Yuum*, "Wondrous Lord," a Maya version of Jesus Christ, and *Jajal Dyos*, "True God." They are the laborers who aid humans in their farming and forest activities.

Humans may be taken into the villages of the guardian spirits to receive esoteric teachings or when the spirits want to make doubters understand who brings the rains and why offerings are necessary. Getting lost in the forest is an experience that often triggers such a journey, although the paths leading up to the spirit villages do not seem to go through a specific topography or sensorial landscape (Vapnarsky 2013). There are stories, however, that relate how those who have been "taken" by the *yuuntsilo'ob* come to look down on their land from on high. In these stories, the *yuuntsilo'ob* are said to be in the sky, on the fringes of the first celestial layer, where they hop among the clouds to unleash the rains, "watering the milpas" from their inexhaustible gourds. They carry off those who doubt their existence, and these doubters take some time to understand that what they see is an aerial view of their own field. One story tells of a poor boy who escaped the *yuuntsilo'ob* village only to be caught hanging from a *chiikam* (*Pachyrhizus erosus*) root that had been planted in their milpa, which he had tried to climb down to get back to his own village. Although the *yuuntsilo'ob* move about every day in forested areas (which are considered to include fields), they remain anchored to the two frontiers of the *yóok'ol ka* terrestrial world: the space adjoining the first celestial layer and the half-buried *múul*.[7]

To better understand the spatiotemporal, memorial, and living properties of *múul* mounds, further comprehension of the nature of their main occupants and life-givers, the *yúuntsilo'ob*, is required. Based on reports of experiences that mention their presence, the behaviors adopted toward them, and stories that describe their various exploits, the *yuuntsilo'ob* appear to be entities possessing certain typical traits of spiritual ontologies: they are said to be of the winds or airs (*íik'*)[8]; they do not touch the ground; they are physically moved by the very mention of their own names (hence the restrictions surrounding their names, which can only be uttered by a specialist during ritual ceremonies); they cannot be seen (except when they assume the appearance of familiar beings), but they can see us; they communicate to each other by whistling; for humans, they exist as collectives, without any specific individuality (besides that of belonging to their subcategory); they live on earth, but in liminal spaces; they are immortal: *xma'xuul kuxtal, mina'an kíimil ti'o'ob*, "their life is without limit, they do not know death."

And yet, on the other hand, they closely resemble humans: they possess a human form, although slightly taller; they wear hats and white cotton clothes, much like the grandparents, the "big people," the *nukuch máako'ob*, the name most commonly used to refer to them, and which, as we have seen, can designate living elders, deceased relatives, and ancestors, as well as spirits; they eat a particular variety of tortillas (*x tuuti waaj*, a type of ritual bread prepared specially as an offering during ceremonies in their honor); their forest homes and villages are laid out in the same way as human settlements[9]; and they have their own milpas and livestock (the cries heard coming from the *múul* are invariably those of domesticated animals: chickens, roosters, turkeys, horses, and occasionally sheep). Each spirit has its own personality, which can be more or less severe. Those called upon or referred to during rituals or in stories are male *yuuntsilo'ob*; they are the workers with whom humans interact. But when I inquire, I am told that they must also have their women waiting for them back in the *múul*. And they probably speak Maya among themselves. In fact, the very idea that the *yuuntsilo'ob* might communicate in Spanish seemed so outlandish to one of my Maya friends, so at odds with what we might call the inherent, defining Indigeneity of these spirits, that when I suggested it, she burst out laughing uncontrollably.

Given the traits attributed to them, the Yucatec *yuuntsilo'ob* seem to represent a clear example of the Mesoamerican tendency to project one's own society onto mountains or other spaces (see for instance the prehuman *baatsik'* beings among the Teenek, Ariel de Vidas 2004). They do, however, differ from other groups, such as the Tseltal of the Chiapas highlands, another Maya group studied by Pitarch (1996) and also described in this volume (Becquey and Chosson, chapter 3). For the Tseltal, the mountain interior *ch'iibal* embodies the Other and is strewn with *lab*, which constitute the many souls of each individual while simultaneously representing colonial and Ladino power, as well as their excess, wealth, and modernity materialized by reproductions of non-native species and artifacts. Thus, according to the Tseltal, the *lab* sit in the tall chairs of the colonial authorities rather than on traditional stools, and their animal or vegetal incarnations are of the *kaxlan*, "castilla" type. Furthermore, the most modern objects, from televisions to helicopters, can be found in these mountains, sometimes even viewed as skyscrapers (Pitarch 1996, 107, 110–23). In contrast, the *yuuntsilo'ob* of the Yucatec Maya are traditional and solemn. Rather than Others or outsiders, they are insiders, in terms of both lifestyle and space, for they are not found in distant mountains or beyond the horizon, as in Chiapas; instead, they reside close by, in a shared space of daily interactions.[10]

The *yuuntsilo'ob*, eternal beings and guardian spirits of surrounding spaces, are tightly linked to the past, due not only to the characteristics mentioned above but also to the process of habituation (*suuk*) associated with them (Hanks 1999, 234; Vapnarsky, Yvinec, and Becquey, 2022). Indeed, anyone seeking to use a new plot of land has to adapt their offerings to what the *yuuntsilo'ob* have previously "been accustomed to." It is not uncommon for a *jmeen*, ritual specialist, to claim that an illness befell an adult or a child because the spirits did not "accept" (*ma' tuk'amo'ob*) the offering as it did not meet their expectations. In such cases, the *jmeen* will then prescribe a ritual with newly defined offerings (type of food, number of calabashes, how often, etc.) that should be more in keeping with the habits of the *yuuntsilo'ob*. At the same time, those making the offering can, by their own individual actions, partially change the nature of these gifts or when they should occur, thus not only perpetuating but transforming the habits. Through their habituation to these places and the ritual practices dedicated to them, the spirits both represent and continue a local and intergenerational history of human occupation of and generative interaction with the lands they use and live on.

The ritual speeches used to summon the *yuuntsilo'ob* further demonstrate these clear links to territorial space and a local and experiential memory. To bring guardian spirits to the altar to accept the offerings laid out for them, the ritual specialist must project his voice into the surrounding space to seek them out in the specific locations within the territory to which they are spatially attached. Most of these locations correspond to former dwelling places: some are *múul* mounds, while many others are *xla'kaaj*, abandoned villages (Vapnarsky and Le Guen 2011). Although *xla'kaaj* are clearly distinguished from *múul* by the type of material construction and their temporality, the spiritual entities that inhabit them may overlap, thus establishing a close relationship between these two kinds of places.

In the course of conversations with my Maya interlocutors, other signs emerged that confirmed this veiled yet concrete connection that the *yuuntsilo'ob* have with the predecessors and the recent dead. For instance, when I enquired what becomes of *jmeen* ritual specialists when they die, although most answers expressed uncertainty, I was told a few times that they probably become guardian spirits themselves. While the link between ritual specialists and *yuuntsilo'ob* is sustained insofar as the latter teach the former during dreamlike or ecstatic encounters in the forest, it also seems to express the hazy continuity that the Maya have more generally established between themselves and these spirits. This continuity can also be seen by the temporal complementarity of the souls of the dead and the *yuuntsilo'ob* guardian spirits.

While the recent dead are mentioned by name during the rituals performed annually for their souls, after about two generations they become part of a generic collective known as the *pixano'b*. Thereafter, they are no longer called upon during family rituals and instead are only invoked collectively at the end of the prayers for the dead in church rituals offered by the village (Le Guen 2003). Whereas the souls of recently deceased people often interact with the living, the collective of generic souls no longer manifests as such in the Maya's lives and experiences. This absence of interaction contrasts with encounters with the souls of those who died more recently and who are still individuated by name, but also with encounters with *yuuntsilo'ob* spirits, whose presence outside the village, and inside it after nightfall, is clear to all.

I will mention one final revealing example on this subject. The road leading from the village where I stay to the next one, barely four or five kilometers distant, runs alongside a village that had been abandoned following an epidemic and other grim events two or three generations earlier. People were reluctant to travel this stretch of road at dusk for fear of "being frightened there." Old Don Sidro knew the history of this village well, since he had been a child when it was abandoned. In particular, he remembered the day when a man lost his senses there during a first fruits ritual, driving him to kill his own brother while he believed he was hunting a deer. For years after, whenever Don Sidro or his friends passed by the place at nightfall, they sensed that something was throwing sticks or stones at them. This was undoubtedly the soul (*pixan*) of the dead man, Don Sidro explained. Later, a woman was said to have found a way to protect herself and her two daughters by taking off their clothes before passing through. Not only did the *pixan* not attack them, this also seemed to put an end to the nocturnal confrontations. The powerful effect of the sight of naked women is typical of accounts about the *yuuntsilo'ob*; narratives include violent scenes of irrepressible attraction experienced by *yuuntsilo'ob* obliging them to leave the premises. A similar dramatic effect is found with the *arux* (also known as *alux*), clay figures often associated with *múul*, which people say grandparents would fashion to protect their crops, setting them in the earth and invigorating them with their blood to bring them to life. The *arux* often became too demanding of their masters, and in this case, putting them in the presence of a naked woman was considered one of the only ways to destroy them: they would explode (Vapnarsky and Le Guen 2011, 202).[11] Almost fifty years after the village had been deserted, our friends still feared to pass by it at dusk because of the whistling (*xoob*) they could hear nearby, which, they said, the *yuuntsilo'ob* spirits use to communicate with humans and alert them to dangers.

This story shows that, while *pixano'ob* souls and *yuuntsilo'ob* spirits may be distinguished linguistically and in metadiscourse, they are implicitly connected through actual practice, and perhaps even related in their very essence, insofar as the former seem to merge imperceptibly into the latter in stories and memories.[12] From this, we might deduce, in contrast to the Yucatec process of ancestralization that has previously been suggested (Le Guen 2003), that, after two or three generations, the dead typically undergo a process of "generification"—that is, they become generic—and spiritualization, in the transition from *pixano'ob* souls to *yuuntsilo'ob* forest spirits. Whereas souls at first remain attached to their name, their family home (where offerings are made to them), and their grave, they gradually become detached from these anchor points. They are no longer mentioned during family rituals, they no longer enter the homes of their descendants to be fed (which now occurs in church during a collective ritual), and their graves are no longer maintained and become overgrown.

It is worth noting that the house (*naj*)/home (*otoch*) plays a central role in this process, for the named souls of the recently deceased as much as for the *yuuntsilo'ob* spirits. In addition to the bond with their descendants' homes, to which still-identified souls regularly return, the burial site, as Le Guen (2003) has argued convincingly, is seen as the house (*naj*) of the deceased: first, the dead are buried in their home (or, if they must be buried in a cemetery, this considered an extension of the home); second, the grave itself can be treated as a home, notably by erecting a structure of wood and palms that resembles a house (Le Guen 2003, 187; Redfield and Villa Rojas 1934). Similarly, the stone circles marking the graves are described as *u koot*, like the low wall surrounding a residential compound. Based on these observations, the *múul*, home of the *yuuntsilo'ob* spirits, appears as a spatiotemporal and ontological transposition of a grave, the first home of the *pixano'ob* human souls.

The spirits residing within the *múul* of inhabited areas are thus incarnations, or at least indexes, of a relatively recent past. By contrast, the entities who reportedly built these ruins are often associated with distant times. Indeed, the *múul* bear certain intriguing features that Maya observers use as material clues to their great age. *Úuchben, úuchben, jach taaj úuchben, ooraako' mina'an che', chen lu'um yéete tuunich*: "They are old, they are old, they are very old, at that time, there were no trees, only earth and rocks," Delio once told me in his milpa, while demonstrating how the roots of the trees grow over the piles of stones and showing me traces of ancient ceramics (*k'aat*) scattered around them. He continued without hesitation: if trees had existed at the time, their roots would grow underneath the stones. For some, this means that these *múul* predated modern humans and were built by the *Ch'ilankabo'ob*, people from another age with extraordinary abilities. Others, including Don Yano, a renowned ritual specialist, claimed instead that the *múul* had been fashioned later, during the earth's redemption by *Ki'ichkelem Taata* (or *Yuum*), the "Wondrous Lord." Once he had finished creating the earth, he is said to have lain down these stones, which are thought of as the earth's bones, its skeleton.

> *Ma' umeyaj ch'ilankabo'ob bin, ma' umeyaj máakobi', es kee u meyaj Ki'ichkelem Taata . . . jebix le múulo' kawiliko' ma' chen máako' meentbili', lete' ka' foormarnaj yóok'ol ka', lete' ka' beetab le lu'uma', leti' ka' wa'akúunsa'a(b) tun beya'.*

> "This is not the doing of the *ch'ilankabo'ob*, nor the doing of people, it is the doing of *Ki'ichkelem Taata* . . . the *múul* that you see, men did not make them, it is when the surface of the earth was formed, when the earth itself was created, that is when they were arranged like this."

These divergent interpretations reflect not so much individual differences in knowledge as the intermediary position that the *múul* of inhabited spaces occupy between two other types of place that also take material form: first, the *xla'kaaj*, abandoned villages, associated with recent generations and a common personal, familial, and communal memory that is both agentive and experiential; and second, the *rwiinas*-type *múul*, belonging to distant times and spaces, and attached to a different type of regime of memory altogether, one which we will now explore.

MYTHIFIED RUINS AND PETRIFIED PEOPLE: LATENCY

The term *múul* can also refer to grander ruins, ranging from large structures still hidden under forest cover to monumental *rwiinas*-type *múul*. The word *rwiinas* is borrowed from the Spanish *ruinas*, "ruins," which is commonly used in Mexico and in wider Latin America to designate archaeological sites—particularly those open to the public and popular among tourists—of which there are a significant number on the Yucatán Peninsula. Most of the Maya I met in my villages of study had only ever known about these *rwiinas* through hearsay, but now images of iconic archaeological sites reach them even in their remote villages via television, tourism commercials on billboards, political ads on T-shirts, or Coke cans. Relatively recently, schools have started taking children on field trips to some of these established tourist sites, such as Tulum; yet most adults, even those working in local hotels, have not had the chance or indeed the inclination to visit them themselves.

The Maya from the villages I frequent remark in passing that these *rwiinas* were built by humans of past eras, the *Ch'ilankabo'ob* and the *P'uus*, some of whom were petrified (*tuunichajo'ob*, "they have turned to stone") and remain buried beneath the half-crumbling structures. It is said that one day they will come back to life and take the place of modern humans once the latter have been annihilated by a cataclysm similar to those that destroyed people from previous ages or when a statue holding a trumpet finally brings the instrument close enough to its mouth to blow it, thus signaling the beginning of the prophesied war. At this point, the *úuchben máako'ob*, the ancient men, will return to form an alliance with today's Maya and fight alongside the British and the Americans against the Mexicans. *Biin ka' súunako'o' ya'ala, tumen leti'o' kun ba'te'o', ma' to'oni'*, "It is said that one day they will return, for it is they who will fight, not us." This prophecy is directly related to the history of the Maya during the Caste War and to the alliances they formed with the British Crown, based in Belize, and those they sought to establish with Americans through archaeologists in the region (Sullivan 1989). It is in keeping with other widespread prophecies that predict a return to war after the current period of truce, the Amistad, a war that will finally restore power to the Maya (Sullivan 1984; Vapnarsky 1996). Other stories surrounding these ruins are more widespread, having long been reported in the ethnography of the Yucatán peninsula (Redfield 1932; Redfield and Villa Rojas 1934; Tozzer 1907, 153–54; Villa Rojas [1945] 1987, 438ff). It is said, for instance, that Chichen Itza' was connected to Tulum by a *kuxa'an suum*, a "living cord" forming a celestial arched road that bled from its middle. The kings of the Maya and those of the *Ts'úul* (rich white Spanish men) challenged each other to carry a hot tortilla from Tulum to Mérida; a Maya knight won by using this celestial *sak beej*, "white road," a fact often recalled with a big smile.[13] Sadly, however, the cord was cut, and so bled to death, or at least disappeared.

On a wider scale, these accounts of ruins being inhabited by humans of past eras who are destined to return represent a recurring theme in Mesoamerican mythology. They are found in many ethnographies, ranging from Maya to Pueblo territories, including central Mexico, where they have been widely documented, and masterfully summarized by Alfredo López Austin (2011). This motif is based on the disappearance underground of early beings—often thought of as giants in central Mexico, or variants thereof[14]—and their transformation to stone, frozen in a state of latency. These beings, like those in our accounts, are said to have miraculously built the archaeological ruins. Additionally, in many cases they are embodied by the figure of a king who is often described as an avatar of Montezuma, whose foretold return will allow the petrified beings, temporarily vanquished, to reclaim their power from the forces of oppression in an instance of political millennialism (López Austin 2011; 2015, 191) reminiscent of the prophecies of future alliances and war against the Mexican government found in our region.

Rwiinas-type *múul*, like the more subtle *múul* dotting the local landscape, are living places where animal cries can also be heard on certain nights, but, unlike the common *múul*, it is their state of latency that is emphasized, manifested through this temporary petrification. They represent a macrohistorical horizon that is clearly defined, removed from the present, yet freshly delineated by recent interethnic relations shaped by twentieth-century political alliances that emerged from the earlier Caste War. Moreover, while the story of the tortilla race along the celestial cord between the Spanish and the Maya may be only vaguely remembered, its very survival as one of very few narratives we have relating to the *rwiinas* confirms the significance of these places as motifs carved from the memory of the political conflicts that have shaped the long history of the Maya.

VESTIGES AND SPIRITS: INDEXES OF MAYA MULTITEMPORALITIES

Whereas Maya ethnographies that describe vestiges generally mention these mythical or macrohistorical accounts, the data and analysis presented here show that beneath the *múul* are hidden beings that personify a rather different relationship to the past and to historicity. On one hand, the *yuuntsilo'ob* instantiate history on a microcollective and personal level, based on people's lived experiences and immediate surroundings. They are alive, immortal, hypermobile, active (they work in their own villages, work to help humans in their fields, protect the forests, alert humans to danger, etc.), and occupy an inhabited, dynamic space. Above all, they are linked to the past of current, living humans and, as such, are subject to rituals and continual negotiations. In ritual discourse, they are invoked, summoned, manipulated, and rewarded; there are also countless detailed narratives of their deeds and misdeeds, whether generically speaking or on a more biographical level (Vapnarsky 2013). Yet, on the other hand, the *úuchben máako'ob*, "ancient people," of the *rwiinas*-type *múul* belong to the greater macrohistory of the Maya cycles of creation and destruction of successive humankinds. They have disappeared, are frozen in a state of latency, simultaneously dead and alive. In contrast to the mobility and agency of the *yuuntsilo'ob*, the *úuchben máako'ob* are static and passive, hidden away in their inaccessible *múul* and other distant places, as far removed in time

TABLE 2.1. Contrasting properties of entities dwelling in living ruins

	Yuuntsilo'ob	Úuchben máako'ob
Life	Living	Gone (latent)
Agency	Action	Inaction
Mobility	Hypermobile	Static; petrified
Visibility	Invisible	Petrified
Communication	Sounds (whistling); dream or forest visits; human appearance	Silence, mute
Narrativity, type of discourse	Ritual discourse; detailed and reinvented stories	Prophecies; succinct, unchanging stories
Time—History	Microcollective	Macrocollective
	Current humans	Past humans
Space—Territory	Inhabited, active, used space	Distant, imagined space
Vestiges	*Múul* and *xla'kaaj* (mounds and abandoned villages)	*Rwiinas*-type *múul* (mounds-ruins)

as they are in space, since they derive from past human eras. Framed within succinct, almost telegraphic, and highly stereotyped narratives, these men of bygone ages are most commonly evoked in prophetic statements that serve to interpret typical present-day behaviors and events, ranging from politics at the collective level, as we saw above, to moral judgments, sometimes conveyed in expressions close to proverbial sayings. So, the *P'uus*, ancient hunchbacks said to have disappeared as a result of their depraved mores, are often cited by elders to criticize new practices. One elder, lamenting the youth's inability to correctly express ritual requests, remarked: "*Bey ich le p'uuso' le bu'ulobo' beyo', bey kukáaja úuchu béejla'*," "Like the *P'uus*, who were drowned, it's beginning to happen again." Another, disapproving of a man's marriage to his own cousin, exclaimed rather more crassly, "*Puuta! tun ka' suut uraasa le p'uuso'obo'*," "Shit! Here come the *P'uus* all over again!"

Múul operate as a macrocategory of stone vestiges that articulates two separate temporalities—recent memories and daily experiences framed in a life process of regeneration, and ancient historical pasts seeping from a life in latency—and the distinct ruptures each involves. To better understand the form of temporalization that *múul* operate, we can look at how these places function like the Yucatec Maya temporal particle *úuch*, meaning "previously, long ago." This particle signals a temporal stepping back of several days or more, and can extend as far back in time as needed; it is used as often for the recently deceased as for the most distant times of past humans. Yet the distance that *úuch* expresses is not only temporal; it is also praxical, experiential, and/or emotional. This is why, for example, the recently deceased tend to be temporalized using *úuch* only after a particular series of rituals has been performed, which allow the individual to become aware of his or her death and the living to separate themselves from their kin. Similarly, *múul* both imply and express these ruptures that transform humans into ontologically (*yuuntsilo'ob*) or historically (*úuchben máako'ob*) distinct beings.

And, as does the temporal particle *úuch*, *múul* connect these two types of beings in a way that seems to combine them and distinguish them at the same time. They have marked contrasts as detailed above, yet both are linked to *múul*, which are their *naj*, "homes," and both are designated by the same term *nukuch máako'ob*, "big people," and considered to be *íik'*, "air" or "winds." *Nukuch máako'ob* expresses the generational and historical relationship between these beings and present-day humans despite historical and ontological ruptures.[15] In contrast, *íik'* points to their different experiential and sensorial makeup, in terms of visibility, mobility, communication, and temporality, that distinguishes these beings from present-day humans.

THE *MÚUL* CHURCH AND THE CLOISTERED SAINT

The Maya story of *rwiinas*-type *múul* is consistent. Whether distilled through comparisons with contemporary events or condensed into concise narratives, it has withstood the modern, pyramid-imbued phantasmagoria of the political and tourism machine. But are these two visions in fact so different? After all, on the surface, the enduring, typically Maya conception of past and departed humans fits rather well with the Western myth of the complete and cataclysmic disappearance of the ancient Maya. It also reflects the gulf that has been created between the ancient, pre-Hispanic Maya and their present-day descendants by national policies that prefer to see the latter as peasants or workers in an insistent effort to create a homogenized mestizo society. Another rupture between human eras. And the ancestors of old are as buried away beneath the ruins for today's Maya as they are for archaeologists, tour operators, and political decision makers, although, for the Maya, internment does not equal annihilation and may indeed be only temporary. From another perspective, the affinity that the Maya have built between themselves and these different incarnations of past humans, despite the ontological and historical differences detailed above, could be seen to echo, albeit loosely, the idea of continuity and endurance espoused by most heritage and restoration programs, which embrace these vestiges from the past. Yet, on closer inspection, the Maya and Western views on vestiges and "cultural heritage" are fundamentally divergent.

Not far from a Maya village in my area of fieldwork there stands an imposing stone structure variously designated *nojoch múul*, "big *múul*," *nojoch rwiinas*, "big ruins," or *igleesya*, "church," and also known by its proper name: the Tampak'. Hidden within the forest, this structure is theoretically quite accessible, about a kilometer from the village and barely a hundred meters from the main road. For the Maya, this is obviously an ancient structure, although how and by whom it was built remains unclear. The Tampak', "adobe wall" (a common toponym for these types of structure on the peninsula), is associated with a particular tale and its many variations: at this place, a hunter once came across a saint, *x Ki'ichpam maama K'an le' oox*, brushing her long blond hair. Strikingly, and quite unusually, this saint bears the name of one of the very few deities still called by her Maya name, despite being described with features more typical of a medieval princess.[16] Here, the hunter also discovered and stole a hoard of gold guarded by two enormous serpents, an act that led to his death and, more important, to the place being sealed off from the outside world. Another version tells of a man pursued by soldiers during the war between the Maya and the Mexicans who took refuge in the Tampak'. The beautiful saint protected him and gave him a bag of provisions so he could continue on his way. Once outside, however, the man was captured and forced to reveal where the bag had come from. The soldiers, armed with hammers and shovels, then found their way to the Tampak', where they destroyed an outer wall while trying to gain entry. The house within has been closed off ever since; the hole created by the armed men is still visible.

I myself was escorted to the Tampak' with great caution by Don Juan, an old man who was one of my main interlocutors during the first months of my stay in the region, when I was living in a neighboring hamlet. Convinced of my sincere interest in the stories from the times of war, but also that I must be an emissary of the British Crown or other allied nations, he offered to take me in secret to the Tampak', whose stones, he said, guarded ancient writings that I, with my knowledge of English, would no doubt be able to understand. Over twenty years later, having significantly expanded my network of acquaintances and friends throughout the surrounding villages, I came to realize what a privilege this visit had been. Indeed, few Maya from outside the Tampak' *ejido* had ever been there.[17]

Now fully sealed, the Tampak' remains home to *x Ki'ichpam K'an le' oox*. Cloistered within the stones, visible only to those rare people destined to see her, she protects the surrounding area, which the local people also conserve

FIGURE 2.5. *Tampak'* structure with its modern altar protected by a plastic sheet. Photo: Valentina Vapnarsky, 2015.

to protect her. In particular, one should not hunt or gather plants in the area, except sparingly. This has allowed a microforest ecosystem to develop, rich in flora and fauna, eliciting joy and admiration among the villagers, who visit rarely and only when strictly necessary. Snakes reportedly swarm the path in such numbers that one can hardly avoid walking on them. But one walks without fear, for the saint prevents misfortune for those who come with good intentions. The *Tampak'* is an important site of local worship where various rituals are performed, including the *k'eex*, "exchange," to protect children,[18] and the *looj*, a major collective ritual normally held in a central church for those villages without a *Tampak'*. These rituals are addressed to *x Ki'ichpam K'an le' oox* but also, famously, to the local *yuuntsilo'ob* spirits. Indeed, the *k'eex* and *looj* rituals involve unique associations between these two types of beings. The *k'eex* are normally addressed to the *yuuntsilo'ob*, but, given their relation to children—in a place where the Virgin, *Ki'ichpam maama* par excellence, looks after the young—local logic dictates that a female saint should also be invoked. Meanwhile, *looj* are the only community rituals in the region in which offerings are made to both the *yuuntsilo'ob* and the saints, strictly alongside one another and at the same time, each on a separate altar inside the church,

Figure 2.6. *Offerings for the kʼeex ritual at the Tampakʼ*. Photos: Valentina Vapnarsky, 2015.

presided over by two distinct ritual specialists, with specific incantations for each respective group of entities.[19]

A whole series of interweaving stories surrounding the Tampakʼ present various external attempts, by biologists, botanists, and no doubt archaeologists and soldiers, to study, clear, and restore the ruins. Despite these outsiders' determination to intervene and preserve the site, the villagers have always systematically refused, which at times has led to violent clashes. For them, there is no doubt that allowing outside interference would lead the *Ki'ichpam maama* to shut herself away once and for all, deeper still than when the soldiers had breached the wall to gain entry to the ruins.

In essence, the Tampakʼ consolidates, rather paradigmatically, the memorial and historiographical power of *múul* as topoi—in both the literal and the rhetorical sense—that encompass the integration, conversion, and assimilation of past experiences. It should not surprise us that local Maya villagers—despite their involvement in tourism and artisanry—seek to guard the site from external eyes and actions, which would break the transactional bond that they maintain so closely with the powerful beings associated with it. Moreover, and perhaps more crucially, outside intervention could rupture the very ruptures that the Maya have conceived and honed to assimilate, by distance and separation (both historical and ontological), the foundations of their very long (hi)stories: of historical cycles of humankinds and (inter)ethnic relations (the *rwiinas*-type *múul)*; of more local and intergenerational themes (the simple *múul*); and, finally, of the structures, such as the Tampak', that combine the two. Thus, any emphasis on continuity would in fact deprive the *múul* not only of their interpretive historical power but also of their political and ritual power.

THE RUPTURES AND INTERLOCKING TEMPORALITIES OF LIVING RUINS

This chapter has dealt with how present-day Yucatec Maya people relate to what we call vestiges. Amplifying previous descriptions, I have let my thoughts linger on a variety of ancient ruins and places that are significant to Maya eyes, beyond the major temples and buildings to which tourists now flock. These meaningful places consist mostly of old stones, ranging from plain circular rock arrangements marking relatively recent burials and promptly devoured by the forest, to small mounds, to abandoned villages cloaked in vegetation, to imposing structures. Some are simply left to decay in the forest, others are visible but barely noticed, and still others are objects of great attention. Analysis of historical and biographical local Maya narratives concerning such places, combined with close scrutiny of the daily practices surrounding them, has shown that each type is liable to activate specific links between past and present and specific visions of future.

What is particular about vestiges referred to as *múul* is that they at once encompass and distinguish two orders of memorial inscription: first, that of macrohistory and politics, and, second, that of biography and land use, which stone carves into different cosmological and temporal configurations. In this way, some *múul* (of the *rwiina* type) function as major historical anchor points in the frame of cyclical history, characterized by interruptions and recurrences rather than by continuity. Ancient humans are petrified in these ruins as they wait to come back to life in the next historical cycle. In the meantime, for the Maya of Quintana Roo I have lived with, there is no interaction between these stone figures and present-day people, no negotiation, no dialogue, no ritual investment—only repeated prophecies of resurgence that build hope for new freedom and Indigenous political emergence. A state of latency.

In contrast to the temporal and interactional inertness of major faraway ruins, small mounds are teeming with life and activity. Far from the grand cyclicity of macrohistory, the most mundane of Maya vestiges—the ancient mounds found in the forest and in cultivated plots—embody the tenuous and generative relationships uniting humans of previous and current times. Although considered, as are major ruins, to have been built by humans of bygone eras through miraculous or forgotten techniques, they are, above all, the live houses of the guardian spirits that inhabit and protect the area and collaborate with humans in their agricultural, silvicultural, and hunting activities. Since the guardian spirits are also attached to the *xlaj-kaaj*, abandoned villages whose builders were humans of more recent times, they also pertain to the contemporary historical era. Furthermore, all these mounds of both decay and life are connected materially and conceptually with graves. Because of this connection and other properties, I have argued that guardian spirits implicitly incarnate dead people's souls. Through their spiritual inhabitants, the more discreet and local *múul* instantiate processes of habituation, domestication, and regeneration.[20]

In both cases, *múul* are marked by ruptures of various kinds: historical and interactional for the distant *rwiinas*, and mostly ontological for the proximate *múul* mounds. For the latter, it is worth mentioning that despite the many features and transformative processes that link the guardian spirits to past humans, there is no explicit discourse drawing a continuous line between these two kinds of entities. Instead, people say that guardian spirits were created by True God at the beginning of the present era and have lived ever since in their parallel, though accessible, world. In fact, this Christian version reinforces the otherness of the ruin dwellers, and hence the sense of rupture associated with all *múul*, which, from a Maya point of view, is an absolute prerequisite for significance and salience to be ascribed to these places.

Thus, the relationship with humans of past eras who inhabit *múul* should not be conflated with a link to ancestors. In the many ritual, formal, and informal discourses that I witnessed over the years in the villages, no mound building or occupation was ever attributed to "our ancestors." This differs from what has been reported in other regions of the Yucatán Peninsula. In particular, the "ancestral" stance seems to have become predominant among the younger Maya generation living near major sites like Chichen Itza'. In these places, although it took a few generations, interaction with archaeologists, national institutions, tourists, and New Agers has led to a radical reformulation of the relationship with ruins and remains, now associated with "Maya ancestors" (see Armstrong-Fumero 2011, 73, and the introduction to this volume).

By contrast, ethnographies from the early days of archaeological exploration, such as Robert Redfield's famous account of the Maya from Chankom, show that the Maya living in the vicinity of Chichen Itza' at that time told quite different narratives about these ruins and interacted with them in diverse ways (Redfield 1932; Redfield and Villa Rojas 1934). People used to ascribe these sites to humans of previous historical eras—who still live under the ruins, very much like our guardian spirits—and so feared contact with ancient artifacts that they smashed them to avoid entering a domesticating relation with them. At the same time, they reused other artifacts in a very practical way, such as taking old carved stones from pyramids to build new houses. Thus, the Maya living in the vicinity of Chichen Itza' a few generations ago related to the *múul* and other remains in ways similar to what we still observe in our area today, combining the properties of the two types of *múul*.

Could the distinction between the two types of *múul*—*rwiinas* and ordinary *múul*—be another consequence of the fact that the Maya have been dispossessed of some of their major ruins as a result of archaeological and tourist-focused programs? It is quite remarkable that, according to my data, only the ruins characterized by latent beings are called *rwiinas* in Maya. Latency and petrification follow from Maya historical cycles (characterized by the disappearance of the people of each age), but they also fit well with the broken relationship between the Maya and their *múul* brought about by programs that enclose vestiges in the untouchable sphere of "cultural heritage" (untouchable for local inhabitants, though very manipulated by foreign experts). Thus, whereas in the villages I frequent, more distant from and less affected by the tourist-archaeological turmoil than other regions, cultural heritage programs have not (yet?) resulted in an "ancestral" reformulation, they may nevertheless have reinforced the properties of latency and frozenness of some ruins, but also, in a complementary manner, intensified the projection of interactional and ritual relationships onto small mounds. This has arguably led to two inverse dynamics: on one hand, a sort of "zombification" (see Santos-Granero, chapter 1) of major ruins and, on the other hand, the reinvigoration of more intimate *múul*. Zombification, however, does not always imply defilement. Sites such as Chichen Itza' and Tulum remain highly salient historically even for faraway Maya. The rupture created by cultural heritage programs may even have reinforced the historical rupture that is so foundational to the meaning of those sites for the Maya. Much more than mere indexes of the past, these sites continue to catalyze events and political relations, projecting them into the long-term, cyclical before-and-after of present-day people.

This sense of rupture also accounts for the eagerness of some Maya communities to protect local ruins from being explored, studied, rebuilt, or turned into tourist attractions, as was illustrated in the case of the local Tampak' ruins. As a place where a saint, enclosed in stones, is associated with guardian spirits, in new sets of ritual exchanges with local inhabitants, the Tampak' reveals a recent ceremonial community reinvestment of vestiges that combines, in addition to secrecy, the two temporal modes of latency and regeneration.[21] This complex multitemporal frame that articulates different forms of ruptures and estrangements is what, from a Maya perspective, eventually makes ruins more meaningful and alive.

NOTES

1. This chapter largely came about as part of the ANR project Fabriq'Am: The Making of "Heritages": Memory, Knowledge, and Politics in Amerindia Today, with different versions of the text having been presented at its meetings ("La fábrica del 'patrimonio' en las sociedades amerindias: regímenes de temporalidad, historicidad y transmisión," Buenos Aires, December 7–8, 2015, and "Culture: Modes d'emploi—La patrimonialisation à l'épreuve du terrain," Paris May 30–June 1, 2016). The film mentioned below (currently being edited) was shot in 2015 with Patrick Deshayes as part of the same project. I would like to thank the participants of these meetings for their comments.

2. In the region under study, the maximum difference in elevation is 23 meters.

3. Despite its being illegal, I have witnessed since 1994 several burials in people's yards, especially for younger children or for older relatives who expressly ask this of their families before dying. Although against the law, this practice renews its popularity whenever the village authorities show tolerance for it. Grave sites are normally a short distance from the house, in the middle ground separating the domestic space and the forest. See also Le Guen (2003).

4. However, this is not the case in the *xka'ka'lu'um* or *box lu'um*, "black lands," the most fertile, low-lying areas, albeit prone to flooding.

5. In their study of Maya agricultural practices, carried on in Xoken, a village in the eastern limit of Yucatán, Teran and Rasmussen (1994, 139) also note that the soils considered the most fertile are those that were inhabited in old times or located in more recently abandoned gardens.

6. References to noises coming from such places are common across all parts of Mesoamerica (Lopéz Austin 2015, 184).

7. It is worth noting that *múul* may also refer to a mound of earth without stones, such as the *múul saay*, termite mounds; these, however, are said to lead to the

underworld home of the devil *kisin*. Mocking a *jmeen* ritual specialist, one man commented that the shaman had found his *sáastun* divinatory crystal on a *múul say*. This meant he was working with the devil rather than with the guardian spirits, since such crystals should be found on *múul*, where the *yuuntsilo'ob* spirits (and certainly not termites) "give" them to their discoverers. Accordingly, the presence of some sign of rock formation seems essential to a *múul*'s function as a point of attachment for the *yuuntsilo'ob*, and for the historicity that they imply, as we will see below.

8. *Íik'* refers to the air one breathes, air streams, or winds. It is also used to designate invisible spiritual entities of different sorts.

9. See also Villa Rojas ([1945] 1987, 293).

10. The Yucatec *yuuntsilo'ob* spirits' otherness relates them more to the forest world than to the Ladino one: their stools are said to be curled snakes and their tortillas the large, ear-shaped, white mushrooms that grow on trunks.

11. Redfield (1932, 305) also remarks that the Maya from Chankom associate the ancient clay artifacts found in the ruins with the *alux* and tend to conflate them with the *balam* guardian spirits, who are henceforth (re)located in the ruins.

12. Villa Rojas ([1945] 1987, 299) also notes that such *íik'* are souls forced to wander in divine retribution for their bad behavior in life, a more Catholic and moralistic explanation of the transformation at play.

13. In another version of the tale, the knights are replaced by a squirrel (the Maya) and a horse (the Spanish).

14. Versions with giants are also found among the Maya.

15. Ultimately, these uses of *nukuch máak*, encompassing everything from what we have translated as past humans of previous historical eras to present-day humans and spirits, invite us to reconsider what the category of *máak* "person" may refer to among the Yucatec Maya.

16. This is *x K'an le' oox*, "green breadnut tree (*Brosinum alicastrum*) leaf," linked with maize and crop fertility.

17. An *ejido* is an area of communal land used for agriculture, on which community members individually farm designated parcels and collectively maintain communal holdings. In the region under study, each *ejido* is associated with one main village.

18. The *k'eex* "exchange" is a common ritual among Yucatec Maya people, performed when someone's disease is attributed to guardian spirits having taken their soul or energy (a small wax figurine standing for the patient is offered along with gifts of drink and food in exchange for the person's liberation, hence the ritual name). Noticeably, in the village adjoining the Tampak', the *k'eex* seems to have generalized into a ritual held for any child in the first months of life to ensure their protection by the Ki'ichpam maama and the other spiritual entities invoked.

19. See Redfield and Villa Rojas (1934, 173–74), for instance, for a brief description of this ritual.

20. Archaeological, ethnohistorical, and some ethnographical data show that, in Mesoamerica, mounds and pyramids were often related to mountains (Halperin 2014; López Austin and López Luján 2009; among others). Interestingly, this metaphor is absent from my data, where there appears to be no link between *múul* and the famous Maya concept of *wits*. Moreover, Maya people clearly distinguish between artificial mounds (purposely built by previous people) and others, which simply result from growing stone accumulation (at most, at God's hand, but with no human intervention). A connection can nevertheless be found in the fact that present-day Yucatec people say that societies of living spirits are located in *múul*, and the Highland Maya (e.g., the Tseltal) say that living soul societies are located in mountains. The most striking contrast is, as argued above, that the Yucatec *muul*'s spirit societies reflect inwardly to traditional imagery, whereas the Tseltal Maya inner mountain world of soul societies projects outwardly to colonial and highly modern technologies and imageries.

21. The combination of temporal modes is reminiscent of the Lacandons' uses of ruins. For the Lacandon, closely related to the Yucatec, ruins such as Palenque, Yaxchilán, and Bonampak were until recently the home of gods, and there the Lacandon celebrated rituals, burned incense, and gave offerings. Moreover, they believed, and many of them still do, that souls of the dead pass through vestiges to reach their final realm, which is close to the gods' abodes. Like guardian spirits, gods also make their home in living ruins, which look to the gods like the ordinary thatched-roof houses humans live in.

REFERENCES

Ariel de Vidas, Anath. 2004. *Thunder Doesn't Live Here Anymore: The Culture of Marginality Among the Teeneks of Tantoyuca*. Boulder: University Press of Colorado.

Armstrong-Fumero, Fernando. 2011. "Words and Things in Yucatán: Post-Structuralism and the Everyday Life of Mayan Multiculturalism." *Journal of the Royal Anthropological Institute* 17 (1): 63–81.

Balsanelli, Alice. 2018. "Jach Winik y winik: la construcción de la identidad y de la alteridad entre los lacandones de la selva chiapaneca." PhD diss., Escuela Nacional de Antropología e Historia (ENAH), México.

Basso, Ellen B. 1995. *The Last Cannibals: A South American Oral History*. Austin: University of Texas Press.

Begel, Johann, Marie Chosson, and Cédric Becquey. 2022. "Materiality and Agentivity of Structure Building Rituals: An Ethno-Archaeological Approach." In

Materiality in Rituals: A Deep History of Ritual Practice, edited by Rosemary Joyce and Lisa Johnson. Louisville: University Press of Colorado.

Bloch, Maurice. 1998. *How We Think They Think: Anthropological Approaches to Cognition, Memory, and Literacy*. Boulder, CO: Westview Press.

Boremanse, Didier. 1998. *Hach Winik: The Lacandon Maya of Chiapas, Southern Mexico*. Albany: Institute for Mesoamerican Studies, University at Albany, State University of New York.

Castañeda, Quetsil. 1996. *In the Museum of Maya Culture: Touring Chichén Itzá*. Minneapolis: University of Minnesota Press.

Fausto, Carlos, and Michael Heckenberger. 2007. *Time Matters: History, Memory and Identity in Amazonia*. Gainesville: University of Florida Press.

Franchetto, Bruna. 1993. "A celebração da historia nos discursos ceremoniais kuikúro (Alto Xingu)." In *Amazônia etnologia e história indígena*, edited by Eduardo Viveiros de Castro and Manuela Carneiro da Cunha, 95–116. São Paulo: NHII/USP, FAPESP.

Halperin, Christina. 2014. "Ruins in Pre-Columbian Maya Urban Landscapes." *Cambridge Archaeological Journal* 24: 321–44.

Hamann, Byron. 2002. "The Social Life of Pre-Sunrise Things: Indigenous Mesoamerican Archaeology." *Current Anthropology* 43 (3): 351–69.

Hanks, William F. 1990. *Referential Practice: Language and Lived Space among the Maya*. Chicago: University of Chicago Press.

Le Guen, Olivier. 2003. "Quand les morts reviennent . . . Réflexion sur l'ancestralité chez les Mayas des Basses Terres." *Journal de la société des américanistes* 89 (2): 171–205.

López Austin, Alfredo. 2011. "Los reyes subterráneos." In *La quête du Serpent à Plumes: Arts et religions de l'Amérique Précolombienne: Hommage à Michel Graulich*, edited by Nathalie Ragot, Sylvie Peperstraete, and Guilhem Olivier, 39–56. Brepols: Turnhout.

López Austin, Alfredo. 2015. "Los gigantes que viven dentro de las piedras." *Reflexiones metodológicas: Estudios de cultura náhuatl* 49: 161–97.

López Austin, Alfredo, and Leonardo López Luján. 2009. *Monte Sagrado-Templo Mayor: El cerro y la pirámide en la tradición religiosa mesoamericana*. México: Universidad Nacional Autónoma de México, Instituto de Investigaciones Antropológicas.

López Luján, Leonardo. 2019. "Pretérito pluscuamperfecto: Visiones mesoaméricanas de los vestigios arqueológicos." Lección inaugural, El Colegio Nacional, México.

Oakdale, Suzanne. 2005. *I Foresee My Life: The Ritual Performance of Autobiography in an Amazonian Community*. Lincoln: University of Nebraska Press.

Pitarch, Pedro. 1996. *Ch'ulel: una etnografía de las almas tzeltales*. México: Fondo de cultura económica.

Pitrou, Perig. 2015. "Life as a Process of Making in the Mixe Highlands (Oaxaca, Mexico): Towards a 'General Pragmatics' of Life." *Journal of the Royal Anthropological Institute* (n.s.) 21: 86–105.

Redfield, Robert. 1932. "Maya Archaeology as the Mayas See It." *Sociologus* 8: 299–309.

Redfield, Robert, and Alfonso Villa Rojas. 1934. *Chan Kom: A Maya Village*. Washington, DC: Carnegie Institution of Washington.

Stanton, Travis, and Aline Magnoni, eds. 2008. *Ruins of the Past: The Use and Perception of Abandoned Structures in the Maya Lowlands*. Boulder: University Press of Colorado.

Sullivan, Paul. 1984. "Contemporary Yucatec Maya Apocalyptic Prophecy: The Ethnographic and Historical Context." PhD diss., John Hopkins University.

Sullivan, Paul. 1989. *Unfinished Conversations: Mayas and Foreigners Between Two Wars*. New York: Alfred A. Knopf.

Teran, Silvia, and Christian Rasmussen. 1994. *La milpa de los mayas*. Yucatán: DANIDA.

Tozzer, Alfred Marston. 1907. *A Comparative Study in the Mayas and the Lacandones*. New York/London: Archaeological Institute of America/McMillan.

Vapnarsky, Valentina. 1996. "The Voice of Prophecies: Expressions and Visions of Time in Yucatec Maya." In *Los Mayas de Quintana Roo*, edited by Ueli Hostettler, 13–39. Bern: Institüt für Ethnologie.

Vapnarsky, Valentina. 2013. "Le passif peut-il éclairer les esprits? Agentivités, interactions et esprits-maîtres chez les Mayas." *Ateliers d'Anthropologie* 39 (2). http://ateliers.revues.org/9449.

Vapnarsky, Valentina. 2017. *Senses of Time: Exploring Temporality in Mayan Discourses, Experiences and Remembrances*. Habilitation à Diriger des Recherches, EHESS.

Vapnarsky, Valentina, and Olivier Le Guen. 2011. "The Guardians of Space and History: Understanding Ecological and Historical Relations of the Contemporary Yucatec Maya to Their Landscape." In *Ecology, Power, and Religion in Maya Landscapes*, edited byy Christen Isendahl, and Bodil Liljefors Persson, 191–206. Markt Schwaben, Germany: Verlag Anton Saurwein.

Vapnarsky, Valentina, Cédric Yvinec, and Cédric Becquey. 2022. "'Culture': Say It with Grammar! The Expression of Notions Related to 'Culture' in Amerindian Languages." *Anthropological Quarterly* (95)3.

Villa Rojas, Alfonso. (1945) 1987. *The Maya of East Central Quintana Roo*. Washington, DC: Carnegie Institution of Washington.

Vogt, Evon. 1969. *Zinacantan: A Maya Community in the Highlands of Chiapas*. Cambridge, MA: The Belknap Press.

3

Deserted Ruins?

Maya Tseltal and Ch'ol Engagement with Salient Spaces

CÉDRIC BECQUEY AND
MARIE CHOSSON

In the Mexican state of Chiapas, as in the whole Maya region, the landscape is dotted with monumental vestiges, the oldest of which date back to the first millennium BC (Sharer 1994, 81). Despite this ubiquity, these structures are subject to varying levels of symbolic or emotional interest. This region's different Maya linguistic communities (Lacandon, Ch'ol, Tojolabal, Tseltal, and Tsotsil) sometimes display surprisingly contrasting practices and representations. While bibliographic references report that some of these groups make ritual use of ancient artifacts and hold ceremonies on archaeological sites, others seem to place little or no value on vestiges. Closer inspection of these differences raises questions about the reasons that determine whether salience is attributed to these sites. Could this be related to the sites' possibly being magnets for nonhuman entities? In this chapter, we will use "salient space" to refer to any remarkable site that is an object of collective interest, through the attribution of physical and/or symbolic characteristics that make it distinctive on the community landscape. By focusing on the spatial rooting of social memory, we intend to highlight the diversity of memorial anchoring places in the communities concerned. A review of local conceptions of historicity and ancestrality will allow us to examine the important role that the projected presence of certain entities plays in humans' relations with vestiges, and more broadly with space.

https://doi.org/10.5876/9781646422869.c003

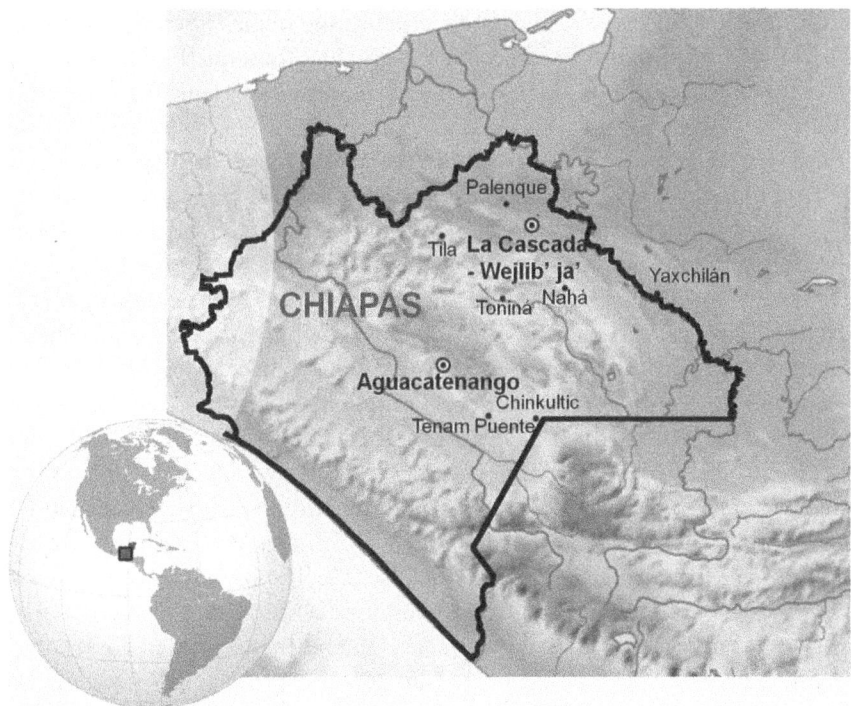

FIGURE 3.1. *Map of Chiapas and the main sites mentioned in the article. Background map: Sémhur / Wikimedia Commons / CC-BY-SA-3.0 (or Free Art License)*

CONTRASTING CASES

In the vast ethnographic literature on the region, different Maya groups' relations with vestiges have been unevenly documented. The most extensive works are those exploring the Lacandon Maya community of Nahá and the Yaxchilán archaeological site. They describe how important these buildings are to a group that conducts intense ritual activity in them. Documentation of such practices started in the late nineteenth century, with Désiré Charnay noting that "they went there [the ruins] in crowds to perform ceremonies" (1885, 399), and Anne and Alfred Maudslay stating that "the Lacandons . . . still . . . hold the place in reverence" (Maudslay and Maudslay 1899, 238). Didier Boremanse (1998, 203) and Jon McGee (2002, 149) reported that these buildings are important as salient sites of historical memory, citing stories that present them as the scene of an earlier humanity's destruction. Furthermore, Lacandons regard pre-Columbian buildings as special sites of interaction with supernatural entities. They are viewed as the homes of celestial entities, and "gods live in palm thatched houses, just like those of the Hach Winik (Lacandon Maya). But to human eyes, these godly houses look just like stones" (Boremanse 1998, 202).

More recent works by Enrico Straffi (2013; 2014) have shed light on ritual practices performed on or near vestiges by other Maya groups in Chiapas. Straffi presents two other case studies, in Tojolabal and Tseltal areas. These examples are markedly different from those observed among the Lacandons, particularly owing to their lack of historical depth. Straffi mentions that a group of Tojolabal people from the Francisco Sarabia *ejido* (communal lands) began holding ceremonies on the Tenam Puente archaeological site in either 1940 or 1962, according to two different consultants. One version of the origins of a ritual protocol on that site specifies that it followed the erection of a cross on the very spot where lightning had struck, a divine reminder to respect the site. Furthermore, this cross was sourced from "a forest considered enchanted, being home to the elders" (Straffi 2013, 265). In his second example, Straffi reports the existence of a ceremony held on the Toniná site since 1994 by a Zapatista Tseltal group. In that case, the introduction of these practices was part of a broader process of identity assertion and Indigenous empowerment, in which Maya ruins were "the symbol and presence of the people's wisdom, of our peoples, our ancestors" (Straffi 2014, 123)—words that are clearly strongly influenced by the militant political or religious networks in which this particular Tseltal group was involved.[1]

Most of these works give us a glimpse of each group's very particular relationship with archaeological sites that "play the role of sacred sites appropriate for relating with supernatural beings," in which the structures act as magnets, special sites where these entities converge, but also as particularly salient elements, places that have "spiritual value" (Straffi 2014, 241) and are a source of historical memory. In his conclusion, Enrico Straffi (2014, 240) even suggests that:

> Archeologists physically alter what is generally considered a sacred site. Its transformation from a sacred status to that of an archeological site . . . overlooks the value system traditionally assigned to ruins . . . , by encouraging the transformation of its symbolic capital from religious to patrimonial, the reciprocity principle is destroyed and replaced by principles of Western economic relations.[2]

These studies therefore offer a comprehensive overview of a set of practices and beliefs relating to ruins, which has supposedly had a kind of continuity since the pre-Hispanic era and is particularly threatened by the nation's desire to exploit them as archaeological sites. However, given the ubiquity of pre-Hispanic vestiges on the Chiapas landscape, a comparison with other case studies shows that these examples are far from conveying the whole gamut of relationships that Indigenous Maya groups have with vestiges. In fact, other Tseltal and Ch'ol examples conversely reveal a lack of symbolic or emotional interest in vestiges. Two case studies will illustrate this. They will also contrast with the aforementioned cases insofar as the populations concerned are not involved in militancy centered on the valorization of their tangible and intangible heritage.

The first case study details this reality among the traditionalist population of the Tseltal village of Aguacatenango (see figure 3.1). This segment of the population, also defined as *católicos de costumbre*, "customary Catholics," claims to follow a traditional lifestyle and respects the customary politico-religious organization.[3] The latter still represents the most important authority within the village, controlling the justice system and the distribution of communal land, among other things. This majority is opposed to other groups (converts to neo-Protestant movements, temporary urban migrants, etc.), who wish to break free of or overhaul the traditional system. The geographic particularities of this one-by-two-kilometer lakeside village, surrounded by hills and inhabited by a population of 3,000, partly explain why the population density has been so high since the precolonial period. Excavations conducted by archaeologists—led by Arturo Guevara Sánchez (1981), Joaquín García Bárcena (1986), and others—and the presence of pre-Hispanic structures confirm the age of the human settlement on that site, which is still considered one of the region's first population centers. The historical depth of this concentration, which is exceptional within a region characterized by a scattered form of settlement, suggests long-standing continuous occupation.

The second case study will highlight how the inhabitants of the Ch'ol village of La Cascada (*Wejlib'ja'*) relate to vestiges. This village, administratively dependent on the *municipio* of Palenque, is located in the Ch'ol historical area, documented at the beginning of the sixteenth century when the Spanish arrived (Lenkersdorf 1995; Vos 1995). In the aftermath of the Spanish conquest, this microregion of the Rio Chancalá was gradually abandoned by the Ch'ol communities, who were displaced and concentrated farther west following the *reducciones* that began in 1528. The reoccupation of this eastern area by the Ch'ol only took place on the occasion of major agricultural reforms at the beginning of the twentieth century, which gave rise to a redistribution of land. The last phase of this redistribution in the 1970s saw the birth of the village of La Cascada, currently home to 900 people, mostly migrants from the Ch'ol *municipio* of Tila. Tila, the only historical center of the Ch'ol population at the time of the Spanish conquest (Bassie-Sweet, Hopkins, and Laughlin 2015, 14), is still a pervasive identity referent for the inhabitants of La Cascada. While some institutions such as the "cargo system" have not been recreated at the local level in La Cascada after the migration, this population considers itself to be Ch'ol traditionalist. Today it is this part of the population that controls the supreme organ of the locality, the *ejidal* (communal land) assembly.

Despite these different historical trajectories, the two village groups seem to share a certain disinterest in the vestiges of past human activities. This lack of any particular symbolic or emotional interest is all the more remarkable in that both villages contain vestiges of ancient pre-Hispanic structures. La Cascada is in an area where a Ch'ol-speaking[4] pre-Columbian Maya civilization flourished in the Classic era (AD 250–900). The village is right in the middle of a large archaeological site containing relatively well-preserved pyramid/temples (figure 3.2). These ruins, like those of many pre-Hispanic cities in that area, were abandoned in the tenth century AD, unlike those of the northern highlands (Tseltal, Tsotsil, Tojolabal areas), which endured until the Spanish conquest. Aguacatenango itself is on the periphery of an area dotted with Maya sites such as Tenam Puente and Chinkultik, from the Postclassic era (AD 900–Spanish conquest). As in much of the region, there are some surviving small structures that the inhabitants of Aguacatenango call *montículos*, from the Spanish word for "mounds."

Yet, in neither of these two villages are vestiges subjected to any care or any particular ritual protocol. They are generally located in the surrounding *monte* "forest" area, which is considered wild. In La Cascada, some of these vestiges are on a corn-growing field or livestock grazing plot, with one or another of these uses encroaching upon the structures themselves. Unlike buildings on patrimonialized sites that are isolated and protected within the circumscribed space of the site, those in Aguacatenango and La Cascada, like those in Quintana Roo (Vapnarsky, chapter 2), are integrated into the landscape, often hidden by vegetation. The wild or agricultural spaces in which they are found are not excluded from the village territory but rather spaces that complement the residential area and are just as suitable for social occupation. While they provide inhabitants with indispensable resources like firewood, they are also—similarly to what has been mentioned in works on other groups—home to many entities with which humans interact. Since the village territory, like the earthly world as a whole, is a place where a multitude of beings converge, the presence of nonhuman entities forces human beings to conduct regular negotiations with them to maintain the fragile balance of that universe. Through a fusion of topographical elements with certain entities tied to them, the landscape is personified, alive,

FIGURE 3.2. *Pyramid/temple in La Cascada* (Wejlib' ja'). *Photo: Cédric Becquey, 2009*

and dynamic, influencing people's fate and behavior. It also becomes a source of memory, since events from the local historiography (to which we will return later) that are considered important are often projected on the mental map of the elements regarded as salient on the symbolic landscape. These conceptions being widespread among all Maya groups, it is worth examining the divergences between the cases documented so far and the two village communities under consideration, concerning the status and characteristics attributed to vestiges. In light of the preceding case studies, it is useful to more precisely review the historical and cosmological conceptions of extended time and its actors, which elsewhere shape relations with ruins.

TWO REGIMES OF TEMPORALITY: CH'OL AND TSELTAL

Studies of Chiapas oral tradition have highlighted, among the historical and cosmological conceptions of these groups, the existence of two or three previous humanities—see Calixta Guiteras Holmes (1961, 255) or Gary Gossen (1974, 148–55) on the Tsotsil area (communities neighboring the Tseltal), and

Jesús Morales Bermúdez (1999, 130) and Augusto Gebhardt Domínguez (2001) on the Ch'ol area. These previous humanities, either because of their poor behavior or because they neglected their duties to the supernatural entities, were destroyed, transformed into other entities, or relegated to the Chthonian world. On our two field study sites, however, stories about these previous humanities are rare and not very detailed. In La Cascada, only a few allusions are made to them, whereas in Aguacatenango several humanities are clearly distinguished. One of them, obviously failed and completely destroyed, consisted of humans that had no mouths and only one leg and arm. Others met with a less tragic end, like the one said to have been turned into monkeys, or the only one to have been attributed a name: the *ahch'al pixol*, "the mud *sombreros*," now living in an underground world penetrated by the nocturnal sun.

Ch'ol and Tseltal stories collected in La Cascada and Aguacatenango also mention another humanity directly preceding the current one. Although physically similar to today's people, they differed in that they lacked social organization. Those humans allegedly "walked without knowing where to go, talked constantly without making any sense, and had no work. They didn't know where to eat, and had no *milpa* [cornfield]."[5] According to the Tseltal, this humanity with zero sociability was also devoid of any ritual interaction with nonhumans. Although there is no destruction or transformation story about this humanity, it is clearly specified in Aguacatenango that it, too, was punished for its inability to fulfill the divine entities' expectations with regard to rituals or appropriate social behavior. To correct these flaws, the latest creation—today's existing humans—coincided with the founding of the village by the Virgen de Natividad in the case of Aguacatenango. In La Cascada, this imperfect humanity endeavored to attract a divine entity to take advantage of its good deeds by building several buildings able to accommodate him. This initiative concluded with the Lord of Tila deciding to move in to the building he found most attractive, corresponding to the current church in Tila, the town from which La Cascada's inhabitants originate. It was only after these Tseltal and Ch'ol entities chose to live in their respective churches that new humans settled and organized around those buildings. This settlement was facilitated by these entities' bestowal of corn, as well as the protection they granted on the condition that humans take care of them and the other saints accompanying them.

It should be noted that, for the Tseltal and Ch'ol, in addition to this division into alternating sequences of creation, destruction, or transformation of different humanities, long time is also marked by other ruptures that led to moments of cosmological organization. In Aguacatenango, the story of Jesus Christ's victory over the Jews is a good example of this. Probably as a result of an unusual interpretation of colonial evangelical discourse, the Jews were incorporated into the Tseltal pantheon as deviant supernatural entities that caused a lot of damage in the course of their long persecution of Christ. To put an end to this torment, Christ suggested they set up a test, which he won. This victory gave Jesus the privilege of reigning from heaven, while he gave Jews the responsibility of administering earthly space, turning them into de facto *ajwaliletik*,[6] masters of the earth. Similarly, in La Cascada, it is told that humans once provoked a flood as punishment for destroying the surrounding environment. Humans survived the flood, but God decided that masters of the earth, *witso'/ch'eño'*, would be put in place to control how humans act upon it. According to the story, "a new [world] started again . . . there were already people there but new masters were formed. They were the masters of the mountains."[7] Thus the Indigenous Ch'ol and Tseltal cosmos underwent a number of reorganizations, transformations, and reattributions of the roles of human and nonhuman entities, shaping the current landscape.

Let us therefore explain the place that vestiges occupy in this long time. Inhabitants of La Cascada and Aguacatenango agree that these structures, whether imposing ruins or simple *monticulos*, are vestiges of past human activity. The humans to whom they are referring are those born of the latest creation, still surviving today. However, probably because of the differences in their historical trajectories, the two groups diverge when it comes to how the builders are linked to the current inhabitants. In Aguacatenango, everyone shares the idea that their ancestors, *jme'tik tatik*, "our mothers' fathers," are the originators these buildings. Conversely, in La Cascada, a recent migration site, the paternity of vestiges is attributed to the men who once occupied that area according to oral tradition. Although they frequently link the creation of the latest humanity with the founding of their home village, the various village groups also believe that this humanity developed elsewhere with different characteristics or traditions. The current inhabitants of La Cascada believe that the men who once occupied this territory were from the latest creation, but they do not have direct filiation links to them, which explains their cultural differences. The men who once occupied their territory, who are referred to as "Maya" probably because of the influence of the discourse of outside actors (teachers, tour guides, etc.), are sometimes compared to Lacandons, a group with which the Ch'ol historically have a complex relationship and whom they characterize as *lak-ichañ*, "our (maternal) uncles," or as *karibe*, borrowing the Spanish word for cruel and inhuman people (see Real Academia Española 1992). This association can be partly explained by the fact that this Indigenous ethnic group is attributed customs that greatly differ from those of the Ch'ol.

Among their most dissimilar traits, the Lacandons are known for their hostility, their nomadism, their alleged consumption of raw, unsalted meat, and their traditional dress—a broad, white, unornamented robe. Furthermore, seen from Tila, the place from which most inhabitants of La Cascada originate, the territory of this new village is closely associated with that of the Lacandons, since both are located far to the east.

The material chosen by these "Maya" to build the ruins is explained—according to most of our Ch'ol interlocutors—by the strong cooperative relations that existed in the distant past between humans and the Chthonian entities that are the masters of the earth. In fact, according to these interlocutors, "We [the humans and the masters of the earth] were once similar. We all made up one house, one village like this one."[8] This similarity even favored sexual relations between humans and the daughters of these entities, who assumed the form of a human during the day and of a boa at night. Out of annoyance, the masters of the earth "closed people's eyes."[9] They went to live on the mountain, rendering their world and its inhabitants invisible to human eyes, appearing only rarely. However, their past cooperation made it possible to erect hewn stone buildings whose very imposing dimensions rule out the possibility that these resulted solely from traditional Ch'ol know-how. It is also said that it was precisely the masters of the earth who, at that time, lightened the weight of stones so that these "Maya" could build their houses, enclosures, kitchens, etc. The Ch'ol see the decorations on buildings constructed by these men, the ubiquitous representation of jaguars and snakes—animals associated with the masters of the earth—as additional proof of their substantial link with Chthonian entities. By the same token, some pre-Columbian buildings are interpreted as enclosures for these same animals.

The use of stone for these structures has also been questioned by the Tseltal inhabitants of Aguacatenango. They mention the theory that the *monticulos* might be traces of men's aborted attempts to imitate the architectural style of what they consider the village's first and only ancient stone building: the church. This ambition seems futile to them, insofar as everyone knows that the church could only be built thanks to the will of the Virgen de Natividad—who brought the stones to life so they could move by themselves—and with the help of possums, who came and welded them together. Unlike the Ch'ol, who believe that these churches were built by men to attract protective entities, the people of Aguacatenango think man is incapable of erecting a stone building:

> The church is only made of stone. It has received no cement, no mixture. But since all the stones are scattered here, they were not carried. Little by little the

large stones came [alone] grouping together. .... It can't possibly be people who have climbed up there [in order to pile the stones to build the church]. They can't. It's the possums that climbed up there.[10]

In their view, this powerlessness explains why the *antiwo na*, old houses, were abandoned in favor of traditional construction techniques using adobe or timber.

THE "TIME OF THE ANCESTORS"

The lack of interest in these structures is echoed in the low value placed on other types of past human production. In Aguacatenango, one anecdote is particularly illustrative of this attitude. The inhabitants remember major archaeological excavations between 1977 and 1985. If they essentially recall the rumor that skeletons and even a treasure were found, they still joke about the researchers' interest in other artifacts from the past:

> People say they found some old knives. Those are our ancestors' knives, but why would anyone want to keep them? I don't think they still cut, and we have our own knives. If I throw away my machete because it's broken, do you think my grandchildren want to keep it? (Translated from Spanish)

This lack of interest often translates into vestige deterioration and even plundering. In La Cascada, the presence of numerous tourists visiting the archaeological site of Palenque and surrounding area is an incentive to search for sellable artifacts, a particularly lucrative trade in this region. For example, a panel covered with inscriptions found in the main pyramid was initially left in the tourist center at the waterfall, then sold to passing tourists. Alongside this trade activity, artifacts considered unmarketable are simply thrown away or reused for other purposes, like the smooth, cylindrical *mano* from a pre-Hispanic metate left on a patio and occasionally used as a bench.

It would therefore seem that no value is attributed to traces or artifacts of past human activities beyond utilitarian and economic value, and this disinterest is also found in the local historiography. In the two village groups, a number of stories make up what, in the local typology, is considered the *scuentoil jlumaltik*, "the story of the village," in Tseltal, and the *oño' ty'añ*, "words of the elders," in Ch'ol. This oral literary corpus groups a heterogeneous set of narratives set in the period after the founding of the village. Yet most of these stories recount episodes in which the principal actors are non-human entities, including saints, masters of the earth, or Jesus Christ. These stories recall the origins of certain customs or, as we saw earlier, provide information about distinctive features of the landscape. In Aguacatenango, the shape of a mountain is explained by its master's desire to reach another faraway mountain/master that stole a golden ring from him, while a cave entrance was revealed by a *ijk'al*, a malicious entity, in a desperate attempt to escape the persecution of men. In both groups, men only appear in these stories in the context of an interaction with these entities. For the Tseltal, the only individually remarkable human being, Juan Lopez, acquired his role after a transformation into a nonhuman entity gave him the ability to throw lightning bolts, among other powers. In this historical register of the oral tradition, generations of men seem to have crossed the course of history without leaving a mark on the historical landscape in terms of significant, chronologically identifiable events.

The human protagonists of these stories are designated by the generic term *jme'tik.tatik* in Tseltal and *laktyaty lakña'* in Ch'ol, "ancestors (literally our mothers and fathers)" in both languages, and are never individually identified. This generic group designates all unidentified deceased individuals belonging to what the Tseltal and the Ch'ol consider their village community. In the case of La Cascada, a recent migration site, these ancestors are associated with the Tila community. Since genealogical memory does not reach back more than two or three generations, this group is distinguished from their forefathers, the identified or identifiable dead, referred to as *lakyum/lajko'*, "our forefathers" (literally our grandfathers/grandmothers), in Ch'ol, *muk'ul tat/muk'ul me'*, "our forefathers" (literally grandfather/grandmother), or more rarely *mam*, "grandfather," in Tseltal, linked to familial groups. In some of the stories of the local historiography, the presence of ancestors is important insofar as these narratives are considered teachings on the behavior to adopt toward nonhuman entities. They therefore serve as practice in remembering human experiences that are seen as critical because they offer keys that enable mankind to survive and sustain the fragile world of the village community. According to the logic of successively created humanities, inappropriate behavior could lead to a new destruction. According to a Ch'ol saying, "If this world were to become ruined again, if God wanted to destroy us again . . . , lightnings [forces controlled by the masters of earth] would also strike the heavens [to protect the World and its inhabitants]."[11] According to a Tseltal man, "If the period [of our humanity] does not die, that's because it's protected [by men who take care of it]."[12]

References to the ancestor group as an information source or protagonist are common in discourse that corresponds to what we could call different genres: stories, tales, myths, descriptions of beliefs or practices, etc. One characteristic of speech in Tseltal and Ch'ol, and in Maya languages more broadly, is that they are strongly marked by terms of evidentiality. The source of all information must be scrupulously identified. The lack of an evidential marker automatically implies that the speaker is taking subjective responsibility for the truth of their assertions. The choice to attribute responsibility for an utterance to the ancestors confers an indisputably truthful character upon it and places it within the institutionalized framework of collective knowledge and tradition. Although this truth regime presupposes that the assertions are accepted as true by the whole community, this does not mean there are no contexts in which mentioning the ancestors as the source can be exploited for practical purposes. Authorities can use the manipulations made possible by this type of discourse to introduce innovations into the shared knowledge by creating continuity where there is discontinuity, or to incorporate new facts into their collective history, for example, when making land claims. The "living" character of discourse attributed to the ancestors, as well as its truth value, are highlighted by the use of evidential expressions (e.g., 1.a and 1.b) that involve the imperfective (ICP) construction of the verb "to say," which is unbounded in time and, in this context, would be translated into English by simple present constructions with their interpretation of general truth.

1.a. *che' mi y-äl lak-tyaty lak-ña'*
(Ch'ol) thus ICP 3A-to say[-3B] our-fathers our-mothers
"Thus say our ancestors."

1.b. *Te namey   ya yal te j-me'-tik.j-tat-tik*
(Tseltal) DET once ICP 3A-to say[-3B] our-fathers our-mothers
"In the past, our ancestors say."

In stories of past events, identification of the information source is often accompanied by a temporal contextualization. The analysis of temporal deixis markers in these stories recalls the previously mentioned distinction made between forefathers and ancestors. Stories reporting datable facts are distinguished from those narrating undatable events rooted in an undefined past. Datable facts—whether the dating is absolute (the date is mentioned) or approximate ("I was still that small," "when there was still a forest here," "when my grandfather was a child")—correspond to individual/personal experiences or those reported by the forefathers. The source(s) of the information are still identified by name or are identifiable (from "I" to a group of various forefathers). This "recent past" is opposed to the "ancestors' past." In Tseltal, this latter time is marked by the deictic (*te*) *namey*, literally "distant past." In

Ch'ol, this ancestors' past is usually introduced by the deictic *(tyi) wajali*, "in the past." However, this marker is not very specific since it can just as well refer to a recent past of a few months earlier as to a more distant past going all the way back to mythological times. It is therefore exclusively by referring to the ancestor group as an information source that the story can be rooted in the distant past of the ancestors. However, in this language there are deictic markers specific to the ancestors' time that only appear in contrastive contexts, that is to say they emphasize the fact that one is shifting from a story set in the recent past to a story from a more distant time. These markers correspond either to the parallelistic pair *(tyi) wajali (tyi) oñi(yi)*, in which *oñi(yi)* is an archaic form for "a very long time ago" that no longer appears in any but this context, or to the derived form *antepasado* ("ancestor" in Spanish), which specifically designates "the time of the ancestors."

As we have seen, the local historiography of long time is characterized by a suppression of human individuality that tends to simplify human actions. However, this conception should not be seen as attributing no importance or utility in these actions. In fact, in the collective memory, past human experiences are the medium of knowledge and know-how that represent the customs of the village group, which the people of Aguacatenango designate by the expression *te sbeil yu'un jme'tik jtatik*, "the path of the ancestors," and which all must follow. Despite this exemplary function of their actions transmitted by oral tradition, the ancestors only rarely show themselves to people, interactions with them being limited to a single occasion: the festival of the dead. Their move to their current location and their relative immobility reinforce this relational rupture and these entities' disconnection from vestiges. The Ch'ol believe that upon the ancestors' death, their souls were assembled a place called *ch'ujulb'ä ajñib'äl*, "sacred/holy/divine place," which is a transposition of the Christian concept of heaven. The Tseltal of Aguacatenango believe that as long as they have respected custom, their souls will find the path to a cave, *Jtojkeptik*, that houses not only the souls of ancestors and forebears but also those of the living, in an extracorporeal form. In any case, the ancestors are confined to a specific space in the community's landscape, and have few direct relations with living humans. Therefore, their presence no longer occupies the spaces and buildings it once did. On the contrary, the nonhuman entities that are the principal actors of these stories of long time can, on their own initiative, move and interact with humans in everyday life. They are also often associated with places that, because of this projection of presence, these groups consider important.

SALIENT SPACES IN THE LANDSCAPE

For the Tseltal of Aguacatenango, although the various nonhuman entities are capable of moving through space, they are systematically tied to what is regarded as their place of residence, which is clearly defined. Celestial space is home to thirteen entities, including Jesus Christ/God/the Sun. The reproduction of *The Last Supper* owned by many inhabitants is interpreted as a representation of these celestials. These entities are differentiated from the guardian saints who live in the *ch'ul naetik*, the churches. If these buildings house representations of celestial entities, churches are above all conceived as the voluntarily chosen home of the saints tied to the village community. The physical figures of these saints kept in the church benefit from special care and precautions insofar as they are considered, contrary to representations of the heavenly entities, as the bodies of these saints, who have the ability to move about and communicate with other entities through their *ch'ulel*, the impalpable essence of beings who have the power to go outside their carnal sheath, although their physical presence is confined to the limited space of the church. Other entities, like the *ijk'al* already mentioned, live in the Chthonian world, only leaving it at specific times, such as at night.

For the Ch'ol of La Cascada, this strict division between different spaces is less pronounced. The world of men on the surface of the earth is a space of confluence of the heavenly and Chthonian spheres of influence. These two groups of nonhuman entities are liable to appear (*mi'sub' ib'ä*) or more rarely stay temporarily (*mi yajñel*), but they do not live there. However, earthly spaces where these entities have assumed a human form and lingered for a while are marked by their presence, a trace of their spirit, *ch'ujlel*, which is rooted there, bestowing a sacred character, *ch'ujul*, upon these earthly spaces. While the spaces occupied by this presence can be scattered throughout the territory, the church is seen as a building constructed by humans specifically to attract and accommodate earthly manifestations and representations of these entities. This particular conception explains why it is possible for one entity to project its presence in several spaces, as illustrated by the example of the Lord of Tila. This black Christ, a manifestation of God's heavenly divinity on earth, deploys his presence both in the church (his place of residence and where his representation is found) and within the cave *Yäxb'ä ch'eñ*, "the very green/humid cave" (where he took refuge during outside attacks on Tila), and also on a cross (where he watched the arrival of danger). Thus, he occupies all three levels of the Ch'ol cosmology: celestial, earthly, and Chthonian.

In this overview of the entities' spatial rooting, another category of beings is clearly distinguished: the masters of the earth. In Aguacatenango, the *ajwaliletik*, which are individualized and named, divide up the management of earthly space among themselves. They delimit plots, each associated with a natural element of the territory, a relief, mountain, or watering place. The region's hilly landscape favors the proliferation of these actors, which abound in the area. The village's indigenous toponymy recalls this omnipresence of the masters of the earth. In addition to its Spanish designation, every district takes the name of the *ajwalil* on which it depends, preceded by the word *y-ahlan-i(l)*, "under." The literal translation being "under X," it is likely that these expressions refer to the most salient element (usually a mountain) dominating the *ajwalil*'s area of control, which is also where it lives. The *barrio* Benito Juarez, for instance, is called *Yahlani Kolinton*, the *barrio* San Antonio is called *Yahlani Nahch'i*, the *barrio* del Carmen is called *Yahlani Pomtik*, the *barrio* de Santa Maria is called *Yahlani Hu'ub*, etc. The Ch'ol of La Cascada believe that the masters of the earth make up a generic group that they designate by the pair *witso'/ch'eño'*, "mountains/caves," marked by the plural of human referents. They are thought to live inside the natural elements to which they are connected, and there they store treasures like gold and jewels and also, the Tseltal believe human *ch'ulel*, "spirits," in which they take a special interest. Any openings to the outside are considered "windows," intermediate spaces between the earth's surface and the underworld. However, in Aguacatenango, a spirit's power to control a space extends beyond its residence, covering a zone that is, nevertheless, delimited by its boundary, with the zone dependent on another *ajwalil*. The Ch'ol believe that more than being simply an area of control, the earth's surface constitutes their body. By contrast, the Tseltal *ajwaliletik* often move from one place to another, particularly to visit each other. In both communities, these entities also have the ability to assume human form in order to interact with people. These appearances are particularly feared because, as we have seen, their purpose is usually to warn, frighten, or even punish humans for inappropriate behavior. Some topographical elements therefore stand out as particularly salient through their association with these various entities.

> They [the mountains] are all sacred. All of them are like temples. Those mountains are like churches. Where there are caves, that's where everything is. It's completely alive. It's where everything they [the masters of the earth] own is assembled.[13]

According to both groups, these masters of the earth are the sole "owners" of earth, which humans only hold in usufruct, something that must be negotiated, as is the case throughout Chiapas. June Nash (1970, 16–18) has highlighted how in the Tseltal village of Amatenango "a meal is given to the spirit of the house earth" at the moment of its inauguration but is also given every time "a severe illness is diagnosed as being caused by the devil eating the soul of the patient," this devil being suspected of having benefited from a pact with the master of earth, enabling it to enter the house. In fact, the "tenants expect nothing [from the landlord] in return for their offerings but freedom from harm." In his description of the Ch'ol house-founding ritual, Cédric Becquey (2017, 249) likens it to an "almost notarial deed made up of clauses" in which "ritual discourse resembles the pleas made by a lawyer (the ritual specialist) defending the inhabitants of the house against the hostility or inaction of the masters of the earth." In the Tsotsil village of Zinacantán, Evan Vogt (1979, 90) describes the necessary protocol for offerings of food and prayers to the masters of the earth prior to sowing cornfields. Thus, every occupation of space, whether domestic or agricultural, requires a ritual protocol that aims, on the one hand, to appease masters of the earth disturbed by human activity and, on the other hand, to get them to protect this space from other entities regarded as evil. Although these rituals enable humans to occupy a very delimited space and receive protection there, this propitiation can also extend beyond it. These ceremonies are also a chance to ask for special protection from other entities, particularly celestial ones whose field of action is not limited to one specific territory but instead covers the whole of the earth's surface. Interactions with these entities happen in a special way, in their place of residence—churches—or in the presence of ritual materials consecrated there, such as holy water and candles.

In the two communities studied here, the fact that humans' good living is subject to negotiations with various entities helps explain the symbolic and ritual interest in certain elements of the landscape. The salience of certain sites, in the oral tradition as well as in the ritual sphere, is explained by their association with beings with which humans must interact to ensure not only a pleasant, productive life but sometimes also their survival. The importance of churches and topographical elements associated with the masters of the earth, which are symbolically comparable, springs from the projection of their presence onto these spaces. The only sites receiving special attention are those benefiting from the effective presence of entities that live in them, and not necessarily those that were the scene of memorable events in a bygone past. Under this logic, the very concept of places of remembrance in the sense in which Western societies understand them, that is to say as the material heritage of an emotionally and symbolically charged collective history, does not seem relevant. Remembrance practices and the oral transmission of the ancestors' teachings aim precisely to preserve the memory of those sites where it is possible to visit entities that are liable to move about to conduct constantly renewed negotiations relevant to present concerns.

CONCLUSION

Unlike most ethnographies on the Maya of this region, the two case studies (Tseltal and Ch'ol) presented in this chapter reveal an indifference to vestiges. A review of concepts relating to long time and its actors showed that these buildings are not sites with specific ties to the souls, ancestors, and entities that make up the spiritual landscape of these two communities. Furthermore, the fact that these entities are tied to other salient elements of the landscape explains why nowadays, despite being mentioned in the oral tradition relating to the community's history, these vestiges are not attractive sites conducive to communication with these entities. Nor are they places to be avoided or subject to any particular caution. In fact, they may even be found within a space being exploited by people, without it being necessary to implement a ritual protocol any different from the one applied when any kind of space is being occupied or used.

Although this lack of interest would seem to set the Ch'ol of La Cascada and the Tseltal of Aguacatenango apart from other Maya groups in the region, as described in the existing literature, these contrasts should not be seen as major differences in conceptions of historicity or ancestrality. Instead, they reveal a differently oriented spatial anchoring of nonhuman entities. In the Lacandon examples cited earlier, the authors pointed out that symbolic and ritual interest in vestiges in Yaxchilán derive from their being considered the residence of certain celestial entities (Boremanse 1998, 202). Therefore, it is possible to draw a parallel between the function and value attributed to these vestiges and that attributed to churches in La Cascada and Aguacatenango.

In the same way, the rituals performed in Tenam Puente also highlight, in our view, dynamism and mobility in these nonhuman entities, recalling scenarios observed in the villages studied. A new ritual protocol was implemented on this archaeological site following a lightning strike there (Straffi 2013, 265). Many Maya groups see this type of event as a way nonhuman entities express themselves. Depending on the context, it is interpreted either as the mark of a dispute between entities or as an expression of dissatisfaction with humans. Not long ago in Aguacatenango, lightning struck next to a neglected cross placed stunningly close to the home of individuals who had converted to a new religious referent. This event was experienced as a condemnation, as well as a reminder to follow the ancestors' path and take care of divine entities.

Similarly, in a village close to La Cascada, a lightning strike was said to have left a mark depicting the figure of Christ, causing a de facto transformation of the site into a ritual space, a special place for interaction with this entity, drawing more visitors every year. Thus, the mobility of nonhuman entities, and especially their ability to interact with humans, can lead to the reactivation or creation of new salient spaces.

It seems noteworthy that new saliences, illustrated by the cases of Tenam Puente and Tonina, are rooted on or near vestiges specifically located in archaeological zones patrimonialized by the state. There is no way to tell if, as Enrico Straffi has postulated, the exploitation of archaeological sites threatens practices and beliefs relating to ruins or if, on the contrary, state-induced patrimonialization triggers a new form of reappropriation by neighboring Indigenous groups, giving them added (contemporary) relevance by circulating what is often new discourse on these buildings.

Our study presents cases in which vestiges are attributed value neither by local groups nor by the authorities in charge of archaeological heritage. The rooting of nonhuman entities, and the ritual staging of contact with them, is much more readily tied to other salient sites on the community's landscape: a church, unbuilt spaces, elements of the local topography. However, the dynamic and mobile nature of these entities, and constant nurturing of relations with them, facilitate the possibility that new salient sites will emerge, often in connection with a desire to regain control of those spaces. Thus, in all documented cases in Chiapas, any possible symbolic and emotional interest in vestiges depends above all on their residential occupation by entities with whom interaction is an unavoidable necessity.

NOTES

1. In the original version, the Spanish term *pueblos* was used. Here it was translated as "peoples," but it also has the semantic value of "villages."

2. This position is similar to that of Fernando Santos-Granero (in the present volume), who even speaks of the staining of sites.

3. Also called "cargo system" by the Mesoamerican researchers, this is a model system of customary government in which members of the village community take turns occupying religious and political positions.

4. A group of languages of the Maya family that includes Ch'ol, Chontal of Tabasco, Ch'orti', as well as classic Ch'olan, the language of Maya glyph writing in the Classic era.

5. Translated from Tseltal: "*Ben, ben pe ma' sna' ba baht, la spas wulwunel, puro bol k'op, ja'nix ma'yuk ya'tel. Ma' sna' ba xwe', ma'yuk sk'inal.*"

6. The Tseltal term *ajw-al-il-etik* is constructed through a derivation from the root *ajaw*, meaning "guardian, master, ruler," and the plural *-etik*. In Aguacatenango, whereas the *ajaw* root can refer to other entities, particularly celestial ones, the term *ajwaliletik* solely designates the masters of the earth. For more details on the semantic variety of the *ajaw* root, see Aurore Monod-Becquelin (1996).

7. Translated from Ch'ol: "*yamb'ä tsihi'b'ä ta' cha'tyehchi, tsa' cha'tyehchiyo' he'el, añix kristyaño pero ta' cha'tyehchi yamb'ä yumälo', iyumo' wits.*"

8. Translated from Ch'ol: "*lajal añoñloñb'i la wajali laj juñp'eb'i lakotyoty pueblob'i b'ajche' ili.*"

9. Translated from Ch'ol: "*ta' mich'äyo'i tab'i ilajmäkb'eyo' iwuty jente.*"

10. Translated from Tseltal: "*Och stehk'anik la ts'in ch'ulnae, pere como pura ton yich'oj, ma'yuk yich'o cemento, ma'yuk yich'oh mezcla, puro ton. Pere como puhk bel ton spisil, ma' yu'un kuchbiluk, xbalahan xlaj baht la te muk'ul tonetik . . . Pere yu'un ma' xmoh te gente me yu'un lo mismo te uch moh.*"

11. Translated from Ch'ol: "*mib'i tyi kaji tyi cha' asiyel ili pañmil, mi yom icha' jisañoñla lakyum dyosi, hiñixb'i jiñ chajk je'eli muxb'i b'ajb'eñ pañchañ je'el.*"

12. Translated from Tseltal: "*Ja' hichuk ma' xch'ay, ja' hich ay mak stup' tiempoil, ja' ya yich' kantaelbi.*"

13. Translated from Ch'ol: "*pejtyel ch'ujul, pejtyel b'ajche' lajalb'i b'ajche' templo, lajal b'ajche' iglesya jiñi ili wits. B'aki añ ch'eñ, b'aki añ pejtyel, laj kuxul, ya' laj lotyol pejtyelel chuki añ icha'añ.*"

REFERENCES

Bassie-Sweet, Karen, Nicholas A. Hopkins, and Robert M. Laughlin. 2015. "History and Conquest of the Pre-Columbian Ch'ol and Lacandon Ch'ol." In *The Ch'ol Maya of Chiapas*, edited by Karen Bassie-Sweet, 3–28. Norman: University of Oklahoma Press.

Becquey, Cédric. 2017. "Rituel de fondation de la maison chez les Chols: une étude ethnolinguistique." In *(Re)Fonder: Modalités du (re)commencement dans le temps et dans l'espace*, edited by Philippe Gervais-Lambony, Frédérique Hurlet, and Isabelle Rivoal, 243–57. Paris: Editions de Boccard.

Boremanse, Didier. 1998. "Representaciones metafóricas de los antiguos mayas en mitos y ritos religiosos lacandones." *Journal de la Société des Américanistes* 84 (1): 201–9.

Charnay, Désiré. 1885. *Les anciennes villes du Nouveau-Monde: Voyages d'explorations au Mexique et dans l'Amérique (1857–1882)*. Paris: Librairie Hachette.

García Bárcena, Joaquín. 1986. *El Precerámico de Aguacatenango: Chiapas, México*. México: Instituto Nacional de Antropología e Historia.

Gebhardt Domínguez, Augusto. 2001. "El origen de la creación según los ch'oles." *Tlalocan* 13: 49–58.

Gossen, Garry. 1984. *Chamulas in the World of the Sun: Time and Space in a Maya Oral Tradition*. Long Grove, IL: Waveland Press.

Guevara Sánchez, Arturo. 1981. *Los talleres líticos de Aguacatenango, Chis*. México: SEP INAH.

Guiteras Holmes, Calixta. 1965. *Los peligros del alma: Visión del mundo de un tzotzil*. México: Fondo de Cultura Económica.

Lenkersdorf, Gudrun. 1995. "La resistencia a la conquista española en Los Altos de Chiapas." In *Chiapas: Los rumbos de otra historia*, edited by Mario H. Ruz and J. P. Viqueira, 71–85. Mexico: Universidad Nacional Autónoma de México, Centro de Investigaciones y Estudios Superiores en Antropología Social.

Maudslay, Anne Cary, and Alfred Percival Maudslay. 1899. *A Glimpse at Guatemala, and Some Notes on the Ancient Monuments of Central America*. London: John Murray.

McGee, R. Jon. 2002. *Watching Lacandon Maya Lives*. Boston: Allyn and Bacon.

Monod-Becquelin, Aurore. 1996. "Une hypothèse sur la nature du terme 'ajau': Un sens qui change de traduction." *Ateliers* (Nanterre: Laboratoire d'ethnologie) 17: 139–69.

Morales Bermúdez, Jesús. 1999. *Antigua palabra: Narrativa indígena Ch'ol*. Mexico: Plaza y Valdés/UNICACH.

Nash, June. 1970. *In the Eyes of the Ancestors: Belief and Behavior in a Mayan Community*. New Haven, CT: Yale University Press.

Real Academia Española. 1992. *Diccionario de la lengua española: Vigésima primera edición*. Madrid: Espasa-Calpe.

Sharer, Robert J. 1994. *The Ancient Maya*. 5th ed. Stanford, CA: Stanford University Press.

Straffi, Enrico. 2013. "Interpretaciones mayas de los sitios arqueológicos: un análisis." In *XV Encuentro de Latinoamericanistas Españoles, Nov 2012, Madrid, España*, 252–71. Madrid: Trama editorial/ CEEIB.

Straffi, Enrico. 2014. *Los Mayas de hoy y los sitios arqueológicos: interpretaciones y actividades rituales*. Quito: Abya Yala Publications.

Vogt, Evan Z. 1979. *Ofrendas para los dioses: análisis simbólico de rituales zinacantecos*. México: Sección de obras de Antropología, Fondo de Cultura Económica.

Vos, Jan de. 1995. "El lacandón: Una introducción histórica." In *Chiapas: Los rumbos de otra historia*, edited by Mario H. Ruz and J. P. Viqueira, 331–61. Mexico: Universidad Nacional Autónoma de México, Centro de Investigaciones y Estudios Superiores en Antropología Social.

4

Where Past and Future Meet

Abandoned Village Sites as Cruxes of Political, Historical, and Eschatological Narratives among the Chácobo of Bolivian Amazonia

Philippe Erikson

In the Amazon lowlands of Bolivia, *Xabaya* is an abandoned village site where no living person dares set foot. It is nevertheless an essential historical landmark for the Chácobo, a Panoan-speaking people who maintain a strong relationship with this no-longer-existing place. Although now deserted, *Xabaya* is often mentioned in conversations and, as we shall see, plays a major role in historical as well as political and cosmological narratives. Because many people have died there, *Xabaya* is closely associated with death; as such, it the last place anyone would ever want to go. However, it also stands out as the symbolic embodiment of the group's unification and is therefore spoken of with great respect, as the place that witnessed the birth of what is now officially recognized in Bolivia as *la nación indígena*, "indigenous nation," Chácobo.[1]

In this chapter, I argue that although the Chácobo have no monuments or memorial places, ruins of former dwelling places such as *Xabaya*—and, to a lesser extent, archaeological vestiges such as antique funerary urns—are key to the forging and reshaping of their eschatological beliefs. Widening the scope of the argument, I contend that such connections with invisible ruins and virtual memorials represent a fairly typical means of recounting the past and envisioning the future in lowland South America. This chapter looks at the impact of past political events on contemporary ideas regarding the afterlife. But, above all, it concerns the intricate relationship between time and space as

https://doi.org/10.5876/9781646422869.c004

mediated by death, which is why it starts off with the description of a funeral and considerations about Chácobo eschatology.

MARO'S FUNERAL

In 2003, in the height of the dry season, Maro, a Chácobo teenager, was bitten by a snake while helping his parents clear a patch of forest to plant a new garden. Hoping he might spontaneously recover—and lacking the means to do so—his parents did not take him to the hospital. Although his condition seemed to improve at first, the young man died just a couple of days later. The ensuing funeral was an emotionally intense, tragic, and literally haunting moment. All the more so on a personal level, because Maro had been one of my elder son's playmates. The funeral lasted a full day and a full night, with constant, heartbreaking chants. Following a typically Amazonian pattern, each individual mourner sang on their own, never attempting outright synchronization.[2] Yet, a strong feeling of togetherness permeated. Throbbing ritual wailing, outbursts of sobs, and hoarse voices saturated the air, creating an indescribable, albeit unforgettable, emotional frenzy.

Incessantly repeated hour after hour, the monotonous lyrics of the funeral songs finally gave way to phonetically reduced forms, until eventually turning into barely audible yet constant mumbling. This gradual decrescendo of the laments, although due to physiological exhaustion, also seemed to suggest the gradual fading away of the deceased youth's soul (*yoshini*), as if diminishing vocal intensity signified progressive distancing from the land of the living. Long before daybreak, the parents' hypnotical litany "*noho baquë yama, noho baquë yama . . .*" (my son is no more, my son is no more . . .) had given way to "*no-bak-rama, no-bak-rama . . . ,*" uttered in raucous voices with obvious effort to overcome tremendously sore throats.[3] Emotionally speaking, such endurance in self-inflicted physical pain and such open display of sheer misery had a contagious effect. They spread out a generalized feeling of awe, making a frightfully iconic statement about the inner devastation of Maro's relatives and friends. Broken voices for a broken life. Such rampant display of tangible sorrow obviously carried a message. There was no escape from tears and crying. And, indeed, wails could be heard from every household in the village. At various moments, the coffin was carried from house to house, making it easier for everyone to wail in its proximity. People swarmed around the body, eager to get the best possible look at the corpse, even toward the end of the funeral, despite the increasingly foul stench. Such physical manifestation of grief, with people literally bumping into one another to get as close as possible, is reminiscent of the manner in which the nearby Wari' pile up around the deceased's body during their funerals, eventually forming human lumps above it (Conklin 2001). In Amazonia, despite the blatant contrast with Western notions of due solemnity and appropriate demeanor in similar contexts, such swarming is deemed the best way to pay funerary respects (a point to keep in mind, for reasons explained below).

Formerly, Chácobo mourners—especially family members—used to run in circles around the deceased's body, punching bystanders, forbidding access, as if to keep them away from the corpse. Ritualized hand-to-hand wrestling sometimes ensued, especially if close kin suspected members of the visiting party to be responsible for the death (Prost 1970, 89). This custom is no longer followed. However, other traditional means of regulating the typically mixed emotions associated with grief are still available. Occasionally, for instance, while the rest of the crowd either listens or goes on with regular singing, one mourner might dramatically replace the standard lyrics with spontaneous speech, chanted out in tune with the song's rhythm. This offers an opportunity to vent anger, speak harsh words, scold those deemed responsible for the tragedy, or even proffer accusations of witchcraft in a formalized—and therefore irrefutable—manner. In such instances, the anthropologist experiences the eerie feeling of flowing amid an Amazonian rendition of an ancient Greek chorus, the lead wailer (usually a woman) declaiming devastating statements in artistic staccato, punctuated by the crowd's highly standardized—and therefore semantically shallower—weeping bass line.[4] But Maro's death gave rise to no apparent conflict. His bereaved parents were not held responsible for being poor, young, and inexperienced. What stood out was the collective ritual wailing's strong bonding effects, frequently enhanced by acts of mutual head-rubbing, a ceremonial form of mourning-related greeting common among Amazonian peoples and frequently performed during Maro's funeral wake.

XABAYA: HAZY LAND OF THE DEAD

The following morning, shortly after Maro's body had been interred in the village graveyard, there was a small cloudburst and a few thunderclaps were heard. This, to my agnostic ear, stood out as rather incredible. We were still weeks away from the rainy season and I couldn't recall a single drop of water pouring from the sky in the past few weeks. A true challenge to my incredulousness. However, as would be expected, my Chácobo friends found such timing perfectly natural. Like many other Amazonian peoples, they consider thunder a token of a deceased soul's safe arrival in the afterworld. In this

FIGURE 4.1. *Chácobo panpipe orchestras.* Photo: Philippe Erikson, 1993.

particular instance, I was told that Maro's soul (*yoshini*) had arrived in a place called *Xabaya* (also known as *Xaba Xobo*), where his namesake grandfather, the also recently deceased and much respected elder known as *taita* Maro, was welcoming him with a great feast, replete with manioc beer, boisterous laughter, and panpipe orchestras twirling around. The thunder was caused by the dancers' stomping feet.[5]

Overwhelmed by the previous night's emotions, I took this for yet another example of the importance of namesake relationships among the Chácobo (Erikson 2003), and yet another example of how belief systems can be strongly reinforced by a mere coincidence, such as unexpected rainfall and thunder in the dry season. I was also impressed by the fact that, in real life, during ritual drinking feasts such as the one *taita* Maro allegedly hosted to welcome his junior namesake, panpipe orchestras dance in circles around ceremonial beer jars, which are said to attract the *yoshini* spirits, eager to drink from them. And doing so, all while playing, the orchestras compete to get as close as possible to the central beer pot, following a pattern strikingly similar to that displayed during the ceremonial fighting that formerly occurred during the mourning ceremonies.[6] This analogy seemed ever more striking considering that most of the ceremonial beer is stored in a coffin-like canoe, which is deemed to attract thirsty *yoshini*—in fact, shamans even used to summon them in the form of winds. And,

FIGURE 4.2. *Coffin-like beer trough carved in the forest out of a* mapajo *tree and brought back for a ritual. Photo: Philippe Erikson, 2001.*

remarkably, this beer trough is carved out of a tree of the *Bombacaceae* family, in other words one bearing close resemblance to those in which—as we shall see—some of the souls, in past times, were said to be trapped.[7]

When I first heard about Maro's eschatological whereabouts, it triggered a mental frenzy of connections between funerary rituals and drinking feasts, eschatology and shamanism, and other such neostructuralist niceties. But it was years before I finally became aware that *Xabaya* might also actually exist in the physical world we live in. And, by yet another coincidence, that it might even be found in the very location where Austrian anthropologist Wanda Hanke (1958, 115), who visited them in 1958, was told:

> When a Chácobo dies, his soul flies up to a big house in the sky where all the souls are gathered. It is surrounded by beautiful forests filled with plentiful game and rivers filled with the most delicious fish. The Chácobo are all alone in this Paradise devoid of either God, or "taita" or chiefs, or Whitemen.

Hanke is probably the first Westerner to report about the Chácobo souls' celestial abode. Though she doesn't give its name, her description of this "Paradise" of sorts sounds likely to be *Xabaya*, a designation that, at least at first sight, is both insignificant and obvious. In Chácobo, *xaba* simply refers to open spaces. It is most commonly used for patches of savanna (locally called *pampa*), which, in their environment, alternate with forested parts. The suffix *–ya* is a locative morpheme, meaning something like "where there are." (The Chácobo's main village, for instance, is known as *Tapaya*, because of its numerous *tapa*, i.e., "Brazil nut trees.") In that perspective, *Xabaya* simply means something like "a savanna-like place" or "a place where savanna abounds."

Etymologically speaking, the alternative name, *xaba xobo*, is just as unremarkable and means just about the same thing. *Xobo* simply means "house" or, by metonymic extension, "group of houses" or "village." In toponyms that stress the abundance of a particular feature in the surroundings of a dwelling place, *xobo* is preferred to the ordinary term for "village" (*yaca*). *Xaba xobo* could therefore simply be "a village surrounded by savanna." However, in this instance, rather than referring to the specific definition of *xaba* ("savanna"), *Xaba xobo*'s name probably stems from its generic meaning ("open spaces"). This seems even more likely given that the lexeme *xaba* also conveys the general idea of haziness, such as the mist one encounters while paddling on a lake in the early morning. *Xaba* can refer to foggy landscapes, where all is level, monotonous, or at the very least devoid of notable landmarks to fix one's eye on. Spaces that are paradoxically infinite—because devoid of any visible enclose—but, at the same time, lacking any vanishing line. By extension, *xaba* can also refer to the concept of time. Zingg's Chácobo-Spanish dictionary (1998) provides examples such as *yonocoti xabaca*, "time for you to work" (literally "the space cleared out for working"), and *mi nati xabaca*, "time for you to die":

Yonoco-ti   xaba-ca
work-SUBS   xaba-LOC
Lit.: the space (= time) cleared up for work
Time for working

Mi   na-ti   xaba-ca
2.pers to die-SUBS xaba-LOC
Lit.: the open space of/for your death
The moment of your death

Although it most commonly refers to the *pampa*, *xaba* therefore also has more metaphorical connotations such as "nimbus," "mist," "halo," and, by extension, "time span" or "time slot." The morpheme *xaba*, as it appears in *Xabaya* and in *Xaba Xobo*, therefore provides an apt metaphor to designate the wonderful-yet-mysterious place where souls gather to dance around beer troughs while playing their panpipes. As an abstraction, its meaning is close to "sometime/somewhere." Yet, as we shall see, *Xabaya* is also the name of a very specific locality, a village site full of bittersweet memories where the Chácobo's ancestors lived in the mid-1950s, where many of them encountered tragic death, and where crucial events totally reshaped their collective history.

XABAYA: ACTUAL HISTORICAL LANDMARK

When I first heard about young Maro's arrival in a heavenly abode called *Xabaya*, I failed to make the connection with any particular terrestrial location. There are numerous reasons for this. In the first place, it seemed logical that the recently deceased's soul should travel to an abstract place with a generic name, rather than to an actual place with a specific name. So why bother to investigate further? Second, in narratives I had heard or read about *Xabaya* as a historical place, it usually bore its Spanish name: Núcleo (an abridged form of *Núcleo Indigenal Ñuflo de Chávez*, a lay mission created in the early 1950s by the Bolivian government on the banks of the Benecito River to "civilize" the Amerindians). I was therefore rather unfamiliar with the Chácobo name of this place. And even so, *Xabaya* was nondescript since savannas, alternating with patches of gallery forest, are plentiful around Núcleo.[8] Finally, another reason why I initially failed to connect celestial *Xabaya* with terrestrial *Xabaya*/Núcleo is because it was neither young Maro's nor his namesake grandfather's birthplace. Neither of them had any particular connection with that place, which leaves me wondering: if biographically unrelated to the place, why would they congregate there in their afterlife?

I have no definitive answer to that puzzling question, only hunches I will detail below. Although it took me a decade to realize it, I am now quite certain that when told Maro's *yoshini* had reached *Xabaya*, I had been given the actual name of the actual place his soul traveled to, and not just a generic name for a vague postmortem destination. This was made clear to me in a conversation about the political turmoil that followed a particularly violent witchcraft-related execution (Erikson 2016). During the interview, to my utter surprise, my close friend Paë Chavez (alias Paëcito) answered my eschatologically oriented questions by recalling hunting expeditions we had taken part in many years ago. When he spontaneously mentioned *Xabaya*, I asked where that might be. "Papa Felipe," he answered, "without even knowing it, on one of those long treks we used to make, heading out east toward the Benecito, you once nearly saw *Xabaya* with your very eyes. If we hadn't chanced upon that herd of white-lipped peccaries and turned back, we probably would have made it all the way there."[9] In other words, Paëcito was talking about the afterworld (which had triggered our conversation) with recollections of hunting trips embedded in the actual landscape.

This recalled another conversation, this time about historical events, that I had once had with another good friend, Paë Davalos. While telling me about various historically significant places on the Benecito and Yata Rivers, Paë gave detailed and lengthy descriptions of many former village sites; but when he mentioned *Xabaya*, he just said (in Spanish) that it was a very windy place, that no one lived there anymore, and that people (especially Chácobo) traveling in the vicinity didn't care to stop over, for fear of the many spirits/ghosts/souls (*yoshini*) lurking there. At that time, I thought Paë was referring to the tremendous amount of suffering and death his people had experienced in Núcleo, whose ill repute was bad enough to entail its inclusion in the *White Book of Ethnocide* (Beghin 1972) and about which oral tradition has even more—and worse—to say. A mere two generations ago, in the name of civilization, exploitation, abuse, and sometimes even murder, rape, torture, and other acts of sheer sadism took a heavy toll on the Chácobo, not to mention inner strife related to witchcraft accusations. To make matters even more tragic, a series of deadly epidemics occurred. People were buried inside their houses, beneath constantly lit fires, on the opposite side of the entrance door.[10] As Paë told me, at one point, so many people had died that houses were replete with funeral hearths, to the extent that the living space for survivors was restricted to just a tiny space near the exit—as if the dead were gradually pushing them out, which eventually happened when Núcleo had to be resettled elsewhere, as we shall see.

No doubt, then, that historical *Xabaya* is perfectly qualified to epitomize the shadowy land of the dead, and that contemporary travelers avoid staying there. Yet, the question remains: why should recently deceased people, even youngsters like Maro, return to that specific place rather than, for instance, to the Chácobo's original lands farther south, near the lake Rogoaguado, where their forebears' presence is still recalled (cf. Nordenskiöld 1911)? Why do ghosts of today reunite with those of the past in that specific place? A brief look at the events that took place near and around the Benecito in the mid-1950s provides clues, and a possible explanation, for this intriguing turn taken by Chácobo eschatology.

NÚCLEO, PUERTO LIMONES, AND CHÁCOBO ETHNOGENESIS

Historically, forebears of the people now known as Chácobo occupied a vast territory running along both banks of the Guaporé/Mamoré River. Their lands extended from the northern parts of contemporary Bolivia and adjoining parts of Brazil all the way south to the outreaches of the region known as Llanos de Mojos. The southernmost branch of the Panoan linguistic family, the Chácobo's ancestors had full control over a vast region stretching from the Beni River up north to the region surrounding Rogagua and Rogoaguado Lakes down south. Oral tradition still recalls the names of the mighty chiefs who, a mere few generations ago, allegedly exercised unrestricted authority over places such as Riberalta and Guajará-Mirim, which have since become regionally important towns. Tumi Chucua, where Protestant missionaries of the Summer Institute of Linguistics (SIL) had their Bolivian base—and where archaeological ruins are found in the form of raised fields and ditches—is also claimed to have formerly been a "Chácobo" stronghold (Erikson 2014).[11]

In the past, southern Panoans were usually lumped together under general headings such as Pacaguara (on the Bolivian side) or Karipuna (on the Brazilian side).[12] "Chácobo," as a general name for part of these groups, seems to have been in use for over a century, but it was mainly used as an exonym by Spanish-speaking outsiders.[13] Though speaking closely related dialects of the same language and following very similar customs, the southern Panoan people probably never considered they might all belong to one vast "nation." Rather, their social organization rested upon a series of named groups known as *maxobo* (*maxo*/head + -*bo*/collective). Each of these "headings" had a distinct name, such as *isa nohiriabo* (porcupine people), *xëna nohiriabo* (worm people), *isko nohiriabo* (oropendola people), *capë nohiriabo* (caiman people), etc. Each had slightly different customs, used distinct patterns for their face paint, different styles for their bark-cloth garments, a different musical repertoire. Each even supposedly had very specific physical, intellectual, or emotional characteristics: some were stereotyped as chubby and sluggish, others as svelte and quick; some as generous, others as bad-tempered; some were deemed warlike, others peaceful, etc. All of these groups are said to have lived rather independent lives and to have followed relatively endogamous marriage patterns. Some were mutually hostile, others on good terms or even engaged in close alliances. However, no mention ever seems to have been made of any kind of federation of the different *maxobo* at any point in history and, in all likelihood, none of their members ever self-identified as "Chácobo," "Pacaguara," or "Karipuna," even though they probably knew full well that "white-nosed" people labeled them thus.

In the early 1950s, due to depopulation brought about by epidemics, colonial oppression, the rubber boom, cattle ranchers, abusive bosses, and many other detrimental factors, people still remembered what *maxobo* their family theoretically belonged to. Yet, the latter no longer had political significance. On the Brazilian side of the border, the Panoan-speaking Karipuna were on the brink of extinction, and their last words were being eagerly collected by sympathetic government-sponsored as well as independent foreign lexicographers (Barbosa de Faria 1947; Hanke 1949). On the Bolivian side, people lived in dispersed family groups, in sorry condition, living rather isolated lives. They were culturally and physically vulnerable. Some, such as those now known as the Roca family, had been living with and working for ranchers for so long that they were no longer aware that other Panoan speakers could be found nearby. They were encountered by chance and gladly welcomed to come to live with the rest. In other words, in those days, what came to be known as the "Chácobo" were no more than a bunch of scattered, scared, and scarred families, ready to surrender their destiny to powerful outsiders—or at the very least ready to accept life under their influence. This is precisely what happened in and around *Xabaya*.

In 1952, the Bolivian government, intent to "civilize" the local "savage" population, established a so-called *Núcleo indígena*—a secular *reducción* of sorts—some ten miles away from Puerto Limones, on the Benecito River. It was led by the notoriously infamous José Martorell, who bullied the Chácobo in the most creative and sadistic ways. The Native population initially consisted of only twenty-eight people, led by "Capta" Paë, whose wife of Movima descent, Mama Tohë (a.k.a. Hortensia Durán) spoke fluent Spanish. A couple of years later, SIL missionary Gilbert Prost and his wife, Marian, started to act in the vicinity, and their less aggressive demeanor, as well as their impressive logistics, gave them an obvious advantage over Martorell. In 1956, Núcleo was transferred some fifty kilometers to the west, on the Ivon River. The government establishment finally vanished, but the Chácobo who had moved there stayed.[14] A few years later, in 1964, the vast majority of the Chácobo migrated westward, led by Capta Paë—who apparently had stayed with Papa Jicho (a.k.a. Gil Prost). Several other groups joined the move, leaving only a small group from the Yata and Benecito Rivers to stay behind. Most of the migrants settled in what is now the Chácobo's main dwelling place: *Tapaya*, known as "*Alto Ivon*" in Spanish and only a few hours' walk from the new Núcleo.

To make a long story short, apart from those who stayed on the Yata/Benecito River (and are still found there), nearly all of the Chácobo started living together on the Ivon River, where pressure (and oppression) from the outside world was far less than on the larger rivers they used to live by.[15] This is also the time when the Chácobo began to acknowledge the authority of one paramount chief (*chama chamaria*), the first having been Capta Paë, succeeded after his death by his wife, Mama Tohë, followed by *taita* Huara and finally Maro Ortiz, who still holds the office. In other words, a nation was born, and the Chácobo had finally become one people, self-defined as such, formally acknowledging (if not obeying) a single leader. This was done under the influence of, but also as a form of resistance against, Western pressure of all sorts.

Jonathan Hill (1996, 1) defines ethnogenesis as "the historical emergence of a collectivity defining itself in terms of shared language and culture," arguing that this can often be understood as a reactive process, especially in the case of domination by states or colonial powers. This seems to be precisely what happened with the different *maxobo* in the savanna regions of the Benecito River. Yet, as Brightman (2016, 6) recently stated about such forms of exo-affiliation among Carib Peoples of the Guianas, "hav[ing] become officially recognized as 'tribes' or 'ethnic groups' by nation states, they have become increasingly real as categories of identity, and the traceability of their historical construction makes them no less significant." This also holds true for the present-day Chácobo and can help explain recent changes in their eschatology.

WHY ARE SOULS EXILED TO *XABAYA*?

I have no definite answer to this initial question. In fact, because I started visiting the Chácobo twenty-nine years ago and only have privileged access to information provided by "elders" of my own age group, I am not even sure what type of postmortem destinies are imagined by the younger generation (or those living on the Yata River). Important changes are undoubtedly brought about by the growing impact of Christian values and the fact that people are now buried in cemeteries. Time will tell, with the probable help of younger anthropologists. Yet, in the absence of certitudes, I do have a few hypotheses.

My first hunch was that, at least for members of the older generation, the *yoshini*'s systemic exile in the ruins of a deserted village on the Benecito River might be related to the modus vivendi negotiated with the missionaries. The

FIGURE 4.3. *Shaman's drum (left) and beer jar of similar make (right), around which people dance. Photo: Philippe Erikson, 2001.*

latter had protected the Chácobo from abusive bosses, helped them acquire a land title in the Ivon, and were influential in helping them acquire the economic and political autonomy they enjoy today. In return, minimal allegiance to Christian values was required, especially around the graveyard; spirits were therefore expected to travel to ancient dwelling places.

It is hard to say how profoundly converted the Chácobo have been over the past fifty years. Most of the converts belong to the one family, which now holds most of the major salaried positions and the ensuing power. In other words, Chácobo schoolteachers, merchants, male nurses, teachers, local officials, etc. mostly belong to the one and only openly converted family (Erikson 2018). Yet, in terms of religious positioning, they seem to have adopted a midway stance, as if Alto Ivon were a sort of spiritual no-man's land, where neither Jesus nor *yoshini* ruled unchallenged. This struck me in the early 1990s, when I heard the Chácobo preacher warn his congregation, during his Sunday morning sermon, that *yoshini* were indeed powerful and helpful but should no longer be summoned since people were now following Jesus. In a similar vein, in the mid-1980s, Swiss missionaries[16] tried to encourage the use of Native instruments, drums in particular, to accompany the singing of hymns. This attempted indigenization of gospel songs was firmly rejected by those Chácobo who were converted enough (or perhaps should I say "ill-converted enough") to see it as heretic. Drums were meant to summon *yoshini*, and that is precisely what one should not be doing in church! For the same reason, by contrast with the communities that stayed behind in the Benecito/Yata area, drums are no longer played in Alto Ivon, even during manioc beer festivals.[17]

Obviously, the *yoshini* are not always welcome in Alto Ivon, and I first thought that might explain why their dances must be staged in *Xabaya*. This, however, is a rather weak argument, considering how eminently volatile *yoshini* are. Just like the wind—or perhaps even as the wind, in wind form—they move around a lot. Ghosts (*yoshini*) do appear in Alto Ivon. Years after his passing, *taita* Maro's daughter claimed to have seen a human-shaped form clearly wearing her late father's favorite sweater, and a few weeks later, my wife reported a group of women on their way to the gardens being literally spooked by a couple of hens running toward the graveyard. Everyone was convinced they were being herded off by the *yoshini* of a highly respected woman, Cai Jëma, who had passed away the year before. In other words, Christian influence is only part of the story, and *Xabaya* still a mystery.

Another clue to the enigma of postmortem exile to *Xabaya* could be found in the ancient belief that a *yoshini*'s final destiny was to end up trapped in a *shono*: a majestic tree of the *Bombacaceae* family that abounds in forests off the shores of the Benecito and Yata but are not found in the vicinity of Alto Ivon (Bergeron et al. 1997, 155). Admittedly, I have been told that such entrapment was an accident of sorts that might occasionally happen to a soul and was far from systematic. Yet, there is plenty of evidence that the forebears of present-day Chácobo (or at least previous occupants of the region) buried their dead in funeral urns beneath such trees. Traveling on the Yata and Benecito Rivers, I heard from Spanish-speaking riverine dwellers that when *mapajo* trees, tumbled by erosion, fell in the river, urns were commonly uncovered. And of course, as we have seen, another clue stems from Chácobo *mapajo* beer troughs being used as ghost traps of sorts (see note 7).

Be that as it may, ontological tracks seem misleading when it comes to solving the *Xabaya* enigma. It is probably more interesting to consider how people relate to history and perceive their ethnic identity than to linger on their relationship with spirits. In fact, from an ethnotheological perspective, warding spirits off to *Xabaya* is a rather awkward move, going against the grain of mainstream Chácobo mortuary practices and beliefs. As we have seen (see

FIGURE 4.4. Shono (Ceiba *sp.*) *tree in the Javari basin. Photo: Philippe Erikson, 2000.*

note 10), remnant connections with the dead are important, and the tendency is to keep the deceased close by. Bodily remains, in particular, are clung to, to the extent that Paë Davalos recalls that in his childhood days on the Benecito, when so many people died that his people decided to resettle a few miles away, they took some of their deceased parents' bones along with them.[18] And nowadays, photographs of the dead are keenly sought after and sometimes used for postfuneral ritual mourning, a phenomenon we might label secondary wailing, by analogy with secondary funerals. So, once again, we are left with an enigma and must look for alternative explanations for the exile of souls to *Xabaya*.

RAGE AND REVENGE, POST HOC AND POSTMORTEM

To sum up, I argue that souls might still be exiled to *Xabaya* for emotional rather than mystical reasons. Possibly as a means to make a political statement of empowerment by reconquering *Xabaya*, albeit in a retrospective and purely imaginary way, thereby stressing that formerly dispersed, isolated, roughed-up people have finally managed to find unity in life and death, past, present, and future. Although eschatology might not radically reshape the course of history, it might at least symbolically rectify its ontological consequences. *Xabaya* would therefore appear to be a means to settle postcolonial accounts, even if only remotely and vicariously. A hypothesis of such nature, of course, is not something anyone could ever prove. Yet, the notion of cosmology as a means to get even, to level out past torts, not only made sense but even sounded somewhat obvious when I heard my Chácobo interlocutors recounting stories of the past to account for contemporary acts.

My friend Rabi Ortiz, for instance, often recalled episodes of his youth on the Benecito, featuring local bosses of the worst abusive kind. According to him, just for fun, such people would shoot their guns at his mother's ceramics (hard work), wasting her beer supply (hard work), and there was nothing she could do or say (harsh feelings). But, as recounted elsewhere (Erikson 2017), Rabi Ortiz has become a successful local businessman and respected political leader. He therefore concluded his stories with a punchline such as: "Hey, but look at me now. I even have white men working for me now . . ." One of these employees, a Brazilian man who happened to have previously worked for the Salinas family (one of the infamous Benecito River *patrones*), had been employed for more than a decade as warehouse supervisor in Alto Ivon when he was buried alive by the family of a woman who had accused him of sorcery just before she died. When the police came to investigate, I was told, stories of the Benecito were constantly put on the forefront. "Back then, we were unorganized, and you killed many of us, but those days are gone, now we are united, have our own leaders, and will accept no interference in our internal affairs, even if a white man has been killed." In other words, the crutch of the argument was: "In *Xabaya* you killed many of us, so don't make such a fuss because we have now (rightfully) killed one of you." This is certainly the reason why, in 2015, while investigating this particularly violent witchcraft execution that had occurred a decade earlier, my close friend Paëcito constantly merged the issues of past violence (much of which happened in *Xabaya*) and narrations about the ultimate destiny of present-day souls (for whom *Xabaya* happens to be the point of entry in the afterworld). As if *Xabaya* were both a place of (past) death and a place for the (future) dead and, as such, a virtual memorial place, an intangible landmark, where past and present conflate.

In this respect, and in an assumedly Marxist perspective, Chácobo eschatology emerges at the end of the day as a reflection of recent political history, if not a product of pre- and postcolonial sufferings and struggles. This is reminiscent of Bonilla's (2009) analysis of the Amazonian Paumari's contemporary conception of the afterlife as governed by rules replicating the patron-client relationship implemented during the rubber boom. Another parallel situation can be found in the Javari basin, in Brazil, among the people known today as the Marubo. This "ethnic group" results from the amalgamation of various previously autonomous communities and "commercial collectives" set up during the rubber era. And, strikingly, even today, their postmortem destiny is attached to the place where this amalgamation took place: a now-abandoned village called *Kapi vana wai* where, in the 1930s, a charismatic leader known as João Tuxaua convinced different groups, each bearing a different name, to jointly transfer their longhouses to a newly established territory and thereby "become" the Marubo. In the words of Helena Welper:

> Strictly speaking, the Marubo did not exist prior to João Tuxaua's reformation. His "good talk" urged the abandonment of warfare and the formation of a single moral community. He exhorted the people to surrender the political autonomy of their isolated groups and gather into a single village settlement—a village that today figures not only as the birthplace of the Marubo but also potentially as a posthumous destiny. "When we die here," the shaman Arnaldo Mashempapa explained, "our doubles go to the spirit-land, they go to *Kapi vana wai*." (in Fausto, Xavier, and Welper 2016, 54)

In short, and using an assumedly Lévi-Straussian rhetoric: João Tuxaua and *Kapi vana wai* are to the Marubo what Capta Paë and *Xabaya* are to the Chácobo. Mutatis mutandis, of course, since both groups—although speaking related Panoan languages—live some 500 miles apart, in different countries and with different histories.

CONCLUSION: LIVING RUINS

I started working with the Chácobo in 1991, have lived with them for extended periods of time, and return to visit on a regular basis. Yet, it took me nearly twenty years to discover the strong connection between *Xabaya* as the place where the Chácobo were united in the late 1950s, under the leadership of a missionary and their first paramount chief, and *Xabaya* as the landing place where afterlife begins for contemporary dead people. Twenty years to find out that a historical landmark can also be an eschatological destination. To find out that *Xabaya* was at once both initial and final. Yet, my previous ethnographical experience with the Matis of the Brazilian Amazon, as well as recent ethnography such as that discussed in this volume by Virtanen and Stoll (chapter 5), should have prepared me for the idea that former dwellings and their surrounding gardens are places that Amazonian people are prone to symbolically reinvest long after having abandoned them (Erikson 2007). To state it slightly differently: for many Amerindians, secondary growth is a primary source for ancestral spirits. Cultivated palm trees, in particular, are regularly associated with beneficial spirits, most probably because their fruit are typically harvested many years after the people who planted them have died, in locations where abandoned dwellings have since given way to densely reforested areas (Erikson 1996; Rival 1998). Fermented beverages made from palm fruit grown there are typically shared with these ancestral spirits, reestablishing contact with them a reasonable number of years after their "fresh" ghosts cease to be perceived as a dangerous. In many ways, if my interpretation is correct, the recent evolution of Chácobo eschatology is but a modernized variant of this scheme.

Recent history has had a tremendous impact on Chácobo religious beliefs, in particular by reassigning afterlife to a village where their formerly dispersed ancestors had been successively mistreated, decimated, missionized, but finally united. Though paradoxically created on the initiative of Spanish- or English-speaking foreigners, that place nonetheless became the focal point of shared identity, the place where a feeling of communality emerged and is now assumed, perhaps even "commemorated," each time someone passes away. Freshly departed souls, previously dispersed in large *shono* trees along the riverine gallery forest, are now said to all congregate (or at least mark a stop) in just one place, *Xabaya*. Remarkably, the alpha of the group's unity therefore came to stand for the omega of individual destiny. Could Chácobo eschatology therefore be considered a form of cryptohistorical narrative? Be that as it may, Chácobo narratives seem keen on having both history and eschatology congregate in this virtual milestone that bears a doubly predestined name: *Núcleo* ("the core") and *Xabaya* ("the drab clearing").

However contingent and clearly circumscribed in time, the events that took place in *Xabaya*, because they led to Chácobo ethnogenesis, turned this initially rather inconspicuous location into a virtual memorial site. The place where scattered groups initially came together now stands for ultimate reunification, and each individual death seems to provide an opportunity to proffer a cryptic narrative about collective identity. History seems to have profoundly impacted Chácobo eschatology, transmuting the real place where destiny once politically united their groups into a virtual locus of postmortem family meetings. Perhaps transmuting a place of past tragedy into one of future bliss, but in any case, placing *Xabaya*—a living ruin of sorts—at the crux of Chácobo political, historical, and eschatological narratives.

NOTES

1. The Chácobo are a Panoan-speaking group of approximately 1,000 members, living in twenty-seven villages in the Department of Beni, Bolivia (Provincias de Vaca Díez, Yacuma y Ballivián). Over the past twenty years, an increasing percentage of the population has migrated to the nearby town of Riberalta. However, for subsistence, most of the Chácobo still rely on agriculture and, to a lesser extent, hunting and fishing. Cash income derives mainly from the sale of forest products such as Brazil nuts (*Bertholletia excelsa*), timber, *palmito* (heart of palm), and, until recently, natural rubber (*Hevea brasiliensis*). Largely thanks to the efficient action of their leaders at the head of the Central Indígena de la Región Amazónica de Bolivia (CIRABO), their territory has expanded from the 43,000 hectares, originally obtained in the early 1970s with the help of the Summer Institute of Linguistics, to the 510,895 hectares now covered by the Chácobo-Pacahuara TCO, or Tierra Comunitaria Originaria (Original Comunitarian Land) (Herbas Araoz and Patiño Fernandez 2010).

2. For a more general picture of ritual wailing in Amazonia, see Allard (2013), Beier, Michael, and Sherzer (2002), Graham (1986), Lea (2004), Shepard (2002), and Urban (1988).

3. Throughout the text, spelling of Chácobo words follows the conventions adopted by missionaries of the Summer Institute of Linguistics and the Swiss Evangelical Mission (Zingg 1998). For a more technical and phonologically sophisticated description of Chácobo linguistics, see Tallman (2018).

4. In one such case I witnessed, during a woman's funeral, the mother of the dead woman verbally chastised the deceased's son for having hit her just before she died (of diabetes). The person in charge of serving manioc beer very subtly diminished the ostracizing effect by including the son in the round of drinks when his turn came around. The gratitude in his tearful eyes was just as moving as his grandmother's Choephore-like speech.

5. The Chácobo also say that when someone is critically ill and hears thunder, it means their father is calling them and they are about to die. When thunder roars, widows typically stop what they are doing and think about their lost spouse. Yet, when a little girl nearly got killed by lightning, I was told it was just because someone had imprudently used a discarded copper wire as a clothesline. (I was expecting an ethnographically richer explanation, given that the wire was a remnant of an antenna that had once belonged to *taita* Maro, whose ghost sometimes appears.)

6. Having to circle around a desired goal, struggling against obstacles or competitors to reach this central target, seems to be a major trope of Chácobo ritual life, as previously argued in Erikson ([2000] 2010). Although lacking Native discourse to back this speculation, I can't help but wonder if this importance of twirling motions in Chácobo ceremonial life might not be related to the intricate relationship between spirits and strong winds, both called *yoshini* (Villar 2004).

7. Although the tree used for troughs is called *pora* whereas the residence of souls is called *shono*, both trees belong to the *Bombacaceae* family and are known as *mapajo* in regional Spanish. Such trees, in Native Central and South America, are common figures of the axis mundi uniting the upper (celestial) and lower (terrestrial) worlds.

8. This apparently anodyne toponym seemed not only adequate but perhaps even slightly cheeky, considering it was applied to the very place where contact with the white man's world was consolidated, and that before the derogative nickname *rëquë oxo* ("white noses") came into fashion, white people were called *xabaca nohiria*, "savanna people."

9. Despite the quotation marks, this citation is by no means literal. It has been reconstructed as faithfully as possible based on memory and field notes. Technically speaking, the precise location of the spirits' dancing grounds is somewhat obscure to me, since they seem to be simultaneously in the ruins of a former village and somewhere in the sky. Perhaps just straight above *Xaba Xobo* . . .

10. According to SIL sources, people were still buried beneath their hearths in the early days of the mission. In 1970, Marian Prost wrote of the recently deceased: "*Por lo general está enterrado debajo del lugar donde el finado solía dormir. Si una persona de una aldea se muere en otra, la entierran en la selva cerca de la aldea que visitaba. Hubo dos casos de esto en nuestra aldea, los cadáveres fueron sepultados en la antigua aldea que hoy prácticamente es selva, y a unos 60 metros de la actual*" ("People are usually buried just beneath

the place they used to sleep. If someone from one village dies in another, they are buried in the forest next to the village they were visiting. There were two such cases in our village, and the bodies were buried in the former village site, which is now practically totally overrun by forest again, some 60 meters away from the present village." Prost 1970, 88–89).

11. Tumi Chucua's Panoan name was *Pamahuaya*, and its last Native headman was known as Boca. *Jënë shiniya* (Guayaramerin) was led by Mahua *tëhui tëtëca*, and *Xëbiya* (Riberalta) by Mahua *maxoquiri*.

12. The Panoan Karipuna are not to be confused with their homonyms of the Tupian linguistic stock, who still live on the other side of the border, in the Brazilian state of Rondônia. According to Pierre and Françoise Grenand, the term *karipuna*, of probable Arawakan origin, came to designate various groups of acculturated Amerindians in different parts of Brazil (in Nimuendajú [1926] 2008, 41).

13. Judging from writings by early nineteenth-century explorers, the term "Chácobo" was in use as early as 1844 (Palacios [1875] 1976). For a more detailed history of southern Panoan ethnonyms, see Córdoba and Villar (2009).

14. Chácobo people still live in this village, which is still called Núcleo. They are mostly descendants of a man called *taita* Huara, rather than *taita* Maro's kin. Probably in a desperate attempt to circumvent its failure and move slightly away from the American missionaries, the original Núcleo had already changed location on the Benecito. Present-day Núcleo (on the Ivon River) is therefore the third in a series. A rather puzzling onomastic loyalty, considering the terribly negative feelings associated with the name.

15. A more detailed account of Chácobo migrations can be found in Córdoba (2008). Erikson (2018) provides further information on the recent history of Chácobo leadership and missionary influence on its (re-)emerging.

16. After nearly a quarter of a century in Bolivia, the SIL were expelled from the country, and the Prost family was replaced by the Zinggs, from the Misión Evangélica Suiza, who stayed until the mid-1990s. The mission is now run by Spanish-speaking locals, much less intent on learning the Native language, much less well-funded, and whose influence is dwindling, especially in the very specific political context of Evo Morales's election. For a more detailed picture of Chácobo evangelization, see Villar (2015).

17. Having heard that, out of sheer nostalgia, a woman had manufactured a clay drum, and because I wanted to hear it played along with the flutes as people once did, I bought this item from her and tried to get someone (anyone!) to play it. The attempt proved to be a total failure, and though it was not enough to spoil the party, I had obviously made a major blunder. Drums as a major means of summing spirits seems be a widespread Amazonian pattern (see Descola 1986, 159).

18. Keeping and carrying your forebears' bones is a custom typically associated, for lowland South America, with people of what David Jabin (2016) has referred to as the Sirionoïd complex (Siriono, Yuqui, Yora, etc.), some of whom were former neighbors (albeit enemies) of southern Panoans.

REFERENCES

Allard, Olivier. 2013. "To Cry One's Distress: Death, Emotion and Morality among the Warao of the Orinoco Delta." *Journal of the Royal Anthropological Institute* 19 (3): 545–61.

Barbosa de Faria, João. 1947. "Vocabulário dos índios caripuna (El'OÉ) do Rio Madeira organizado com o concurso do índio Vicente Bocamuller da tribo Caripuna." In *Conselho Nacional de Proteção aos Índios, Publicação No.2, Comissão de Linhas Telegráficas Estratégicas de Mato-Grosso ao Amazonas ("Comissão Rondon"). Anexo No. 5. História Natural: Etnografia pelo General Cândido Mariano da Silva Rondon*. Rio de Janeiro: Imprensa nacional.

Beghin, François-Xavier. 1972. "Exactions à l'égard des Indiens d'Amazonie." In *Le livre blanc de l'ethnocide en Amérique*, edited by Robert Jaulin, 143–92. Paris: Librairie Arthème Fayard.

Beier, Christine, Lev Michael, and Joel Sherzer. 2002. "Discourse Forms and Processes in Indigenous Lowland South America: An Area-Typological Perspective." *Annual Review of Anthropology* 31: 121–45.

Bergeron, Sylvie; Jërë Ortiz, Bari Ortiz, and Kako Soria. 1997. *El uso de las plantas por los Chácobos (Alto Ivón, Beni, Bolivia)*. La Paz: Ediciones IBIS Dinamarca.

Bonilla, Oiara. 2009. "The Skin of History: Paumari Perspectives on Conversion and Transformation." In *Native Christians: Modes and Effects of Christianity among Indigenous Peoples of the Americas*, edited by Aparecida Vilaça and Robin M. Wright, 127–46. Farnham, UK: Ashgate.

Brightman, Mark. 2016. *The Imbalance of Power: Leadership, Masculinity and Wealth in the Amazon*. London: Berghahn Books.

Conklin, Beth. 2001. *Consuming Grief: Compassionate Cannibalism in an Amazonian Society*. Austin: University of Texas Press.

Córdoba, Lorena. 2008. "Parentesco en femenino: género, alianza y organización social entre los Chácobo de la Amazonía boliviana." PhD diss., Universidad de Buenos Aires.

Córdoba, Lorena, and Diego Villar. 2009. "Etnonimia y relaciones interétnicas entre los Panos meridionales (siglos xviii–xx)." *Revista Andina* 49: 211–44.

Descola, Philippe. 1986. La *Nature domestique: symbolisme et praxis dans l'écologie des Achuar*. Paris: Les Editions de la Maison des sciences de l'Homme.

Erikson, Philippe. 1996. *La griffe des aïeux: Marquage du corps et démarquages ethniques chez les Matis d'Amazonie*. Paris: Peeters.

Erikson, Philippe. 2003. "Cana, Nabai, Baita y los demás . . . Comentarios sobre la onomástica Chácobo." *Scripta Ethnologica* 23: 59–74.

Erikson, Philippe. 2007. "Faces from the Past: Just How 'Ancestral' Are Matis 'Ancestor Spirit' Masks?" In *Time Matters: History, Memory and Identity in Amazonia*, edited by Carlos Fausto and Michael Heckenberger, 219–42. Gainesville: University of Florida Press.

Erikson, Philippe. (2000) 2010. "Dialogos à flor da pele . . . Nota sobre as saudações na Amazônia." *Campos, Revista de Antropología Social* (Curitiba) 11 (2): 9–27.

Erikson, Philippe. 2014. "El ritual como máquina del tiempo: ejemplos Chácobo (Amazonía boliviana)." In *Antes de Orellana: Actas del 3er Encuentro Internacional de Arqueología Amazónica*, edited by Stephen Rostain, 399–406. Lima: Instituto Francés de Estudios Andinos (Actes et Mémoires de l'IFEA, tome 37).

Erikson, Philippe. 2016. "'Si matamos a un brasileño, ¿en qué le concierne al gobierno?': Análisis de un caso de brujería entre los chácobo." In *Apus, caciques y presidentes: Estado y política indígena en los países andinos*, edited by David Jabin, Oscar Espinosa, and Alexandre Surrallés, 179–94. Copenhagen: IWGIA.

Erikson, Philippe. 2017. "La carrera política de un líder chácobo de la Amazonia boliviana o de cómo Rabi 'Yobëca' se volvió Alberto 'Toro' Ortiz." In *Política y poder en la Amazonia: Estrategias de los pueblos indígenas en los nuevos escenarios de los países andinos*, edited by François Correa, Philippe Erikson, and Alexandre Surrallés, 146–61. Bogotá: Centro Editorial de la Facultad de Ciencias Humanas de la Universidad Nacional de Colombia.

Erikson, Philippe. 2018. "Traductores, pastores, conversos . . . ¿jefes? Reflexiones sobre el fundamento evangélico del poder político entre los Chácobo (Amazonía boliviana)." *Boletín del Instituto Francês de Estudios Andinos* 47 (3): 335–48.

Fausto, Carlos, Caco Xavier, and Elena Welper. 2016. "Conflict, Peace, and Social Reform in Indigenous Amazonia: A Deflationary Account." *Common Knowledge* 22 (1): 43–68.

Graham, Laura. 1986. "Three Modes of Shavante Vocal Expression: Wailing, Collective Singing, and Political Oratory." In *Native South American discourses*, edited by Joel Sherzer and Greg Urban, 82–118. Berlin: Mouton de Gruyter.

Hanke, Wanda. 1949. "Algumas vozes do idioma karipuna." *Arquivos: Coletanea de documentos para a história da Amazônia* 3 (10): 3–12.

Hanke, Wanda. 1958. "The Chácobo in Bolivia." *Ethnos* 23: 100–25.

Herbas Araoz, Amparo, and Marco Antonio Patiño Fernandez. 2010. *Derechos Indígenas y Gestión Territorial: El ejercicio en las TCOs de Lomerío, Mosetén y Chácobo-Pacahuara*. Santa Cruz: PIEB (Programa de Investigacion Estrategica en Bolivia).

Hill, Jonathan, ed. 1996. *History, Power, and Identity: Ethnogenesis in the Americas, 1492–1992*. Iowa City: University of Iowa Press.

Jabin, David. 2016. "Le service éternel: Ethnographie d'un esclavage amérindien (Yuqui, Amazonie bolivienne)." PhD diss., Université Paris Nanterre.

Lea, Vanessa. 2004. "Mebengokre Ritual Wailing and Flagellation: A Performative Outlet for Emotional Self-Expression." *Indiana* 21: 113–25.

Nimuendajú, Curt. (1926) 2008. *Les Indiens Palikur et leurs voisins*. Paris: Éditions du comité des travaux historiques et scientifiques/Presses Universitaires d'Orléans.

Nordenskiöld, Erland. 1911. *Indianer och Hvita y Nordöstra Bolivia*. Stockholm: Albert Bonniers Förlag.

Palacios, José Augustín. (1875) 1976. *Exploraciones de Don José Augustín Palacios, realizadas en los ríos Beni, Mamoré y Madera y en el lago Rogoaguado, durante los años 1844 al 47: Descripción de la Provincia de Mojos*. La Paz: Instituto Boliviano de Cultura.

Prost, Marian. 1970. *Costumbres, habilidades y cuadro de vida de los Chácobo*. Riberalta: I.L.V. y Ministerio de Educación y Cultura de Bolivia.

Rival, Laura, ed. 1998. *The Social Life of Trees: Anthropological Perspectives on Tree Symbolism*. Oxford: Berg.

Shepard, Glenn. 2002. "Three Days for Weeping: Dreams, Emotions, and Death in the Peruvian Amazon." *Medical Anthropology Quarterly* 16: 200–29.

Tallman, Adam. 2018. "A Grammar of Chácobo." PhD diss., University of Texas at Austin.

Urban, Greg. 1988. "Ritual Wailing in Amerindian Brazil." *American Anthropologist* 90(2): 385–400.

Villar, Diego. 2004. "La noción de Yoshini entre los Chácobo de Bolivia: una interpretación." In *Los mundos de abajo y los mundos de arriba: individuo y sociedad en las tierras bajas, en los Andes y más allá*, edited by Maria Susana Cipolletti, 165–201. Quito: Abya-Yala.

Villar, Diego. 2015. "Procesos de evangelización en la Amazonía Boliviana: Un drama misionero en tres actos." *Boletín Americanista* (Barcelona) 1 (70): 113–31.

Zingg, Philipp. 1998. *Diccionario Chácobo-Castellano, Castellano-Chácobo con bosquejo de la gramática Chácobo y con apuntes culturales*. La Paz: Ministerio de Desarrollo Sostenible y Planificación, Viceministerio de Asuntos Indígenas y Pueblos Originarios.

5

The recent discoveries of precolonial geometric earthwork complexes (geoglyphs) in southwestern Amazonia and "dark earths" (*terras pretas*, anthropogenic fertile soils) elsewhere in Amazonian rainforests have contributed to a new understanding of lowland South America's Indigenous past, giving rise to discussion among researchers, civil servants, and public bodies about the need to protect these sites and promote them as Amazonian cultural heritage. Meanwhile, a number of studies have pointed out that, far from being self-contained, heritage only exists in a vast network of social, economic, political, and cultural relations encompassing local residents, landowners, politicians, companies, archaeologists, anthropologists, and others (Berliner and Bortolotto 2013; Gallois 2012; Guillaud et al. 2016; Suremain 2015).

This chapter examines the production of cultural heritage among Indigenous and riverside populations in Brazilian Amazonia, discussing the issue through social relations involving nonhumans, local knowledge, and practices of administrative agents of national society. We draw on ethnographic material produced with Indigenous communities in the states of Amazonas, Acre, and Pará and a riverside population in Pará. Ethnographic research has been carried out among the Apurinã (Pupỹkary) and Manchineri (Manxineru) of Amazonas and Acre—in the upper and central Purus River region where geometric precolonial earthworks have recently been identified—and among riverine

Grounds for Political Claims

Earthworks and Anthropogenic Soils as Cultural Heritage and Sources of Territorial Legitimation in Brazilian Amazonia

PIRJO KRISTIINA VIRTANEN
AND EMILIE STOLL

https://doi.org/10.5876/9781646422869.c005

peasants and Indigenous people living in areas characterized by the presence of dark earths in the lower Tapajós area, Pará.

Dark earths have been associated with precolonial settlements and anthropogenic soil management (Arroyo-Kalin 2014; Glaser and Woods 2004; Lehmann et al. 2003; Smith 1980), while geometric earthworks embody precolonial ceremonial sites and social networks. Both have become popular foci of attention and research among those studying the cultural and ecological history of lowland South America. In this context, earthworks and dark earths, as material vestiges, have been increasingly discussed and addressed by our local Indigenous and riverside interlocutors as indicators of their ancestors' presence, and have also been used to advance and advocate Indigenous politics and territorial demands.

Several legal instruments protect Brazilian cultural heritage (such as the 1988 Federal Constitution's Article 216, Law 4845 from 1965, Decree 3551 from 2000), and discussion of the best tools for this purpose has been actively promoted. In Brazil, archaeological sites are considered public heritage (*bens da União*) by Law 3924 from 1961 and by the Constitution's Articles 20, 23, and 24.[1] In terms of the registration of cultural heritage, there are increasing numbers of collaborative attempts with local communities, while so-called "cultural heritage education," to be conducted collaboratively with local actors during any archaeological research project, is now a legal requirement.

UNESCO has recognized the cultural heritage of Indigenous peoples at the international level, and several sacred sites were acknowledged when designing the 1972 World Heritage Convention. However, at that time, the recognition of cultural and natural heritage sites pertained to separate categories. In 1992 a new category of Cultural Landscape was introduced, recognizing places of specific human-environment interaction. The first property to be recognized as Cultural Landscape was the Tongariro National Park (Aotearoa, New Zealand), inhabited by the Maori, who had a spiritual relationship with the mountain at the heart of this territory. Convention for the Safeguarding of the Intangible Cultural Heritage (2003) defines intangible cultural heritage as "the practices, representations, expressions, knowledge, skills—as well as the instruments, objects, artefacts and cultural spaces" of communities and individuals. Indigenous perspectives on collective cultural heritage entered the discussion at the 2000 World Heritage Indigenous People's Forum. They later appeared in the draft principles and guidelines on the cultural heritage protection of Indigenous peoples, according to which Indigenous cultural heritage includes both tangible and intangible creations, manifestations, and productions collectively developed and maintained. The UNESCO Convention on the Protection and Promotion of the Diversity of Cultural Expressions (2005) mentions member states' responsibility to support Indigenous peoples in producing and disseminating their cultural heritage (articles 1 and 19). The cultural heritage and sacred sites of Indigenous peoples are protected by articles 12 and 31 of the UN Declaration on the Rights of Indigenous Peoples (2007).

Indigenous cultural heritage protection often mobilizes a similar rhetoric in Brazil, such as the protection of Indigenous knowledge and practices. Examples of this are found in IPHAN's (Instituto do Patrimônio Histórico e Artístico Nacional, National Historic and Artistic Heritage Institute) recent registration of the intangible heritage of the agricultural systems of the Amerindian populations of the Rio Negro (Van Velthem and Emperaire 2016), the *kusiwa* designs of Wajãpi communities (Gallois 2006), and the Iauaretê waterfall, a sacred place of the Indigenous peoples of the Uaupes and Papuri Rivers. Previous studies addressing the notion of cultural heritage among Amazonian Indigenous peoples have pointed out its ontological elements, such as invisible shamanic body paintings and ornaments of spirits (see Coelho de Souza 2009; Miller 2009), thereby highlighting the complexity of the concept (see also Porsanger and Virtanen 2019). Brazil's 1988 Constitution promotes multiculturalism and allows specific cultural and collective land rights for Indigenous people. Land demarcation, ruled by Law 6001 of 1973 and Decree 1775 of 1996, and today organized by the state Indigenous affairs' agency FUNAI (the Indigenous National Foundation), is a complex and still actively debated issue and process in Brazil (Ramos 1998). The first stage of legal land demarcation involves anthropological expertise whereby an anthropologist is employed to gather information pertaining to and demonstrating a "traditional occupation" in a particular territory, by a specific group. Local knowledge on the history of human occupation in the area, traditional economic activities, and natural resources used and currently necessary for the group are a central part of the report. Archaeological vestiges may then comprise evidence of ancestral human activities to support Indigenous demands for the creation of an Indigenous territory—*Terra Indígena* (as in the recent identity claims of the Tapajós discussed in this chapter).

In this chapter, our aim is to examine local claims made on cultural heritage and heritage values in political processes. Sources for this study have been produced in the states of Acre and Amazonas in 2005–2016 and in Pará in 2011–2019. Our ethnographic focus has allowed us to notice how invisible agencies in certain places narrate the history of the communities, especially through long-term interactions with nonhumans. Additionally, we will show how the narratives about the past take shifting forms in today's cultural heritage discussions and political processes in the two locations, southwestern Amazonia and Lower Amazon, and with the state.

GEOMETRIC EARTHWORKS IN THE UPPER PURUS AND GROUNDS FOR POLITICAL CLAIMS

Geometric Earthworks and Nonhuman Agencies

A number of geometric precolonial earthworks are located on the interfluvial (*terra firme*) plateaus of the tributaries of the Purus and Madeira Rivers, mostly in the Brazilian states of Acre and Amazonas. They are made up of ditched enclosures of different geometric shapes and varying sizes in association with exterior and sometimes interior embankments. The forms of the geometric ditches are diverse, but circular and quadrilateral shapes predominate. Ancient roads, delineated by low earthen banks, frequently connect the separate earthworks and link them to adjacent streams. The construction and use of these geometric earthworks, established largely for ceremonial purposes, spans approximately 3000 to 1000 BP (Pärssinen, Schaan, and Ranzi 2009; Saunaluoma 2012; Saunaluoma and Schaan 2012; Schaan 2012a; Watling et al. 2017). To date, more than 800 earthwork formations have been identified, especially along the deforested BR 317 highway (Martti Pärssinen, personal communication).

Launched in 1977, the PRONAPABA project (Programa Nacional de Pesquisas Arqueológicas da Bacia Amazônica) was the first attempt to study the sites, and focused on the findings of ceramics and their different styles (see, e.g., Dias 2006). There were some other studies in the region, but it was not until 1999 that paleontologist Alceu Ranzi (personal communication) identified the extent of these numerous earthwork sites by aerial reconnaissance and reinitiated broader-scale studies. The research team consisted of Brazilian and Finnish archaeologists who consequently began working in the area. The first author (Virtanen) has been working on the team as an anthropologist, collecting research material with the local Indigenous population, and the area has become a place of study for various multidisciplinary teams. Studies of the upper Purus geoglyphs have shown that they were ceremonial in nature and that they had a complex organizational system (Saunaluoma and Virtanen 2015). To date, a few precolonial residential settlements have been identified in this region, often as mound formations, but the record of cultural material related to earthworks is still scant. Studies of the earthwork sites have also argued that they were multiethnic ritual spaces, drawing on the design of the sites and the precolonial ceramics with different cultural traditions (Saunaluoma and Schaan 2012; Virtanen and Saunaluoma 2017).

The sites' use declined gradually (Saunaluoma et al. 2018), and since colonization, the diversity, numbers, and social organization of Indigenous peoples has changed drastically. The sites recently identified lie principally in deforested areas, and these are also the places that have been the most affected by settler colonialism and extractivism. Precolonial earthwork complexes are increasingly cut by roads, even by paved highways; they are used for pasturing animals and agriculture; and different types of erosion have weakened and eradicated the enclosures. Therefore, archaeologists and other scientists have claimed that their protection as cultural heritage is urgent, as is cultural heritage education—given that knowledge of the precolonial heritage in the area is still scant (see also Ranzi 2011). For the scholars and others working to protect precolonial archaeological sites, the inclusion of the Earthworks of Acre (where most of the identified sites are situated) on the UNESCO Tentative List in 2015 gave hope for their protection and acknowledgment as precolonial heritage (UNESCO 2015). However, how this protection should take place has not been agreed upon, while the views of Indigenous peoples have rarely been presented in the state discussions. The contemporary Indigenous territories closest to the earthworks are those of the Arawak-speaking Apurinã and Manchineri peoples, with whom Virtanen has been working.

Even though considerable time has passed since the construction of the geoglyphs, the forms of the sites and the objects found in their contexts are not unfamiliar or strange to the Manchineri and Apurinã. The latter live in almost thirty Indigenous territories in the state of Amazonas, and number some 10,000 persons. While it is difficult to identify earthwork sites in forested areas, two Apurinã territories are critically traversed by the BR 317 highway: the Boca do Acre (also called Aldeia 45) and the Apurinã km 124–BR 317 (Manhē and Camapã being its main villages)—in which some precolonial geometric earthworks have been officially registered in the IPHAN reports (in an area next to the state of Acre). Yet, according to the Apurinã, many more earthworks, situated in forested areas, can be found in their Indigenous territories. Similarly, earthworks have been identified in the Camicuã reserve, especially during so-called "ethno-mapping" of Indigenous territories.

But how do the Apurinã perceive these geometric ditched enclosures? A long-term ethnographic study has shown that for the people in the villages next to the BR 317 highway (Boca do Acre and Apurinã km 124–BR 317) and in its vicinity (Camicuã), the earthworks are generally regarded as "places of spirits," such as of the past shamans, and "powerful" places (*kymyrury*). Overall, these places usually generate respect and avoidance, and are therefore never used by the Apurinã for housing or everyday activities, although surrounding

FIGURE 5.1. *Geometric earthwork site revealed by deforestation and the highway BR 317 in the Apurinã territory. Photo: Diego Gurgel.*

non-Indigenous populations (mainly small and large farmers) do use the sites for diverse agricultural and cattle herding activities (see Virtanen and Saunaluoma 2017). The geometric earthworks obviously have an important place in Apurinã memory as well as in their protective actions. They were crucial sites of transformation, dangerous and powerful in an ambivalent way. The elders recount that they had to be respected and remembered how their parents had advised them to pass by quickly and not to linger in their vicinity.

The deforested areas along the BR 317 highway have already been a focus of archaeological studies, especially in the form of excavations and aerial images produced to study and register the earthwork sites. Furthermore, several state-sponsored studies have been carried out by a number of consultants (geographers, anthropologists, agricultural experts) on the BR 317 highway's impacts on the local Indigenous people whose demarcated territory it traverses: Boca do Acre, Apurinã km 124–BR 317, and Camicuã (all demarcated in 1991). The highway has not been paved in the sections that pass through the Indigenous territories of Boca do Acre and Apurinã km 124–BR 317, because the Apurinã have called on the government to first fulfill its obligation to provide necessary education and health services and environmental protection in these Indigenous territories (Apurinã 2019). This has been a recurring request since the declaration of the territories (the first step in a demarcation process) in the 1980s.

During the recent state archaeological studies on the impact of the BR 317 highway, governmental consultants asked Apurinã to identify the places that should be protected from the impacts of the highway to be surfaced. They also collected local information about existing geometric earthwork formations. Consequently, the Apurinã have started to hear about the sites referred to as geoglyphs with increasing frequency. Apurinãs' knowledge about the sites is partly mentioned in the official reports, but not their ideas about their significance as "sacred places."

The sacredness of similar sites was also noticeable in the Tumiã Indigenous territory, several days' journey by boat from the Indigenous reserves traversed by the highway to the lower river, where Virtanen has worked more extensively. There, people also regard similar ditches as places of spirits. This Apurinã community firmly claimed a knowledge of the existence of these sites during collaborative research, even if they had no previous contact with officials documenting earthwork sites. Community members tell long, elaborate narratives about the geometrical "holes" and "ditches."

Such stories are a crucial part of the oral histories of the Tumiã River (a tributary of the central Purus River). For instance, it is said that one of the "holes" was inhabited by a giant *taia* fish. When visiting these sites with a small group of Apurinãs, Virtanen was told that the monster *taia* had once pushed people into its hole, and as a result many had become sick or even died. People could not pass the place in canoes; they had to be portaged to bypass the giant creature's domain and survive. Eventually, a shaman managed to calm the fish spirit through a dream. Virtanen was also invited to the ditch of a *mapinkuari*, a monstrous hairy being that had claimed the lives of many people. According to the story, one day, the villagers banded together and attacked him. When the being finally died, all the Apurinã felt his death in their own bodies. The holes were in fact the "houses" of different spirit beings (in a similar way that will be described in the lower Tapajós example below), and the narrations about powerfully transformative nonhumans were highly detailed and similar to other narrations concerning different types of "owner" spirits[2] closely linked to the management of forest resources. Owner spirits of forest animals, fish, stones, and certain trees have to be respected whenever traveling through the forest (Virtanen 2015, 2019).

Relationships to the earthwork places were experienced quite similarly in the body or in embodied ways in all the Apurinã communities of this study, despite differences in ways of living. Even communities that live alongside the

BR 317 highway, and where Apurinã is rarely spoken and traditional stories seldom told, regarded the sites as places of both power and danger. Nonetheless, the stories about the earthwork sites were guarded by elders, while many community members knew about their existence. The Apurinã living along BR 317 did not interact and travel as much within the forest, as it offered fewer resources; they used buses and motorbikes to go to schools and salaried jobs, to purchase groceries, and for visits. Furthermore, they experienced prejudice against Indigenous population by the dominant society on a more daily basis. This seems to have affected how knowledge and memories of landscape have been shaped and lived. Yet, none of the cultural heritage and land demarcation reports have explained why the earthwork sites were crucial for the Apurinã.

Another Arawak-speaking people, the Manchineri, is also one of the contemporary Indigenous groups located closest to the earthwork sites. They live along the Yaco River, a tributary of the upper Purus, and number some 900 persons. Though none of them has actually visited theses places, they associate the landscape of the earthworks with the places of their ancestors and palm spirits, who are considered to live in very similar locations in *terra firme* areas. Interaction with invisible beings (spirits) requires great care and attention. The Manchineri see the large ritual plazas of the geometric earthworks as places for ritual interaction with nonhuman beings, although these sites are also available for many other purposes, including human interaction (see Virtanen and Saunaluoma 2017).

Multidisciplinary studies have shown that the builders of precolonial ditched enclosures used a number of resources provided by palm trees (Pärssinen et al. 2021; Watling et al. 2017). Seeds, especially those of palm trees, have been extensively found in earthwork excavations. A long-term collaborative study shows that for the contemporary Indigenous people in the region, the fruits of various palm trees, such as uricuri, jarina, moriche, peach palms, patauá, and açai are still a good source of protein, and they apparently also were the major source of nourishment in the past (especially uricuri, jarina, and peach palms). Palm trees are used to prepare nutritious soups and drinks, often combined with corn, fish, and many other riches of the Amazon rainforest. Palm fruit–based beverages are also ceremonial substances, consumed in abundance by many Indigenous communities during late-summer feasts. Palm trees also provide raw materials for constructing houses and manufacturing such as bows and arrows (Virtanen 2011).

Furthermore, artifacts, musical instruments, and other items made from palm trees play a central role in contemporary rituals and ceremonies. In the oral tradition of the Manchineri, the owner spirits of palm trees are considered

FIGURE 5.2. *Geometric earthwork site Tequinho in Acre. Photo: Martti Pärssinen.*

to bring strength, health, and power to those who take good care of them. These same palm-tree spirits produce the geometric designs that the Manchineri see in visions that commonly occur when consuming hallucinogenic substances in ritualized contexts (Virtanen 2011). These designs are vehicles for a contemplation of the presence of certain nonhumans, and the very same forms can be seen in the compositions of geoglyphs: circular, rectangular, semi-rectangular, and so forth. These forms are typical for many Indigenous peoples of the region, and their geometric shapes are intimately related to other beings, such as nonhuman entities that are considered to give and ensure the reproduction of game, fish, and natural resources in general. They can also connect people to their ancestors, and thus to their past. The geometric designs are based on the principles of the shamanic world—processing power, relating to the other, and transformation between humans and nonhumans. They mark the presence of nonhuman entities that can become manifest and visible (see Virtanen 2011; Virtanen and Saunaluoma 2017). The importance of palm trees is highlighted by the fact that many local Indigenous peoples in the geoglyph regions mention certain palms in their myths of origin and as their spiritual agencies.

The invisible realities of the spirit world are rarely discussed because of their sacred nature (Virtanen 2019). However, their materiality is clear evidence of Indigenous presence and has recently been mustered as a ground for political claims. Those Apurinã whose socioeconomic situation has suffered from the impact of BR 317—especially from rapid deforestation and the cattle ranches that circle their territories—have started to speak more about the earthworks in their territories, even if earlier they were avoided because of their transformative powers. As more sites are discovered and discussed by the authorities and public, their existence has become a new resource in political discourses for the local Indigenous population. Territorial claims to protect Indigenous lands and to guarantee adequate education and health services increasingly refer to the earthworks as signs of occupancy by previous generations of their Apurinã forebears. Thus, protecting the sites also serves the political aims of contemporary Apurinãs.

Territorial Legitimation in the Communities: Forests as Ancestors' Vestiges

In the state of Acre, as already noted, when local authorities produced official reports about the regional Indigenous people's cultural heritage needing protection—when assessing how surfacing the highway might impact it—only the material vestiges, the visible material traces, of the Apurinã past were included. According to the official reports, the communities of Boca do Acre and Apurinã km 124–BR 317 indicated their recent cemeteries and ancient village locations to communicate the present community's relations with the ancestral territory.

Shifting narratives could be seen in the reports and between the level of everyday lives and more complex narrations of past practices. During fieldwork discussions, the elders told Virtanen that the use of cemeteries was in fact a recent practice, because they had lived mobile lives in the past, leaving their dead behind without marking their graves. The Apurinã did not have fixed cemeteries but buried their people as they trekked, before moving on to new locations. Ethnography produced with the Apurinã underlines mobility in a large area, in which revered places and nonhuman agents were taken into consideration in the meshwork of movement and historic times.

Overall, long-term collaborative research has shown that for both Apurinã and Manchineri, particular localities refer to specific historical times, calling up memories of beings and events. When talking about evidence of past generations, the Apurinã and the Manchineri most frequently referred to their anthropogenic forests as vestiges of their past. For both peoples, certain trees and vegetation, such as palm and fruit trees, indicate where their ancestors actually lived (see also Strang 1997; Virtanen 2019). The ancient swidden cultivations were also remembered by their Apurinã owners. Pieces of ceramic vases and plates are often found in these places. Anthropogenic forests were difficult for nonresidents to identify, and consequently so were the material vestiges attached to them.

Besides anthropogenic forests, the earthwork sites, which conjured up powerful beings, were linked to events in the past, and thus the community memory. In this sense, certain Amazonian cultural landscapes are deeply personalized, with owner spirits of places affecting people still today. For the Apurinã and Manchineri, the earthworks are linked to invisible agencies, embed transformations, and create relations with other beings. The earthwork sites reference powerful spirits and the relationality of a world that has to be maintained in balance, and consequently these sites are avoided. For the Apurinã, the localities linked to past community events often exhibit the presence of nonhumans that have shaped the lives of previous generations. But their transformability and ambiguity as both dangerous and powerful seemed too complex to handle in claims regarding territorial legitimation. As Marcela Coelho de Souza (2009) has argued, many traditional practices are based on the reality of the invisible, which rarely matches cultural heritage categories.

On the other hand, Apurinã memories of earthworks in the different Indigenous territories show how the material natural environment, and its continuing sustainable management, affect memories of the past. When an environment is largely deforested, as is the case with the Apurinã territories next to the BR 317 highway, the historical knowledge embedded in the forest and its vegetation can be lost. However, from the local perspective, the places of the spirits, earthworks carved in the soil, remain. In the past, they were rarely talked about with outsiders (Virtanen 2019), but now, being all that is left after deforestation, they are taken as signs of the presence of previous Indigenous generations. Therefore, some Apurinã communities facing state-led infrastructure and development projects as well as extractive economics and infrastructure have started to refer to the earthworks as a source of evidence in claims to protect their lands from resource extraction.

DARK EARTHS AND THEIR MULTIPLE "MASTERS" IN THE LOWER TAPAJÓS

Human and Nonhuman "Masters" Negotiating Land Occupation across Generations

Residents of riverside villages in Santarém, in the lower Amazon state of Pará, willingly show curious visitors the archaeological vestiges they have recently found in their yards. These pottery sherds appear on the surface from time to time, and one can simply bend down and pick them up. That is how the famous anthropologist Curt Nimuendajú, traveling in the region in 1922, after hearing that children were playing with some ancient *caretas* (faces) pottery, came to begin excavations in Santarém and its vicinity (Nimuendajú 1948; see also Stenborg, Schaan, and Amral-Lima 2012). Between 1923 and 1926, he discovered sixty-five archaeological sites in the Aldeia quarter of Santarém, in Alter-do-Chão, Samaúma, Arapixuna, Curuai Lake, and along the Arapiuns River (Nimuendajú 1948, 9–11). According to Nimuendajú, these sites were precolonial Indigenous villages. Further excavations followed, highlighting the well-known Santarém culture ceramics (*Tapajônica*). According to archaeological studies, the current location of the city of Santarém was the epicenter of Santarém culture and society (AD 1000–1500) before the arrival of Europeans (Gomes 2011; Nimuendajú 1948; Schaan 2012b; Stenborg, Schaan, and Amral-Lima 2012). This horticultural society had a rapid population growth toward the end of the precolonial period, introducing fixed settlements (which produced the dark earths) and complex chiefdoms (Roosevelt 1993).

Today, the region of Santarém is mostly inhabited by riverside communities of people of mixed origins (also referred to as *caboclos* or *ribeirinhos*) resulting from marriages between Natives and migrants from various places. These Amazonian populations have experienced the social and economic marginalization depicted in Indigenous history books (Moreira Neto 1988). Thus, in a quest for historical compensation, some communities have recently engaged in identity claims to make the state recognize them as Indigenous peoples and demarcate their lands (Bolaños 2011). In this region, to a certain extent, both riverside and Indigenous people share similar historical and cultural backgrounds, and there are many similarities in their relationships to the land and to precolonial vestiges. However, as observed by Emilie Stoll, their narratives are formulated differently for different audiences and according to context. External actors, such as researchers, NGO activists, or state officials, hear different stories when the discussion is about legitimizing landownership, cultural heritage, or Indigenous land demarcation processes (see also Gomes 2011).

Lower Tapajós populations are aware of the significance of dark earths and other precolonial manifestations as vestiges of past inhabitants. For the contemporary local population, the frequent presence of dark earth and pottery sherds in people's yards, gardens, and fields demonstrates continuity of human occupation from precolonial times. "This is an Indigenous object!" is often said whenever a piece of an ancient vessel is found. However, the so-called "local Indians from the past" (*os índios antigos daqui*) are said to be dead or gone. Stoll heard statements such as: "That may be why they broke all their vessels

FIGURE 5.3. *Island in the floodplain of the Curuai Lake. Photo: Emilie Stoll, 2015.*

before they left." "Indians from the past" are not thought to be the ancestors of the current dwellers, though many relate to them because both past and current residents participate in the same network of sequential transmission of mastery of these places. All are therefore legitimate dwellers and "owners," because they are all locally considered to be "masters" of the place (*donos do lugar*), even if there is no genealogical continuity between them. The concept of mastery is significant in lowland South American societies, in particular in Amerindian cosmologies. It refers to a "generalized mode of relationship that applies to humans, non-humans, and things" (Fausto 2008, 329).

In the lower Tapajós region, the territorial dimension of mastery is a crucial aspect of people's relationships to their land. According to the local people, several types of masters coexist in the same places. They include contemporary human families whose occupation is recognized as legitimate by their neighbors, as well as spirit masters in the form of subaquatic enchanted beings (the *encantados*) such as the giant enchanted anaconda, and the "Indians from the past" recognized through precolonial pottery. All of these masters are hierarchized on a topographic axis: some live on the earth, others at subaquatic levels in an "enchanted city" (*cidade encantada*). Terrestrial and subaquatic homes are thought of as superimposed, implying a kind of co-residency. The connection with precolonial pottery shows that the masters of places are also hierarchized by a temporal dimension as they are related to past and present dwellers. Therefore, as the first owners of a place, "Indians from the past" are given a prior right of mastery over the land in relation to the actual human dwellers of the riverbanks.

From a microlocal perspective, reciprocal interactions between "masters of the place" and human families living in the same location determine the permanency and/or the exclusion of human groups. An example of such a situation occurred when, during a drought, Stoll was staying with a family on an island in the floodplain of the Curuai Lake in the municipality of Santarém (see figure 5.3). The head of the family, a middle-aged woman, had inherited from her father a piece of land called Maloca. Her family is recognized in the neighborhood as the master or owner (*dono*) of Maloca—a local term referring to a circular collective Indigenous house. This place name was most probably chosen because the ground there is densely covered by pottery fragments placed in a circular pattern, implying a precolonial Indigenous residential site. Each year, the island is physically submerged, and when the floodwaters subside, more ceramics rise to the surface, making more visible several layers of former occupation (see figure 5.4). One day, Dona Maria told a story about another family who, some years earlier, had settled on Maloca without asking anyone's permission. One night, a girl from the family went into a trance, possessed by the giant enchanted anaconda that lived underneath the island. This spirit master ordered the intruding family to leave within fourteen days, as they had settled on her property without authorization, and the noise they made was disturbing her. Dona Maria further explained that "the Maloca belongs to the Indians [of the past], and Indians dislike being invaded." Then, based on her own criteria, she added that the newcomers were from another island and had no right to establish themselves on that one. In this example, the co-presence of different human and nonhuman masters makes it necessary, from a local point of view, to obtain all parties' authorization before any given family may legitimately occupy a piece of land.

In the region of Santarém, riverside people and Indigenous populations live on archaeological sites, perpetuating a continuous occupation of these places through time. As each place is managed by several human and nonhuman masters, the families' occupancy over time depends on the good relations maintained between "Indians of the past," enchanted spirit masters, and current human settlers. More than the land tenure documentation, in practice,

FIGURE 5.4. *Precolonial pottery covering the ground of Maloca island. Photo: Emilie Stoll, 2015.*

what truly legitimizes occupation in a place are peaceful interactions with its co-owners, including enchanted spirits and precolonial occupants.

Significance of Vestiges in the Lower Tapajós and Contemporary Heritage Discourses

The combination of local conceptions of what is culturally relevant in the environment and the expectations of institutional bodies (mostly IPHAN and FUNAI) or actors (such as archaeologists, anthropologists, NGOs) in charge of heritage inventories produces complex challenges. For the local population, however, heritage discourses and processes offer the chance to relate to the state. In addition, engagement between Native populations and anthropologists, archaeologists, and government agencies involves translation efforts, but also negotiations and shifting power relations.

In the lower Tapajós region, current identity claims and reinterpretations of precolonial pottery provide insights into the political dynamics of the area.

An example is provided by the archaeological excavations that were carried out in Parauá, a village of approximately 500 inhabitants on the left bank of the Tapajós River, some 100 kilometers south of the city of Santarém (Gomes 2011). Parauá villagers recognize themselves as one of the "traditional populations,"[3] in contrast with another village nearby, where the inhabitants identify themselves as Indigenous. The archaeologist Denise Gomes recounts that excavations in Parauá were a memorable experience due to both internal village conflicts that limited research and to the unexpected way the extracted precolonial pottery was understood by the non-Indigenous villagers.

> The archaeological remains obtained indicated various elements in common with the current population. . . . However, these findings were not seen by the local population as a connection with the past. People's response stressed an alterity in relation to Indigenous peoples, describing the pieces as "the Indian's pot," "the Indian's house" or the "Indian's coffin" (a funerary urn). (Gomes 2011, 308)

To Gomes's surprise, not all of the local people identified with the precolonial Indians, as they—as explained earlier—did not see any consanguine continuity with them. For Gomes, discovering vestiges of a horticulturalist society showed a similar way of life to that of the regional populations, and it could have been used as evidence to support (or awaken) regional Indigenous identity claims (Gomes 2011, 309). Yet, as pointed out above, these populations related continuous occupation of the land and relevant relationships to the idea of "mastery." The lack of understanding on both sides resulted in a great deal of frustration for both the community and the archaeologist.

In this region, equally awkward dialogues also occur in Indigenous villages claiming land demarcation. In the same way as in the Parauá case mentioned above, the meaning of the assertions was initially unclear to the researchers. An Indigenous leader would say: "Look at these Indians' *caretas*. We are here on Indian land. So, we are Indians." In this statement, the link between precolonial inhabitants and the current residents of the place was not explicit. How can land in the Tapajós River area be claimed by the present-day population as Indigenous land, with Indigenous roots, if there is no consanguine continuity with Indigenous inhabitants from the past? It is striking that in the lower Tapajós region, where there is so much evidence of precolonial occupation, archaeological artifacts found there by the population are rarely mentioned in the land demarcation reports. Indeed, this argument damages Indigenous claims, as all the inhabitants (Indigenous and traditional) insist on emphasizing a discontinuity with the precolonial occupants of their lands. Yet, this discontinuity, carefully elaborated, carries nonexplicit cosmological agencies (constituting a chain of past or present human and spirit masters) within which the legitimation of their occupation of the land is embedded. This interaction through time is their main argument in favor of demarcation.

Master Spirits versus Material Vestiges in Political Processes

While the dark earths and precolonial vestiges are rarely mentioned in the lower Tapajós' land demarcation reports, Indigenous claims explicitly point to nonhuman agencies embedded in the landscape, which are signs of a specific relationship with the land. This contrasts with the Apurinã case (as described above), where narratives referencing master spirits are rarely present in political processes, despite Apurinã history in the Purus River region being inscribed in the landscape in the form of certain vegetation and landscape formations, essentially nonhuman actors.

To fulfill administrative process requirements, Indigenous peoples from different ethnic backgrounds in Brazil, such as the Apurinã or the Indigenous people from Tapajós, have tended to highlight elements that are easily categorized as material vestiges or as past community activities, including cemeteries. Along the lower Arapiuns River (a tributary of the Tapajós River), Indigenous populations also pointed out places inhabited by emblematic spirit entities, such as the giant enchanted anaconda, Cobra Grande, which gave its name to the Indigenous territory *Terra Indígena Cobra Grande* (see Stoll 2016, 2019). Specific features of the riverine landscape, owned and inhabited by enchanted beings, became Indigenous sacred sites in the land demarcation report, associated with spirit entities that include enchanted people, animals, or artifacts (the enchanted fiancé, a ship, a cockerel, etc.). These "sacred sites" delimit the Indigenous territory.

As "the real masters of these places," these enchanted spirits legitimize the occupation of the land by specific human families. However, in political discourses, enchanted beings such as giant anacondas often take on a different meaning as they are presented as the "guardians" of a collective territory rather than as partners engaged in interpersonal interactions. In the Indigenous Territory Cobra Grande, for example, one of these enchanted beings is a giant anaconda called Merandolino, who inhabits the Toronó sandspit. Before becoming an enchanted being, Merandolino was in fact a powerful and talented healer of the Arapiuns River. At the beginning of the twentieth century, he maintained a specific bond with the Toronó area. He is said to have been born in the vicinity and was doing business with the owner (or human master) of this specific sandspit and of a tradepost. Today, Barbosa's children still live in Toronó, recognize themselves as Indigenous people, and head the land demarcation process. They keep alive the memory of the interactions between Merandolino and their ancestors, as both a human being in a remote past and as an enchanted entity today. They recount how their great-grandfather would go fishing or would travel in a boat with Merandolino in the 1930s; how the healer once invited him to visit his enchanted house underneath the water; or how he was the godfather of one of Barbosa's daughters. Today, new stories are produced about displays of Merandolino's presence in Toronó spit as an enchanted being: when he makes himself visible (as a ghostly apparition) and frightens hunters at night, or when boats are disturbed by swirling water when they cross the Toronó spit.

These stories about (past and present) interactions between Toronó's inhabitants and Merandolino have been and still are transmitted through generations in the extended Barbosa family as a family heritage. Thus, the status of these narratives started to change after the land demarcation process. Merandolino's spirit, incorporated into an enchanted anaconda living underneath the Toronó, became an "Indigenous entity" and the sandspit owned by the Barbosa family turned into a "sacred site," interacting now with other spirit masters and other places of different families, and contributing to the Indigenous community cultural heritage as a whole. Merandolino's story then entered the public sphere and he started to be thought of as a guardian entity of not just one place (the Toronó sandspit owned by one specific family) but rather of a collective Indigenous territory (the Indigenous Territory Cobra Grande). Consequently, such political processes created a living collective heritage, as well as perpetuating the stories about enchanted beings that are today taught in the Indigenous schools of the Cobra Grande territory, endorsing the community's cultural heritage. The story about Merandolino Cobra Grande is now part of the school curriculum in the four villages that are included in this territory. It was also turned into a song, which was later adapted for a specific choreography (the giant anaconda dance) performed during the festivities surrounding Saint John the Baptist Day (in June).

The local sense of place as historical continuity, and the occupation of specific places as stemming from the chain of mastery of a specific family, is elided in the political process. The narratives of enchanted master spirits belong to families and have rarely been shared with other people. Now, because of challenges to territorial rights claims, mastery emerges as a major topic, although the strong link between the spirit masters and the land is perpetuated through a more generic connection between the Indigenous people and their guardian entities, such as the giant anaconda and other enchanted beings.

DISCUSSION

Our study has demonstrated how the Amazonian past is active in the lives of its nonhuman residents, in its forests, waters, and land. In addition to recent theories about the human occupation of the Amazon and the anthropogenic nature of its forests and soils, information about the past can also be obtained from the local records of nonhuman agencies. Archaeologists have stressed the need to work with Indigenous people and to include their conceptions of territory, as well as their ideas and conceptions of the past, objects, and landscapes in academic analysis, as Juliana Salles Machado (2013, 79) has observed about "collaborative archaeology" in Brazil (see also Ormon-Parker 2005). Our study shows that the idea of territory includes diverse invisible aspects that are historically situated. Narratives about nonhuman beings play a central role in constructing a sense of place and territory. Discussions on cultural heritage should pay more attention to understanding them in respectful ways.

After the traumatic experiences of the rubber boom and assimilation, several Indigenous peoples have attempted to participate in state decision-making. This has meant reassessing what "cultural heritage" means for the dominant society, and how its preservation could be used as a resource and power. In this process, several shifting narratives have appeared, as different strategies are used. Anthropological and archaeological knowledge are increasingly being used in the service of guaranteed land-rights protection, while the signs of past generations, which ancestral forests or land itself richly incorporate, are rarely given space in discussions between Indigenous peoples and the state authorities.

However, for the Apurinã and Manchineri, these signs in the environment and vegetation often count as the vestiges that most affect their memories and current practices. These elements from the past empower and offer knowledge to contemporary Indigenous generations. They highlight how the previous generations have managed the forests and related to certain tree and plant subjectivities, and how this is still a crucial part of the communities' social relationships (Virtanen 2019). While this can be observed in the environment and provides evidence of a profound heritage of knowledge about how to interact with different entities, it still requires considerable time, knowledge, and effort to frame the evidence in terms of existing official cultural heritage concepts, both tangible and intangible. Instead, in such situations, the Apurinã and Manchineri often build on the tangible and irrefutable evidence of previous occupations in the form of the earthworks carved in the land or found pieces of ancient ceramics.

On the other hand, the anthropogenic material vestiges in the Tapajós region did not find resonance in political claims, as Indigenous and traditional communities nowadays disconnect present inhabitants from "Indians from the past." Instead, as can be seen through the example of the enchanted anaconda Merandolino, they would rather insist on a historic continuity between themselves and the enchanted spirit masters. Merandolino was a Native from the Toronó spit region, and had relatives and friends there. After he died, he eventually turned into an enchanted being who continues interacting with the new generations of masters of this place. Nevertheless, how people relate to enchanted master spirits in a mastery network draws attention to aspects that are difficult to communicate to others, as our case study shows; consequently, when the master spirits are mentioned in local claims, it places them at a distance, as guardians. By not revealing the relationships with master spirits in the course of political processes, it distances them, thereby avoiding and limiting unexpected transformative powers to take part in territorial legitimation processes.

For the Apurinã and Manchineri, as well as for the riverside and Indigenous populations of the lower Tapajós, the past, the present, and the future are constantly intertwined, through temporal and topographic dimensions. Furthermore, we must consider that memories of the past and of past beings are not necessarily restricted to specific places, because they constantly shift with contemporary practices and ritual acts. The use and practice of medicinal plants, traditional designs, ways of learning, and certain foods and substances can actualize relations with ancestors and spirits or open up a pathway to their knowledge.

Therefore, Indigenous inclusion in cultural heritage nomination, decision-making, and management is crucial. There are good examples of how that can be done based on Indigenous values and principles, offering co-learning (e.g., Ford 2017). Amazonian Indigenous peoples should be allowed to play an active role in heritage discussions with their own perspectives and languages.

State officials rarely have opportunities to carry out long-term fieldwork, and instead their knowledge is based on information gained during a brief consultation visit to the area. Although researchers act as principal agents in the official cultural heritage initiatives connected with understanding and preserving earthwork sites, cattle raising, new roads, and agricultural plantations constantly work to destroy them. Meanwhile, Indigenous people continue to interpret their own history and have their own "historicities," which according to Neil Whitehead (2003, xi), refer to "the cultural proclivities that lead to certain kinds of historical consciousness within which such histories are meaningful." Their material and immaterial culture, such as ideas of mastery, ways of traveling, use of space, ceremonies, management of natural resources, and geographical art still produce an Amazonian Indigenous living heritage today. Only by guaranteeing Indigenous lands can Indigenous cultural heritages be protected. Therefore, safeguarding of Indigenous peoples' land and cultural heritage should always go hand in hand.

Acknowledgments. We would like to thank several projects: "United in Diversity, Monumental Landscapes, Regionality and Cultural Dynamism in Precolonial Western Amazonia," Research Funds of the University of Helsinki, the Academy of Finland, fieldwork funding by Local Heritage and Governance unit (Paloc, IRD/MNHN) and the French Research Institute for Sustainable Development (IRD); the French ANR Project Fabriq'Am—The Making of "Heritages": Memory, Knowledge, and Politics in Contemporary Amerindia Today (LESC/Mondes Américains); and the CAPES-Cofecub project Land Tenure Reconfigurations and Identity Claims in the Brazilian Amazon. We are grateful to Indigenous and riverside research collaborators, as well as to Sidney Facundes, Martti Pärssinen, Sanna Saunaluoma, Denise Schaan (in memoriam), Alceu Ranzi, Valentina Vapnarsky, Anath Ariel de Vidas, Philippe Erikson, and Patrick Menget (in memoriam).

NOTES

1. See also Law 25 from 1937; CONAMA Resolution 001 from 1986; and IPHAN Order 001 from 2015.
2. See also the work of Fausto (2008) on owner spirits.
3. In Brazil, "traditional populations" is a legal category defined as "culturally differentiated groups that recognize themselves as such, who possess specific forms of social organization, who occupy territories and use natural resources as a condition for their cultural, social, religious, ancestral and economic reproduction, using knowledge, innovations and skills generated and transmitted through tradition" (Decree 6.040 from 7 July 2007, Art. 3-I).

REFERENCES

Apurinã, Francisco. 2019. "Os 'limites' da rodovia federal BR-317 e os povos indígenas: Do licenciamento ambiental à licença dos espíritos." PhD dissertation, University of Brasília.

Arroyo-Kalin, Manuel. 2014. "Amazonian Dark Earths: Geoarchaeology." In *Encyclopedia of Global Archaeology*, edited by Claire Smith, 168–78. New York: Springer. https://link.springer.com/referenceworkentry/10.1007%2F978-1-4419-0465-2_2252.

Berliner, David, and Chiara Bortolotto. 2013. "Introduction: Le monde selon l'Unesco." *Gradhiva: Revue d'anthropologie et d'histoire des arts* 18: 4–21.

Bolaños, Omaira. 2011. "Redefining Identities, Redefining Landscapes: Indigenous Identity and Land Rights Struggles in the Brazilian Amazon." *Journal of Cultural Geography* 28 (1): 45–72.

Coelho de Souza, Marcela Stockler. 2009. "A cultura invisível: conhecimento indígena e patrimônio imaterial." *Anuário Antropológico* 1: 149–74.

Dias, Ondemar. 2006. "Estruturas Arqueológicas de Terra no Estado do Acre—Amazônia Ocidental, Brasil: Um Caso de Resiliência?" In *Estudos Contemporâneos de Arqueologia*, edited by Ondemar Dias, Eliana Carvalho, and Marcos Zimmermann, 59–168. Belford Roxo: Insituto de Arqueologia Brasileira. Palmas: Universidade do Tocantins.

Fausto, Carlos. 2008. "Too Many Owners: Mastery and Ownership in Amazonia." *Mana* 4 (2): 329–66.

Ford, Violet. 2017. "The Self-Governing of Inuit Cultural Heritage in Canada: The Path So Far." In *Indigenous Peoples' Cultural Heritage: Rights, Debates, Challenges*, edited by Alexandra Xanthaki, Sanna Valkonen, Leena Heinämäki, and Piia Nuorgam, 199–217. Leiden: Brill.

Gallois, Dominique Tilkin, ed. 2006. *Patrimônio Cultural Imaterial e Povos Indígenas: Exemplos no Amapá e norte do Pará*. Macapá: Iepé.

Gallois, Dominique Tilkin. 2012. "Donos, detentores e usuários da arte gráfica kusiwa." *Revista de Antropología* 55 (1): 19–49.

Glaser, Bruno, and William I. Woods, eds. 2004. *Amazonian Dark Earths: Explorations in Space and Time*. Berlin: Springer.

Gomes, Denise Maria Cavalcante. 2011. "Archaeology and Caboclo Populations in Amazonia: Regimes of Historical Transformation and the Dilemmas of Self Representation." In *Indigenous Peoples and Archaeology in Latin America*, edited by Cristóbal Gnecco and Patricia Ayala, 295–314. Walnut Creek, CA: Left Coast Press.

Guillaud Dominique, Dominique Juhé-Beaulaton, Marie-Christine Cormier-Salem, and Yves Girault, eds. 2016. *Ambivalences patrimoniales au Sud: mises en scène et jeux d'acteurs*. Paris: IRD/Karthala.

Lehmann, Johannes, Dirce C. Kern, Bruno Glaser, and William Woods, eds. 2003. *Amazonian Dark Earths: Origins, Properties and Management*. Dordrecht: Kluwer Press.

Machado, Juliana Salles. 2013. "História(s) indígena(s) e a prática arqueológica colaborativa." *Revista de Arqueologia* 26 (1): 72–85.

Miller, Joana. 2009. "Things as Persons: Body Ornaments and Alterity among the Mamaindê (Nambikwara)." In *The Occult Life of Things: Native Amazonian Theories of Materiality and Personhood*, edited by Fernando Santos-Granero, 60–80. Tucson: University of Arizona Press.

Moreira Neto, Carlos de Araújo. 1988. *Índios da Amazônia. De maioraia a minoria (1750–1850)*. Petrópolis: Vozes.

Nimuendajú, Curt U. 1948. "Os Tapajó." *Boletim do Museu Paraense E. Goeldi* X: 93–106.

Ormon-Parker, Lyndon 2005. "Indigenous People's Rights to Their Cultural Heritage." *Public Archaeology* 4 (2/3): 127–40.

Pärssinen, Martti, Denise Schaan, and Alceu Ranzi. 2009. "Precolonial Geometric Earthworks in the Upper Purus: A Complex Society in Western Amazonia." *Antiquity* 83 (321): 1084–95.

Pärssinen, Martti, Evandro Ferreira, Pirjo Kristiina Virtanen, and Alceu Ranzi. 2021. "Domestication in Motion: Macrofossils of Pre-Colonial Brazilian Nuts, Palms and Other Amazonian Planted Tree Species Found in the Upper Purus." *Environmental Archaeology* 26 (3): 309–22.

Porsanger, Jelena, and Pirjo Kristiina Virtanen. 2019. "Introduction: A Holistic Approach to Indigenous Peoples' Rights to Cultural Heritage." *Alternative: International Journal of Indigenous Peoples* 15 (4): 289–99.

Ramos, Alcida Rita. 1998. *Indigenism: Ethnic Politics in Brazil*. Madison: University of Wisconsin Press.

Ranzi, Tiago Juruá Damo. 2011. *Geoglifos do Acre e a proteção arqueológicos no Brasil*. Rio Branco: Printac.

Roosevelt, Anna Curtenius. 1993. "The Rise and Fall of the Amazon Chiefdom." *L'Homme* 33 (126–28): 255–83.

Saunaluoma, Sanna. 2012. "Geometric Earthworks in the State of Acre, Brazil: Excavations at the Fazenda Atlântica and Quinauá Sites." *Latin American Antiquity* 23 (4): 565–83.

Saunaluoma, Sanna, and Denise Schaan. 2012. "Monumentality in Western Amazonian Formative Societies: Geometric Ditched Enclosures in the Brazilian State of Acre." *Antiqua* 2 (1): 1–11.

Saunaluoma, Sanna, and Pirjo K. Virtanen. 2015. "Variable Models for Social Organization of Monumental Earthworks in Upper Purus, Southwestern Amazonia: Archaeological and Ethnographic Perspectives." *Tipití: Journal of the Society for the Anthropology of Lowland South America* 13 (1): 23–43.

Saunaluoma, Sanna, Martti Pärssinen, and Denise Schaan. 2018. "Diversity of Precolonial Earthworks in the Brazilian State of Acre, Southwestern Amazonia." *Journal of Field Archaeology* 43 (5): 362–79.

Schaan, Denise. 2012a. *Sacred Geographies of Ancient Amazonia: Historical Ecology of Social Complexity*. Walnut Creek, CA: Left Coast Press.

Schaan, Denise, ed. 2012b. *Um porto, muitas histórias: objetos arqueológicos do Porto de Santarém e seus contextos: Exibição, do 18 avril ao 20 mai 2012*. Santarém: Museu João Fona.

Smith, Nigel J. H. 1980. "Anthrosols and Human Carrying Capacity in Amazonia." *Annals of the Association of American Geographers* 70 (4): 553–66.

Stenborg, Per, Denise Pahl Schaan, and Márcio Amral-Lima. 2012. "Precolumbian Land Use and Settlement Pattern in the Santarém Region, Lower Amazon." *Amazônica* 4 (1): 222–50.

Stoll, Emilie. 2016. "La fabrique des entités: récits sur l'enchantement d'un riverain extraordinaire en Amazonie brésilienne." *Cahiers de littérature orale* 79: 23–50.

Stoll, Emilie. 2019. "'Vamos segurar nossas pontas!' Paisagem em movimento e domínio dos lugares no rio Arapiuns." In *Paisagens Evanescentes: Estudos sobre as percepções das transformações nas paisagens pelos moradores dos rios amazônicos*, edited by Emilie Stoll, Edna F. Alencar, Ricardo T. Folhes, and Chantal Medaets, 137–62. Belém: Editora do NAEA.

Strang, Veronica. 1997. *Uncommon Ground: Cultural Landscapes and Environmental Values*. Oxford: Berg.

Suremain, Charles-Édouard de. 2015. "Fabric-acteurs, recherche, patrimoine: une relation sous haute tension." In *Fabric-acteurs de patrimoine: implication, participation et postures du chercheur dans la patrimonialisation*, edited by Charles-Édouard de Suremain and Jean-Christophe Galipaud, 5–17. Igé: L'Etrave.

UNESCO. 2003. *Convention for the Safeguarding of the Intangible Cultural Heritage*. https://ich.unesco.org/en/convention.

UNESCO. 2005. *Convention on the Protection and Promotion of the Diversity of Cultural Expressions*. https://en.unesco.org/creativity/sites/creativity/files/passeport-convention2005-web2.pdf.

UNESCO. 2015. *Geoglyphs of Acre*. https://whc.unesco.org/en/tentativelists/5999/.

UN Declaration on the Rights of Indigenous Peoples (UNDRIP). 2007. https://daccess-ods.un.org/tmp/4879102.70690918.html.

Van Velthem, Lucia Hussak, and Laure Emperaire, eds. 2016. *Manivas aturás beijus: o Sistema Agrícola Tradicional do Rio Negro: Patrimônio Cultural do Brasil*. Santa Isabel do Rio Negro: ACIMRN.

Virtanen, Pirjo Kristiina. 2011. "Constancy in Continuity: Native Oral History, Iconography and the Earthworks of the Upper Purus." In *Ethnicity in Ancient Amazonia: Reconstructing past Identities from Archaeology, Linguistics, and Ethnohistory*, edited by Alf Hornborg and Jonathan D. Hill, 279–98. Boulder: University Press of Colorado.

Virtanen, Pirjo Kristiina. 2015. "Fatal Substances: Apurinã's Dangers, Movement, and Kinship." *Indiana* 32: 85–103.

Virtanen, Pirjo Kristiina 2019. "Ancestors' Times and Protection of Amazonian Biocultural Indigenous Heritage." *Alternative: International Journal of Indigenous Peoples* 15 (4): 330–39.

Virtanen, Pirjo Kristiina, and Sanna Saunaluoma. 2017. "Visualization and Movement as Configurations of Human-Nonhuman Engagements: The Geometric Earthworks of the Upper Purus, Brazil." *American Anthropologist* 119 (4): 614–30.

Watling, Jennifer, José Iriarte, Francis E. Mayle, Denise Schaan, Luiz C. R. Pessenda, Neil J. Loader, F. Alayne Street-Perrott, Ruth E. Dickau, Antonia Damasceno, and Alceu Ranzi. 2017. *Impact of Precolonial "Geoglyph" Builders on Amazonian Forests: Proceedings of the National Academy of Sciences of the United States of America* 114 (8). http://www.pnas.org/content/early/2017/01/31/1614359114.

Whitehead, Neil L. 2003. "Introduction." In *Histories and Historicities in Amazonia*, edited by Neil L. Whitehead, vi–xxi. Lincoln: University of Nebraska Press.

6

Inca Vestiges

From Prehumans to New Agers

Antoinette Molinié

Despite its incomparable charm, the village of Yucay, located in the Sacred Valley of the Andes, north of Cuzco, bears a name that suggests a certain amount of ambiguity: "*Yúkay*: deception, a deceptive action or trick. To deceive, to lead into error. To produce illusions. To amuse, distract, hoodwink, seduce . . . *S'kkhrakk yukáskkan*: Seduced by the demon."[1] The monumental Inca terraces, built from stones assembled without mortar, run across the foothills of the gleamingly snow-capped cordillera. Here and there, lush orchards hide the alignments of stones, which reappear under the cornfields and start to ripple again on the strawberry patches. The water flowing along the clever network of canals leaps from one terrace to another in cascades inset in the carved stone, punctuating this mineral, florid world with Moorish garden melodies, with the foliage of Norman hedges. Yucay was home to princes. In fact, the Sacred Valley that shades this village did not belong to any of the four provinces of the Inca Empire but was under the direct control of the royal family.[2]

In 1972, after a few months of investigation in Yucay, I became intrigued by recesses in the rocks towering above the sumptuous Inca terraces. Their inaccessibility, suspended as they were above the terraces, made them particularly mysterious. The villagers said these were very ancient tombs in which the remains of their ancestors had been placed. Some of them reluctantly informed me that they had found mummies and treasures there, but they refused to provide details, citing the danger surrounding these tombs and past problems with archaeologists, who had identified these cavities as Inca tombs ornamented with pictographs. One beautiful June morning, I went up there on horseback, intending to photograph and sketch the tombs. After arriving on the crest, I was contemplating the village of Yucay winding between the Cyclopean stones of the terraces and the sparkling water of the Urubamba River, when I was assailed by shouting rising from the cornfields. Realizing that the invectives were directed at me, I hurried down to the village. When I arrived in the main plaza, my horse suddenly bolted, making a sharp turn in midgallop and throwing me to the ground. People rushed to help me: one of my ankles was in bad shape. My friends informed me that I was probably the victim of the prehuman ancestor housed in the tomb I had intended to explore. I had not followed the required ritual prescriptions for gaining access to those places, whose very special status I was beginning to understand. The prognosis was fatal: not only would my joints snap open to release the ancestors' bones, which have been eaten away by time, but since my *animu*[3] had probably been taken away, I was going to perish little by little. From that moment, my nights were haunted by Rascar Capac as he appears in the episode *The Seven Crystal Balls* in *The Adventures of Tintin* (Hergé [1948] 1962). I seized the opportunity to get treatment from a local specialist.

It was by undergoing the magic cure that I understood the crucial role that these Inca tombs played, not only in the everyday life of Yucay farmers, but also in their representation of space and time.[4] By virtue of their position between the communal, unfarmed highlands (the *puna*) and the private, cultivated land of the terraces at the bottom of the valley (the *quechua*), they belong to two eras and two worlds.

PREDATORY VESTIGES THAT STRUCTURE THE SPACE AND TIME OF AN ANDEAN COMMUNITY

The opposition between *puna* and *quechua*, and more generally between high and low, lies at the root of every Andean expression of the environment. At every level of the cordillera, farmers distinguish between high and low, and even on the Yucay terraces, parcels located at heights differing by only a few meters are subject to this sort of distinction. Yucay territory is thus divided into two opposing categories. The upper *puna* is home to evil creatures that need to be warded off and supernatural beings that need to be won over. It is from the *puna* that the *condenados* descend, those fire-tongued giants expiating the sin of incest committed when they were humans. At night they devour foolhardy pedestrians. The *puna* is also where it is possible to encounter the flying heads of women whose hair gets tangled up in the brambles. Responding to their supplications can prove fatal. The *ñakaq* or *pishtaku* also wander about those gloomy parts: they can put the traveler to sleep and extract the fat from his lifeless body in order to sell it to priests who will use it to make bells and to computer specialists to lubricate their hardware.[5] The upper territory is also the realm of the mountain gods (*Apu*), who may be benevolent or malevolent depending on the offerings made to them. To pacify them, one must make at least one offering of brandy and coca (called *t'inkay*) when spotting them. And an appeal has to be made to them when working the fields, since they can determine the outcome. These *Apu* in the heights make pets of animals that humans consider wild: their dogs are foxes, and sometimes the farmers spot deer carrying loads similarly to llamas or horses, usually packages of gold and silver being transported for the mountain gods. This underscores the opposition between the two levels of the territory.

On the other hand, the people who populate the valley floor are at the heart of human history. Their stories refer to events in the lives of Inca ancestors or Spanish colonists, taking us into the real history of characters who lack the supernatural or mythical dimension of *puna* creatures. The invention of irrigation is recounted as follows: a *cacique* offers his daughter's hand to a hero who can bring water to his land, and the three competitors are the inventors of the three terrace irrigation systems. Another story celebrates the love life of the Marquis of Oropesa. Most toponyms refer to historical events. The site called Quriwayrachina was home to a "tribe" led by a female *cacique* named Maria Paicoc Sisal whose authority inspired universal fear. She made gold nuggets fly in front of her house, which still stands on one of the terraces. Its toponym (*quri wayrachina*: a place where a golden wind blows) preserves this memory.

The valley's two ecological levels are the foundation for two categories defined by myths and beliefs connected with each of them: above is the wild part of the territory, the age of chaos of an unsocialized nature, but also the realm of the mountain gods; below is the domesticated part of history and society, the era of order in a culture with strict categories that govern both the arrangement of the Inca terraces and the distribution of the plots.

These two categories of space and time are mediated by a particularly effective boundary. The valley farmers believe that the caves I saw at the foot of the cliff were the seat of the *machu*. These prehuman ancestors lived without any social order in the era before the appearance of the sun, in a kind of twilight between day and night. They were burned when the sun appeared, inaugurating today's humanity. The solar era marked the end of their undifferentiated world. To avoid getting burned by the sun—which some describe as divine, since it is closely connected with the Inca sun god—the *machu* took refuge in those caves. The farmers believe that the mummies in these caves are the charred remains of these prehuman ancestors. Other *machu* managed to flee into the tropical forest, where they are still hiding today. However, some *machu* escaped the sun fire and, from tombs that have become refuges, they can snatch foolhardy passersby like myself who failed to take the necessary ritual precautions. They can inflict serious illnesses like those that I was threatened with after my fall. This is why it is advisable to make regular offerings and avoid their dangerous caves.

The *machu* in its evil form—the one it took when I fell from my horse—is a *suq'a*, a prehuman ancestor seeking revenge for his annihilation by solar fire. He is male and can be a *suq'a machu*, *suq'a pukyu*, or *suq'a wayra*. The first can have sexual relations with his victim and give her a *suq'a wawa*, a child who may be either handicapped, mutilated, or stillborn. The *suq'a pukyu* is the prehuman ancestor's manifestation in the springs. His origins lie in the mythical period of the *machu*: many of them took refuge in watering places to protect themselves from the solar fire. When a woman crosses a stream, the *suq'a pukyu* can assume the form of a snake and enter her vagina, provoking pain, vomiting, and the symptoms of pregnancy. In men, the *suq'a pukyu* can cause tumors and boils. The *suq'a wayra* is a pathogenic wind tainted by contact with *machu* mummies. The *suq'a paya* is the female equivalent of the *suq'a machu*, a succubus who can make herself look like the wife of her male prey in order to copulate with the poor fellow, who will die upon the birth of the son he fathered with the perfidious *suq'a paya* seductress.

The *suq'a* usually "catch" their victims during a fall caused by the fright they provoke (*susto*). In addition to lethargy and depression, it provokes a strange illness. The joints swell, especially the knees and ankles, and then wounds open up, secreting blood that carries the small, yellowish, burned bones of *machu* ancestors. At the same time, the *suq'a* takes its victim's *animu* to the upper Yucay territory. This is the dual illness I was threatened with after falling from my horse.

The link between these symptoms and their etiology is plain to see. The skin—the boundary with the outside—bursts at the joints, and the prehuman ancestors flow out in the form of their bones. The structural homology is clear between, on the one hand, the boundary that the *suq'a* draws by means of the vestiges they haunt between the *puna* and the valley and, on the other hand, the boundary that the skin constitutes between the interiority and exteriority of the body targeted by the *machu*. The source of the illness affecting the liminality of a victim's body was his failure to recognize the role played by the liminality of vestiges to which they did not make the necessary offerings. Thus the mishap is rooted in a breach of the vertical categories of space and time. The confusion of fundamental categories harms the victim's flesh and takes away their *animu*, which needs their distinction to stay alive.

The treatment depends on the seriousness of the illness. First a *paqu* will be summoned, a doctor that many ethnologists refer to as a shaman. To the mountain gods this healer will make an offering called *pago* or *despacho*: this consists of a collection of food products, codified objects, and alcohol set out on a *mesa*, that is to say on a suitable ritual cloth.[6] This must be burned at the end of the cure. If this offering fails, one places oneself in the hands of an *altumisayuq* who has the power to get the *Apu* to intervene directly. It is worth noting that this high-ranking shaman is singled out by lightning: he blacks out when struck by a lightning bolt, and when he regains consciousness, he finds the paraphernalia he needs for cures. The thunder god *Illapa* was a liminal Inca divinity, an intermediary between *hanan pacha* (the upper world), *kay pacha* (the world here), and *ukhu pacha* (the lower world). Thus there is a remarkable structural homology between:

the two categories of territory mediated by Inca vestiges
the inside and outside of the victim's body mediated by skin
the *Apu* and the patient mediated by the *altumisayuq*
the *Apu* and the *altumisayuq* mediated by *Illapa* the thunder god

It is tempting to link the ambivalent nature of *machu* ancestors to the liminal location of the Inca vestiges they haunt. When benign, the *machu* is the benevolent ancestor of our humanity, and is therefore linked to the domesticated lower part of the territory divided into Inca terraces; when evil, he descends from a humanity that preceded ours, corresponding to the wild upper territory. He is on the boundary between humanity's two spaces and two eras.[7] Let us now take a look at those cultivated, productive vestiges of the lower level. Yucay's Inca terraces are fertile lands producing corn of exceptionally high quality, as well as other vegetables and fruits. But they also form an archaeological site protected by the National Institute of Culture. These vestiges, "cultivated" in both senses of the word, are not only a fertile soil but also an unconscious, fantastic medium of pre-Hispanic memory.

VESTIGES AS MEMORY: YUCAY'S INCA TERRACES AS A SYSTEM

It is said that, chosen by the royal household, the earth of the various Inca terraces was transported from the four regions of Tawantinsuyu by *mitimaes*, laborers deported from the northern empire, who made up most of the population of the valley. However, to the economic functions of these vestiges, which are alive to say the least, a classificatory dimension was added.

It was by analyzing the toponyms designating these terraces that I discovered their symbolic value. My study was based on the hypothesis—later broadly verified—that the Andean landscape is the medium of a conception of the world, a way of "persevering in one's being," a tool for remembering tradition. This space-division activity is particularly remarkable for the meticulousness with which Andeans distinguish topographical elements by naming them, not necessarily according to their physical features. If the Andean landscape is treated as a thought aid, one can see that the many toponyms marking out the terraces in Yucay do not just refer to topographical elements but constitute a system with its own organizational logic.[8] This approach is all the more justified in the case of the Inca terraces in Yucay insofar as they constitute not just a landscape but a complete construction that replaced most of the original slopes. This paucity of topographical signs frees the toponymy from the constraints that the landscape could have imposed upon it. At once landscape and architecture, the Yucay terraces as a whole could reflect a symbolic system, or maybe an aesthetics, through the organization of its many toponyms.

To test this hypothesis I recorded 277 toponyms over 404 hectares of cultivated Inca terraces, marking them on an aerial photograph. I also located these toponyms in archive documents. They have demonstrated a remarkable permanence: most of them are in Quechua and can be found in documents dating as far back as the sixteenth century. Next I was able to determine how each of them related to the ethnography of myths, beliefs, visions, and rites. The results of this lengthy process, which I only reference in broad terms here, are presented in Molinié (1996).

A meticulous study of toponyms reveals that they are repeated from one section of the terraces to another (see figure 6.1). I was able to demonstrate a dualist structure duplicating the one that organizes the whole Yucay territory into *puna* and valley, the two levels mediated by the Inca tombs that house the *machu*. This dualism is essentially based on the organization of the irrigation system, which I have described elsewhere (Molinié 1982, 1996). It is primarily manifested in the repetition of toponyms on both halves of the terraces, either identically or with a variation in the referential suffix indicating a topographical variation. For example, Saqsabamba and Saqsapata are found below, while Saqsabamba and Saqsamuqu are found above (*saqsa* meaning "speckled," in reference to a particular species of corn, and *bamba, pata*, and *muqu* being referential suffixes). Another toponym rooted in Spanish—Mediocalzón (Half-Pants)—is found identically repeated above and below, just as a repeated pair

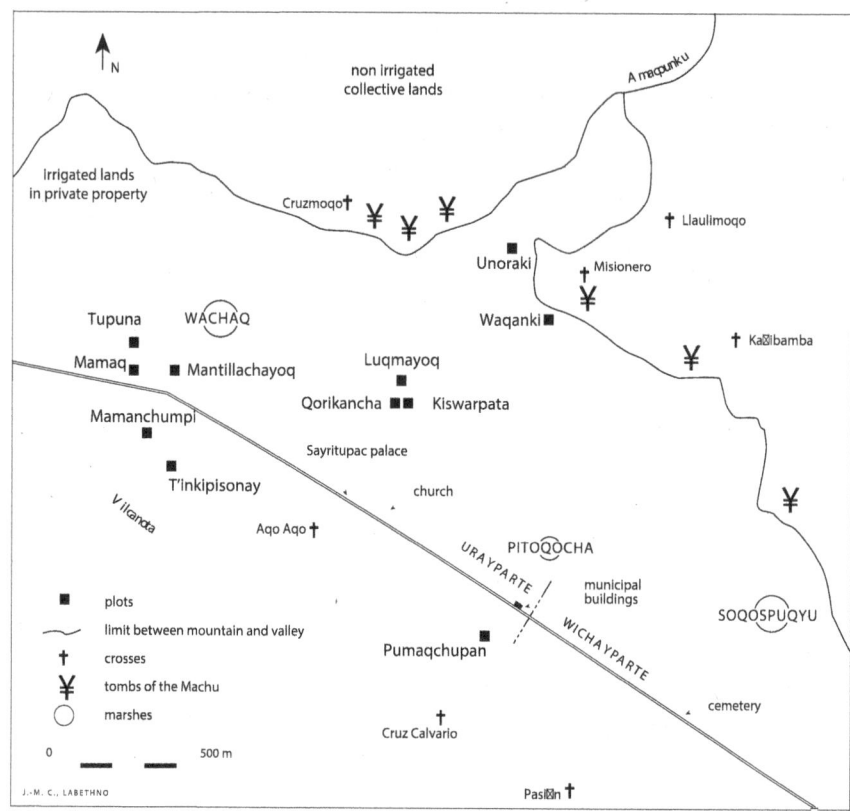

FIGURE 6.1. *Map of the most important toponyms in the symbolic structure of the Inca terraces of Yucay.*

like Mesapatagrande and Mesapatachico can be found on each of the two halves. Many other examples could be provided.

This dualism has a remarkable particularity: the halves have a gender, with the male half above and the female half below. This gendering of halves is reflected in the meaning of the toponyms of each half, as well as in the myths linked to them. I have already separated Maria Paicoc Sisal, from the place called Quriwayrachina in the lower half. For that same half, a story is told that a princess from Urubamba wanted to build a church, for which she coveted the beautiful stones of Yucay's terraces. For this reason she seduced the prince. The lovers hid in the place known as Pakacalle (*pakay*: to hide); the princess became pregnant in Chichubamba (*chichu*: pregnant), and gave birth in Wachaq (*wachay*: to give birth). As for the male half, people often recount the myth of the invention of the irrigation system, which sees three champions entering into a virile competition for the hand of the daughter of the *cacique* of Yucay. The names of these four mythical heroes formed the toponyms Wayrapunk'u, from the *cacique*'s name Wayra and *punku* (door), Wilkabamba where the suitor Wilka came from, Turukuntur from the name of the glacier that crowns the summits of Yucay, and finally Phaqcha, son of the *cacique* of Phaqchayoq.

I was able to determine the boundary between the two gendered halves through the very particular toponyms that characterize the terraces' median zone (see figure 6.1). The place known as Qurikancha takes its name from Cuzco's Temple of the Sun, which was at the center of Inca cosmogony. Kiswarpata refers to Kiswarkancha, the name of the Temple of Viracocha in Cuzco.[9] Thus these two toponyms, designating two juxtaposed sites in the middle of the terraces, refer to the temples of the two major divinities of the Inca state. The other toponyms of this median zone refer to the sanctuaries that made up the *ceque* system (the calendar of the imperial city), such as Qolqanpata, Pilcobamba, Ninabamba, Sunchupata, Porotoqolqa, and Pumamarca (Zuidema 1964).[10] Through their link with the sanctuaries in the capital of the Inca empire, these toponyms are infused with the sacredness that generally characterizes frontiers in the Andes (Molinié 1986–87).

Furthermore, whereas across the terraces as a whole place-names are duplicated from one half to the other and produce symmetry, on this particular boundary zone, several toponyms have a pair connotation. It is as if this specular repetition were concentrated into single terms like Wispan (Twin) Wakanqui, which designates a magic spell uniting two lovers (Duviols 1967, 23); Pitoqocha (swamp couple); and paradoxically Sapana, which comes from *sapa* (single), that is, to say the opposite of a pair.

This median zone also stands out because of exceptional characteristics. This is the only place where the wildness of two-and-a-half-meter-tall boulders disturbs the perfect geometry of the Inca terraces. Close examination reveals that some of them are sculpted. Archaeologists see them as puma heads.[11] This feline is a boundary symbol in Andean culture.

Furthermore, there is a magnificent tree growing in this intermediate zone, a *lucuma* (*Lucuma obovata*, of the *Sapotaceae* family), which has the special characteristic that it is sterile, and gives its name to one of the terraces (Luqmayoq). In Yucay they claim it is ungendered, giving by symmetry confirmation of the gendered character of each of the halves. Farmers are quick to stress its longevity, and they claim the *lucuma* in Yucay has been there since the time of the Inca terraces. A *lucuma* appears in the first episode of the life of the god Cuniraya Huiracocha as told in the myths of Huarochiri (Taylor 1987, 55–57), a story that confirms the ambiguity of its gender, as well as its supernatural character. The divinity Cahuillaca, a beautiful young virgin, is weaving under a *lucuma*. The god Huiracocha turns into a bird and perches on one of the tree's branches. He places his sperm into a very ripe fruit and drops it near Cahuillaca. She picks it up, eats it, and soon notices she is pregnant, having never been touched by a man. Thus she gave birth while remaining a virgin. In this myth, a god impregnates a virgin through a *lucuma* fruit carrying his semen. It seems clear that the *lucuma* trees in Huarochiri and Yucay are sexual intermediaries, one between a virgin and a god, the other between the male and female Inca terraces.

This *lucuma* tree is the site of visions that some farmers reported to me. One of them found an enormous ear of corn beneath its branches. One night, another farmer saw a sparkling man dancing in its foliage as the surrounding land blazed. The tree is considered particularly dangerous during a thunderstorm because it can attract lightning like a magnet. It is known that lightning is a recurrent symbol of boundaries: we have seen that it designates the shaman who serves as an intermediary between humans and the mountain gods. But the most frequently recurring apparition is a monstrous two-meter-high toad, which presents itself on stormy nights and mysteriously disappears at the end of the storm. It so happens that the sculpted stones standing in this median zone of the terraces near the *lucuma* are called *hamp'atu*, which means "toad." This name is a specific reference to the land toad (*Bufo spinulosus*), not to be confused with its aquatic counterpart. This amphibian is designated by three other revealing nouns. *Saqra*, which could be loosely translated as "devil," indicates its supernatural and dangerous character. The ancients thought toads were demonic creations that brought misfortune (Urton 1981, 180). Its second name, *pachakuti*, designates the other side of time and space marking the transitions between different eras in Andean history; this word refers to the spatial reversibility of the animal, which comes out of the ground during the rainy season and then spends the dry season in the underworld. Finally, *pachawawa* designates it as one of the sons of the earth, since it stays underground throughout the dry season. These toads also have a special characteristic: they eat their own sloughed skin.[12] Thus the quintessential symbol of liminality, located in the median zone of the Inca terraces, reflects the boundary between the inside and outside of its own body: as if this monstrous toad were making it known that, in the construction of dual categories, there was no going beyond the liminality in which it resides. This symbolic function of skin is reminiscent of the illness that strikes foolhardy visitors to the *machu* tombs: like the toad, their skin dissolves to reveal the bones of prehumans. Thus the creature that symbolizes the mediacy between the land's male and female halves devours its own boundary with the outer world. This is the typically Andean comparative logic of interlocking dualisms, involving skin in this case, the smallest of the liminal elements, giving access to no other, but sufficient unto itself.

In this monumental Inca terrace space, controlled both in terms of its ecology and its symbols, there is a swamp on either side of the median line that we have just been exploring. This forms two uncultivated zones, and the dangers they present make them like an echo of the Inca graves. The *suq'a machu* can catch you there and inflict the same illnesses as in the prehumans' tombs. In a way, the two swamps reproduce, in the domesticated part, the role played by *machu* tombs throughout the territory. They do not draw a separation line as the *machu* tombs do, but through the beliefs with which they are connected, they contribute to demarcating the two halves of the Inca terraces. And this is primarily because their names confirm the gender dimension of the two halves. The swamp on the lower, female half is called Wachaq (from the verb *wachay*: to give birth), and the one on the male side is called Soqospukyu, which means "the source with reeds." Since there is not a single reed to be found in the swamp, one detects a phallic connotation here. It should be noted that these are very old toponyms: both are mentioned in eighteenth-century documents like "Guachapuquio, hacienda del valle de Yucay"[13] and "Hacienda San Miguel de Socospucyu."[14] The names of saints that the Spanish added to them—probably to ward off their curse—do not contradict the gender opposition of the earlier toponyms: the Wachaq hacienda is also called Santa Beatriz, while Soqospukyu became San Miguel in the seventeenth century, as if the warrior archangel had been called to fight the demons in these sinister parts.

Between these two swamps is a small pond named Pitoqocha: *qocha* means "stretch of water" and *pito* designates a couple. The pond's toponym seems to suggest a union of the two swamps' toponyms. A hydraulic fact supports this hypothesis. The water from Soqospukyu is carried through canals to an area near Wachaq and Mamanchumpi. *Chumpi* designates the woolen belt that women wrap around their newborn. Many other toponyms in this area make reference to women's clothing, like Mamaq, Mantillachayoq (place having a female shawl), and Tupuna, which refers to the broach holding together the two sides of a *mantilla*. In Andean fertility rites, there is a well-known link between canal water and fertilizing sperm (Isbell 1978). Thus the toponyms use this homology in combination with a hydraulic fact to establish a link between the two lagoons and, by extension, between the male and female halves in which they are located.

The two swamps are also linked by a remarkable vision that is rooted in the pre-Hispanic past and confirms the dualism of the Inca terraces' categories. Farmers say they have seen a rainbow with its two ends touching the two

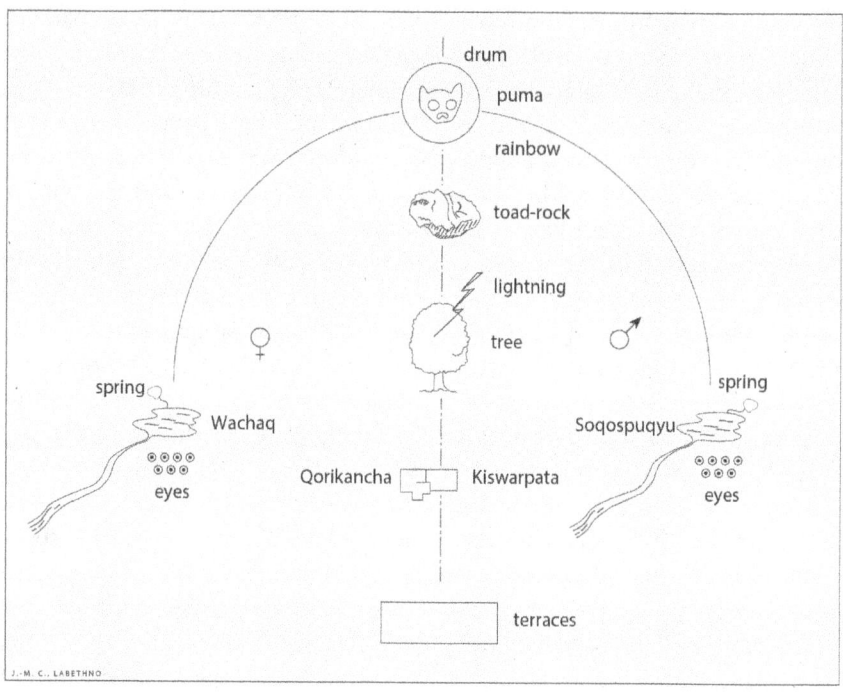

FIGURE 6.2. *Symbolic structure in the Inca terraces of Yucay.*

water sources, uniting Wachaq on the female half and Soqospukyu on the male half. This rainbow between the two sources evokes the one surrounding the scene in the famous anonymous painting at the Museum of the University of Cuzco, depicting the execution of the Inca Atahualpa by Spanish soldiers. Both rainbows link two water sources, but the one in Yucay has another characteristic revealed by those who have seen it in visions: it is a *wankark'uychi* because a puma head in a large drum appears at its center. The rainbow/puma connection is a common iconographic motif in various Andean cultures. In the Inca version, it is a recurring symbol of mediation in space and in time (López-Baralt 1986). This vision therefore supports the dualist structure of Yucay's vestige-land. The two sources that, as we have seen, are connected in the underworld are also interlinked by a threefold symbol of mediation (see figure 6.2) consisting of the rainbow springing from each of them; the puma that, let us not forget, also appears on the toad boulders; and finally the drum, which is played in Inca rites of passage such as the initiation of young noblemen during the Capac Raymi (Zuidema 1985).

We have seen that the Inca tombs overlooking the terraces are the refuge of prehumans who appear as *suq'a* predators when they do not receive the offerings they are due. But the predation that characterizes them has an important structuring function: the alignment of the Inca tombs draws the boundary between two realms (those of chaos and culture) and also between two eras (the prehuman era prior to the appearance of the sun and the human era afterward). Can we really speak of vestiges when it comes to remains that have a contemporary function in representations of space and time?[15] As for Yucay's Inca terraces, it is difficult to see them as mere vestiges, not only because they provide the community with food but also because they are the subject of a sophisticated symbolic elaboration, as evident in toponyms, myths, beliefs, and even visions. The classificatory activity that I have just outlined also contributes to the reproduction of society, as well as to the Yucay villagers' memory.

A CRUCIFIED MEMORY: CROSSES ON THE VESTIGES

We have seen that the Inca tombs that dominate the village of Yucay are presented as a danger. This is exploited to structure the community's space and time. The efficacy of the boundary that these vestiges draw between the categories of Nature and Culture is reinforced by another powerful symbol that is inseparable from the Inca tombs. On the foothills of the mountain that dominates the terraces, above the Inca tombs, stand seven crosses housed in small chapels. Their location so close to the prehuman caves is no mere coincidence: missionaries were in the habit of extirpating pre-Hispanic deities by imposing crosses or saints. It is even conceivable that the dangerousness of the Inca tombs, and the presence of the *suq'a machu* instead of peaceful ancestors, were designed to drive Yucavinos away from their pagan cults. This is why the alignment of these crosses cannot be separated from the alignment of the Inca vestiges.

We have seen how dualism characterizes not only the representation of the whole territory with its division into the *puna* (above) and valley (below)—categories mediated by the Inca tombs—but also the order of the Inca terraces at the bottom of the valley, divided into an upper/male half and a lower/female half. The village of Yucay itself reproduces this partition into Wichay ("high" and male) and Uray ("low" and female). During the Cruzvelacuy celebrations on May 3,[16] the seven crosses are brought down to the village to be worshipped. Each of them is celebrated in its own half by its own population in conformance with the system of responsibilities (*cargos*).[17] Each cross stands at the home of its *mayordomo* of the year, who must invite the neighborhood for a feast and dance. On the night from Sunday to Whit Monday, the seven crosses are solemnly carried in a procession to the village church according to a strict hierarchical order. The following day, with great pomp, they are taken back up to their chapels near the Inca vestiges, each following its own specific ritual path: Cruz Calvario, Aqo Aqo, Cruzmoqo, and Misionero are celebrated by the Uray (lower) half, and Llaullimoqo, Kañibamba, and Pasión are celebrated by the Wichay (higher) half. The seven crosses carry not the figure of Christ but silver objects that distinguish them from one another. Covered in suns, moons, flowers, and birds, these crosses look like totems. Now, those faithful to the same cross usually live in the same district of the village, and this district constitutes the identification with the pre-Hispanic *ayllu*.

An archive document states that in 1558, seven *ayllu* of the region were "reduced" into the village of Yucay[18]: Cuzco, Yanacona, Acosca, Chacho, Cachi, Pomaguanca, and Chicon. In 1595, the names of the *ayllu* changed, but there were still seven of them: "Yngas Cuzco, Guaraca, Paca, Yanacona con don Alonso Puchana de principal, Yanacona con don Juan Ayrambo de principal, Ancaypuro y Ananpa."[19] In the eighteenth century, Yucay still had seven *ayllu*: Paca, Collana, Lancha, Librecañari, Aliaga, Guaraca, and Cosco. And in the nineteenth century (in 1830 and 1841), these seven *ayllu* still had the same names.[20]

A few years ago, there were still a few elderly people who could show where each of the *ayllu* that existed in the early twentieth century would be located in today's districts. Although Yucavinos do not associate the individual crosses with individual districts of their village, they do distinguish between the crosses of the Uray moiety and those of the Wichay moiety, particularly during their ritual manipulations. This dualism of the crosses is the last remaining expression of the village's division into *ayllu*, as shown by parish archives from the early twentieth century that mention the Urayparte *ayllu* and the Wichayparte *ayllu*. Thus the distribution of the crosses between the moieties links them to the memory of the *ayllu* that took refuge in this bipartition. The celebration of the crosses, with their separate *cargos*, gives them the same scope as the districts to which the *ayllu* were reduced. The hierarchy, manifested in their decorations and their order in the procession, individualizes them and recalls the order of the reduced *ayllu*. One cross, Cruz Calvario, plays a very special role in their bipartition. It leads the procession, its silver jewels are more sumptuous, and all of the other crosses are prostrated in front of it on the threshold of the village church. It appears in the farmers' dreams, always in a position of authority.[21] But what interests me most is that its "responsibilities" (*cargos*) give access to the political management of the community. This direct relationship between a political responsibility and a religious responsibility recalls the link between *mayordomos* and the authorities of the colonial social units, which were none other than the *ayllu*.

The crosses' distribution between the moieties of the village in which the memory of the *ayllu* survives, their celebrations through separate *cargos* corresponding to the districts to which the *ayllu* were reduced, their hierarchy manifested during processions, their journey from the outside to the inside of the village, the equivalence between the promotion each of the *carguyocs* and that of the *ayllu's* colonial authorities, the fact that the *cargo* of Cruz Calvario—the main cross before which the others are prostrated—gave access to the political management of the community only a few years ago: all of these structures expressed in the ritual make the crosses symbols of the *ayllu*. Furthermore, all of the crosses have a double in Yucay's church, just as the divinities of the provinces of the empire had their doubles in the Temple of the Sun in Cuzco.

One can see how the boundary that the Inca vestiges draw between the categories of time and space is strengthened by these seven crosses: the Inca vestiges refer to the prehuman time above, while the crosses refer to the domesticated time below. Moreover, this dual boundary is turned into missionary discourse: the appearance of the sun that burned the prehumans is often mixed into mythical discourse on the apparition of the solarized Christ.

Finally, in their ritual displacements between the church and their chapels near the Inca vestiges, the crosses commemorate the essential event when the previously dispersed *ayllu* were reduced to the village. They testify to the pre-Hispanic location of the *ayllu*, but this is not to say that the site on which each stands—on the foothills of the mountains near the Inca tombs—corresponds to the location of each of their corresponding *ayllu*, nor even that each cross is the present symbol of an *ayllu*. It is not a term-to-term relationship. It is the whole set of crosses and their liminal position in relation to the prehuman tombs that constitutes a metaphor for the disjunction between the pre-Hispanic *ayllu* and the reduced *ayllu*. This is how the memory of the reduction is crucified.

This is connected with the creation of humanity through the Inca vestiges, through the presence of the prehumans destroyed by solar fire. The rite commemorates the *ayllu's* transition from dispersion to *reducción*; the myth that the tombs represent conveys the memory of a buried prehumanity. The *reducción* of the *ayllu* and the appearance of a social humankind seem to be united in the superimposition of an event and a myth: the transition from dispersed *ayllu* to reduced *ayllu*, on the one hand, and the transition between the two phases of humanity, on the other hand. One tradition is preserved in memory by two voices, one speaking through the rite, the other through the myth. This conjunction between a mythical event and a historical fact gives the latter a cosmic value: the disjunction between the dispersed *ayllu* and the reduced *ayllu* becomes the equivalent of the transition from a wild era to a domesticated era. The advent of the *reducción* assumes the dimension of the appearance of the sun or the solarized Christ. The prehuman tombs infuse the crosses with a mythical message. By giving the crosses a cosmic dimension, the Inca vestiges reinforce their classificatory efficacy and strengthen their contact metaphor. History and myth are connected through ritual.

Thus Yucay's Inca vestiges proved to be powerful classification instruments. The symbolic efficacy of the *machu* tombs essentially stems from the *machu*'s predatory activity. The Inca terraces themselves convey the memory of an Andean aesthetic, that of two gendered halves, mediated by a murky zone: the one that Verónica Cereceda showed in her work on Andean fabrics, most of which consist of two halves linked by a median motif called *k'isa*, presented as a heart (Cereceda 1978, 1987). On those cultivated vestiges, the predation carried out in certain highly circumscribed areas by the *suq'a machu* from the Inca tombs has a structuring function, as we have seen.

Let us now continue our journey through the Urubamba Valley: about thirty kilometers past Yucay, we are dazzled by the Pisac fortress.

NEW AGER PREDATION AT THE PISAC ARCHAEOLOGICAL SITE

Unlike those in Yucay, the Inca vestiges to which we now turn our attention constitute an official archaeological site visited by many tourists. We do not have space here to fully describe the wild beauty of this fortress carved into the rock on the flank of the cordillera overlooking the river, nor give a sense of the emotion that grips anyone who undertakes the vertiginous descent from these terraces that form a prodigious balcony overlooking the abyss. Let us now take a journey in both space and time: if the data collected in Yucay date to the 1970s, we now visit the Pisac site thirty years later—in the 2000s. We are no longer in the company of village farmers whose understanding of the marvels left to them by their Inca ancestors we will never know, but are instead visiting with New Age followers from North America.

The Pisac archaeological site is a must for the mystic tourists inundating the Cuzco region in search of positive energy left by the Incas. Agencies organize rituals on archaeological sites, officiated by neo-shamans who draw from traditional Andean practices as well as from publications by anthropologists, recycling their works as neo-Inca ceremonies (see Galinier and Molinié 2013; Molinié 2018). A veritable Andean New Age is being created based on two corpuses: on the one hand, that of the Andeans, which has grown out of a fusion between pre-Hispanic culture and Christianity, and on the other hand, that of the New Age movement, introduced mainly through mystic tourism. Since we cannot go into all aspects of the Andean New Age here, I will look only into matters concerning the treatment of vestiges.[22] Pisac is one stop on a circuit linking various Inca vestiges in the Cuzco region. This "initiation journey" was devised by a former professor of anthropology at the University of Cuzco who claims to have followed the initiation stages to the highest grade of shaman: his master taught him a "coronation of a sacred king" rite (Nuñez del Prado 1998, 45). The stops on this archaeological itinerary are those of the revelation of the future Inca who will govern in the next era, as the New Age predicts. This ritual cycle, a cross between a pilgrimage and an initiation ceremony, is a good example of confluence between New Age messianism and the Andean myth of the return of the Inca. It also shows the role that anthropology plays in local reformulations of the New Age.

Prior to the Pisac stop that interests us, the mystical circuit begins at the Cuzco cathedral, where two divinities of local Catholicism are solicited from the *hanaqpacha*[23]: La Virgen de la Natividad la Antigua welcomes believers at the entrance, in the blinding light of the Plaza de Armas, and Taytacha Temblores, deeply venerated in Cuzco, is beseeched in the half light of the altar candles amid the murmurs of Natives' supplications. New Agers attribute the harmony of the yin and yang to this pair of divinities. They produce complementary energies, one male and the other female, which the New Agers fervently collect. These icons are not inventions: both divinities have in fact been receiving prayers from the people of Cuzco for centuries.[24] However, it should be noted that followers of the Andean New Age draw not only from the pre-Hispanic past reinvented by the neo-Incas but also from local Christianity, the product of a fusion with pre-Hispanic beliefs.

That is not all. Here at the cathedral, a New Age group is appealing to a strange divinity that is probably older than the two preceding Christian images. It is an oval stone holding open the enormous cathedral door, which gives way onto Plaza de Armas. It is reputed to be Inca and is the most minimal of all vestiges. Measuring around one and a half meters in diameter at its widest point and sixty centimeters high, it is thoroughly polished and has a cavity in its center. According to the neo-shaman accompanying the New Agers, this stone is a *khuya*. He is referring to an Indigenous belief that I have observed elsewhere.

Khuya, which are also called *inqa*, *inqaychu*, *ylla*, or *khuya rumi*, are miniatures of each of the animal species they represent (Flores Ochoa 1977; Ricard

Lanata 2007)[25]: shepherds have a *khuya* for each herd they breed (cows, sheep, llamas, or alpacas) and also for certain plants they cultivate, like corn. These amulets are presented as marvels of nature, and in fact they are often polished and even paradoxically sculpted so that they acquire their exceptional character. The *khuya* carry an "essence in actuality" proper to each animal, a "life power" that impels this essence to actualize itself (Ricard Lanata 2007, 206). Shepherds hide them in precious fabrics, feed them, and potentiate them through rituals held on specific dates. The *Apu*, the mountain gods, animate animals and plants through these *khuya*—"fulfillment forces" that they give to humans (Ricard Lanata 2007, 205).

It is true that the stone holding the cathedral door is presented as a giant *khuya*. Yet it is the object of a discreet Native devotion. A few years ago, it was relegated to the corner of one of the cathedral's chapels. The priests made several attempts to get rid of it, but objections from Natives forced them to bring it back, this time as a doorstop. This does not discourage certain believers who come from remote communities to make offerings to it, particularly in August when the earth is open, and especially at dawn when the cathedral doors open, when no one will see them. Sometimes they get permission from the sexton to leave llama fat or coca leaves next to the sacred stone. Most people in Cuzco are unfamiliar with this worship, since its believers are few, and they often limit themselves to raising their hands for a few seconds while murmuring an invocation, with that persecuted look so characteristic of the *Runa*.[26]

Juan Nuñez del Prado, the inventor of the ritual circuit I am describing, calls this stone/*khuya* Hatun Taqe Wiraqocha, the name of the Inca divinity. Abraham Valencia Espinoza (1991), an anthropologist from Cuzco, has compared this ovoid to the oval in the famous drawing of the god Wiraqocha by chronicler Joan de Santa Cruz Pachacuti Yamqi ([1613] 1950, 226). According to New Agers, the stone has the ability to absorb negative energies (*hucha*). Here and elsewhere, the *Runa* and the New Ager have a reverse relationship with the sacred. The former makes an offering; the latter gets rid of his negative energy. We are thus witnessing the abrupt shift from Indigenous worship to a New Age worship. The Native *khuya* became the New Age *khuya*, its transformation involving nothing more than being hidden behind a door. Will the children of Aquarius return to the *Runa* a god extirpated by the cathedral's priests? Just as Juan Nuñez del Prado was explaining that this stone had to be rubbed to free oneself from "heavy energy," an old Indian woman got down on her knees beside it, removed her hat, and gently rubbed the whole surface with llama fat, murmuring prayers. Finally, the Natives' *khuya*, which a neo-Inca text identifies as the supreme god Wiraqocha, is thus shifting from its official function, as a doorstop and unofficial offering receptacle, to simply functioning as an energy trashcan.

The second stage of the New Agers' initiation tour led us to Q'enqo, an Inca site near Cuzco where the mystics find themselves on a "light platform" on which they will rid themselves of "residual heavy energy." Then in the Amaru Machay cave, the future initiates are asked to imagine their own conception in their mother's womb. This is how they succeed in "transferring their energetic umbilical cord from their parent to the *Pachamama*," an Andean variant of Mother Earth. They are now "brothers" and "sisters," being "children of the same mother."[27] Their journey continues with a stop at Lake Huacarpay, which they are told is the birthplace of Huascar Inca: here they can connect with the spirit of the last sovereign of Tawantinsuyu. Next the initiates will devote themselves to the spirit of Pachacuti amid the Cyclopean stones of the Saqsayhuaman citadel.

Next, the group takes the road to Pisac and scales the majestic Inca buildings on the cordillera hillside. The heavy bodies of the New Agers wobble on the precipitous rocks and slip on the palace's paving stones, overlooking the void. None of them seems to be struck by the amazing panorama on offer, nor by the minimal beauty of the barely sculpted stones of the majestic buildings. To capture the energies of the summits surrounding the site, the Inca calendar is summoned, which does not make things easier for the ethnographer of the New Agers, who is asked to give a scientific backing to the Inca vibrations. One of the rituals that the mystics performed in front of me consisted of capturing the "energy of the *ceques*." Here it is necessary to provide some information on the Inca *ceques* system, which is essential for understanding the ritual being performed by these mystics.

In the Inca Temple of the Sun in Cuzco (Quricancha), there was a convergence of forty-one alignments (*ceques*) of 328 sanctuaries (*huacas*). The points on the horizon that these alignments of sanctuaries or *ceques* pointed to were determined by astronomical observations. These lines were displayed around the Temple of the Sun according to the position of the stars: thus, the *ceques* corresponded to months of the year, forming around the city of Cuzco a giant calendar that was at once sidereal and synodic (see figure 6.3).[28] Rites were held in these aligned sanctuaries on the corresponding calendar dates. They were the responsibility of each of Cuzco's social units, which were in charge of this or that *huaca* on this or that *ceque*. The alignments of the sanctuaries were, then, not merely an enormous calendar around the imperial city; they were also a series of references to geographical points on Cuzco's territory, as well as a register of its social units, because it was among these units that the services

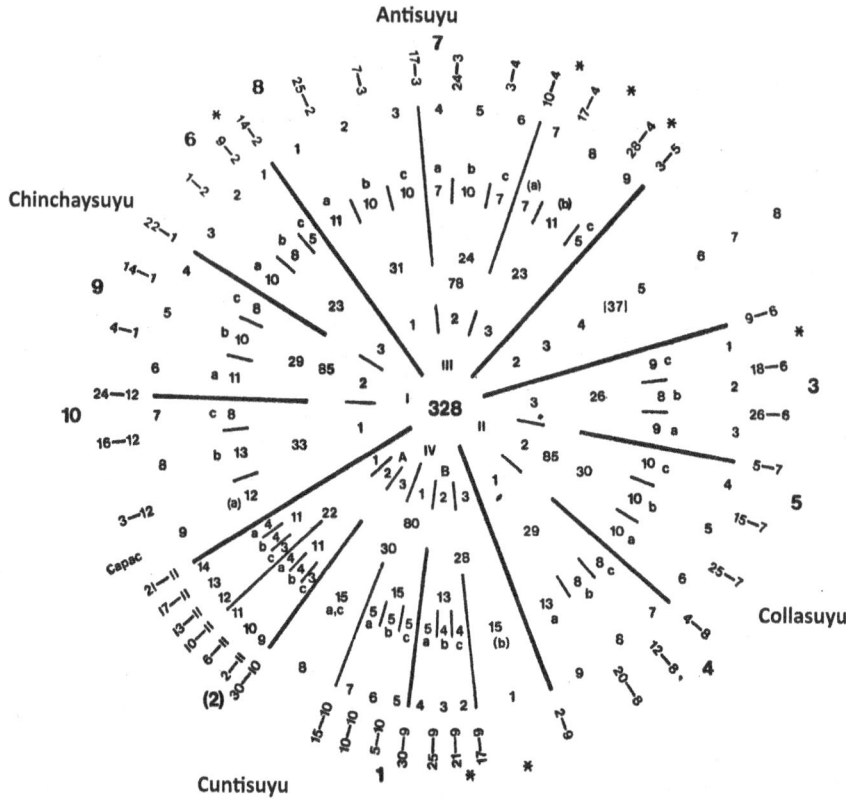

FIGURE 6.3. *The 328-day calendar of the* ceque *system (according to Zuidema 1986, 94).*

conducted in each of the aligned sanctuaries were shared out. Thus, the system organized the imperial space, regulated time through the ritual calendar it formed, and ordered the society that conducted the services of worship.

Here on the Pisac archaeological site, the New Age mystics have turned the sanctuary alignments making up that vast Inca classification and governance system into mediums of energy to be captured in the niches of the Inca walls facing the summits that both New Agers and the *Runa* consider divinities (see figure 6.4). Thus we discover New Age *ceques* that establish a mysterious connection between living *Apu* and Inca vestiges: a relationship between the contemporary Andean gods and the ancestors of today's Natives, among whom the future New Age sovereign is sought through this rite—a striking encounter between pre-Hispanic history, Andean religiosity, and New Age mysticism. In the prayers of the mystics—their heads stuck into the niches of the Inca temple

FIGURE 6.4. *At the Inca ruins of Pisac, Mystic New Agers capture the energy of the ceques. Photo: Antoinette Molinié, 2002.*

of Pisac—there was something like the outline of a fantastical genealogy, with the added "scientific" but truncated reference to the work of the anthropologist Tom Zuidema, recycled as a spiritual guide despite himself. In the Pisac vestiges, New Age culture based on anthropology becomes fully coherent: the notion of a recycled *ceque* acquires an extraordinary symbolic efficacy.

We are then asked to form two energy-circulation circles, one female and one male. By sitting in two circles on one of the superb esplanades of the Inca site, we form a *yanantin* system (according to our spiritual guide), whose gender complementarity is the Andean form of the yin and yang.[29] Some mystics ensconce themselves between two sculpted stones to get rid of their negative energy, inadvertently evoking a more basic biological operation, while other more ambitious mystics press up against the Huayna Capac temple to capture good energies.

We continue our quest in Ollantaytambo. Here again, the New Agers seem indifferent to the astounding beauty of the Inca archaeological site. They are busy opening the "eye of their throat" to let in the spirit of the wind, surging in gusts at Wayrapunk'u (the Gate of the Wind), facing Verónica's superb snowcapped peak. The initiation continues at Machu Picchu, which is swarming with esoteric groups. They are squabbling over the temples, in a similar way as the churches in Jerusalem fight to celebrate mass on Jesus Christ's tomb. Some groups sneak in at night, occasionally falling victim to accidents that are inevitable on such a steep site. Archaeologists complain of the irreparable damage they cause. In these sumptuous ruins, there are temples that are identified by the "master" yet are unknown to archaeologists. He enters the Temple of the Condor, explaining that this animal represents the collective spirit of all Andeans. The "master" says that the North Americans making up the group bear the spirit of the Eagle. We should therefore make use of the *yanantin* energy generated by the couple formed by the Condor and the Eagle.

The next stop on the initiation circuit is the gigantic Temple of Wiraqocha, a few kilometers from Cuzco. Whereas in Cuzco the mystical tourists "worked" with this world (*kaypacha*), and in Machu Picchu they worked with the underworld (*ukhupacha*), now they are going to tackle the *hanaqpacha*, the world above. They are told that in this temple, the twelve royal families met to choose the next Inca from among twelve candidates. This Inca would be distinguished by a supernatural aura: that of a sixth-grade priest. It is during this final stage that candidates for the role of Inca should arise.

FROM PREDATORY VESTIGES TO VESTIGES AS PREY

On the Pisac site, we have observed relations with Inca vestiges that are worth comparing with the conceptions of Yucay's farmers. First of all, the New Agers' search for the next Inca connects with the Andean messianism of the return of the executed sovereign. One tradition predicts that Inkarrí, king of Tawantinsuyu, will return to Peru one day to restore the Native population. From his head—buried somewhere in the cordillera—his body is growing back bit by bit, and when it is complete, Inkarrí will stand up and seize power.[30] Some people tell of how Inkarrí defeated his brother Jesus Christ, who is called Sucristu or Españarri depending on the version.

There are also certain Andean notions that are compatible with the idea of energy, a central New Age conception.[31] Many prophecies predict that the arrival of the Age of Aquarius will be accompanied by the profound upheavals described in the Book of Revelation. A cataclysm will bring a "Great King" whose accession will be like a return of Christ and will initiate a new Golden Age. This belief has a clear connection to the belief in the return of the Inca, who is supposed to "turn the world upside down" to reestablish Tawantinsuyu, which is presented as a paradise. The Andean and New Age conceptions of the story are curiously quite similar. The Quechua notion of *pacha* expresses both time and space. For Andeans, history is not linear but is made up of different *pacha*, universes separated by *pachakuti*, that is, to say reversals (*kuti*) that take the form of catastrophes.[32] This notion of *pachakuti* is similar to New Age representations. The children of Aquarius have a comparable cyclical view of the future. They believe that each cycle consists of four successive ages of gold, silver, bronze, and iron and that humanity has arrived at the cusp of a new age. Like New Age time, that of the Andeans works in a bipolar, cyclical way.

Other Andean concepts are so similar to New Age notions that they seem to have been influenced by Aquarius. The Quechuas' notion of *yanantin* expresses opposition between elements that are opposite but complementary, their constant imbalance requiring perpetual adjustment. It is a "mirror-symmetry relation" (Platt 1978, 1098). The word is used in reference to organs that come in pairs (like the eyes), and in particular for a human couple. This notion is echoed by that of the yin and yang in its New Age sense, that is to say, an ideal of complementarity applied to genders, colors, or temperaments.

Furthermore, the New Age notion of "energy" accords with certain ideas in the Andes that, though complex and not widely known, are transposable and even translated by New Age Quechua terms like *sami* for "refined energy," *huaca* for "sacred energy," *hucha* for "heavy energy," *puq'pu* for an energy "bubble," and *kausay* for "energy hanging in the world." One sees how this single New Age term "energy," when combined with an adjective, expresses particularly varied, heterogeneous Andean notions. Thus, globalization proceeds by homogenizing and reducing Indigenous concepts.

From the Native Andeans, New Agers have learned the practice of *despacho*, which is to reestablish the balance of the *animu* captured by the *suq'a machu*, as we observed in Yucay. We saw that according to a very precise code, ingredients are placed on a consecrated fabric (*mesa*). A specialist addresses the *despacho* to the summits, which are worshipped, or to the earth divinity, from whom good harvests are requested. For a decade, the *despacho* rite has seen a meteoric rise in popularity among the *mestiza* and the white populations of Cuzco, who until recently scorned these "idolatrous manipulations" as much as they despised the "Indians" who practiced them. The *despachos* of the Andean New Age are now performed by "masters" from Cuzco who also teach the rite in training courses given in the United States, northern Italy, Scandinavia, and Catalonia.

One feature radically distinguishes the New Age *despacho* from the Andean original. The *Runa* burn the offering they have carefully prepared for the gods, while the New Age mystics prepare an energy-filled packet that is placed on the patient's head or solar plexus (figure 6.5). He then feels "the energy penetrating him from head to toe," "a burning sensation on his head," "a very strong feeling of communion with his fellow men," or "the feeling of becoming a snake." Other officiants have had visions of "a group of Tibetan monks penetrated by a silver ray" or "a solar eclipse with a golden ring and a space shuttle travelling in intense heat."[33]

In this sense, the New Age officiants' process is very different from that of the Andean specialists: whereas the latter make the *despacho* into an offering to the mountain gods or to the earth, the "master" of the New Agers captures the "Inca energy" from the Inca vestiges and keeps it inside the *despacho* for New Ager consumption. The *Runa* give in order to receive; the New Agers take in order to improve their life. The Andean *despacho* is the vehicle of a gift: it is a sacrifice. The New Age *despacho* contains the sought benefit in its very substance. In the Andean tradition of exchange, its constituent objects are intended to feed the gods. In the New Age version, the *despacho* is charged with captured "energy," that of Inca vestiges and that of the "tradition" fed by millions of Natives who are thus turned into energy vehicles through the rites they perform. This energy predation is based on a theory far removed from any Quechua conception. New Agers believe that the vestiges they visit are infused with positive energy left by the Inca, and this energy can be captured for them by a neo-shaman whose Inca ancestry gives him this ability for predation. Today's Natives can also help recharge the energy that New Agers seek to capture. They infuse the Andean landscape with their positive energies through the major rituals they perform. The rituals themselves are of no interest to New Agers, despite their spectacular nature. What they are fond of is the energy produced by these ceremonies, and when they make their way to the Quyllur Rit'i pilgrimage—something that is demanding in terms of athletic performance and dollars—they wait for the *Runa* to return to their communities before proceeding with the predation of the energies the *Runa* produced through their prayers and dances. It is as if the landscape, in its terrestrial materiality, preserved something of the sacredness of these Indigenous practices, which New Agers prey upon in the form of "energy."

This very odd predation naturally brings us back to the Yucay vestiges, in which the *suq'a machu*, the malevolent prehuman ancestor, seizes the unscrupulous walker who has neglected the offerings that he should make. In that case, the vestige is the predator and the visitor is the prey. The visitor assumes the role of offerer through a *despacho*, with the help of a sacrificer, whose sacrifice is directed at the *Apu*, the mountain god. In Pisac, the roles are reversed: in the first phase, the benevolent vestige acts as an energy resource for the *despacho*, and the neo-shaman acts as a predator on behalf of the New Age recipient. In the second phase, the neo-shaman delivers the energy collected from the vestiges, captured in the *despacho*, to the New Agers.

FIGURE 6.5. *Inca ruins of Pisac. Energy predation through a New Age ritual of "pago." Photo: Antoinette Molinié, 2002.*

Furthermore, the predatory function of Yucay's local traditional vestige is an indication of a structuring of a space-time boundary. Indeed we saw that the alignment of the Inca vestiges and the crosses separates two spaces and two temporalities: above is the space-time of the prehuman ancestors, and below is that of humanity. Pisac's global New Age vestige is structured by relations with other archaeological sites producing positive energies. In the former case, the predatory vestige presents a boundary structuring space-time, and in the latter case, the vestiges are structured as stops along a circuit in search of a global Inca.

The meaning of the Native vestige is reproduced through the succession of predation and sacrifice. A New Age vestige gets its meaning through a predation whose theory seems to be based on a virtual energy that is infinitely renewable by Inca ancestors who demand no offerings—unless the neo-shaman from Cuzco is an intermediary working on behalf of his ancestors, collecting dollars that would make up a *despacho* offering. The *Runa* infuse their terrestrial landscape with energy consumed by New Agers, but without getting anything in return. As they have always done with other goods, for other predators in other times. But now it is a virtual good, comparable to the value that neoliberal capitalism produces through international finance.

NOTES

1. "*Yúkay: engaño, acción engañosa o de astucia. Engañar, hacer caer en un error. Producir ilusión. Entretener, distraer. Embaucar. Seducir . . . S'kkhrakk yukáskkan: Seducido por el demonio*" (Lira 1944, 1189). This dictionary is sometimes a bit fanciful, but Father Lira lived in Yucay for a long time and left many children.

2. Even though private property was then extremely rare, most of the Yucay terraces were the personal property of Huayna Capac, the second-to-last Inca. Similarly, Tupac Inca Yupanqui owned private property there (Rostworowski de Diez Canseco 1962). The inhabitants of the Sacred Valley were *yana*, servants directly connected to the Inca. Francisco Pizarro took possession of them as an *encomienda*, and his son Gonzalo was his successor (Wachtel 1971). After his surrender and his return from Vilcabamba in 1558, and in exchange for his collaboration with the occupying forces, Sayri Tupac was granted the Yucay *encomienda*, which extended from the Ollantaytambo area to Urquillos and Maras-Chinchero on the plateau. Seven *ayllu* (prehispanic lineages) were then reduced there by Damián de la Bandera (Villanueva 1970a). In 1560, Sayri Tupac was succeeded by his daughter, Beatriz Coya. The inhabitants of Yucay then enjoyed a fortunate situation. To avoid tax, almost all of Doña Beatriz's taxpayers declared themselves *yana* of Francisco Chilche, Pizarro's right-hand man. Beatriz Coya's husband demanded that the taxes be handed over to his family. In 1572, the matter was passed to the Corrregidor de Cuzco, who referred it to the Concejo de Indias in Spain (Villanueva 1970b). In 1613, a debt certificate from Felipe III ordered that 418 taxpayers be given back to the *encomendera* Ana Maria, daughter of Doña Beatriz, who received the title Marquise de Oropesa (Lohmann Villena 1948). She was soon exiled by the king of Spain, who wished to remove the descendants of the Incas. Five marquis succeeded him, the last dying in 1741. The haciendas developed from the late sixteenth century in the context of the *encomienda*.

3. The *animu*, which evokes the Spanish term *alma*, the soul, is a person's vital breath, their "actualization force" (Ricard Lanata 2007, 206–7).

4. For a detailed study of this cure, see Molinié (1979).

5. In Andean communities, it is also said that the fat of Natives is used to lubricate airplane engines and make lipstick. They also say that in Lima, the Peruvian government collects Native fat sent by *pishtaku* throughout the country and uses the proceeds from its sale to pay off the national debt to the International Monetary Fund (see Molinié 1991).

6. See the full list of products making up my offering and my whole cure in Molinié (1979).

7. For a more detailed study of Yucay's time-space dualism, see Molinié (1985).

8. This hypothesis is brilliantly demonstrated by Martinez (1989).

9. *Pata* and *kancha* are topographical suffixes, the former indicating a high, flat surface and the latter indicating a closed area.

10. For a precise identification of the toponyms corresponding to the names of the *ceques*, see Molinié (1996, 215–16).

11. Personal correspondence from Ruben Orellana.

12. Personal correspondence from Billie Jean Isbell and *Encyclopédie du monde animal* (Vallardi 1962, t. II: 526).

13. Archivo General de la Nación de Lima, Real Audiencia, leg. 13, cuaderno 66.

14. Archivo Departamental de Cuzco, Diezmos (noncatalogue).

15. On the link between the handling of vestiges and the regime of historicity, see Molinié (1997).

16. On May 3, Christians celebrate the Invention of the Holy Cross, which commemorates Saint Helena's more or less mythical discovery of the instrument of Jesus Christ's torture. This feast is celebrated in Spain, especially in Andalucía and Extremadura, often through unorthodox ceremonies that reference fertility rites more than the Passion of Jesus (see Caro Baroja 1979; Molinié [2016] 2021).

17. The responsibilities system regulates the social life of Andean societies. The worship of the virgins, Christs, and saints is led, on a specific day of the year, by a community member who must organize the festivities and cover any costs they entail. These responsibilities or *cargos*, which vary in importance, create a hierarchical system, and community members take turns assuming them. Religious responsibilities very often give access to political responsibilities.

18. *Visita y Numeración de los Indios del valle de Yucay y sus anexos que practicó Damián de la Bandera el 30 de junio de 1558 mandando que se redujesen en sus respectivos pueblos* (in Villanueva 1970a).

19. Archivo Departemental del Cuzco, Archivo Notarial de Urubamba, leg. 2, 3; *Repartos de tierras en 1595, Revista del Archivo Histórico del Cuzco,* no. 8, 1957.

20. Archivo Departamental del Cuzco, *Tesorería fiscal* nos. 3, 4, 8.

21. For an analysis of Cruz Calvario's role in the bipartition of the crosses, and to understand how seven crosses are compatible with bipartition, see Molinié (1985).

22. For a study of the genesis and rituality of the Andean New Age, see Molinié (2009, 2012, 2016). The ethnographic data of the analysis that follows was collected in 2002 on the Pisac site. The practices of New Agers are evolving very quickly, and it is possible that some have undergone changes of which I am not aware.

23. The "world above," one of the components of the tripartite division of the Andean world into *hanaqpacha*, *kaypacha* (this world), and *ukhupacha* (the underworld), as anthropological tradition would have it. In reality, most Andeans only consider the latter two levels.

24. Taytacha Temblores, Lord of the Earthquakes, is worshipped especially on Easter Monday. In prayers he is spoken of as a mountain god, and as such, he might even appear on the ritual table of a high-ranking shaman (Valencia Espinoza 1991).

25. These beliefs certainly have pre-Hispanic origins, as shown by Gonzáles Holguín's dictionary ([1609] 1952, 366).

26. In Quechua, *runa* means "human being" or "person." Quechua use this term to identify themselves in contrast to the *misti*, which designates the white man.

27. I am quoting the neo-shaman who served as guide.

28. The *ceque* system has been described by Tom Zuidema (1964). Brian Bauer (2000) established a cartography of the system through archaeological excavations.

29. The notion of *yanantin*, which could be translated as "complementarity," is central to Andean traditional conceptions and rites (Platt 1978, 1098).

30. *Inkarrí* comes from the Spanish *inca rey*. There are many variants of this myth. The first version was recorded in Cuzco in 1955 during an expedition organized by the University of Cuzco (Nuñez del Prado 1973). The Quechua version was published in Spanish and later in Quechua (Arguedas 1968). A volume edited by Juan Ossio (1973) assembled several versions recorded in various regions of Peru. See also Burga (1988), Flores Galindo (1986), Ortiz Rescaniere (1973), and Valderrama and Escalante (1995).

31. On New Age ideas, see Ferguson (1981).

32. On the notion of *pachakuti*, which is too complex to explore here, see Bouysse-Cassagne and Harris (1987).

33. Personal accounts collected from members of a group of mystical tourists in June 2002.

REFERENCES

Arguedas, José Maria. 1968. *Los mitos quechuas posthispániscos*. La Havana: Casa de Las Américas.

Bauer, Brian. 1998. *The Sacred Landscape of the Inca: The Cusco Ceque System*. Austin: University of Texas Press.

Bouysse-Cassagne, Thérèse, and Olivia Harris. 1987. "Pacha: en torno al pensamiento aymara." In *Tres reflexiones sobre el pensamiento andino*, edited by Thérèse Bouysse-Cassagne, Olivia Harris, Tristan Platt, and Verónica Cereceda, 11–61. La Paz: Hisbol.

Burga, Manuel. 1988. *Nacimiento de una utopía: muerte y resurección de los Incas*. Lima: Instituto de Apoyo Agrario.

Caro Baroja, Julio. 1979. *La estación de amor*. Madrid: Taurus.

Cereceda, Verónica. 1978. "Sémiologie des tissus andins: les talegas d'Isluga." *Annales ESC* 33 (5–6): 1017–35.

Cereceda, Verónica. 1987. "Aproximaciones a una estética andina: de la belleza al *tinku*." In *Tres reflexiones sobre el pensamiento andino*, edited by Thérèse Bouysse-Cassagne, Olivia Harris, Tristan Platt, and Verónica Cereceda, 133–231. La Paz: Hisbol.

Duviols, Pierre. 1967. "Un inédit de Cristobal de Albornoz: La instrucción para descubrir todas las guacas del Pirú y sus camayos y haciendas." *Journal de la Société des Américanistes* 56 (1): 7–39.

Ferguson, Marylin. 1981. *The Aquarian Conspiracy: Personal and Social Transformation in the 1980s*. London: Routledge & Kegan.

Flores Galindo, Alberto. 1986. *Buscando un Inca: Identidad y Utopía en los Andes*. La Habana: Casa de las Américas.

Flores Ochoa, Jorge. 1977. "*Enqa, enqaychu, illay khuya rumi.*" In *Pastores de puna: Uywamichiq punakuna*, edited by J. Flores Ochoa, 211–37. Lima: Instituto de Estudios Peruanos.

Galinier, Jacques, and Molinié, Antoinette. (2006) 2013. *The Neo-Indian: A Religion for the Third Millennium*. Boulder: University Press of Colorado.

Gonzáles Holguín, Diego. (1609) 1952. *Vocabulario de la lengua general de todo el Peru llamada lengua qquichua o del Inca*. Lima: Instituto de Historia.

Hergé. 1962. *The Seven Crystal Balls*. Methuen. Translation of *Les sept boules de cristal*, Les aventures de Tintin no. 13, 1948. Brussels: Casterman.

Isbell, Billie Jean. 1978. *To Defend Ourselves: Ecology and Ritual in an Andean Village*. Austin: University of Texas Press.

Lira, Jorge. 1944. *Diccionario kkechuwa-español*. Tucuman: Universidad Nacional de Tucuman.

Lohmann Villena, Guillermo. 1948. "El señorio de los marqueses de Santiago de Oropesa en Perú." *Anuario de Historia del derecho español* 19: 347–458.

López-Baralt, Mercedes. 1986. "The Yana K'uychi or Black Rainbow in Atawallpa's elegy: A Look at the Andean Metaphor of Liminality in a Cultural Context." In *Myth and the Imaginary in the New World*, edited by Edmundo Magaña and Peter Mason, 288–96. Amsterdam: Centrum voor Studies en Documentatie van Latijns Amerika.

Martinez, Gabriel. 1989. *Espacio y pensamiento: Andes meridionales*, t. I. La Paz: Hisbol.

Molinié, Antoinette. 1979. "Cure magique dans la Vallée Sacrée du Cuzco." *Journal de la Société des Américanistes* 46: 85–98.

Molinié, Antoinette. 1982. *La vallée Sacrée des Andes*. Paris: Société d'ethnographie.

Molinié, Antoinette. 1985. "Tiempo del espacio y espacio del tiempo en los Andes." *Journal de la Société des Américanistes* 71: 97–114.

Molinié, Antoinette. 1986–87. "El simbolismo de frontera en los Andes." *Revista del Museo Nacional (Lima)* 48: 251–86.

Molinié, Antoinette. 1991. "Sebo bueno, Indio muerto: la estructura de una creencia andina." *Bulletin de l'Institut Français d'Etudes Andines* 20 (1): 79–92.

Molinié, Antoinette. 1996. "The Spell of Yucay: A Symbolic Structure in Inca Terraces." *Journal of the Steward Anthropological Society* 24 (1–2): 203–30.

Molinié, Antoinette. 1997. "Buscando una historicidad andina: una propuesta antropológica y una memoria hecha rito." In *Arqueología, antropología e historia en los Andes: Homenaje a María Rostworowski*, edited by Rafael Varón Gabai and Javier Flores Espinoza, 689–708. Lima: Instituto de Estudios Peruanos.

Molinié, Antoinette. 2009. "Del Inca nacional a la internacional inca." In *El regreso de lo indígena*, edited by Valérie Robin and Carmen Salazar, 237–64. Lima: Institut Français d'Etudes Andines.

Molinié, Antoinette. 2012. "Ethnogenèse du New Age andin: A la recherche de l'Inca global." *Journal de la Société des Américanistes* 98 (1): 171–99.

Molinié, Antoinette. (2013) 2016. "The Invention of Andean New Age: The Globalization of Tradition." In *New Age in Latin America: Popular Variations and Ethnic Appropriations*, edited by Renée De la Torre, Cristina Gutiérrez Zúñiga, and Nahayeilli Juárez Huet, 291–315. Leiden/Boston: Brill.

Molinié, Antoinette. (2016) 2021. *Sevilla, del rito al inconsciente*. Sevilla: Athenaica/Universidad de Sevilla.

Molinié, Antoinette. 2018. "'Indian' Identity and Indigenous Revitalization Movements." In *The Andean World*, edited by Linda J. Seligman and Kathleen S. Fine-Dare, 373–88. London: Routledge.

Nuñez del Prado, Juan. 1998. *Camminando nel cosmo vivente: Guide alle tecniche energetiche e spirituali delle Ande*. Cesena: Macro Edizioni.

Nuñez del Prado, Oscar. 1973. "Versión del mito de Inkarrí en Q'eros." In *Ideología mesiánica del Mundo Andino*, edited by Juan Ossio, 275–80. Lima: Ed. Ignacio Prado Pastor.

Ortiz Rescaniere, Alejandro. 1973. *De Adaneva a Inkarrí*. Lima: Ed. Retablo de papel.

Ossio, Juan. 1973. *Ideología mesiánica del Mundo Andino*. Lima: Ed. Ignacio Prado Pastor.

Platt, Tristan. 1978. "Symétries en miroir. Le concept de *yanantin* chez les Macha de Bolivie." *Annales ESC* 33 (5–6): 1081–1107.

Ricard Lanata, Xavier. 2007. *Ladrones de sombra: El universo religioso de los pastores del Ausangate*. Lima/Cuzco: Instituto Francés de Estudios Andinos/Centro Bartolomé de Las Casas.

Rostworowski de Diez Canseco, María. 1962. "Nuevos datos sobre tenencia de tierras reales en el incario." *Revista del Museo Nacional* 31: 130–59.

de Santa Cruz Pachacuti Yamqi, Joan. (1613) 1950. "Relaciones de antigüedades deste Reyno del Piru." In *Tres relaciones*, edited by Jiménez de la Espada, 207–81. Asunción: Ed. Guaraní.

Taylor, Gérald. 1987. *Ritos y tradiciones de Huarochiri, manuscrito quechua de comienzos del siglo XVII*. Lima: Instituto de Estudios Peruanos/Instituto Francés de Estudios Andinos.

Urton, Gary. 1981. *At the Crossroads of the Earth and the Sky*. Austin: University of Texas Press.

Valderrama, Ricardo, and Carmen Escalante. 1995. "El inka vive." *Revista del Museo e Instituto de Arqueología* 25: 241–70.

Valencia Espinoza, Abraham. 1991. *Taytacha Temblores, patrón jurado del Cuzco*. Cuzco: Centro de Estudios Andinos.

Vallardi, Francesco, ed. 1962. *Encyclopédie du monde animal*. Paris: Librairie Aristide Quillet.

Villanueva, Horacio, ed. 1970a. "Visita y numeración de los Indios del valle de Yucay y sus anexos que practicó Damain de la Bandera en 30 de junio de 1558, in Genealogía de Sayri Tupac." *Revista del Archivo Histórico del Cuzco* 13: 55–148.

Villanueva, Horacio, ed. 1970b. "Auto seguidos pore el capitán D. Martín García de Loyola y la Coya Doña Beatriz su mujer, con el fiscal de S.M. sobre los indios yanaconas del valle de Yucay (1574), in Genealogía de Sayri Tupac." *Revista del Archivo Histórico de Cuzco* 13: 55–148.

Wachtel, Nathan. 1971. *La Vision des vaincus: Les Indiens du Pérou devant la Conquête espagnole 1530–1570*. Paris: Gallimard.

Zuidema, Tom. 1964. *The Ceque System of Cuzco: The Social Organization of the Capital of the Inca*. Leiden: E. J. Brill.

Zuidema, Tom. 1985. "The Lion in the City: Royal Symbols of Transition." In *Animals, Myths and Metaphors in South America*, edited by Gary Urton, 194–201. Salt Lake City: University of Utah Press.

Zuidema, Tom. 1986. *La civilisation inca de Cuzco*. Paris: Presses Universitaires de France.

7

The Topography of Time

Pre-Hispanic Ruins, Topographical Vestiges, and the Controversial Andean New Year (North Potosí, Bolivian Andes)

LAURENCE CHARLIER ZEINEDDINE

In 2009, Evo Morales, the president of the Plurinational State of Bolivia, proclaimed the day of the winter solstice in the southern hemisphere a national holiday. June 21 was to be officially dedicated to the Andean New Year, an allegedly ancient Aymara celebration going back more than five thousand years but perfidiously abolished by the Catholic Church in the aftermath of the Spanish conquest. In the year 5523 (i.e., 2015),[1] the Andean New Year was celebrated on eighty archaeological sites. The biggest event took place at Tiwanaku, declared a World Heritage Site by UNESCO in 2000 as the "spiritual and political center of the Tiwanaku culture." Significantly, Evo Morales, the first Amerindian president, had chosen Tiwanaku as the location for his inaugural speech on January 21, 2006. The Andean New Year ceremony consists of waiting for the first rays of the sun and making offerings (sometimes *wilancha*, animal blood sacrifices) accompanied by libations to *Pachamama* (Mother Earth) and the mountains to obtain good harvests. This ceremony, organized by the *Viceministerio de Descolonización* (Vice Ministry of Decolonization), was presented as a restoration of an age-old ancestral Aymara tradition, that of "our Aymara ancestors"; not to commemorate a date but to establish a ritual practice with an eminently political goal in view: decolonization. The intention is not only to contest the imposition of the Gregorian calendar and the colonial order more generally but also to further the process of decolonization by ritual means.

https://doi.org/10.5876/9781646422869.c007

The *Viceministerio de Descolonización*, a branch of the *Ministerio de Cultura* (Ministry of Culture), frames the decolonization of Andean culture in terms of interculturality, exemplified by the 2014 decision to reverse the direction in which the time is read on the country's official clocks.[2]

The combination of Indigenism, nationalism, and pre-Columbian roots is nothing new in Bolivia, and the political use of Tiwanaku in relation to the Andean New Year long predates the presidency of Evo Morales. The Bolivian celebration of the Andean New Year dates back to the 1930s and the archaeologist Arthur Posnansky (Sammells 2012a). Posnansky quickly realized the potential political benefits of inventing a Native calendar. By interpreting the inscriptions on the sun gate at Tiwanaku as a calendar based on the sun,[3] the archaeologist hoped to root Bolivian national identity, namely that of the elites, in the glorious pre-Columbian past. For Posnansky, Tiwanaku stood out as the center of pan-American pre-Columbian civilization. From 1930 on, after founding the Sociedad Arqueologica de Bolivia, he established the first tours to Tiwanaku to attend the September 21 (equinox) celebration and gave this date as the starting point of the Tiwanaku calendar (Sammells 2012a).[4] Like President Morales, Posnansky wanted to replace the Gregorian calendar with a pre-Columbian one, but with a different purpose: that of creating a more rational, predictive, and scientific calendar, conducive to international trade and thus able to give Bolivia its place in what appeared to be an increasingly liberal world (Sammells 2012a).[5]

In the 1970s, a fusion of national identity and Aymara identity emerged. In the battle for political use of the calendar, the elites yielded to the Indigenous populations. Tiwanaku became a stronghold of Indigenism in Bolivia. Long an event of national importance, from 1992 onward the celebration of the Andean New Year in Tiwanaku became a pan-Indigenous event attended by representatives of the Indigenous peoples of the Americas, Asia, and South Africa (Sammells 2011). Archaeological sites in other Bolivian regions hosted ceremonies. But for Clare A. Sammells, the celebration was mainly focused on the struggle for the creation of a primevally Aymara nation: "the solstice proclaims Bolivia to be an Aymara nation" (2012b, 124). The Aymara intellectual Inka Waskar Chukiwanka (2016) also played a well-known role in spreading Indigenous and anti-colonialist ideas via the reinstatement of the Andean New Year and the construction of an Aymara national identity. While the 2003 solstice celebrations were attended by a wide range of individuals (Aymara activists, Indigenous pilgrims, foreigners, university students from La Paz, seekers of spirituality, politicians, archaeologists) and for equally varied reasons (entertainment, mystical revelation, pride in Aymara roots, nationalism),[6] the fact remains that "making the pilgrimage to see the Solstice was part of their affirmation of being Aymara, or being Bolivian, or both" (Sammells 2012b, 120).

But how is this phenomenon experienced by the Aymara populations in rural areas? One evening in July 2015 in the Chaparé region, while we were peeling potatoes for dinner, my *compadre* asked me what I thought of the Andean New Year. He seemed worried. The object of his concern was not decolonization or ethnicity but rather chronology, the links between archaeological remains and Aymara ancestors, the present-day necessity to relate with these ancestors, and the interoperability of such a plan with Pentecostalism. For my companion, what did it mean to go back to the time of the Inca, five thousand years ago? What did he consider to be the vectors of social memory? My focus here is to examine the reactions of the Aymara populations of Northern Potosí to the state promotion of the Andean New Year and an alleged return to precolonial times. My research is based on ethnographic data from the rural communities of the Aymaya and Kharacha *ayllus*[7] of Northern Potosí. This region was conquered by the Incas in the fifteenth century and then by the Spanish in 1538 after a long struggle against the Pizarros (Platt 1988, 1999; Platt, Bouysse-Cassagne, and Harris 2006). This explains why Northern Potosí is largely Quechua-speaking today, despite being in the territory of the former Aymara chieftaincy of Charkas, as illustrated by the fact that most of the toponyms are in Aymara. However, that language is currently disappearing and being replaced by Quechua and, more recently, Spanish.[8]

The Indigenous populations of Northern Potosí greet the process of creating national heritage with utmost surprise, and sometimes even outright refusal, which derives from their conceptions of temporality and space, memory practices, and means of "bringing together" or what might be labeled "presentification." My research has revealed two kinds of rupture that contrast (and explain the clash) with the underlying continuity assumed by the implementation of the Andean New Year: (1) a historical rupture between the presolar era—the ancient era associated with the Andean New Year—and the solar era; (2) a rupture in the relationships maintained with presolar ancestors and the beings of the distant past.

A HISTORICAL RUPTURE: THE APPEARANCE OF THE SUN
The Time of the Ch'ullpa

In Northern Potosí (as in the entire Andean area), archaeological remains are considered evidence of a previous form of humanity: that of the *ch'ullpa*.[9] The *ch'ullpa* are called the "people of before" (*ñawpaq runas*). They are considered to be predecessors rather than ancestors. In the region, descent is referred to by the Spanish term *abuelo* (sometimes Quechuaized) preceded by either *tata*[10] or *ñawpaq*. Contemporary ancestors or those of preceding generations are therefore *tata abuelos* or *ñawpaq abuelos*. However, unlike *abuelo*, which emphasizes genealogical ancestry, *runas* (people/humans)—used here to refer to the *ch'ullpa*—emphasizes their ontological status as human beings, albeit of different kind.[11]

This ontological difference corresponds to a historical rupture. For those I spoke to, the time of the *ch'ullpa* dates back to a very distant period ("thousands of years ago"), one that has definitively ended: "We are not of that time." Small in stature (*juch'uycituslla*), the *ch'ullpa* are believed to have lived in a presolar era, only lighted by the moon: "It is said that these people had never seen the sun. When the sun came out, they died immediately" (*Chay ñawpaq runas mana inti rikuq karqa nin chayta inti huk lluqsimun wañurapun nin*).

This time of the *ch'ullpa* is also known as the "time of the Inca" (*Inkas timpu*) or "time of the Aymara" (*Aymara timpu*). Indeed, the *ch'ullpa* are often confused with the Inca: "The *ch'ullpa* come from the Inca [from the time of the Incas]. The sun killed them all" (*Ch'ullpa: Inkasmanta. Inti q'alitu wañurapun*); "The *ch'ullpa*, the Incas, it's the same thing" (*Ch'ullpasqa, Inkasqa kikin*).[12] Finally, the ethnonym "Aymara" is often used to mean "Native Americans," which explains why the Inca are considered Aymara: "Yes, of course, the Inca were Native Americans, they were Aymara."[13]

The time of the *ch'ullpa* corresponds to the period when, against the backdrop of interethnic wars, the *ayllus* were formed. This is indicated in the origin myth of the Kharacha *ayllu*: long before the arrival of the Spanish, "a long time ago" (*unayña*), when the inhabitants of the region were at war (*ch'aqwa*) against the *ayllus* of the neighboring department of Oruro, two condors[14] from Lake Poopó appeared, turned themselves into humans, and helped the people win the battle in exchange for each receiving a virgin woman and land. This gift provided them with a line of descent and marked the birth of the Kharacha *ayllu* (Charlier Zeineddine 2015). As in this origin story, the time of the *ch'ullpa* is linked to the time of conversions, when the guardian mountains (*apu*)[15] and ancestors of the *ayllu*, like the condors, took on human form and communicated in a verbal and reciprocal manner with humans.[16]

Finally, the time of the *ch'ullpa* is associated with lithomorphoses.[17] For the inhabitants of the region, these herald the end of the presolar, lunar era. In the Highlands of the Aymaya *ayllu*, the "valley road" is marked out by geological formations (mountains, rocks, stones) identified as the result of various lithomorphoses.[18] Most of the rocks mentioned are in the Kharacha or Aymaya territories, with which they are associated.[19] In this sense, they are reminiscent of the famous *wanka* described by Pierre Duviols (1979): anthropomorphic or zoomorphic rocks that were the stone doubles of the ancestor of the *ayllu* who founded the territory and cultivated its land. Upon his death, this cultural hero split himself in two: his corpse, which was to be mummified, and his petrified self (*wanka*). The *wanka* then became the subject of worship. It was believed to protect and promote the agricultural cycle and to safeguard the field and its harvest (*chacrayoc*), and was also considered the guardian and protector of the territory (*marcayoc*) (Duviols 1979). Similarly, the lithomorphoses may be interpreted to form an enduring and mutual link between the founders of the *ayllu*, the antecessors and the community. Today, some of the stones described as petrifications are also deemed to have power, which the Aymaya or the Kharacha can summon to defeat the *ayllus* of the opposite half (Laymi, Puraka, Chullpa, and Jukumani) during ritual battles (*tinku*) or wars (*ch'aqwa*).[20]

Lithomorphic History

A great number of lithomorphoses are evoked by the inhabitants of the Aymaya and Kharacha *ayllus*. Prominent among them is the stone called *q'ala warmi* ("naked woman"), described as a woman from La Paz who came to sell coca leaves from the Yungas[21] in the valleys of San Pedro: "This woman is sitting down and you can clearly see her vagina, she's sitting like this [her legs apart], completely naked." Next to her is a stone that resembles a pile (*tawqa*) of coca leaves (figure 7.1).

Another rock, *kimsa yuqalla* ("the three boys"), can be found on the way down from Qhuchini (Kharacha *ayllu*). It is featured in the *Atlas de los ayllus de Chayanta* (Mendoza, Willer, and Letourneux 1994, 40), marking the frontier of the Kharacha *isla* in Chayantaka territory.[22] Several meters tall, it is considered to have "come from below" (*uramanta lluqsisqapuni*), implying that it was not humans who carved it or transported it here (figure 7.2). This rock "from the time of the Incas" represents three men, considered by some to be three different ages: a youth, an adult, and an old man:

> Before, these stones were people and they were in the habit of greeting people, those who were walking in the valleys to or from the *Puna*. Once, a man was walking along and he met another man: "Hello friend. Where are you coming from?" he said to him. The man replied, "I live far away. My home is in the mountain." That's how the walker knew that it was a stone. He got to his knees and said, "Forgive me, forgive me." Because, you see, the "home in the mountain" was like a

FIGURE 7.1. Q'ala warmi *(naked woman) (left) and the pile of coca (right)*, Irpi irpi, Charcas province, Northern Potosí. Photo: Laurence Charlier Zeineddine, November 2017.

FIGURE 7.2. Kimsa yuqalla *(the three boys)*, visible below the level of the road, to the left of the image. Jist'arata Quchini, Bustillo province, Northern Potosí. Photo: Laurence Charlier Zeineddine, November 2017.

code to understand what he was. Afterwards, it was just then that he saw, far away, two more people, two stones. Afterwards they stayed in that place. They no longer appeared as people. (Canción, inhabitant of the Urur Uma community, 2000)

Another mountain, close to Uncía (Kharacha *ayllu*), is famous: Cerro Colorado. It is described as a group of women "watching Potosí," the mining center that made Spain rich: "There is a group of women. They turned into stones too. It was the time of the Inca, it was like that (*inca timpu karqa. Jinacha kanman*). And in front of it, there are two hills, there are two young men there who watch Potosí with their dog in front of them. Behind one of them there is a woman with a drum (*huanca*)" (Venancio, Urur Uma, 2015). This petrification is a reference to the Indigenous people's forced labor in the mines (*mita minera*), a system used by the colonial regime to develop an economy that was heavily reliant on mining, by moving people (*mitayos*) to have them labor in the Potosí mines.

The mine[23] in the parish of the virgin of Surumi (Chayanta province, Northern Potosí) has also given rise to stories of lithomorphoses: "On the great mountain of Surumi, one can see a Father in his habit, celebrating mass in front of a crowd of young people who are standing up and listening, themselves also turned to stone." As well as the mining in Surumi, this story also alludes to the shrine of Surumi[24] and the miraculous appearance of the Virgin in 1779 (Platt 1996).

In the words of my interlocutors, in this landscape "each place has its own name; the history is all there": exchanges between several ecological layers, the founding of the *ayllus*, mining, the introduction of Christianity and evangelization. The transmission of memory-based knowledge is made possible by the permanence of the ancestors or predecessors, as seen in the lithomorphoses. But the fixed nature of the topography is here indicative of action that has been interrupted: an impeded action. The landscape does less to express permanence (what has always existed or been there) than to draw attention to an interrupted process: here, topographical permanence provides a visual rendering of the historical rupture brought about by the appearance of the sun. This is why the geological landscape is the object of great symbolic and ritual investment, unlike buildings or artifacts attributed to the *ch'ullpa*, such as the round stone houses attributed to the *ch'ullpa*, which have been left to ruin, or pieces of pottery, which are thrown into the river because "they're not useful for anything anymore." Stripped of any useful value, these ancient structures and artifacts are not conserved or restored, and act only as a secondary medium for historical interpretation, unlike the mountains, rocks, and stones.

These geological formations may refer to the same presolar era, but they also constitute definitive reference points for social memory.

This historical rupture also had a sonic element, as Henry Stobart (2006) and Rosaleen Howard Malverde (1990) have emphasized. A natural consequence of immobility is silence or, more precisely, dumbness (Howard 1990). Howard notes that with the arrival of the sun or the transition from one era to another (*pachakuti*), mythical heroes were not only petrified but also deprived of their ability to speak and hear. Remaining *upa*, deaf and mute, they were forced to reduce their range of sensory interaction: the presolar beings remain visible in their petrified form but are doomed to silence, thus emphasizing loss and impediment. Paralysis and dumbness thus characterize the change of era.

By proposing a return to the time of the "Aymara Incas of five thousand years ago," Morales is therefore proposing a return to the presolar time of the *ch'ullpa*. My consultants had a hard time figuring out what this "return" amounted to. First, because the time of the *ch'ullpa* brings back the era of the *ayllus*'s foundations and concomitant interethnic wars. Territorial and political issues are therefore at stake. Going back "five thousand years ago" would mean returning to an era when space had not yet been socially allocated and was the subject of struggles and vicious fighting. A historical rupture is thus a necessity ("As for us, we are not part of that time"). Second, this return is unthinkable because, as we have just seen, a different form of humanity was characteristic of that era. An ontological disconnection must be maintained between solar humans and presolar beings insofar as the latter were predators, unlike humans who engage in trade. This radical otherness also has terminological repercussions: presolar beings, whether human or not, are included among the *saqra* and, as we will now see, are characterized as belonging to the underworld.

The Underworld

These historical and ontological ruptures are in fact spatially objectivized. The *ch'ullpa* are linked to the subterranean world in the same way as guardian mountains, certain rocks and stones, the Carnival master (the master of the underworld), guardians of specific places (caves, springs), spirits, certain meteorological or natural forces (wind, hail, lightning, rainbows), the spirits of those who have died recently, or certain wild animals and predators (skunks, foxes, reptiles and amphibians, spiders, owls), all referred to as *saqra*. The underworld is therefore a space linked to both the lunar past and the subterranean world, as its Quechua name indicates: *ukhupacha*, "inner world," *pacha* referring both to space and time (Dedenbach-Salazar Saénz 2006; Harris 1987a).[25]

This explains Henry Stobart's observation that, unlike in the Amazon, in the Andes the animated soundscape is internal, buried away, reserved for the underworld: "each sound made audible becomes significant as the expression of the inner state of a sentient being" (Stobart 2006, 105). This contrast, between "constant inner sound" and the "silent external world," is particularly explicit in Northern Potosí in descriptions relating to the recently dead. They are said to live underground in the company of their dog. On All Saints' Day, humans can hear them arriving and heading to the cemeteries to receive the offerings (*t'ika*) that are made to them: "And below the earth, the dog was barking too. That's what I heard" (*Jallp'a ukhumantapis ayñamunman allqupis. Jinata uyarini nin*).

A RELATIONAL RUPTURE: THE LATENT AGENCY OF THE UNDERWORLD

The ability of the recently deceased to move around, and their desire to come and collect the offerings made to them, demonstrates that the underworld is also an agentive space: the *saqra* of the underworld are all potentially agentive. However, these manifestations are neither continuous nor random, which is how they must remain. Indeed, a return to the time "of the Aymara Incas" as proposed by Evo Morales would be perilous, and for some even diabolical.

THE BOUNDARIES OF PRESOLAR TIME

Other than dreams and moments of intoxication, which are believed to be spheres in which encounters with the *saqra* can take place, manifestations of the *saqra* are limited to certain occasions that may be nocturnal (nights of the new moon [*jayri*] or full moon [*urt'a*]), calendar-based (the first of August, Carnival), or ritual. Invocation on the part of humans is also required.

When "the moon disappears" (*killa wañuqtin*), the *ch'ullpa* are thought to begin flying at sunset: "they go to find water while flying and making a noise. When someone breaks a bone, if it is a *ch'ullpa* bone, they say there is blood. If you touch the bone your fingers will be stained. Small veins appear. This blood is alive" (Charlier 2016).[26] For my consultants, this ability to move around explains why the *ch'ullpa* are always "locked away behind glass" in museums.

On moonless nights, the stones and boulders that are described as petrifications return to their initial presolar condition. My companion referred to this nocturnal activity when explaining his brother's decision to move house. His brother lived next to Cerro Colorado but was unable to sleep on nights of the new moon: "They turned into stone in the time of the Inca. When the moon disappears, they walk again, the drum beats, and the water also flows. That's why my brother was unable to sleep."

In the following account, Venancia from the Aymaya *ayllu* talks to her daughter Natalia and refers to the reanimation of a petrified woman in connection with the lunar cycle:

> V.: They say there is a stone. Like you, sitting down. She is still there. A woman in stone. Like a woman. Her braid also in its place. Like that, her legs stretched out. They say she is weaving a belt. . . .
> N.: Is the stone woman still there today?
> V.: "Even today, she is sitting there," people say. This stone would appear to her [she gestures toward me] as a young person. This woman . . . She changes into a woman, she changes into a young person . . . She's weaving. "Oh, the dead moon is dangerous. It's the dead moon. It disappears, the moon disappears, it disappears," people say. That's when our month [menses] comes.[27] "That's where the devil is," people say. Then she transforms into everything, yes. (Venancia and Natalia, Entre Ríos, 2001)[28]

Certain stones are treated in a special way, in particular those described as being petrifications of animals, whether domestic (bulls, llamas) or not (toads): "Going toward the valleys, in Castilla, there is a rock. It's a giant toad, the size of a horse: when the moon disappears, it becomes a toad [*jamp'atuman kutin*], it makes a terrible noise, it scares people a lot." In November 2017, I went to the valleys with my godson's father, and we passed this rock. He explained to me: "This is the place where my grandfather and I used to stop and have a rest with the donkeys. Then he would try to break the toad into pieces. That is why the ground is strewn with broken stones and chips. But he never succeeded. This rock is so hard that it's impossible to break or cause to crumble. If it does break or crumble, it means the person will be rich."[29]

If the toad and bulls are able to recover their animated presolar state during the dead moon, they are also considered to have powers that may be beneficial to humans and their animals. This imputed power is characteristic of all the stones that are remarkable because of their origin, shape, size, hardness, texture, color,[30] or composition. They are associated with the underworld and presolar time ("that which has always existed") and thus are deemed to possess special powers. This is the case of the stones named *illa*[31] or *khuyiris* (compassion stones),[32] remarkable because of their specific shape, most often zoomorphic. They are believed to ensure fertility, the reproduction of livestock, or the

FIGURE 7.3. Jamp'atu *(the toad)*, Castilla, Charcas province, Northern Potosí. Photo: Laurence Charlier Zeineddine, November 2017.

granting of superhuman power to win in ritual battles (*tinku*) or in war. People request these powers during the Carnival period and on the first of August,[33] times when the earth is considered to be "opened":

> Qallinch'aku is the name given to a stone in the shape of a llama in Achachipampa, when you go along the valleys through Colloma, higher up, as you climb the mountain, the place is called Achachipampa. That stone is powerful; we call it *illa*. You can see it from Salinas. That's why we say there are llamas in that place, because of that stone. When they [people] drink alcohol, they remember [*yuyarinku*] this stone. They drink and make offerings: "Give me sheep, or llamas," that's what they ask the stone. (Segundino, 2015)

As this example shows, here the relationship between the stone and the animal is not iconic: the stone in the shape of a llama "doesn't represent anything; it presents itself" (Allen 2016a, 340; see also Dean 2010, 26; and De la Cadena 2015, 100).

Gregorio discusses *khuyiris* stones in similar terms:

> These stones have compassion for people. You chew on coca for these places. If you want livestock, you say to the *khuyiris*, "Please, I need livestock," and they

FIGURE 7.4. Khuyiri *stone: two bulls tied up in an enclosure* (yunta). *Aymaya, Bustillo province, Northern Potosí. Photo: Laurence Charlier Zeineddine, November 2017.*

> give it to you. For example, near Chayanta there are two bulls tied up in an enclosure, that's *khuyiri* [see figure 7.4]. This stone in the shape of a toad. That's *khuyiri* too, you ask it for money. You pronounce the name of the toad, you chew on coca, and it gives it to you. People chew on coca for *khuyiris*, so that they will be generous/show compassion (*Khuyirispaq pichiyarichkan, khuyarimunawanchijpaq*). (Gregorio, Urur Uma, 2015)

As we can see from these examples, the underworld's power of agency is also manifested in a ritual context when humans request its manifestation and its power while thinking of/remembering it (*yuyay*).[34] The emotional and cognitive process expressed by *yuyay* is indissociable, in the ritual context, from offerings accompanied by libations and the chewing of coca leaves (Charlier Zeineddine 2015). *Yuyay* thus constitutes a mechanism for "presentification." To refer to the manifestations of *saqra*, speakers use the term *sut'i*, which literally means "clearly" (i.e., "in the light of the sun, in this world and not the underworld") followed by the locative suffix *pi*, giving *sut'ipi jamusunqa*: he/she will come clearly.[35] This usage invites a translation of *yuyay* as "paying attention," with this effort of attention having the causal effect of making things become "under our own sun in the light of the present."[36] *Yuyay* helps to enable a potentiality (the mobility of a petrified being, for example) become "clear/visible" (*sut'i*); for example, the petrified being becomes animate and moves around. According to the people I spoke to, the *saqra* exist outside the mental representations of people, but can only interact with humans if humans think of them—that is, ultimately, if they become involved with them.[37] The relationship must be reciprocal. It is only through this confirmed reciprocity on the part of the humans that the manifestations of presolar time may become "clear/visible." The confirmation is given during rituals, in and by offerings, meditation, demonstrations of adoration, and various forms of address or solicitation. These mechanisms are also expressed by the notion of invitation (*Kay nuqa invitamuchkaykiqa*, "I am inviting you," one may say to a *saqra*).

From Reading Signs to Forming a Relationship: A Lithomorphic Text?

Certain mechanisms therefore enable the manifestations of this past to be made present and appear in the social world. Despite their petrification, presolar beings are able to act in the world of humans. Consequently, the various geological formations in the region are not merely evocations, representations, or vectors for memory as Keith Basso (1996) wrote about Apache place-names. Whiles places "have a story to tell" (Basso 1996), they are not mere lithomorphic texts from the past.[38] The Andean landscape has given rise to several textual and mentalist analyses by anthropologists. For example, it has been defined as a component of a conception of the world, as a tool for remembering tradition or as a method of transmitting knowledge and ensuring continuity in time and space (Molinié, chapter 6; Howard 2006): "The lithomorphosis of the ancestor is not to be understood as a negative event, tied in with notions of rupture. Rather, such stones ensure continuity in time and space; their power serves to keep cultural knowledge alive, and they are the material evidence of the enduring presence of the past in the here and now" (Howard 2006, 238). Likewise, Howard Malverde considers the dumbness described in the myth to be a symbol: "In the mythical discourse silence, like lithomorphosis, is a symbolic expression of the latent perduration of the powers of the ancestors, and not that of a complete rupture with the preceding order" (1990, 114). Our ethnographic data invite us to develop an analysis of dumbness beyond this "mythical discourse." The dumbness (or imposed silence) of the *saqra*, which characterizes the current era, primarily describes a mode of sensory interaction between the underworld and this world, between humans and the *saqra*. It must therefore be considered a relational mode, involving the experiential rather than the merely textual. Henry

Stobart (2006) rightly comments that sound is an important medium for not only representing but also "making present" the social relationships that people maintain with the underworld and the landscape. Most frequently, while *saqra* are reduced to silence in the underworld, their first manifestations in the world of humans are auditory, and it is through sound that humans infer their presence in the ritual space (Charlier Zeineddine 2015).[39] Similarly, focusing on the study of *wak'a*,[40] Bruce Mannheim and Guillermo Salas Carreño (2015) dissuade us from reducing *wak'a* to "entities" (entification) insofar as they are persons, "place-persons" with whom humans maintain a relationship, in particular by feeding them.

Materiality as Latent Agency

The granting of an objective existence to the sacred (entification) is likely due to the "physical concreteness" of the *wak'a* (Bray 2015). The *wak'a* constitute physical (geological) incarnations of power and cannot be reduced to abstract notions: "such specifically constructed or demarcated landscape features not only materially express networks of social relations but also create and instantiate these by giving them substantive existence through their material form" (Bray 2015, 3).[41]

This observation has led to several analyses on the power of lithic materiality in the ritual context and the close relationship between sacred stones and guardian mountains (*apu*) (Allen 1997, 2016a, 2016b; Howard 2006; Janusek 2015; Randall 1982; Ricard Lanata 2010; among others). For John W. Janusek (2015), the monoliths of the archaeological site of Khonkho Wankane (south of Lake Titicaca, Bolivia) incarnate the surrounding mountains from which they were extracted and which they continue to index. For Catherine Allen (1997, 2016a, 2016b), the stone *illa* is not merely a part of the mountain but also its metonymy. The relationship between the *illa* stone and the *apu* is then fractal in nature, the *illa* being "an instantiation of the *apu*'s animation presence" (Allen 2016b, 434). Rosaleen Howard (2006), meanwhile, emphasizes the relationship of filiation: "the *apu-illa* relationship could be characterized by a genealogical metaphor of parent to child" (Howard 2006, 235). Finally, in the Ausangate region, the *inqa* stones are considered a gift from the *apu* to the shepherd for granting a soul to his animals (Ricard Lanata 2010).

However, we believe that the specificity of the lithic landscape does not only lie in its own perceptible existence. We have therefore not restricted our analysis to the issue of the objectivization of the sacred and its physical characteristics (shape, colors, compositions etc.). It may also be productive to avoid considering this materiality only in terms of a relationship that is thereby substantivized (i.e., where the lithic materiality embodies a metonymic relationship between the stone and the mountain, whether a relationship of family or a relationship of exchange). We propose considering materiality not as an immutable physical characteristic but rather as a temporary state, a situational and relational quality, with materiality merely objectivizing a latency (a potential agency) rather than an essence (a permanent quality). Such an approach will enable the further study of *wak'a* as a point of intersection between materiality, agency, and personhood (Bray 2015, 4).

Rosaleen Howard (2006) has conducted a highly productive ethnolinguistic analysis of petrification. She argues that the Quechua vocabulary and grammatical forms used by speakers[42] to refer to lithomorphoses reveal two groups of concepts: (1) those linked to decline, degeneration, and disappearance; (2) those relating to commencement, generation, and growth. "Stone thus stands at the crossroads between past, present and future; between inner and outer worlds. . . . Lithomorphosis provides the most salient expression of stone as signifying a turning point, whereby arrest of motion at once neutralizes energies and stores them up to be put to future use" (Howard 2006, 234). If lithomorphoses appear to be a coalescence of the underworld and this world, of the presolar and solar eras, this coalescence must be associated with the state of latency. The stones described as lithomorphoses can be defined as a perceptible expression of potentiality, as the material form of a latent agency. The coalescence is thus always manifested in circumstantial and temporary ways. Howard (2006) concludes by referring to another latent quality, that of reversal or *pachakuti*. According to Howard, this latent quality clearly expresses the permeability of spatiotemporal categories, those of the past and the present (thus running counter to a linear conception of time) and of the internal and the external: "Between these two oscillating dimensions sits *kay pacha*—the here and now—at the interface of world, providing the space and time where human beings enact their lives in the latent presence of past and future. Importantly, no rigid boundary is thus conceived between the *pacha*: these are fluid and creative, allowing for transformational movement back and forth between them" (Howard 2006, 242). Further, "the mythic age is not a preterit past, located on a linear path that leads towards later times, but is a temporarily hidden dimension with the potential to re-emerge" (242). However, the discontinuity of categories (underworld and *pacha*, past/present) is not exclusively spatial and temporal. We believe it also results from how the *saqra* act, and more precisely the different types of modes of action: depending on the situation (the moment, attentiveness, or intentions of humans for example), their movement may or may not be arrested, and their sounds may or may not be muted.

FIGURE 7.5. *A special stone,* Aymaya aylla. *Bustillo province, Northern Potosí. Photo: Laurence Charlier Zeineddine, November 2017.*

THE *SAQRA* AS PREDATORS

We have seen that *saqra* have powers that can be beneficial to humans. But the *saqra* are also fundamentally predators, who may eat the souls of humans when hungry. It is difficult to protect oneself against this. Once humans have confirmed the reciprocity of the relationship, the *saqra* are able to interact according to methods and intentions that, this time, are their own (they may be capricious, vengeful, etc.). More than a category of belonging, the underworld is conceptualized as a mode of action: among other things, satisfying one's needs and "taking" without restriction (Charlier Zeineddine 2015). It seems likely that when humans create *saqra* by thinking of them, they run the risk of having their soul devoured. The limitation of their manifestations to nocturnal and ritual spaces, and only at the instigation of humans, therefore serves a prophylactic purpose. While a relational continuity does exist, enabling contact between the era of the first form of humanity and that of the current one, this coalescence must be subjected to numerous restrictions.

In 2015, while I was walking with Mario past one of his pieces of land, he showed me a stone that, due to its imposing size, was regarded as special: "This stone isn't like any ordinary stone. It has power, that's why we don't move it, we leave it here. My father[43] remembered it faithfully, and that way my bull became champion on All Saints' Day" (figure 7.5).[44] This remark was accompanied by a warning: as the first of August was approaching, Mario refused to go near the stone. "We mustn't touch it, or go close to it. It's dangerous. Especially in August, the devil [the underworld] is open. If you believe, if you are faithful and affectionate like that, then you're OK, otherwise it'll kill you. It's a very dangerous month." When I came back in November 2017 on All Saints' Day, I spent the day and night of November 2 in Victor's house. He had died three weeks earlier as a result of a car accident. For most people, he had been eaten by the *illa* stone near his home. Indeed, he had not remembered (*yuyay*) it, he had not fed it, and the stone had eaten him. Later I learned this stone had eaten Victor's aunt twenty years before.

A RUPTURE OF TEMPORALITY: "EL TIEMPO DE LA RELIGIÓN"

Another rupture, radical this time, consists of no longer appealing to the beings of this lunar past. The Pentecostals take this approach. The idea is not to doubt the *saqras*' existence but to "pay them no heed," to avoid being in a relationship with them. They are ignored: "If you believe in the devil, that means you think of him. I believe in God (*nuqa yuyani diospi*), in God alone, God is the only one. The devil exists of course, he's another divinity, but we must not attach importance to him" (Gregorio, Urur Uma, 2015).[45]

This attitude takes the form of a categorical refusal to think (*yuyay*) of the presolar time of the *ch'ullpa*. The evangelicals translate *yuyay* as *creer*, "believe," *tener fé*, "have faith," as the missionaries and administrators of the colonial period did before them (Cuelenaere 2013, 2016). But this verb should not be understood in the rationalist sense of adhering to a propositional content. It conveys the same agentive meaning as previously, "render clear/visible" or "causing things to become 'under our own sun in the light of the present.'" Belief therefore affects temporalities (*según a su fé, según a su creencia*), not as an intellectual attitude (according to a mentalist conception) but as a practical mechanism for relationships (a recollection). The two religious groups thus share the same concept of belief (understood in the sense of *yuyay*), the main difference being that the people in one group neutralize it whereas those in the other seek to activate its perceived effectiveness (Charlier Zeineddine 2013).[46]

We have already seen how the Inca era and the pre-Inca era could be amalgamated into a single era, one that is remote, autochthonous, Indigenous, Aymara, and pre-Hispanic. We have also noted that the era of the *ch'ullpa* is "made present," particularly during rituals.[47] Three periods can therefore be distinguished: (1) the *sut'i* era, that is, the current era of this solar world; (2) the era of Spanish solar colonization (colonization of the *ayllus*, latent petrification of lunar entities); and (3) the remote era of the presolar and lunar *ch'ullpa* (formation of the *ayllus*, conversions). The sun and the petrifications therefore appear as historical and concomitant markers of a single colonization, the Spanish one; the Incan colonization is no longer historically marked, having been subsumed under an Indigenous, non-Spanish autochthony.[48]

However, the evangelicals do not share exactly the same chronology, as they include an additional era. They consider those who still maintain a relationship with the time of the *ch'ullpa* to be in the age of the forefathers (*tiempo de los abuelos*) whereas they consider themselves to be in the age of religion (*tiempo de la religión*):

> When the moon disappears, she [a petrified woman] walks like a person and you can meet her, if you think of her. But people no longer remember. That's how the forefathers thought, that was their faith. These stone statues are still there today but people no longer remember [there are no longer any rituals]. People have changed, they no longer believe, the forefathers believed. Because previously, religion didn't exist, you see, there was no religion. But time has changed, we are evangelical today and so it depends on your belief. Because once, one of them [a petrified man or woman] would appear to someone, and afterwards they would tell their family, their neighbors, and then the next day the neighbor could see the person too, they would appear to them too. (Segundino, Urur Uma, 2015)

The motivation for Pentecostals not to invoke or see the *saqra* is not theological or moral but rather prophylactic. As the *saqra* are hungry, humans must unfailingly feed them (culinary offerings) and run the constant risk of being eaten. But the evangelicals who do not address them are spared and instead enjoy a degree of calm: they cannot be eaten. Further, while their production may be mediocre, it is guaranteed, without any relational constraints: "I can go wherever I like, nothing has appeared to me, because I don't think about it. The devil only appears to those who believe in him, those who think of him," Gregorio confided to me. The account given in Spanish by Moises is illustrative here:

> M.: Before, we were in the habit of believing in everything, in every stone [he picks up a stone]. . . . The *jurüru, illa, khuyiris* helped us, those who believed.[49] They [people who believe] give them tea, sheep's blood, wine, sugar sweets, *q'uwa*[50] as food. And they help them, they do help

those who believe, yes. This power continues, the Huancarani [guardian mountain] still has that power, some people continue to believe, yes. We have to feed the *khuyiris*. We are like women, that's what people say, because we always have to feed them.

L.: What are the *khuyiris*?

M.: A stone in the shape of an animal, like a bull for example, like this [in miniature]. You have to remember it in order to have livestock, plenty of animals. You have to feed them with faith. In Quechua we say *tukuy sunqu si . . . tukuy sunqu kananchij tiyan, tukuy sunqu kani* [With the heart, yes, we must be with all the heart, I am with the whole heart].[51] Like that. As for me, I think of God with faith, with all my faith. If you don't do it with all your faith, he won't help you. You'll buy candles and burn them, and it'll all be in vain.

L.: Do they believe in God these days?

M.: Yes, as I was saying, they used to believe in stones and mountaintops. And those would help you a lot. We used to remember Huancarani on the first of August and the potatoes would be this big [enormous]. These days they're very small. Maybe that's because we no longer remember it. Primitivo [the *yatiri*, shaman] is very good at making it rain. Now it's the time of religion. But it doesn't rain anymore, well, it rains from time to time but it's not regular. It doesn't rain like it used to. We believe only in God.

L.: But the potatoes are small?

M.: Yes, that's true, but we're happy with how it is. For example, me with my earthworms [as fertilizer], we live this way in the countryside with our animals, and with faith too. Because with the mountain and the stones, you have to constantly feed them, you become like a woman endlessly serving them. They do help you, but there are also times when it doesn't work. They'll help you for a bit but they just want to eat. And they might eat you too. God helps too, yes, he helps you. We ask him with faith at the top of the mountain, yes. (Moises, Urur Uma, July 2015)

For the Pentecostals, it is the *abuelos* (referring both to the forefathers and to the elders) who practiced and continue to practice *costumbre* by forming relationships with the time of the *ch'ullpa*. Religious denomination is therefore a temporal marker here. The Pentecostals do not exist within the same temporal sphere as the Catholics: the latter are still connected to presolar time, whereas the evangelicals exist in close proximity to the presolar entities but ignore them, condemning them to live in a world where time can only be linear and rocks are merely the vestiges of a petrified past that has definitively ended. Although they coexist, they no longer live within the same space/time (*pacha*), as this is defined by their relational modes: being in relation with the *saqra* (*tiempo de los abuelos*) or not (*tiempo de la religión*).

For the Catholic inhabitants, these differences can be situated on a synchronic plane. The Pentecostals, on the other hand, assign a vertical and unilinear axis to these differences in belief, which strongly influences how they discuss evolution: "Today, we are civilized, we no longer believe like the forefathers, we no longer remember [we no longer make offerings]." They add: "This era is exhausted, because God is arriving. It will be the end of humanity."[52]

With the creation of the Andean New Year and the return to a precolonial era, Evo Morales is not only promoting continuity with the pre-Hispanic ancestors of the time of the *ch'ullpa*. He is transforming a national heritage project into a decolonization project. But for my consultants, whether Pentecostal or not, the decolonization (as the official speeches present it) is far more akin to a *pachakuti*, a "reversal of time and the world."[53]

CONCLUSION

While the Andean New Year promoted by Evo Morales is founded on the idea of reestablishing historical and ethnic continuity between the period when pre-Hispanic archaeological structures were built and the current period, the inhabitants of Northern Potosí strive to maintain ruptures: a historical rupture between the presolar and solar eras, and a relational rupture with the beings of the distant past who are capable of acting in the current world of humans and carrying out predatory actions.

Local ways of conceptualizing the reference points of social memory reveal other vectors for memory than the great archaeological sites where the Aymara Andean New Year is celebrated. Local history is found in what may be termed topographical vestiges: the rock that is the petrification of a priest leading prayer, or the lithomorphosis of a woman from La Paz who came to sell Yungas coca from the valleys. To retrace history, one must look at the stones. All of them point back to the presolar era. But while the stones of the archaeological structures left by the *ch'ullpa* are mere remnants of this distant past, the geological stones that "come from the underworld" represent the potential to revive an era that is as pre-Hispanic as it is colonial. The basis for history is a mode of engagement with presolar beings whose geological formations exhibit potentiality.

The sacred stones, then, are not merely figures. We have effectively moved from an analysis based on the reading of signs to a more relational analysis: the stones are *saqra* and agents. For Howard (2006), the function of lithomorphosis is to ensure continuity via the transmission of signs, implying that the continuity between the past and present is maintained by solely textual means. But this sign-reading process can be acknowledged if it is agreed that the immobility of the lithic landscape (which encourages textual analysis) is only latent. Rather than pitting symbolic analysis and relational analysis against one another, we must make them converge by considering that the sign (the rock as a particular shape) and the "place-person" (the rock as a social partner that interacts) are both situational qualities, poles indicating the degree of agency. Within this polarity, whether one reads signs (the rock *kimsa yuqalla* that marks the edge of the *ayllu*'s territory, for example) or forms relationships with petrified presolar beings is indicative of the status of the *saqra*'s agency—it is either impeded and interrupted, reducing presolar beings to silence and immobility, or on the contrary actualized in social life by humans.

The underworld is a huge domain, one of potentiality, which only a coalescence of the present and past, this world and the subterranean world, can reveal, or render "under our own sun in the light of the present" (*sut'i*). This coalescence, a condition for the manifestation of the underworld, occurs on full moon and new moon nights, in the Carnival period, and on the first of August, or when humans pay heed to (*yuyay*) their existence, and ultimately consent to their relationship with the underworld being reciprocal. The Pentecostals, on the other hand, have decided not to pay heed to the underworld, thus leaving the era of the forefathers to enter the era of religion. They therefore share a conception of time reduced to linearity. Ignored, the *saqra* of the presolar world no longer appear to humans. They are condemned to remain in their petrified form, mute and immobile. While the Pentecostals and Catholics occupy the same spaces, they have established different mechanisms for their relationship with the *saqra*, enabling them to coexist without inhabiting the same temporality.

NOTES

1. In 1988, the Bolivian press somehow established that the arrival of the Spanish in 1492 happened to coincide with the five thousandth aniversary of the Aymara nation. According to the so-called Aymara calendar, 1988 therefore corresponded to their year 5496, and 2015 was actually 5523.

2. With the creation of a "southern clock" where the hands move backward, from right to left, the government hoped to reinforce the identity of "peoples of the southern hemisphere" where, unlike in the northern hemisphere, the sun moves to the left. In doing so, it sought to break away from the hegemonic codes of time established by the West.

3. The movements of the sun's rays over the Tiwanaku site have been the focus of archaeologists' interest since the 1930s, and of tour guides today. However, in the sun gate's current location, the sun's rays do not pass through it at sunrise, whether on the equinox or the solstice, probably because it was moved by General Sucre in 1825 (Sammells 2012a).

4. According to Sammells (2012a), in the 1970s this celebration of the equinox was replaced by celebrations of the winter solstice in June.

5. On the importance of the solstice celebration among the Inca, particularly in winter, see Zuidema (1981, 2006) and the chroniclers Molina ([1574] 1989) and Cobo ([1653] 1956) in Zuidema (2006). On the Inti Raymi festival in Peru today, see Galinier and Molinié (2006).

6. Sammells (2012b) has shown that the Andean New Year was an urban event (La Paz, El Alto, and Tiwanaku) and usefully highlights the connection between participation in the Andean New Year and the nostalgia of urban residents: through celebration, they act out nostalgia for an authentically Aymara rural world.

7. Group of humans and other-than-human persons with a territorial land base and related to each other by kinship ties.

8. The spread of Quechua in this region is due to the influence of urban centers, the proximity of roads linking communities to these centers, and most important, the mining economy of the twentieth century: in the Potosí mines, numerous workers were migrants from Quechua-speaking areas (in particular, the departments of Cochabamba and Chuquisaca), and Quechua was the language of business and interpersonal relationships. For the purposes of communication and because of its prestigious nature, Quechua was soon preferred by speakers in Northern Potosí when speaking to people they didn't know. In 2000, for example, the elderly were exclusively monolingual (Aymara) whereas those aged around forty spoke both Aymara (their mother tongue) and Quechua; young people and children might understand Aymara but spoke Quechua, which had become their mother tongue. Spanish, meanwhile, is spoken today by most inhabitants due to various migrations (particularly in Cochabamba) and because it is the language of education.

9. In the Andean region, *ch'ullpa* refers to several elements: regional toponyms indicating places where pre-Hispanic archaeological sites are often found (Cruz 2012, chapter 8; Sendón 2010; Wachtel 1990), permanent landscape features (Cruz 2012), funeral tombs, cemeteries, mummies, bones, and unbaptized men (Sendón 2010), among others.

10. *Tata* is used here to convey respect and submission to an authority, as in the case of God, saints, the chiefs/leaders of a community, or an *ayllu*.

11. By contrast, in the Ausangate region (Peru), it seems that the *ch'ullpa* are not relegated to the maximum ontological level of otherness (meaning a different form of humanity). Indeed, Pablo Sendón (2010) and Xavier Ricard Lanata (2010) have noted that the *ch'ullpa* may be identified as ancestors who are *machula* (*abuelo, antepasado*). According to Sendón, this ancestrality is emphasized by the use of the term *awki*, "which also evokes, among other things, the notions of descent in the paternal line, and more precisely of paternity and authority" (2010, 162).

12. Sendón (2010, 162) also notes the identification of the *ch'ullpa* with certain Inca (such as the Inca Pacha Kuraka in the Marcapata region of the Peruvian Andes).

13. On the valorization of *ch'ullpas* in the Indigenous *campesinos* communities of the Uyuni Salt Flat, see Cruz (chapter 8).

14. A recent version I recorded in 2015 featured two yellow bulls.

15. Hence the association in certain regions between the *ch'ullpa* and the *apu* (Ricard Lanata 2010).

16. The Quechua verb used by my interlocutors is *tukuy*: "become/turn into," "finish/end" (She turns into/becomes a woman, she turns into a young person: *Warmimantaq tukun. Jovenmantaq tukun*).

17. The theme of lithomorphoses is present in the myth of the creation of humanity by Virachoca: after rebelling against their creators, the first humans were transformed into stone. For a summary of the different versions of this myth according to various chroniclers, see Urton (1999 cited in Ricard Lanata 2010).

18. Due to the vertical control of ecological layers (Murra [1972] 1975), members of the Aymaya and Kharacha *ayllus* cultivate land in the valleys where they have another residence to obtain resources that are not available on the High Plateaus. The Aymaya *ayllu* still has land in the Mik'ani valleys (south of San Pedro de Buena Vista), and the Kharacha between San Pedro, Kinamara, and Qarasi. On the subject of "bizonal cultivation" and "double residence," see the work of Tristan Platt (1978 and 1981 in particular). Following the agrarian reform of 1953, the number of families practicing bizonal cultivation nevertheless diminished.

19. A woman from the Laymi *ayllu* told me about other lithomorphoses, with the rocks located in Laymi territory.

20. To demarcate territory during the war against the Laymi *ayllu*, for example. In the 1940s, the Aymaya *ayllu* (allied with Kharacha) was at war against Laymi for territorial reasons.

21. Yungas coca is highly prized and considered superior to that of Chapare.

22. Qhuchini is a Kharacha isla, meaning that the community forms a territory that belongs to the Kharacha *ayllu* but is located within the Chayantaka *ayllu*. According

to historiographical sources, this presence of Kharacha within the Chayantaka *ayllu* can be explained by the solidarity and reciprocity between the two *ayllus* (Mendoza, Willer, and Letourneux 1994). The establishment of an isla can also serve a military function. The Kharacha *ayllu* obtained the community of Palqa Uta, an isla south of the Aymaya *ayllu*, a military alliance with Aymaya against the Laymi and the Puraka.

23. This is the Pacajake mine, rich in selenium (Mandarinoite) but commonly referred to as a silver mine (probably because of the silver mines nearby, such as the famous Colquechaka mine) (Dunn, Peacor, and Sturman 1978).

24. Surumi was attached to San Marcos until the miracle of 1779, when it became a separate parish (Platt 1996).

25. For Allen (2016a), the sites where petrifications take place are sources (*unu punku*). Ricard Lanata (2010) also notes that the sources located at the foot of mountains are conceived as doors to the underworld from which domestic animals and rocks emerged.

26. See also Robin Azevedo (2008).

27. On the links between the lunar cycle, the menstrual cycle, and female fertility, see Platt (2002, 643).

27. V.: *Tiyan nin rumi. Qam jina tiyan nin tiyachkanpuni. Warmi rumimanta. Kikin warmi. Sap'anapis ayaqtasqa kay jina jayt'aqparisqa. Chumpita awachkan nin.* . . .

N.: *Warmi rumipi kunankamachu kachkan.*

V.: *Kunankama chaypi chukukuchkan nin. Chay rumi joven payman rikhurinman. Chay warmiqa . . . Warmimantaq tukun. Jovenmantaq tukun. . . . Awachkan. Aïe urt'a peligroso arí. Jaire urt'apiqa chincan nin killa chinkan, chinkan. Chaypi killanchikpis urayk'uwanchik. Chaypi nin supayqa. Chaymanta tukuy imaman tukun arí.*

29. See Harris (1987b).

30. Certain stones are distinguished by their polished appearance and spherical shape (*jurüru*) or their white color (*píña*). These are selected and taken from mountains and rivers because of their "pretty" shape. They are placed in the center of storehouses to ensure that reserves of *ch'uño* (dehydrated potatoes) or wheat, potatoes, or broad beans "never run out" (*mana tukukunanpaq, Pachayan kakusananpaq*).

31. Among the different types of sacred stones or *wak'a*, the ones we mention echo the two types identified by Howard (2006) in her inventory of research in this area: (1) small conopa or *illa* stones, believed to animate plants and shepherd's animals; and (2) rocks or monoliths (*wanka*) that are petrifications of cultural heroes associated with the territory of the *ayllu*.

32. In Northern Potosí, the *illa* stones are also named *khuyiri*. In other Andean regions, they are (often indiscriminately) referred to as *khuya rumi* (compassion stone), *inqaychu*, or *inqa* (Allen 2016b; Ricard Lanata 2010).

33. Taking into account astronomical, agronomic, religious, and symbolic aspects, Gilles Rivière (2002) suggests that this period starts on the feast of Santiago (July 25) in Aymara cosmology.

34. The Quechua verb *yuyay* means both think and remember. Bilingual speakers use either of these verbs in Spanish (*recordar* or *pensar*). In a ritual context, the verb *yuyay* is used with the *-ri* suffix indicating pleasure and tenderness (*yuya-ri-y*: remember with affection, tenderness).

35. Spanish speakers translate *sut'ipi* as "in reality."

36. Here I am borrowing the definition provided by Allen, "under our own sun, in the light of the present," used to describe this world (*kay pacha*): "each pacha—that is, each living materialised moment (whether it lasts for seconds or millennia)—has its own kind of clarity or vision (*sut'i*; see Allen 1994). Events that happen in this world—under our own sun, in the light of the present—are described as *chiqaq* (true, straight), *sut'ipi* (in clarity) and *kunan* (right now)" (Allen 2014, 74).

37. Similarly, Howard (2006, 235) remarks that participation in the general principles and beliefs of the culture is necessary to establish communication between humans and *apu*.

38. On the landscape considered as literature or "primary text," see Arnold (2009) and Astvaldsson (2006).

39. See, for example, rituals where culinary offerings are made. The effectiveness of the ritual then often relies on a sound-based inference ("we heard the noise, so we know that it came to eat").

40. In colonial sources, the term designates places and powerful objects (mountains, stones, mummies, statues, etc.), "sacred objects" (Bray 2015).

41. The chroniclers and extirpators (José de Acosta, Cristobal de Albornoz, Pablo José de Arriaga) also construed the notion of *wak'a* in material terms (Bray 2015; Mannheim and Salas Carreño 2015).

42. In particular, the author draws attention to the different lexical categories implied, whether nominal or verbal: "the fluctuation in syntactic class of the stones terms—shifting as they do between noun and verb status—may throw light on the way stones are conceptualised in Quechua cosmological thought" (Howard 2006, 238).

43. Mario's father is a *yatiri* ("one who knows"): a shaman.

44. The speaker is referring to *toro tinku*, the bullfight that takes place each year in the community on All Saints' Day.

45. For another mode of relation, see the study of the New Age notions and the reversal predatory vestiges/vestiges of prey, by Antoinette Molinié, chapter 6.

46. Unlike Pentecostalism, Andean theology (Teología Andina, a branch of liberation theology) focuses not on the verb "to believe" (the injunction not to think of/ believe in *saqra*) but rather on the content of the belief. Andean theology seeks to

neutralize the *wak'a* in a Christian manner (prayer, acts of faith, forms of healing) to make these beliefs compatible with Christianity. Cuelenaere usefully points out this is a "contradiction insofar as it intends to sanitize the wak'as while seeking to decolonize Christian theology" (2016, 3).

47. In her study of the Huarochiri manuscript, Sabine Dedenbach-Salazar Saénz (2006) examines the uses of the reportative comment suffix *si* (suffix indicating a distant time of the past) and thereby distinguishes the divinities that form part of the experiential world of the narrator and those that are associated with a more distant time, separated from that world. Dedenbach-Salazar Saénz remarks that in the manuscript, contemporary life appears to be greatly influenced by the era of the Spanish and by the era of the pre-Inca Indigenous divinities; the Inca era and that of the oldest mythical events have only a weak influence.

48. According to the ethnographic data I gathered between 1998 and 2002 (well before the presidency of Evo Morales), all the petrifications were considered to have taken place during the Inca period. The Spanish colonization thus appeared as the decisive historical rupture, in that it led to the petrification of the autochthonous world.

49. "Believe" is used here in its transitive form and refers to making offerings.

50. *Q'uwa*: *satureja boliviana*, an aromatic plant burned in braziers.

51. Bilingual speakers translate *sunqu* as stomach or heart. Located in the stomach, the *sunqu* is believed to have functions that are both biological (it enables digestion, breathing and the circulation of blood) and cognitive (it ensures the capacity for thought, memory, and intentionality).

52. See Harris (1987a), Rivière (1987), Szeminski (1993).

53. Translation by Father Cobo (Harris 1987a).

REFERENCES

Allen, Catherine J. 1997. "When Pebbles Move Mountains: Iconicity and Symbolism in Quechua Ritual." In *Creating Context in Andean Cultures*, edited by Rosaleen Howard Malverde, 73–84. New York: Oxford University Press.

Allen, Catherine J. 2014. "*Ushnus* and Interiority." In *Inca Sacred Space: Landscape, Site and Symbol in the Andes*, edited by Frank Meddens, Colin McEwan, Katie Willis, and Nicholas Branch, 71–77. London: Archetype Press.

Allen, Catherine J. 2016a. "Stones Who Love Me: Dimensionality, Enclosure and Petrification in Andean Culture." *Archives des Sciences Sociales des Religions* 174: 327–46.

Allen, Catherine J. 2016b. "The Living Ones: Miniatures and Animation in The Andes." *Journal of Anthropological Research* 72 (4): 416–41.

Arnold, Denise. 2009. "Cartografías de la memoria: hacia un paradigma más dinámico y viviente del espacio." *Cuadernos FHyCS-UNJu* 36: 203–44.

Astvaldsson, Astvaldur. 2006. "Reading without Words: Landscapes and Symbolic Objects as Repositories of Knowledge and Meaning." In *Kay Pacha: Cultivating Earth and Water in the Andes*, edited by Penelope Dransart, 107–14. Oxford: British Archaeological Reports.

Basso, Keith. 1996. *Wisdom Sits in Places: Landscape and Language Among the Western Apache*. Albuquerque: The University of New Mexico Press.

Bray, Tamara L. 2015. *The Archaeology of Wak'as: Explorations of the Sacred in the Pre-Columbian Andes*. Boulder: University Press of Colorado.

Charlier, Laurence. 2013. "Croire, douter et ne pas croire." *ThéoRèmes* 5. https://doi.org/10.4000/theorems.497.

Charlier, Laurence. 2016. "Le point de vue des pilleurs: Ethnographie d'une exhumation de momies (Andes boliviennes)." *Anthropologie et Sociétés* 40 (2): 209–26.

Charlier Zeineddine, Laurence. 2015. *L'homme-proie: Infortunes et prédation dans les Andes boliviennes*. Rennes: Presses Universitaires de Rennes.

Cobo, Bernabé. (1653) 1956. *Historia del Nuevo Mundo*, edited by Francisco Mateos. Madrid: Atlas.

Cruz, Pablo. 2012. "El mundo se explica al andar. Consideraciones en torno a la sacralización del paisaje en los Andes del sur de Bolivia (Potosí, Chuquisaca)." *Indiana* 29: 221–51.

Cuelenaere, Laurence. 2013. "Paradoxes of Belief as Perceived in the Uses of *Creer, Creencia, and Criyincia* in the Northern Bolivian Highlands." *Ethnohistory* 60 (1): 77–100.

Cuelenaere, Laurence. 2016. "The Decolonization of Belief from a Native Perspective: *Wak'as* and *Teología Andina* in the Bolivian Highlands." *The Journal of Latin American and Caribbean Anthropology* 2 (3): 1–20.

Dean, Carolyn. 2010. *A Culture of Stone: Inka Perspectives on Rock*. Durham, NC: Duke University Press.

De la Cadena, Marisol. 2015. *Earth Beings: Ecologies of Practice across Andean Worlds*. Durham, NC: Duke University Press.

Dedenbach-Salazar Saénz, Sabine. 2006. "Pacha, Space and Time in the Huarochiri Manuscript." In *Kay Pacha: Cultivating Earth and Water in the Andes*, edited by Penelope Dransart, 19–28. Oxford: British Archaeological Reports.

Dunn, P. J., D. R. Peacor, and B. D. Sturman. 1978. "Mandarinoite, a New Ferric-Iron Selenite from Bolivia." *Canadian Mineralogist* 16: 605–9.

Duviols, Pierre. 1979. "Un symbolisme de l'occupation, de l'aménagement et de l'exploitation de l'espace. Le monolithe Huanca et sa fonction dans les Andes préhispaniques." *L'Homme* 19 (2): 7–31.

Galinier, Jacques, and Antoinette Molinié. (2006) 2013. *The Neo-Indians: A Religion for the Third Millenium*. Boulder: University Press of Colorado.

Harris, Olivia. 1987a. "De la fin du monde: Notes depuis le Nord-Potosí." *Cahiers des Amériques latines* 6: 93–118.

Harris, Olivia. 1987b. "Phaxsima y qulliqi: Los poderes y significados del dinero en el Norte-Potosí." In *La Participación indigena en los mercados surandinos: Estrategias y reproducción social: Siglos XVI a XX*, edited by Olivia Harris, Brooke Larson, and Enrique Tandeter, 235–80. La Paz: Ceres.

Howard, Rosaleen. 2006. "Rumi: An Ethnolinguistic Approach to the Symbolism of Stone(s) in the Andes." In *Kay Pacha: Cultivating Earth and Water in the Andes*, edited by Penelope Dransart, 233–45. Oxford: British Archaeological Reports.

Howard Malverde, Rosaleen. 1990. "Upa: La conceptualisation de la parole et du silence dans la construction de l'identité quechua." *Journal de la Société des Américanistes* 76: 105–20.

Janusek, John W. 2015. "Of Monoliths and Men: Human-Lithic Encounters and the Production of an Animistic Ecology at Khonkho Wankane." In *The Archaeology of Wak'as: Explorations of the Sacred in the Pre-Columbian Andes*, edited by Tamara Bray, 335–65. Boulder: University Press of Colorado.

Mannheim, Bruce, and Guillermo Salas Carreño. 2015. "Wak'as: Entifications of the Andean Sacred." In *The Archaeology of Wak'as: Explorations of the Sacred in the Pre-Columbian Andes*, edited by Tamara Bray, 47–72. Boulder: University Press of Colorado.

Mendoza Fernando, Flores Willer, and Catherine Letourneux. 1994. *Atlas de los ayllus de Chayanta*, vol. 1, *Territorios del Suni*. Potosí, PAC-C.

Molina, Cristóbal de. (1574–1584) 1989. "Relacion de las fábulas y ritos de los Incas." In *Fábulas y mitos de los Incas*, edited by Henrique Urbano and Pierre Duviols. Madrid: Historia 16 [Crónicas de América].

Murra, John Victor. (1972) 1975. *Formaciones Políticas y Económicas del Mundo Andino*. Lima: Instituto de Estudios Peruanos.

Platt, Tristan. 1978. "Mapas coloniales de la Provincia Chayanta: dos visiones conflictivas de un solo paisaje." In *Estudios Bolivianos en Homenaje a Gunnar Mendoza*, edited by Martha U. de Aguierre and L. Gunnar Mendoza, 101–18. La Paz: [s.n.].

Platt, Tristan. 1981. "El papel del ayllu andino en la reproducción del regimen mercantil simple en el Norte Potosí." *América Indígena* XLI (4): 665–728.

Platt, Tristan. 1987. "Entre ch'axwa y Muxsa: Para une historia del pensamiento politico aymara." In *Tres reflexiones sobre el pensamiento andino*, edited by Thérèse Bouysse-Cassagne, Olivia Harris, Tristan Platt, and Verónica Cereceda, 61–131. La Paz: Hisbol.

Platt, Tristan. 1988. "Pensamiento político aymara." In *Raices de america: El mundo aymara*, edited by Xavier Albó, 365–450. Madrid: Alianza America/UNESCO.

Platt, Tristan. 1996. *Los Guerreros de Cristo: cofradías, misa solar, y guerra regenerativa en una doctrina Macha (siglos XVIII–XX)*. La Paz: ASUR/Plural.

Platt, Tristan. 1999. *La persistencia de los ayllus en el Norte de Potosí: De la invasión europea a la República de Bolivia*. La Paz: Fundación Diálogo.

Platt, Tristan. 2002. "El feto agresivo: Parto, formación de la persona y Mito-historia." *Estudios Atacameños* 22: 127–55.

Platt, Tristan. 2010. "Desde la perspectiva de la isla. Guerra y transformación en un archipiélago vertical andino: Macha (Norte de Potosí, Bolivia)." *Chungara: Revista de Antropología Chilena* 42 (1): 297–324.

Platt, Tristan, Thérèse Bouysse-Cassagne, and Olivia Harris. 2006. *Qaraqara-Charka: Mallku, Inka y Rey en la provincia de Charcas (siglo XV–XVII): Historia antropológica de una confederación aymara*. La Paz: Plural.

Randall, Robert. 1982. "Qoyllor Rit'i: An Inca fiesta of the Pleiades: Reflections on Time and Space in the Andean World." *Bulletin de l'Institut Français d'Etudes Andines* XI (1–2): 37–81.

Ricard Lanata, Xavier. 2010. *Les voleurs d'ombre: L'univers religieux des bergers de l'Ausangate (Andes centrales)*. Nanterre: Société d'ethnologie.

Rivière, Gilles. 1987. "Le pentecôtisme dans la société aymara des Hauts-Plateaux." *Problèmes d'Amérique latine* 24: 81–102.

Rivière, Gilles. 2002. "Temps, pouvoir et société dans les communautés aymaras de l'Altiplano (Bolivie)." In *Entre ciel et terre: Climat et sociétés*, edited by Esther Katz, Annamaría Lammel, and Marina Goloubinoff, 357–73. Paris: IRD/IBIS.

Robin Azevedo, Valérie. 2008. *Miroirs de l'autre vie: Pratiques rituelles et discours sur les morts dans les Andes de Cuzco (Pérou)*. Nanterre: Société d'Ethnologie.

Sammels, Clare A. 2011. "The Aymara Year Count: Calendrical Translations in Tiwanaku, Bolivia." *Ethnology* 50: 245–58.

Sammels, Clare A. 2012a. "Ancient Calendars and Bolivia Modernity: Tiwanaku's Gateway of the Sun, Arthur Posnansky and the World Calendar Movement of the 1930s." *The Journal of Latin American and Caribbean Anthropology* 17 (2): 299–319.

Sammels, Clare A. 2012b. "The City of the Present in the City of the Past: Solstice Celebrations at Tiwanaku, Bolivia." In *On Location: Heritage, Cities and Sites*, edited by D. Fairchild Ruggles, 115–30. New York: Springer.

Sendón, Pablo F. 2010. "Los límites de la humanidad: El mito de los ch'ullpa en Marcapata (Quispicanchi), Perú." *Journal de la société des américanistes* 96 (2): 133–79.

Stobart, Henry. 2006. "The Animated Soundscape and the Mountain's Bones." In *Kay Pacha: Cultivating Earth and Water in the Andes*, edited by Penelope Dransart, 99–106. Oxford: British Archaeological Reports.

Szeminski, Jan. 1993. "La transformación de los significados en los Andes centrales (siglos XVI–XVII)." In *De Palabra y obra en el nuevo mundo: 3. La formación del otro*, edited by Gary Gossen, Jorge Klor de Alva, Manuel Gutiérrez Estévez, and Miguel León Portilla, 181–230. Madrid: Siglo XXI Editores.

Wachtel, Nathan. 1990. *Le retour des ancêtres: Les Indiens Urus de Bolivie, XXe–XVIe siècle: Essai d'histoire régressive*. Paris: Gallimard.

Waskar Chukiwanka, Inka. (2001) 2016. "Origen del actual año nuevo andino amazónico." *Pukara: Cultura, sociedad y política de los pueblos originarios* 10 (119): 8–9. First published as "Restablecimiento del Intiraymi," *Puriniskiwa*, June 2001.

Zuidema, Tom. 1981. "Comment on J. H. Rowe: 'Archaeoastronomy in Mesoamerica and Peru'." *Latin American Research Review* 16 (3): 167–70.

Zuidema, Tom. 2006. "Ritual movements in Cuzco." In *Kay Pacha: Cultivating Earth and Water in the Andes*, edited by Penelope Dransart, 199–205. Oxford: British Archaeological Reports.

8

Disparate Ancestors

Convergent Pasts and the Dynamics of Heritage in the Southern Andean Altiplano (Uyuni, Bolivia)

PABLO CRUZ

This chapter addresses the intense dynamics of cultural and social change seen in Indigenous campesino communities around the Uyuni Salt Flat in Bolivia over the last twenty years, in regard to the valorization of archaeological remains, in particular caves with mummies and pre-Hispanic settlements. Beyond those impacts generated by the development of tourism, like the introduction of a group of new principles and values linked to the concepts of patrimony, cultural heritage, and commodification of culture, here we analyze how these communities reformulate and update their relationships to archaeological remains and, in doing so, articulate different readings and conceptualizations of the past.

Situated in the heart of the southern Andean altiplano, the region around the Uyuni Salt Flat has been one of the most forgotten rural regions of Bolivia. Its traditional economy, based on the cultivation of quinoa, the exploitation of salt, and the raising of llamas, only began its steep growth in the 1980s with the expansion of the tourism industry. Today, nearly 80,000 tourists visit the region each year, making it one of the principal tourist attractions in the country. The development of this new market brought with it the previously nonexistent idea of patrimony, or cultural heritage, with regard to both the natural landscapes and the "culture" of the region's residents. Within this context, and promoted by numerous outsiders, the Indigenous campesino communities began to produce their own tourist attractions centered around on the vestiges of

https://doi.org/10.5876/9781646422869.c008

the past found within their territories, turning these into "material or tangible patrimony," "cultural resources," "archaeological sites and objects": categories that were also previously nonexistent in the region. Thus, in only a few years, numerous caves filled with mummified human remains and ancient objects began to appear, arranged into elaborate scenes, alongside rearranged archaeological sites and newly built small museums and centers. This led local populations on a process, at times conflicted, of intensive repositioning over the different narratives of their past and the historical categories used the construction of those narratives, as well as those elements that define their own culture and identity.

Today, with the salt flat at its center, the Uyuni region is divided between the Bolivian departments of Potosí and Oruro, and again into four provinces, each of which roughly corresponds to ancient ethnic and linguistic territories: to the north of the salt flat, the Aymara speaking provinces of Daniel Campos (Potosí) and Ladislao Cabrera (Oruro); and to the south and east, the Quechua-speaking provinces of Nor-Lípez and Antonio Quijarro (Potosí). Leaving aside the city of Uyuni, the principal population center with 27,000 inhabitants,[1] the permanent population in the rest of the regions ranges from 15,000 to 25,000 people. This variation is due to the high percentage of non-resident members of communities, as well as to practices of labor mobility and multiresidentiality (Laguna 2011; Vassas-Toral 2015). Traditionally, the principal economic activities in the region are the cultivation of quinoa (and potatoes to a lesser degree), the extraction of salt, and the raising of llamas. This is complemented by commercial activity and periods of labor migration to cities and mining centers. From the mid-1980s onward, communities redirected their production to the cultivation of quinoa due to a growing demand in developed countries, and the region became the principal producer of quinoa on the planet (Winkel et al. 2014). The impact of the quinoa boom in the communities has been significant. The agricultural areas dedicated to its production multiplied by incredible proportions, involving nearly all of the communities surrounding the salt flat. Production advanced into pastoral areas, roads, and even community football fields, becoming, in many cases, a vector for conflict and community fracture that has favored the unequal concentration of lands and of the benefits of the boom.

It was in this context of economic and cultural change that I began to work in the region in 2005. I focused on analyzing the impacts of these changes on the relationship that Indigenous campesino communities maintained with those spatialities, material remains, and entities that remit to the ancient past, a past discontinuous with the present, which is generally identified as *ch'ullpa*.

Nevertheless, during the twelve years since I began work in the area, new actors and situations have arisen, many derived from the political and social transformations seen in Bolivia since 2006. These changes, as continual as they are intense and profound, have led communities to new positions on the *ch'ullpa* past, and above all to a new mode of relating to the vestiges of that past, articulating in their position realities that, to Western eyes, may appear incompatible.

HERITAGE, TOURISM, AND MUMMIES EVERYWHERE

Until the mid-1990s, the concept of "cultural heritage" was unknown in the communities that surround the salt flat, and no word in either Quechua or Aymara encapsulates the concept. It was also not prevalent in the national government or in the rest of Bolivia. However, many of the principles and values that were later mobilized with the concept of heritage were already deeply rooted; whether under the concepts of culture, tradition, and folklore, or in the legal figure of the "monument," all concepts that were linked to the construction of the nation-state and Bolivian identity. Official declarations of "national and regional monuments" reveal the evolution of these concepts in recent Bolivian history, with certain moments revealing a particular preoccupation with ideas similar to national heritage and patrimony. Two-thirds of the 181 national monument declarations passed between the years of 1930 and 1991 were passed in only a few specific years: 1930 (43), 1967 (42), and 1970–1976 (35).[2] All were moments of political instability, developmentalist ideas, and nationalist fervor. While the majority of these declarations concern sites, civil buildings, and colonial churches, among them one also finds pre-Hispanic archaeological sites, like Tiwanaku and Samaipata, considered emblematic for the nation, its regions, and its different cultures and civilizations.[3] By the end of the 1980s the idea of "heritage" became generalized, and the concept of "cultural heritage" amplified. With this momentum and validated by international organizations like UNESCO, a dynamic of valorization of heritage developed with the express purpose of promoting tourism. Many sites were then declared World Heritage Sites, including the city of Potosí and the Cerro Rico (1987), the Jesuit Missions of the Chiquitanía (1990), the city of Sucre (1991), the archaeological site of Samaipata (1998), Tiwanaku (2000), the Parque Noel Kempff Mercado (2000), the Carnaval of Oruro (2008), Kalawaya Culture (2008), the Ichapekene Piesta de Moxos (2012), the Qhapaq Ñan or the Inka Road (2014), and the Pujllay of Tarabuco (2014). This wave of patrimonialization was equally manifest at the national level. Between 2003 and mid-2008, no fewer than ninety-six legal designations of patrimony or heritage (historical, cultural, and intangible, etc.) were passed, both national and regional, of which nine concerned pre-Hispanic archaeological sites. Within this framework, in 2005, the national government declared the "*chullpares* and *chullpas*" (mummies) of the Department of Oruro to be "Historical and Cultural Heritage of Bolivia" (Law 2989), and in 2008 it included the archaeological site Alcaya (Law 3880), which will be addressed in detail here.

At the same time, from the mid-1980s, the tourism industry developed rapidly. On the one hand, tourism in Perú—the traditional destination for tourists in the Andes—was seriously affected by political instability and guerrilla activity. Simultaneously, during the second half of the 1980s, the Bolivian state applied neoliberal reforms that deregulated markets and favored the development of small and medium-size companies. In the global context, Bolivia possessed the ideal characteristics for the development of mass tourism for a youth market: exotic destination, relative safety, and political stability—in comparison to its neighbors—and prices that were much more accessible for travelers from the first world (Cruz 2009). At a national level, tourism was organized around three axes: the country's natural attractions, colonial heritage, and urban festivals.[4] Lake Titicaca, the Uyuni Salt Flat, the Yungas of La Paz, and the natural reserves of the lowlands quickly became the principal natural attractions. The cities of La Paz, Potosí, and Sucre became the urban alternatives. This tourism program developed principally around the natural attractions and the colonial past but ignored the Indigenous and campesino face and reality of the country; that face was not the folkloric version brought out to shine during the large festivals (Absi and Cruz 2005).[5] Yet, each of the regions that became the focus of tourism and heritage development was—and is—heavily populated by Indigenous campesino populations.

Today, the nearly 80,000 annual visitors to the region make the Uyuni Salt Flat one of the most important tourist centers in the country. More than seventy-five tourism companies operate within the city of Uyuni, offering tours that vary from two to four days in duration and traverse the salt flat, or the *salar*, and its surroundings, including the Laguna Colorado and Laguna Verde, with overnight stays in small communities (Cruz 2009; Nielsen, Calcina, and Quispe 2003). The tours are conducted in all-terrain vehicles that usually leave from Uyuni, but sometimes depart from La Paz, Potosí, Tupiza, and even San Pedro de Atacama in Chile. More than 400 vehicles circulate on the *salar* each day. The principal tour operators also have their own networks of hotels and lodgings in communities in the area.

While the industry began with shorter tours in 4x4s on the salt flat and then to the Lagunas, from the beginning many included in their packages the

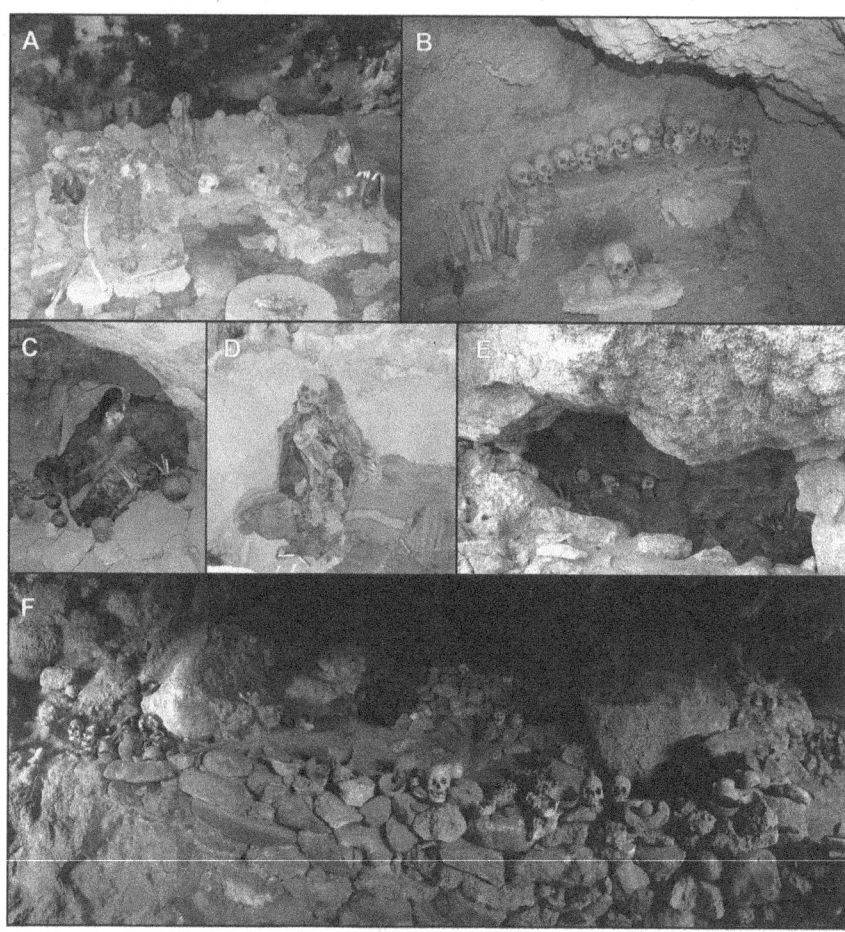

FIGURE 8.1. *Caves with mummies.* (A) *Colchani,* (B) *Chilaco,* (C) *Coqueza,* (D) *Atulcha,* (E) *Jirira (in an archaeological context),* (F) *Ayque.* Photos: Pablo Cruz (A, C, D, and E: 2007; B and F: 2016).

option of a direct experience with mummies and pre-Hispanic archaeological sites. Toward the end of the 1990s, it became more common to see posters in tourist agencies in Uyuni, Potosí, and La Paz that promoted the region using photos of the landscape alongside others that included tourists hugging mummies or holding human skulls. The mummies, while never the principal attraction of the tour, were an essential ingredient in creating the sense of adventure and exoticism tour operators wished to promote.

FIGURE 8.2. (A, B) *Signs advertising* ch'ullpas (A, *Atulcha;* B, *Salinas); (C, D) archaeological sites open to tourism* (C: *Sivingani;* D: *Charali, Saitoco). Photos: Pablo Cruz* (A: *2007;* B, C, *and* D: *2016).*

At that time, the visits to these pre-Hispanic funerary sites did not fully involve the communities but rather depended on direct individual contacts between chauffeurs and guides with a member of a community, who, in exchange for a tip, would lead the tourists to where mummies could be found. In only a few years, with the vertiginous growth in tourism, the number of caves with mummies that were open to tourists multiplied, diversifying the offer to include archaeological sites, museums, overlooks, and so on. A battalion of different actors contributed to this: private companies, governmental entities, NGOs, and international agencies, as well as political leaders, academics, students in tourism programs, and more. They were all involved in the construction of what Marc Augé (1998) called the "illusory kaleidoscope of tourism," promoting the infinite and considerable benefits that tourism could bring in only a few years.

As a result, and only in the communities surrounding the *salar* surveyed in this study, there are fourteen caves with pre-Hispanic mummies (many of which are completely artificial) (see figure 8.1), three caves with natural formations, seven pre-Hispanic archaeological sites (see figure 8.2), eight overlooks, and twelve local museums, with another eighteen similar attractions projected to open to tourists in the coming years (table 8.1, figure 8.3). The manner in which these attractions emerged has been very unequal. On the one hand, attractions like the Island of Incahuasi and the museums of Uyuni and Pulacayo were taken up by municipalities. However, other sites have been developed directly by communities themselves, with the intervention of external agents (NGOs, international cooperation, state programs, tourism companies, etc.). This was the case with the Archaeological Complex at Alcaya, probably the largest project of its kind to date. While the ruins and mummy caves at Alcaya were visited informally by some groups of tourists previously, this project was born after the community recovered an important collection of archaeological objects that had been stolen by a foreign archaeologist, and later confiscated, in the 1980s. With financing from the Department of Oruro and the national government, the Archaeological Complex at Alcaya was completed in 2008 and includes an archaeological park, a network of walking paths, a museum (still being arranged), five cabins, and a restaurant. In 2016, Alcaya was declared a site of Cultural and Natural Heritage for the Department of Oruro (Law 109).

Researchers working in the region also intervened in the development of these projects, like at the archaeological site of Laqaya in Nor-López (Gil García 2005; Nielsen et al. 2003) and the cave of mummies at Atulcha (Cruz 2009). Similarly, in at least one case, the museum at Colchani, development organizations (ASUR and the Italian Agency for Cooperation) initiated the project without community participation, a disarticulation that raised conflicts of interest among community members that had already created their own museum for tourists.

The energy, in financial resources and in physical work, spent in the construction, maintenance, updating, and promotion of these sites has also been

TABLE 8.1. Heritage tourist attractions referenced in the map (figure 8.3)

ID	Location	District	Popul.	MuC	MuA	NaC	Mus	SOL	ArS	Funded
1	Uyuni	Uyuni	27000	–	–	–	A	–	–	Mf, Df, Nf
2	Pulacayo	Uyuni	439	–	–	–	A	–	–	Df, Nf
3	Colchani	Uyuni	250	A	–	–	A	–	–	Ic, As, Df, Nf
4	Jirira	Salinas	50	–	O	–	P	A	O,R	Mf, Df
5	Saitoco	Salinas	120	–	A	–	P	A	A,R	Df, Nf, Ic
6	Alcaya	Salinas	145	A	A	–	A	A	A	Df, Nf, Ic
7	Sivingani	Salinas	–	–	–	–	–	–	A,R	Mf, Df
8	Cheka Cheka	Salinas	0	–	–	–	–	–	R	–
9	Acalaya	Salinas	29 F	–	–	–	–	–	P	Co
10	Puqui	Salinas	140	–	A	–	–	–	A	Df
11	Chantani	Tahua	54	A	–	–	A	–	–	Pe, Co, Mf
12	Ayque	Tahua	28	A	A	–	P	A	A,R	Co
13	Coquesa	Tahua	46	A	–	–	–	–	–	Mf
14	Tahua	Tahua	265	–	–	–	–	A	–	Mf, Df
15	Caquena	Tahua	101	–	P	–	–	–	P	–
16	Incali	Tahua	0	–	–	–	–	–	P	–
17	Isla Incahuasi	Tahua	0	–	–	–	A	A	–	Mf, Ic, Fc
18	Isla del Pescado	Tahua	0	–	–	–	–	P	–	Mf
19	Chiltaico	Tahua	40	–	–	–	–	A	–	Mf
20	Huaylluma	Tahua	–	–	P	–	–	–	P	–
21	Chilaco	Tahua	50	A	–	A	–	–	–	Mf
22	Challacollo	Llica	140	–	–	–	–	–	P	–
23	Pella	Llica	80	–	A	–	–	P	A	Mf
24	Canquella	Llica	125	–	–	–	–	A	P	Mf, Df
25	Huanaque	Llica	221	–	–	–	A	A	A	Mf, Df
26	Chuvica	Colcha K	66	A	–	–	A	–	P	Cf, Mf, Df

continued on next page

TABLE 8.1.—*continued*

ID	Location	District	Popul.	MuC	MuA	NaC	Mus	SOL	ArS	Funded
27	Atulcha	Colcha K	70	A	–	–	A	–	P	Ic, Fc, Mf, Df
28	Aguaquiza	Colcha K	70	A	–	A	A	–	A	Pe, Co, Mf
29	Cruz Vinto	Colcha K	–	–	–	–	–	–	P	–
30	Tanil Vinto	Colcha K	–	–	–	A	A	–	–	–
31	Santiago K	Colcha K	–	–	–	–	P	–	A	Pf, Co
32	San Juan	Colcha K	800	A	A	–	A	–	–	Gc

MuC: Mummies in cave, **MuA**: Mummies in archaeological context, **NaC**: Natural attractions in cave, **Mus**: Museum, **SOL**: Scenic Overlook, **ArS**: Archaeological site. **A**: Active, **P**: Projected **O**: Occasional, **R**: Ritual space, **Co**: Community, **Mf**: Municipal funds, **Df**: Departmental funds, **Nf**: National funds, **Ic**: Italian cooperation, **Gc**: German cooperation, **Fc**: French cooperation, **Pe**: Personal initiative, **Pf**: Private funds, **As**: Association funds.

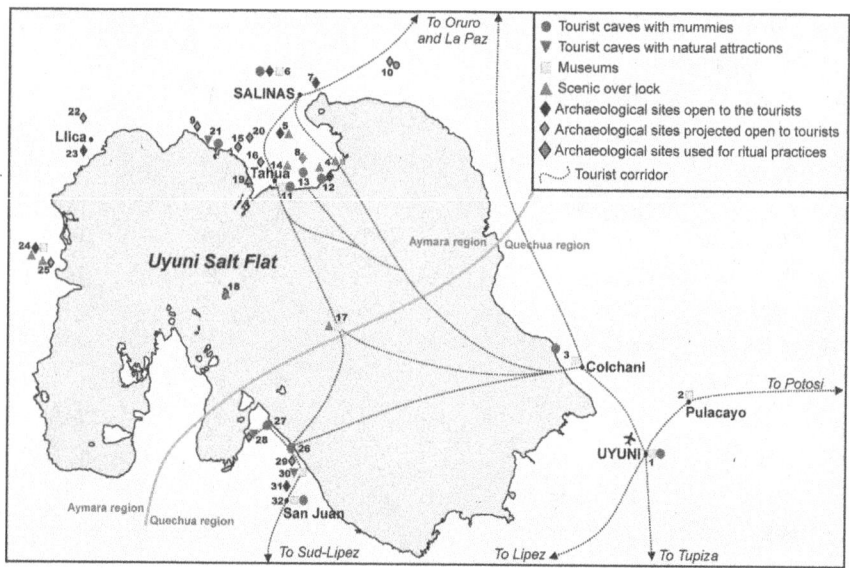

FIGURE 8.3. *Map of the Uyuni Salt Flat with the location of the sites that have been developed and tourist circuits.*

very unequal, and allows one to easily distinguish between those attractions that had external backing and those that—and these are the majority—are sustained only by the communities themselves or by individuals. Among the former, perhaps the best example are the mummy caves at Coqueza that had the support of the German Agency for Cooperation, which also built an impressive portal at the entry to the town. The cave at Atulcha (Q'atinchoo) and the quinoa museum were financed by the Italian Agency for Cooperation with help from the French embassy in Bolivia. The museum at Kawsay Wasi and the necropolis of San Juan, both made possible by the German agency, were also later supported by the municipality and the Department of Oruro.

Community-led projects include large-scale projects like the vast archaeological site and mummy cave in the community of Ayque, medium-size sites like the mummy cave at Colchani, and very small sites like the cave created at Chilaco, where only a few skulls and bones are exhibited. It is worth emphasizing that, in evident contradiction with the principles espoused by the external promoters of the projects, it is not a minority of mummy caves that exhibit idealized re-creations (like Atulcha, Chilaco, San Juan, Colchani, etc.); rather, the majority of them have replaced mummies as they have detoriated from public exposure or have added to the number of mummies in the exhibits by incorporating mummies sacked from other archaeological funerary sites. For example, at least two-thirds of the forty-five tombs shown to the public in the "necropolis" of San Juan are re-creations composed of mummies taken from other sites, including some very distant ones. Moreover, as one resident of Jirira commented, the need to exhibit mummies in good condition has led some communities to disinterr and exhibit "Christian" remains—in other words, more recent human burials than pre-Hispanic mummies. Similarly, aside from preparing elaborate scenes (as in the cave at Colchani), many of the mummies exhibited have been ornamented with elements from different archaeological contexts, including some very modern ones (dog tags, hats, textiles, etc.).

While the financial and labor resources dedicated to these projects may have proportionally increased their potential to attract tourists, other factors, including the antiquity of the attraction, its location within the tourist circuit, and alliances with tour operators and chauffer-guides, are the principal determinants of projects' financial viability. In reality, in the last fifteen years, the business has concentrated around the island of Incahuasi in monopolies that receive nearly all of the tourists to the region. This is followed by a very small number of other sites, like the mummy caves at Coqueza, the grotto of Las Galaxias, the Cave of the Devil in Aguaquiza, and the necropolis and museum at San Juan. These small sites see just enough tourists to guarantee their sustainability. Because the market is oversaturated, the rest of the sites and projects, be they mummy caves, archaeological sites, or museums, receive a small trickle of tourists, frequently going days without a single visitor. Once the initial expectations were crushed, independent of the energy invested, many of these sites stopped staffing reception to receive tourists and charging for entry, as was the case with Alcaya, Saitoco, Sivingani, Atulcha, and Chilaco. Others are temporarily closed to the public, awaiting a change in the situation. Only in a few cases, as in Ayque, the cave at Chiquini (in Chilaca), do they continue to maintain, even at a financial loss, a person to receive potential tourists. However, despite the nonexistent financial success or sustainability, none of these projects have been abandoned. On the contrary, they continue to be maintained, and in many cases improved, including with investment in the construction of new infrastructure. This is surprising considering that these communities, like the nearly eighteen where similar projects are projected to be developed soon, are very conscious of the oversaturation of the tourist market and are aware of the monopolized concentration of tourism around only a few sites. Without discounting the prophetic discourses of the promoters of tourism, everyone in the region has seen the decline in tourism and the slowing of the growth in the sector in recent years. While many have attributed this to poor management by the national government and political instability, none can ignore the global economic crisis and its impact on tourism. However, the development of these sites and their valorization was never only about attracting tourists and making money off them.

THE WORLD OF THE *CH'ULLPAS* AND THE FLUIDITY OF CATEGORIES

For the Indigenous campesino population around the Uyuni Salt Flat, as in much of the Andes, most archaeological remains are vestiges of an extinct humanity, a different humanity, identified in Aymara and in Quechua by the term *ch'ullpa*. This same word is used to identify the bodily remains of this ancient humanity and their burial sites and ancient residences. But the evidence of this *ch'ullpa* past is not limited to these material vestiges; it is a omnipresent in the landscape that includes ancient agricultural surfaces, irrigation canals, paths and roads, spaces with rock art, different geological formations, and spaces in which one finds the ontological explanations of the *ch'ullpa* world and the beings that inhabit it. The *ch'ullpas* are places of social memory (Abercrombie [1998] 2006) that bring together elements that cannot be identified with the genealogical or historical past.

In a narrative that extends across a large expanse of the Andes, the *ch'ullpa* lived in a presolar epoch, a world of shadows where things and colors were not entirely differentiated, where there was an abundance of water, where one could communicate with plants and animals, and where stones could be molded and shaped as if they were made of clay (Cruz 2005; de Vericourt 2000; Wachtel 1990). In the majority of these narratives, this world ended with the rising of the sun and intense heat, which incinerated most of that humanity, or, as the story is sometimes told, with the arrival of a great flood. The few survivors of this universal cataclysm took refuge in caves, houses, and jars or by submerging themselves under the Lauca River, as is said to have been the case with the ethnic group the Uru-Chipaya, whom Aymara consider to be direct descendants of the *ch'ullpa* (Métraux 1935; Sendón 2010; Wachtel 1990).

Like humans today, the spirits of the *ch'ullpas* are jealous of their territory, their constructions, and their belongings; the energy liberated by their presence ensures that no one comes close enough to rummage through their grounds. This energy is the cause of a pathology particular to archaeology sites called *ch'ullpasqa*, something also widely diffused in the Andes, and that can be identified in the affected person by the emergence of cysts or small bone-like protrusions that break the skin. It leads to death without the indicated ritual treatment (see Molinié, chapter 6). Like other similar illnesses of the underworld, *ch'ullpasqa* is a progressive possession that culminates in the transformation of the affected person in *ch'ullpa*, making it dangerous to walk near *ch'ullpas*, remain close to them, especially for women and children, whose spirits are considered to be weaker.

The existence of a past without a sun, inhabited by a humanity different from the present-day one, reveals the perpetuity of an Indigenous vision of time and cosmos, equally expansive throughout the Andean region, which is organized around various cycles of space-time called *pachas*. Each cycle is marked by a cosmic disordering called *pachakuti*. Thus, the period of *purumpacha* is that which preceded the solar order. Within the cyclical conception of the Andean world, the cataclysm that marked the end of the *ch'ullpa* era and the start of the solar era, was a *pachakuti*, a brutal, reordering event, a cosmic cataclysm that gave birth to a regulated society and the hegemony of states. In many regions, the rising of the sun was accompanied by the arrival of the Spanish and Christianity, first characteristics of current-day humanity, while in other regions, such as Potosí, it was the arrival of the Incas and their Empire of the Sun that marked the arrival of the new humanity.

For the *campesinos* in this part of the Andes, the *ch'ullpas* can be distinguished from the dead and from devils because they are spirits of this ancient humanity. Nevertheless, this is not always so clear. *Ch'ullpas*, devils, and other *saqra*[6] entities inhabit, in an undifferentiated manner, the same subterranean universe: the *ukhupacha*.[7] To a great extent, the environmental characteristics of the underworld today are similar to those of the world of the *ch'ullpa*, called *purumpacha* in the colonial chronicles.[8] In the region around the *salar* this is made very explicit in the topology of archaeological sites like *Saqraloma* (Viluyo) and in the choice of peñas and caves (*qaqas*, *maray*) as the scenes and stages for mummies. These spaces are considered to be portals between dimensions (*punkus*) that communicate at certain moments with the underworld and the *saqra* universe (Absi and Cruz 2006; Cruz 2005, 2006). This is not new. In Holguín's Quechua dictionary (1608), which Estensorro refers to (2003, 113–14), *ukhupacha* (*manqhapacha* in Aymara) is defined and includes references to it as a generic terms that designates places like shallow caves, grottos, and caverns. Bertonio ([1612] 1984) utilizes the Aymara term *sakha*, very close to *sakhra* (*saqra*), to identify "apertures in the ground, or pitted rock outcroppings." Bertonio also defines *cacallinca* as "caves in the rock outcroppings or large holes in the ground," *cacani* as "ferocious, cruel," *cacatha* as "to lose consciousness," and *ccaca* "fearful, sad" but also as "ghost that is said to walk at night, and is called by this name because of the stuttering sound it makes." It is thus understandable that in the cave refurbished for mummies located near to Colchani, the dangers of the site are advertised on a sign with a skull and the word "*khakha*" (Aymara). The pathology produced by the *ch'ullpas*, the *ch'ullpasqa*, includes symptoms and presentations similar to those produced by contact with devils and other entities from the *saqra* universe: *mancharisqa* (*susto* or fright), and *jap'isqa* (*posesión* or possession, *pérdida del ánimo* or loss of spirit) (Absi 2003; Cruz 2006). These relations interpellate the Andean cycle of life and death, which is conceived not as a rupture but rather within a dialectic of the wild and the domestic, as two cyclical processes, in that beings socialize from birth on—and with the intervention of rites of passage—and then desocialize at death, losing their identities within the undifferentiated *saqra* universe (Cruz 2005). On the other hand, they evoke a certain continuity in the relation of devils and the dead established early in the colonial period by evangelism and campaigns to eliminate "idolatry" and the ancestor cults. The term *supay*, which used to designate part of the human spirit or ethereal energy that survived the physical death, therefore ended up being translated as "devil" and relocated in the realms of Christian Hell (Estenssoro 2003; Taylor 1980).

It is surprising then, that with many other possibilities, the *campesinos* of the Salar de Uyuni decided to disinter ancient tombs to relocate mummified remains inside caves they have opened for tourists. It is not entirely surprising, however, that the people working shifts at reception at those sites feel very uncomfortable, knowing they are exposed to the energy emanated by the *ch'ullpas*. In fact, with few tourists visiting, the prolonged exposure to *ch'ullpa* energy was one of the principal arguments that led communities to limit time spent at the reception areas or to temporarily close the attractions. In more than a few communities, as is the case in San Juan, some people prefer to pay their fines for not showing up or pay someone to replace them rather than spend too much time in the place. However, the energy liberated by the *ch'ullpas* can be pacified through a protocol of customs, gestures, and ritual practices through which permission is asked to invade the space. The *ch'ullpas* are thanked with libations (*ch'alla*) and offerings that can include coca and cigarettes, a certain quantity of *ajara* (wild quinoa), considered by some to be the food of the *ch'ullpas*, and, rarely, with an animal sacrifice (sheep or llama) or through the calling of an *amauta* (ritual specialist), generally from La Paz. The scale of these customs (the number of participants, expenses, etc.) depends on the power of the *ch'ullpas* and the intensity of the human interventions. While a few coca leaves and a cigarette might be sufficient for a simple visit with a few tourists, the opening of a *chullpar*, the intervention in a cave or the movement or replacement of a mummy, requires various members of the community and could require the investment of a considerable amount of coca, alcohol, cigarettes, ritual mesas or offerings, and animals for sacrifice.

AND ONE DAY THE *CH'ULLPAS* BECAME ANCESTORS

Cheka Cheka (*Chiqa Chiqa*) is a very particular *chullpar*, a pre-Hispanic site (see figure 8.4) located at high elevation, over 4,000 meters above sea level, on the slopes of Tunupa Mountain. The organization of the site, its construction, and the ceramic remains found there are different from the other sites (*chullpares*) in the region. Cheka Cheka was very probably connected to ancient cults and pilgrimages, pre-Hispanic and colonial, surrounding Tunupa Mountain, a sacred volcanic peak that bears the name of the most renowned civilizing hero of the Aymara world, directly linked to the pre-Hispanic lightning divinity. According to Don Carlos N. of Jirira, one of the respected elders of the communities on the north of the *salar*, Cheka Cheka was the most important place in the region, indicated by its name: Cheka Cheka means "the truth of the truth." For this reason, Cheka Cheka is not open to tourism. Don Carlos recounts that before, when the mountains were people who walked and maintained relationships, in Cheka Cheka there lived three brothers. These were none other than San Juan, San Francisco, and Santiago. One day, they decided to come down from Cheka Cheka and split up. San Juan moved to Tahua, San Francisco to Jirira, and Santiago to Churacari, becoming the patron saints of each town. While these are Christian saints, the three-way division and their connection to the mountain remits directly to the pre-Hispanic cults of the mountains and the associated divinities, like lightning, all of which were tripartite in nature (Cruz 2010; Gisbert [1980] 2004; Platt, Bouysse-Cassagne, and Harris 2006). However, a few years ago, for reasons unknown, San Juan abandoned Tahua and returned to Cheka Cheka. Since then, in a reactivation of old memories of the site, residents of Tahua and its surrounding areas return each year to Cheka Cheka for offerings and rituals to their patron saint. Evidence of these accumulate at the site and include offerings and animal sacrifices, as well as metal plaques laid in the stone walls that commemorate the names of the *pasantes* and participants for each year. The oldest plaque dates to 1997.

Though Cheka Cheka is within the community of Jirira in the Department of Oruro, which has a long history of conflict over limits and borders with Tahua (located in Potosí), the return of San Juan, the patron saint of Tahua, and the periodic visits of the faithful from the Department of Potosí present no problem. Quite the opposite. Don Carlos says that only a few years ago, when they climbed up to Cheka Cheka to conduct their rituals, bringing a sheep to sacrifice, they met a group from Tahua who were there for the same purpose with a llama in tow. After each group carried out their sacrifice, they ate and drank together before returning to their communities.

The *pucara* of Charali is a *chullpar* in the community of Saitaco that recently opened to tourists. It is one of the most beautiful and well-preserved archaeological sites in the region. The investment at the site was substantial. Aside from the reconstruction of the ruins, carried out without any consultation from archaeologists, the community members of Saitoco built an access road that stretches over four kilometers, a network of paths, and different meeting and gathering spaces within the site. There are two paths that lead to lookout points on top of the hill and pass by various caves with human remains, a parking lot, and a good-sized building. Nevertheless, like many other sites, the *pukara* of Charali receives virtually no tourists. In all my visits, I have never seen a tourist. Despite this, in October 2016, the site was covered with the remains of offerings, which, while not unusual, testifies to the use of the site for local festivities. When asked about this, Santiago P., who was an authority for the community of Saitoco at that point in 2016, commented that in June, Charali had been the site of a wedding for a young couple from the community, and for the festivities afterward. When asked why that site had been

FIGURE 8.4. *Cheka Cheka, photographs of the site, memorial plaques, offerings, and invitations to the festivities for San Juan Batista, the patron Saint of Tahua. Photos: Paul Cruz, 2016.*

chosen for the wedding and whether it presented any problems for the couple, because it was a *chullpar* after all, Don Santiago responded that they had only conducted the civil wedding there, and that they had carried out many other rituals to pacify the *ch'ullpas*, making Charali more of a sacred place connected to the ancestors of the community. He also told me that only a couple of years before, another wedding had been carried out at Sivingani, another *chullpar* that had been opened for tourism, only about 20 kilometers from Saitoco. He added that he had been able to watch on television the marriage of the vice president of Bolivia, Álvaro García Linera, at the ruins of Tiwanaku.

Ayque is a small community on the northern shore of the salt flat, five kilometers from Jirira. Only fifteen residents live in the community, which is principally dedicated to the cultivation of quinoa and potatoes. As with other communities, the Pucara of Ayque recently opened, including a vast archaeological site and, of course, a cave with mummies. However, in contrast to many other projects, the community members of Ayque carried out the numerous projects and investments at the site, including reconstructions, conditioning of caves, creation of walking paths, construction of an external fence, and a reception desk, entirely without external funding. Despite the scarce and often entirely absent flow of tourists, the community members rigorously keep shifts, under threat of fines, attending to the reception and maintaining the site. Since this work began, members of the Ayque community also began to use the site for their collective acts. They also designed, wrote, and printed a colorful pamphlet for tourists. The front page introduces the "Ayque Archaeological Touristic Site" and follows with different aspects of the site: caves, *chullpares*, archaeological ruins, and ceremonies. The text identifies the site as the ruin of a defensive fort from an ancient civilization descendent from Tiwanaku and thereby from the Aymara culture. It also states that the caves were primitive refuges where the remains of *ch'ullpas* can be found. When asked about the pamphlet, Juan N., a young community member taking his turn at the reception desk and awaiting the unlikely arrival of a 4x4 full of tourists, reaffirmed the sacred nature of the site while making it clear that the site was not only the ruins of the ancestors of the community but also the remains left by the *ch'ullpas*. Without looking up from his internet browsing, Juan commented that he was an IT tech, sympathizer with the Evo Morales government, and had just returned to Ayque after twenty-two years of living in different regions of Chile and Perú. As of January 2017, Juan became an authority in the community of Ayque as part of the obligatory and rotating system of leadership, permitting him access to agricultural lands for cultivation.

Cheka Cheka, Saitoco, and Ayque are examples of the dynamics seen in the region around the remnants of the past and the multiple actors intervening in these processes. With the development of tourism since the 1990s, a group of new ideas, categories, moral principles, and norms linked to the concept of heritage and the commodification of cultural have become rooted in the region. In only a few years, the previously feared vestiges of the extinct world of the *ch'ullpa*, the material testimony of a humanity different than today's, rapidly transformed into mummies, archaeological sites, resources for tourism, heritage, and, something previously unthinkable for Aymara communities, part of their own culture. Considering the importance placed by Aymaras on differentiating themselves from Urus and Chipayas, groups considered to have been descendants of the *ch'ullpas* that survived the cataclysm, this last shift is all the more remarkable. The digestion of all these new concepts and ideas about the world, combined with the need to generate tourist attractions, something promoted by a specific group of actors, fomented an intense debate in communities around the definition of their own culture and which aspects would generate the most tourist interest. In these dynamics the moral principles of patrimony and heritage act as a brake against the new forms of appropriation and dialogue with the past, turning culture into folklore, fossilizing history into a past that can be too distant for local populations. As Gustafson (2006) indicates, this is antithetical to the Indigenous and popular agendas that promote culture as a form of speaking about inequality and consider history as something to be decolonized. In effect, up to the mid-2000s, residents manifested a certain reticence about identifying themselves as Indigenous, preferring to refer to themselves as *campesinos*, *originarios*, Aymaras, or Quechuas. In their words, "Indigenous" was a category systematically related to the near past, that of their grandparents, the customs (rituals, roles, community), foods, and relations to the earth, but also linked to poverty, discrimination, and the relations of domination in which they were subjected. It is not strange, then, that none of the tourist attractions developed in communities considered valuing aspects of the recent past or their customs and practices. This would change, however, and in a very important way.

The ascent to power of Indigenous President Evo Morales Ayma in 2006 marked the beginning of a process of social and cultural change that included profound institutional reforms, among them nothing less than the reformulation of the national constitution, which transformed Bolivia into a plurinational state. The subsequent changes included the creation of a Ministry of Cultures structured around three vice ministries: one addressing interculturality, one addressing decolonization, and another dedicated to tourism. This was no "media show" as some analysts and researchers were tempted to see it: the new president symbolically assuming leadership of the state at the ruins of Tiwanaku surrounded by *amautas* (ritual specialists) before a multitude of Indigenous and social movement leaders sent a clear message about the start of a new era in the country, one in which the Indigenous world that was once subjugated and denigrated would be valued and lauded. The *ch'ullpas*, already placed within the context of heritage or patrimony, would now become a tangible part of precolonial past, a past of autonomy and territorial and political sovereignty, of *buen vivir*, becoming carriers of a set of moral values, spiritualities, and knowledges of the Indigenous world. Some Indigenous intellectuals have identified this as a revitalization of "amautic" thought (Reynaga 1978); others have seen it in a more negative light as emanations of a global discourse very similar to New Age and referred to as "neo-indianism" (Galinier and Molinié 2013) or "*pachamamismo*" (Stefanoni 2011).

The Vice Ministry of Decolonization has played an important role in this return to ancestral sources. In recent years it has been in charge of promoting and coordinating a series of "traditional" ceremonies like the Inti Raymi, the Aymara New Year, and Collective Indigenous Marriages. In June 2013, as part of the government's promotion of the Dakar Rally for 2014, which would pass through the *salar* and surrounding communities, the vice ministry conducted the ancestral ceremony *Waca Taquy Onccoy*. As its name indicates, it was a commemoration of the messianic sixteenth-century movement that proclaimed a return of the mountain cults to the *wak'as*. The purpose was to invoke the ancient deities to ensure the success of the international event. Two years later, in 2015, Evo Morales lead the official celebrations of the Andean-Amazonian New Year 5523 on the island of Incahuasi, also transformed into a ceremonial site (see Charlier Zeineddine, chapter 7). More recently in 2016, the vice ministry handed out 3,000 copies of Fausto Reynaga's book *La Revolución India* to students and professors in the communities around the Uyuni Salt Flat and in the Council of Ayllus in Potosí. Also that year, the vice ministry officially declared the Inti Raymi ceremony, the winter solstice, as the principal celebration of the Indigenous calendar of the southern hemisphere, and included a list of 200 "sacred sites" where the rite should be carried out, among them the most important archaeological sites in Bolivia. Surprisingly, Cheka Cheka is listed as one of the "ceremonial centers," where, in a clear replacement of the myth of the three saints, "history" tells us that the Incas, Tupaj Amaru, Micaela Bastidas, Tupaj Katari, Bartolina Sisa, and Zárate Willka all gathered previously (Viceministerio de Descolonización 2016, 4)—in other words, the forefathers of the Indigenous movement and the new plurinational state. It is not entirely surprising, then, that Tunupa has officially been declared a "Spiritual Energy Center of Bolivia."

Thus, just as is specified in the triptych brochure for tourists at Ayque, the *ch'ullpas*, previously avoided because of the risks associated with exposure to their energies, began to become idealized ancestors, sacred sites, and ceremonial spaces. Proof of the incorporations of these new attributes, the great majority of the mummy caves and archaeological sites are today also spaces for ritual practices (*costumbres*) that previously were carried out in other places or, as is the case in Saitoco and Sivingani, have begun to be used by the communities for ceremonies and festivities. Likewise, in communities and tourist attractions, symbols connected to the Indigenous movement have also begun to multiply, like the *wiphala* and the Andean cross, official emblems of the new plurinational state. Like Tunupa, the Energetic and Spiritual Center of Bolivia, many sites were renamed in accordance with these changes: the Ritual Museum at Incahuasi; the Ceremonial Center at Humani Mountain in Chiltaico; the Museum of the Chullpas or Ancestral Mummies of Aguaquiza; and the Museum of *Kawsay Wasy* (from Quechua, *kawsay*: life, from *Sumaj Kawsay*: Good Life, Ancestral Wisdom, and *wasi*: house). Finally, this recategorization of the *ch'ullpas* as both ancestors and testimonies of an Indigenous past is present, in different frameworks, across much of the Bolivian altiplano, and even beyond that, in parts of northern Argentina and Chile, including in cities and towns. In some regions, these consecutive recategorizations of the *ch'ullpa* past have taken surprising directions, as in Pampa Aullagas, north of the Uyuni Salt Flat, which was formally declared—and promoted to tourists—as the "National Capital of Atlantis." Evidently, this new version of the past came not from the academy or governmental agents but rather from British researcher Jim Allen (1998), who claimed to have found in the area the remains of the famous extinct world. Those voices decrying the ridiculousness of this proposal are irrelevant; the past Atlantis of Pampa Aullagas is today a recognized reality, defended and promoted by the communities, the Indigenous authorities, the municipalities, and the Department of Oruro.

This dynamic, of intense and profound transformation, was potentiated by the exponential growth of technology and forms of communication, in particular the internet and cell phones. Today, these are virtually unlimited in their reach and capacity for the expression, diffusion, construction, and affirmation of Indigenous identities. There are thousands of websites dedicated to information about these communities, along with music and videos referring to their culture and their past. The internet permitted persons from these communities who live in other regions or countries to maintain their connections, to remain integrated, taking on an active role in these dynamics: like Iván I., member of the *ayllu* of Huatari of Alcaya who lives in Toronto and founded the Consejo Andino de Naciones Originarias and who, from his blog, explains the history and traditions of Alcjaya (Alcaya) and their *ch'ullpas*.

SOME (CERTAINLY TEMPORARY) CONCLUSIONS

The dynamics seen in these last decades in the Indigenous campesino communities of the Uyuni Salt Flat surrounding the valorization of the vestiges of the ancient past found within their territories reveal how intensely and quickly cultural change can occur. However, in contrast to similar scenarios seen in other parts of the world, these changes represent not a loss but rather a replacement, in how the communities see, understand, and act in the world and how they identify their own culture and customs. Yes, in a short span of time the *ch'ullpas* and their spaces became tourist attractions, economic resources, heritage sites, archaeological remains, ancestors, etc. At no moment, however, did they cease to be *ch'ullpas*, or be less *ch'ullpa* than before, even though in some cases their energy was managed through ritual practices. Though it is unlikely that the *ch'ullpas* will ever return to being "only" *ch'ullpas* as they were a few decades before. And, while we cannot say whether they will continue accumulating new attributes and categories in the coming years, we know that no limitations exist for this; the Atlantis of Pampa Aullagas tells us that, at least. In any case, the multiple significations and meanings adopted by the *ch'ullpas* today reveal the fluidity and permeability of this category in the minds of local people, as well as the ability with which they simultaneously articulate different realities and discourses about the past (world of the *ch'ullpa*, biblical pasts, archaeology and history, patrimony, etc.), that might seem incompatible, or at least complicated, to outsider's eyes.

Nevertheless, this opening of thought and revaluing of the category of *ch'ullpa* does not explain the enormous efforts exerted by communities in the creation, maintenance, and constant improvements of the mummy caves and the *chullpares*, nor does it explain the long obligatory and rotating shifts worked at reception by members of the community. Neither can it be explained from an economic standpoint. With an oversaturated market and a flow of tourists concentrated and funneled through only a handful of attractions controlled by near monopolies, the great majority of these projects are not sustainable economically and never will be without a radical change in the structure of tourism, something very unlikely. And while the hope that their efforts will pay off with a massive influx of tourists never disappears, the communities are conscious of the limitations of the business. In fact, today, the principal source of income for the region continues to be the cultivation of quinoa, followed by income generated by labor migration and various commercial activities.

However, the dynamic generated around the valorization of *ch'ullpas* can be understood as a confluence of common interests and the reaction of communities before the changes in their ways of life in recent decades. Certainly, the possibility of generating economic resources from tourism, however pitiful the returns, enters into the picture. But equally important, or perhaps more so, the valorization of these sites means a revalorization of the community itself, reaffirming it internally as well as in a local context. In other words, this is a question of self-esteem and prestige as well as positioning in relation to equals; no community wants to be less than its neighbor. Above all, these projects reinforce the basis of the community, not only because they are group initiatives that involve traditional forms of collective work, like the *minka* and obligatory shifts, but also because they achieve a greater degree of involvement of young people and members of communities that were not permanently residing there, including those living in other regions or other countries. That young couples have decided to conduct ceremonies and fiestas like marriages in *chullpares* like Charali and Sivingani is not a minor detail; on the contrary, it is very important. So is the appearance of explanations of the site of Alcaya in a Canadian blog written by a person from Salinas who moved to that country. In this sense, the *ch'ullpas* today create and reproduce community, arresting or mitigating the impacts provoked by those fracturing forces that generate inequality, be it the quinoa boom, labor migration, or tourism itself.

On the other hand, while some projects, like those at Laqaya, the museum *Kawsay Wasi* of San Juan, the island of Incahuasi, and the cave of Atulcha, had the assistance of archaeologists and other heritage specialists in their construction, in the majority of cases, the communities created and have been managing these sites on their own, deciding what gets exhibited, how it gets exhibited, and what gets said about the exhibits. This response is as spontaneous as it is complete: from the profusion of aesthetic values, moral principles, and norms that propagated with the development of tourism and the concept of heritage, and which in many ways came to regulate the social lives of communities and their territories. Moreover, many of these projects, particularly those caves with mummies, challenge some of the fundamental principles of heritage like the preservation and conservation of archaeological remains and the historical authenticity or veracity of the exhibits and information.

Thus, in this part of the southern Andean altiplano, the spirits of the *ch'ullpa* have resisted the onslaught that would have reduced their remains to tourist attractions and cultural heritage sites, finding instead the pathways of ancestrality and recuperating their collective identities and human temporalities, entering once again into history.

NOTES

1. *Vicepresidencia Estado Plurinacional de Bolivia*, July 11, 2016.
2. These happened at the end of the presidential mandate of Hernando Siles Reyes (1926–1930), just before the coup that removed him from power, during the third presidency of General René Barrientos (1966–1969), and during the government of the military dictatorship.
3. Inca Racay (Decreto supremo del 03 de junio de 1937), archaeological ruins of Copacabana and the Isla del Sol (Decreto Supremo del 15 de Febrero de 1941), Tiwanaku (Ley de 8 de enero de 1945), Samaipata (Decreto Ley 2740 [1951], Decreto Supremo 11290 [1974]), Inca Machay (Decreto Supremo 4954 [1958]), Incallajta (Ley 1009 [1988]), Guancané (Decreto Supremo 8171 [1967]), Kalakala (Decreto Supreme 9087 [1970]), Iscanwaya (Decreto Supremo 11034 [1973]), Takesi (Decreto Supremo 12717 [1975]), Tukipaya (Decreto Supremo 14307 [1977]). Source: https://www.lexivox.org, https://www.derechoteca.com.
4. Such as the Carnaval of Oruro, the Virgin of Urkupiña (Cochabamba), the Fiestas of Gran Poder in La Paz, Ch'utillos in Potosí, and Guadalupe in Sucre.
5. It is worth noting that the paths between the centers of tourism in Bolivia are all traveled via airplane or overnight bus, both options that limit the opportunities for tourists to observe the rural regions of the country.
6. The polysemic term *saqra* (*saxra* in Aymara) refers to a category in Andean thought that includes the entities, animating forces, and the spaces of the underworld.
7. Also called *supaypacha* or *saqrapacha*.
8. Absi (2003), Bouysse-Cassagne and Harris (1987).

REFERENCES

Abercombie, Thomas. (1998) 2006. *Caminos de la memoria y del poder: Etnografía e historia en una comunidad andina*. La Paz: IEB-IFEA-Asdi.

Absi, Pascale. 2003. *Les ministres du diable: Le travail et ses représentations dans les mines de Potosí*. Paris: L'Harmattan, Connaissance des hommes.

Absi, Pascale, and Pablo Cruz. 2005. "Patrimonio, ideología y sociedad: Miradas desde Bolivia y Potosí." *Tinkazos* 9: 77–97.

Absi, Pascale, and Pablo Cruz. 2006. "La puerta de la wak'a de Potosí se abrió al infierno: La quebrada de San Bartolomé." *Anuario del ABNB* 12. Archivo y Biblioteca Nacionales de Bolivia, Sucre.

Allen, Jim. 1998. *Atlantis: The Andes Solution*. Cambridge: Windrush Press.

Augé, Marc. 1998. *El viaje imposible: El turismo y sus imágenes*. Barcelona: Gedisa.

Bertonio, Ludovico. (1612) 1984. *Vocabulario de la lengua aymara*. La Paz: Ceres.

Bouysse-Cassagne, Thérèse, and Olivia Harris. 1987. "Pacha: En torno al pensamiento aymara." In *Tres reflexiones sobre el Pensamiento Andino*, edited by Thérèse Bouysse-Cassagne, Olivia Harris, Tristan Platt, and Verónica Cereceda, 217–80. La Paz: Hisbol.

Cruz, Pablo. 2005. "El lado oscuro del mundo: Una cartografía de la percepción de los sitios arqueológicos en los Andes meridionales (Laguna Blanca, Catamarca-Argentina y Potosí Bolivia)." *SIARB Boletín* (La Paz) 19: 38–49.

Cruz, Pablo. 2006. "Mundos permeables y espacios peligrosos: Consideraciones acerca de los punkus y las qaqas en el paisaje altoandino de Potosí (Bolivia)." *Boletín del Museo Chileno de Arte Precolombino* 11 (2): 35–50.

Cruz, Pablo. 2009. "Abarcas campesinas y momias for export." In *Arqueología, tierras y territorios, conflictos e intereses* (Teoría Arqueológica en América del Sur), edited by M. Manasse and P. Arenas, 111–42. Catamarca: Universidad de Catamarca-WAC.

Cruz, Pablo. 2010. "Huacas olvidadas y cerros santos: Apuntes metodológicos en torno a la cartografía sagrada en los Andes del sur de Bolivia (Potosí, Chuquisaca)." *Estudios Atacameños* 38: 55–74.

Estenssoro, Juan Carlos. 2003. *Del paganismo a la santidad: La incorporación de los indios del Perú al catolicismo 1532–1750* (Travaux de l'IFEA t.156). Lima: Instituto Riva-Agüero-IFEA.

Galinier, Jacques, and Antoinette Molinié. (2006) 2013. *The Neo-Indians: A Religion for the Third Millenium*. Boulder: University Press of Colorado.

Gil García, Francisco. 2005. "Cuando vengan los turistas . . . ruinas arqueológicas, turismo y expectativas locales de futuro en Nor-Lípez (Dpto. Potosí, Bolivia)." *Textos Antropológicos* 15 (2): 197–228.

Gisbert, Teresa. (1980) 2004. *Iconografía y Mitos Indígenas en el Arte*. La Paz: Ed. Gisbert & Cia.

González de Holguín, Diego. (1608) 1952. *Vocabulario de la lengua general de todo el Perú llamada lengua quichua*. Lima: Instituto de Historia.

Gustafson, Bret. 2006. "Spectacles of Autonomy and Crisis: Or What Bulls and Beauty Queens have to do Regionalism in Eastern Bolivia." *Journal of Latin American Anthropology* 11 (2): 351–79.

Laguna, Pablo. 2011. *Mallas y flujos: acción colectiva, cambio social, quinua y desarrollo regional indígena en los Andes Bolivianos*. Wageningen: Wageningen University.

Métraux, Alfred. 1935. "Les Indiens Uro-Čipaya de Carangas." *Journal de la Société des américanistes* 27 (2): 325–415.

Nielsen, Axel, Justino Calcina, and Bernardino Quispe. 2003. "Arqueología, Turismo y Comunidades originarias: Una experiencia en Nor López (Potosí, Bolivia)." *Chungara* 35 (2): 369–67.

Platt, Tristan, Thérèse Bouysse-Cassagne, and Olivia Harris. 2006. *Qaraqara-Charka: Mallku, Inca y Rey en la provincia de Charcas (Siglos XV–XVII): Historia antropológica de una confederación aymara*. Lima: Instituto Francés de Estudios Andinos; La Paz: Plural Editores/Fundación Cultural del Banco Central de Bolivia; Scotland: University of St. Andrews/University of London /Interamerican Foundation.

Reynaga, Fausto. 1978. *El pensamiento amaútico*. La Paz: Imprenta Unidas.

Sendón, Pablo. 2010. "Los límites de la humanidad: El mito de los ch'ullpa en Marcapata (Quispicanchi), Perú." *Journal de la Société des américanistes* 96 (2): 133–79.

Stefanoni, Pablo. 2011. "¿Adónde nos lleva el pachamamismo?" *Tabula Rasa* 15: 261–64.

Taylor, Gerald. 1980. "Supay." *Amerindia* 5: 47–83.

Vassas-Toral, Anaïs. 2015. "Movilidades de los productores de quinua y dinámicas territoriales en el Altiplano sur de Bolivia." In *Racionalidades campesinas en los Andes del sur: Reflexiones en torno al cultivo de la quinua y otros vegetales andinos*, edited by Pablo Cruz, Richard Joffre, and Thierry Winkel, 231–80. Jujuy, Paris: EdiUnju, IRD, CNRS.

Véricourt, Virginie de. 2000. *Rituels et croyances chamaniques dans les Andes boliviennes: Les semences de la foudre*. Paris: L'Harmattan (Connaissance des Hommes).

Viceministerio de Descolonización. 2016. "Cartilla. Revalorización de nuestras culturas y sitios sagrados. 21 de Junio 2016, solsticio de invierno. Estado Plurinacional de Bolivia." http://docplayer.es/37021874-Pag-1-21junio2016-descolonizacion-gob-bo.html.

Wachtel, Nathan. 1990. *Le retour des ancêtres: Les indiens Urus de Bolivie, XXe–XVIe: Essai d'histoire régressive*. Paris: Gallimard.

Winkel, Thierry, R. Álvarez-Flores, P. Bommel, J. Bourliaud, M. Chevarría, G. Cortes, P. Cruz, C. del Castillo, P. Gasselin, R. Joffre, and F. Léger. 2014. "Southern Highlands/Altiplano Sur." In *Estado del arte de la quinua en el mundo*, edited by Didier Bazile et al., 362–76. Santiago de Chile: CIRAD/Montpellier: FAO.

Index

abandonment, 9, 140; of landmarks, 58–60
Academia de Lenguas Mayas, 10
Acre, 147, 149; geometric earthworks in, 150, 151, *155f*, 156
action, interrupted, 208, 209
afterlife, afterworld, 131; Amazonian concepts of, 139–40
agency, 3, 18; of stones, 20–21
Age of Aquarius, 192, 193
Age of Reason, 39
agriculture, 6, 107, 149, 224*n18*, 233
Aguacatenango, 14, 16, 107, 108, 114, 116, 120; creation sequences in, 110–11; masters of the earth in, 117–18, 122*n6*; on stone structures, 112–13
Aguaquiza, 241, 251
Alcaya, 235, 252; tourism at, 238, 242
Aldeia (Santarém), 158
Allen, Jim, 251
alliances, Caste Ware, 89, 90
Alter-do-Chão, 158
Alto Ivon, 134; Christian conversion in, 135–36. *See also Tapaya*
Amazonas, 149, 150
Amazonia, 4, 6, 10, 12, 13, 18, 23, 25, 29; abandoned gardens in, 19–20; anthropogenic forests, 156–57; Bolivian, 28, 124; cultural heritage in, 39–40, 147, 165–66; geometric earthworks 15–16, 150–56; territorial mastery in, 159–60
amnesia: genealogical, 12; selective, 27, 62, 63
Amistad, 89
amulets, *khuya*, 187–88
anacondas, enchanted, 159, 160, 163, 164
ancestors, 10, 11, 13, 17, 26, 205, 214; as information source, 114–15; Maya, 80, 97; prehuman, 173, 174–75, 176; in speech/discourse, 115–16
ancestrality, 11, 12
ancestralization, Yucatec Maya, 87
Andean New Age, 10, 17, 30*n6*, 76, 197*n22*; Cuzco region ritual circuit, 186–92; energy predation, 193–95; and Maya ancestors, 97–98; prophecies, 192–93
Andean New Year, 16, 29, 221, 223*n6*, 250; Aymara identity and, 203–4
Andes, 4, 14, 16–17, 18, 22, 23, 25, 29; environmental structure of, 173–74; stones in, 20–21
animacy, animism, 3, 8, 14, 22
animals, 19, 211; *khuya*, 187–88
animation, of petrified beings, 210–11
animu, 173, 175, 193, 196*n3*
anthropogenic forests, in Amazonia, 156–57

anthropogenic soils, 6, 147, 148; Tapajós region, 165–66. *See also* dark earths/soils
antiquities, 3, 8, 19
Antonio Quijarro province, 233
Apinka (Sacaramentaro), 51
apu, 174, 176, 188, 190, 194, 215, 226*n37*
Apurinã, 15–16, 28, 147, 165, 166; anthropogenic forests, 156–57; and earthworks, 151–54
Apurinã km 124–BR 317, 151, 152, 156
Aqo Aqo, 184
Arapixuna, 158
archaeological sites, 11, 25, 233, 251; alteration and exploitation of, 106–7; Andean New Year, 202, 203; in Bolivia, 234, 235, *237f*; in Brazil, 148, 152–53; Maya exposure to, 88–89; Santarém and Tapajós region, 157–61; values of, 113–14
archaeologists, Maya alliances with, 89
archaeology: attitudes toward, 113–14, 162; collaborative, 165
artifacts, 13–14, 31*n10*, 113
Aserr (Iron Person), 48, 58, 67*n6*
Ashaninka (Campa), *49f*, 67*n17*; and Cerro de la Sal, 45, 46, 47, 48; and Juan Santos Atahuallpa, 51, 52; and Palmazú shrine, 42, 43, 57–58
Atlantis of Pampa Aullagas, 251, 252
Atulcha (W'atinchoo), *236f, 237f*, 238, 241, 242, 253
Ausangate region, 215, 224*n11*
awlanchis, 13
axes, stone, 14
ayllus, 205, 224*n18*, 224*n20*; stone ancestors of, 206, 208; at Yucay, 184–85, 186, 196*n2*
Aymara, 16, 31*n10*, 205, 222*n1*, 226*n33*, 233; Andean New Year, 202, 221; identity, 203–4
Aymara New Year, 250
Aymaya, 204, 224*n18*, 224*n20*; lithomorphs, 205–6, 211, *213f*
Aymaya aylla, *217f*
Ayque, *236f*, 242, 248, 249, 251
Aztecs, and ancient artifacts, 13–14

Bailly-Maitre, Luis, 44
Barbosa family, 163–64
Bastidas, Micaela, 250
battles, ritual, 206, 212
Bautista, Espíritu, 62

beer, Chácobo ritual drinking of, 127–28, 142*n4*
beer jars, *135f*
beer troughs, 136; Chácobo, 127–28, *128f*, 142*n7*
behavior: immoral, 56–57; inappropriate, 114
Belize, Caste War, 89
Benecito River, 130; Chácobo on, 134, 138; village on, 131, 132
beverages, fermented, 140
bilingual consultants, 5–6
biosphere reserves, UNESCO, 64–65
Black Christ, Lord of Tila, 117
Boca do Acre (Aldeia 45), 151, 152, 156
body art, 10, 30*n4*
body forms, 18
Bohórques, Pedro, 47
Bolivia, 14, 29, 31*n12*, 132, 133, 222*n1*, 232; Andean New Year, 202–3; Chácobo, 16, 28; cultural heritage, 234–35; decolonization, 202–3; Ministry of Culture, 249–50
Bombacacae, *128*, 136, *137f*, 142*n7*
Bonampak, 9–10, 101*n21*
bones, 19, 22, 23
boulders, ritual activities around, 21–22
boundaries: toads as symbols of, 180–81; Yucay, 174–75, 179, 185
Brazil, 11, 19, 28, 31*n12*, 132, 167*n3*; cultural heritage initiatives, 148, 165, 166–67; land tenure in, 162–63; protection of earthworks, 152–53
breezes, otherworldly, 18
British, alliances with, 89
buildings, as living: pre-Columbian, 105–6
bulls, stone, 211, *213f*
burial sites, 16, 30; in houses, 99*n3*, 142–43*n10*; Maya, 74, 99*n3*

caboclos, 28, 158
Cahuillaca, 180
calendar: Inca, 189–90; Tiwanaku, 203
Camapã, 151
Camicuã reserve, 151, 152
campesino communities, Uyuni Salt Flat, 232–33
Capac Raymi, 182
Capelo, Joaquín, 52
Cárdenas, Gaspar, 44
cargo system, 197*n17*; Yucay, 183–85
Carneiro de Cunha, Manuela, 12

258 INDEX

Carnival period, 212
Caste War, 78; alliances, 89, 90
Castilla, 211
cataclysms, 89, 92
Catholics, Catholicism, 29, 107; as pre-solar, 220–21, 222
católicos de costumbre, 107
Cave of the Devil (Aguaquiza), 241
caves, 116, 117, 251; as boundary, 174–75; with mummies, *236f*, 237–38, 241, 253; relocating mummies to, 244–45; as sacred sites, 245–48
celestial entities, 106, 120; Ch'ol and Tseltal, 117–18
cemeteries, 78, 163
ceques system, 179, 189–90, 191
ceramics, 3, 6, 14, 150; in Santarém, 157–58, *161f*; in swidden gardens, 156–57; Tapajós region, 158–59, 162
ceremonial sites, ceremonies, 28, 250; Cerro de la Sal, 47–48; Palmazú shrine, 42–43, 44
Cerro Colorado, 208; *ch'ullpa* and, 210–11
Cerro de la Sal, 15, 40, 41, *45f*, 58; economic and ritual importance of, 47–49; features of, 45–46, *46f*; protection of, 64–65
Cerro Rico, 234
Cerro Yompor Yompere, 64
Chácobo, 16, 28, 124, 132, 140, 141$n1$, 142$n5$, 142$n6$, 143$n13$, 143$n14$; funeral, 125–26, *127f*; house burials, 142–43$n10$; labor abuse, 138–39; migrations, 133–34; ritual drinking, 127–28; soul and thunder, 126–27; souls, 134–36
Chancalá, Río, Ch'ol in, 107
Chan Chi, Delio, 74, *75f*, *81f*
chapels, on Yucay Terraces, 183, 184
Charali, *237f*, 246, 248, 253
charkas, 204
Chayantaka territory, 206, 224–25$n22$
Cheka Cheka (*Chiqa Chiqa*), 245–46, *247f*, 249, 250
Cheporepen, 42
Chiapas, 27; masters of the earth, 118–19; ruins in, 22, 104, 105–6, 107; stones and incense burners in, 21–22
Chichen Itza' (Chi'ch'e'en Itza'), 77, 80, 89, 97, 98
Chichubamba, 178
ch'iibal, 84
Chilaco, *236f*, 242

Ch'ilankabo'ob, 88, 89
children, protection rituals for, 94, 100$n18$
Chiltaico, 251
Chinkultik, 108
Chiquini, 242
Chiquitanía, 234
Ch'ol, 15, 27, 104, 110, 116, 117, 118, 119; on Lacandon Maya, 111–12; from La Cascada, 107–8, 120; oral traditions, 113–14
Cholan, 10
Christ, solarized, 185, 186
Christianity, 26, 83, 187, 197$n16$, 207, 226–27$n46$, 244; in Chácobo society, 134–36; as temporal rupture, 218–21; in Tseltal society, 107, 110–11, 117
Chthonian entities/world: Chiapas, 110, 117; monument construction, 15, 112. *See also* underworld
chullpares/chullpas (mummies), 245; in Bolivia, 235; treatment of, 246–48
ch'ullpas, 30, 204, 223$n9$, 224$n12$, 254; as ancient humanity, 243–44; *ch'ullpasqa* disease, 16, 22; interaction with, 16–17; lithomorphoses, 205–6; nocturnal activities of, 210–11; and Pentecostals, 218–21; as sacred places, 245–48; social memory and, 242–43; tourism and, 236–38, 249, 251, 252–53; and underworld, 209–10; and Uyuni Salt Flat, 233, *237f*
Churacari, 246
churches, 15, 22, 23, 87, 110, 117; as stone structures, 112–13
clay figures, in *múul*, 86
clothing, and Yucay toponyms, 181
Coba, 15, 74, *75f*, 80
Cobra Grande, 163
coca leaves, as offerings, 43, 47, 213
Cokämkiere, 14, *236f*
Colchani, 238, 241, 244
collective identities, 27, 28
Collective Indigenous Marriages, 250
collective memory, 116
collective self, 25
colonialism, 26, 151; Perené Colony, 48–49
CONAP. *See* Confederación de Nacionalidades Amazónicas del Perú
condenados, 173
Confederación de Nacionalidades Amazónicas del Perú (CONAP), 63

Congreso de Comunidades Nativas Amuesha, 55
Conibo, 42, 49
Consejo Andino de Naciones Originarias, 252
Convention for the Safeguarding of the Intangible Cultural Heritage, 148
Convention on the Protection and Promotion of the Diversity of Cultural Expressions (UNESCO), 148–49
Coqueza, 236f, 241
cornesha', 56
corrals, 19; jaguar, 27, 112
cosmology, cosmogony, 16, 226n33; Chácobo, 138–39; Maya, 77, 82–83, 117–18; previous humanities in, 109–10; ruptures and restructuring, 110–11; Yanesha, 41–42
creation(s), 14; ruptures in, 110–11; Yanesha, 41–42
crosses, at Yucay, 183–85
Cruz Calvario, 184, 185
Cruzmoqo, 184
cultural heritage, 4, 9, 25, 26, 147; Bolivia, 234–35; Brazil, 148, 151, 165; Indigenous, 39–40, 166; land claims and, 11, 166–67; Maya programs, 92–93, 98–99
Cuniraya Huiracocha, 179–80
Curuai Lake, 158, 159f, 160
Cuzco, 179; New Agers in, 187–90

Dakar Rally, 250
Daniel Campos, 233
dark earths/soils, 6, 21, 28, 147, 148, 158, 163; fertility of, 19, 31n8. *See also* anthropogenic soils
dead, the, 87, 138; souls of, 85–86, 101n21
death, 116; time and space and, 124–25, 129–30
decolonization, 250; through ritual practice, 202–3
defilement, 57, 61; of landmarks, 55–60, 62
deities, 58, 93; Yanesha, 41–43, 47, 56–57, 62–63
de la Torre, José M., 44
del Monte, Juan, 59
depatrimonialization, 39
depopulation, Panoan speakers, 133
desoulment, of objects and places, 27, 40
despacho, 193–94; *Runa* and, 195–96
devils, 243, 244
diseases, 18, 22
disremembering, 15, 63

ditched enclosures, 28. *See also* geometric earthworks
divine power, 59
divine revelations, 56
DNA tests, 8
drinking feasts, Chácobo ritual, 127–28
drums, 143n17, 182; Chácobo shaman's, 135, 136
dualism: Inca terraces, 181–82; of memory, 185–86; in Yucay toponyms, 173–74, 177–79, 183–84
dumbness, of *saqra*, 209, 214–15
Durán, Hortensia (Mama Tohë), 133, 134
dwellings, 24, 140

earthquakes, Palmazú shrine and, 58
earthworks. *See* geometric earthworks
Earthworks of Acre, 151
economics, 235; of vestiges, 18–19; of Cerro de la Sal, 47–49
effigies, 23, 59
elders, Maya, 80
enchanted beings: land tenure and, 163–64; in lowland South America, 159–60
enchanted cities, 160
energy, 19, 20, 23, 29; New Age, 193–96, 195f
Enlightenment, patrimonialization and, 60
ensoulment, 8, 76
environment, 11; Andes vertical structure, 173–74
Españarri, 192
Espíritu Soto, Juan José, 62
Estanco de la Sal, 49
ethnogenesis, 26, 134
evangelization, 208. *See also* Pentacostals
evil creatures: *machu* as, 175–76; in *puna*, 173–74
executions, for witchcraft, 131, 138–39
expropriation, of Indigenous past, 26
extractivism, 5, 151

Fabriq'Am, 39
failure/defilement, 40; in Yanesha rituals, 55–57
fallow fields, appropriation of, 13
families, 114, 133; and enchanted beings, 163–64
Federación de Comunidades Nativas Yanesha (FECONAYA), 55, 63–64
feeding: guardian spirits, 82, 87; *khuyiris*, 220; masters of the earth, 119; *saqra*, 219; stones, 218

fertility rites, Andean, 181
festivities, at Charali, 246, 248
field trips, to Maya archaeological sites, 88
figurines: clay, 11, 14; lithic, 21
fire, divine, 43
floods, 111, 243
forced labor, 48–49, 208
forests, anthropogenic, 156–57
France, 61, 241
Francisco, San, 246
Francisco Sarabia *ejido*, 106
French Guiana, 10
Frikel, Protásio, 19
frontier, lithomorph as marker of, 206
fruit trees, anthropogenic forests, 156
FUNAI (Indigenous National Foundation), 149, 161
funerals, Chácobo, 125–26, 142$n4$
funerary urns, 124, 136

García, Alan, 63
García Linera, Álvaro, 248
gardens, abandoned, 140
gender, in Yucay toponyms, 178–79, 180, 181, 183
generification, 87
geoglyphs. *See* geometric earthworks
geologic formations, 29; lithomorphoses of, 205–6
geometric earthworks, 6, 11, 16, 147–48, 150, 157; Apurinã on, 151–53; palms on, 154–55; sacredness of, 153–54
German Agency for Cooperation, 241
ghosts, Chácobo, 136
ghost traps, beer troughs as, 136
gods. *See* deities
graves: as houses, 87; Maya, 78, 99$n3$
Great Britain: and Belize, 89; Perené Colony, 48–49
grief, grieving, Chácobo, 125–26
Guachapuquio, 181
Guajará-Mirim, 132
Guaporé/Mamoré River, ancestral Chácobo on, 132
guardian saints, 117
guardian spirits, 24; characteristics of, 83–85; in *múul* mound, 80–82, 97, 100$n11$. *See also nukuch máako'ob/báalamo'ob; yuuntsilo'ob*
Guatemala, 7, 25, 30$n3$, 31$n12$

Hacienda Palmazú, 44
Hanke, Wanda, 129
Hatun Taq Wiraqocha, 188
heritage programs, 77; Maya region, 92–93
Herodotus, 60
hidden beings, under *múul*, 90
historicity, 4, 25, 60, 77; Yanesha, 61–62
history, 6, 221; Andean, 192–93; continuity of, 166; ruptures in, 208–9
horticultural society, Santarém, 158
hotel industry, Yucatán, 75
house-founding ritual, Ch'ol, 119
houses/homes, 13, 76, 87; burials in, 99$n3$, 142–43$n10$; as living, 81–82
Huacarpay, Lake, 189
huacas, 42
Huara, 134, 143$n14$
Huarochiri, 179, 180
Huascar Inca, 189
Huatari of Alcaya, 252
Huayna Capac temple, 191
Huiracocha, 180
Humani Mountain, 251
human remains, 9; Chácobo treatment of, 138, 144$n18$; dangers of exposure to, 16–17
humans, humanities, 114; of past eras, 89–91, 92; previous, 109–10; in *rwiinas*-type *múul*, 90–91, 96
Hyperreal Indian, 6

Iauaretê waterfall, 149
Ichapekene Piesta de Moxos, 234
illapa, 176
illa stone, 215, 225$n31$, 225$n32$
illnesses: caused by *ch'ullpa*, 243, 244; caused by *suq'a*, 175–76
Inca Empire, 227$n48$; stone terraces, 16, 172
Incahuasi Island, 241, 250, 251, 253
incense burners, Lacandon use of, 21–22
Indians of the past, in Amazonia, 159–60, 162, 166
Indigenism, 203
Indigenous Territory Cobra Grande, 163–64
initiation journey, Cuzco region, 187–90
Inka Road, 234
Inkarri, 192, 198$n30$
Inka Waskar Chukiwanka, 203
inqa stones, 215

Instituto do Patrimônio Histórico e Artístico Nacional (IPHAN), 31*n12*, 149, 161
interethnic wars, and *ch'ullpa*, 205
Internet, 251–52
Inti Raimi, Inti Raymi, 65, 250
IPHAN. *See* Instituto do Patrimônio Histórico e Artístico Nacional
ironworks, at Cerro de la Sal, 48, *49f*
irrigation systems: Inca terrace, 174; Yucay, 179, 181
Italian Agency for Cooperation, 241
Ivon (river), 135
Izaguirre, Bernardino, 44–45, 59
Itza Maya, 10
Iván I., 252

jade, 21
jaguars, monuments as corrals for, 27, 112
Jajal Dyos ("True God"), 83
Jamp'atu, *212f*
Javari basin, 139
Jesus Christ, 192; in Tseltal cosmology, 110–11
Jews, in Tseltal cosmology, 110–11
Jirira, *236f*, 246
Juan Bautista, San, 246, *247f*, 253
Juan Santos Atahuallpa, 15; remains of, 58–59; resistance by, 49–51; tomb of, 40, 41, 51–52, 62
Jukumani, 206

Kalawaya Culture, 234
Kañibamba, 184
kapi vana wai, 139
Karipuna, 132, 133, 143*n12*
Kawsay Wasi museum. *See* Museum of Kawsay Wasy
Kawsay Wasy, 251, 253
Kharacha, 204, 224*n18*, 224–25*n22*; lithomorphs, 205–6, 208
Khonkho Wankane, 215
khuya, at Cuzco cathedral, 187–89
khuyiris stones, 212–13, 220, 225*n32*
Ki'ichklem Yuum ("Wondrous Lord"), 83, 88
Ki'ichpam maama K'an Le'oox, at Tampak', 93–94, 95, 100*n18*
kimsa yuqalla, 206, *207f*, 208, 222
Kiswarkancha, 179
Kiswarpata, 179
Kob Ha' (Coba), 80

Krahô rituals, 14
kusiwa designs, 149

lab (soul), 84
labor, 82, 83; exploitation of, 75, 138–39; Inca terraces, 176–77; Perené Colony, 48–49
Lacandon Maya, 10, 21, 101*n21*, 104, 120; and Ch'ol, 111–12; on pre-Columbian buildings, 105–6
La Cascada (*Welib'ja'*), 107–8, *109f*, 110, 111, 113, 114, 117, 118, 120, 121
La Combe, Ernesto, 51
Ladislao Cabrera, 233
land claims, 10, 11; Yanesha, 54–55
landmarks: defilement and abandonment of, 55–60, 62; Peruvian patrimony, 64–65
land of the dead, Xabaya as, 131–32
land rights, 9, 19; Amazonian, 163, 165; Chiapas, 107–8; cultural heritage and, 166–67; Yanesha, 54–55
landscapes, 4, 6, 28, 214; life and agency of, 20–21; as personified, 108–9; Yucay, 177–79
land tenure, 13; enchanted beings and, 163–64; Tapajós region, 162–63, 165–66
La Paz, 235
Laqaya, 238, 253
Las Galaxias, 241
Last Supper, The, in Tseltal households, 117
Lauca River, 243
La Virgen de la Natividad la Antigua, 187
Laymi, 206, 224*n19*, 224*n20*
legitimization, political and religious, 75–76
life, of stones, 20–22
lightning, 142*n5*, 180; as messages, 120–21
liminality, 29; of skin, 180–81; of vestiges, 24; at Yucay, 175, 176, 185; *yúuntsilo'ob*, 83
Linares, Olga, 19, 30–31*n7*
lithomorphoses, lithomorphs, 20, 23, 214, 216, 222, 224*n17*, 224*n19*; *ch'ullpa* and, 205–6; named, 206–8; place names and, 208–9
llamas, 19, 233; stone, 211, 212
Llaullimoqo, 184
Lopez, Juan, 114
López Austin, Alfredo, 89
lucuma (*Lucuma obovate*) at Yucay, 179–80
lunar cycle, and *ch'ullpa* activities, 210–11, 222

262 INDEX

Macehual Maya, 78
machu ancestors, 22, 174; illness caused by, 175–76; in Yucay tombs, 177, 180, 181, 186
Machu Picchu, 3; New Agers at, 191–92
Madeira River, 150
Makushi, 6
Maloca, 160, *161f*
Mamanchumpi, 181
Mamaq, 181
Manchineri (Manxineru), 15–16, 28, 147, 165, 166; anthropogenic forests, 156–57; earthworks, 151, 154–55
Manhé, 151
Mantillachayoq, 181
Mapinkuari, 153
Marajó, 3
Maro, 127; funeral of, 125–26
Maro (*taita*), 127, 136
Martorell, José, 133
Marubo, 139
masters of the earth, 111, 122*n6*; building with stones, 112–13; concepts of, 117–19
masters of the place, 159–60, 166
mastery, territorial, 159–60
materiality, 5, 77; of lithic landscape, 215–16; of spirit world, 155–56
Matis, 6, 12, 140
Mato Grosso, petroglyphs, 10
Matsigenka, and Cerro de la Sal, 45
Maudslay, Alfred, 105
Maudslay, Anne, 105
maxobo, 132–33, 134
Maya, 20, 121*n4*; ancestors, 97–98; and archaeological sites, 25, 88–89; cosmology, 82–83; heritage programs, 77, 92–93, 98–99; ruins, 74–76; sacred sites, 7, 30*n3*; salient spaces, 27–28; souls of the dead, 85–86
Mediocalzón, 177–78
memory, 27, 60, 105, 109; dual, 185–86; of geometric earthworks, 152, 157; regimes of, 13, 75; Yanesha historical, 61–62
Merandolino, 163–64, 166
mercantilism, 40
Mesa de Diálogo Permanente entre el Estado y los Pueblos Indígenas Amazónicos, 63–64, 67*n21*
Mesapatachico, 178
Mesapatagrande, 178

Mesoamerica, 3, 4, 23, 25; legitimization in, 75–76; stones in, 20–21
"meteorites," 21–22
metonyms, stones and mountains, 215, 216
Metraro (La Purísima Concepción de Metraro), 49–50, 52
Mexico, 31*n12*; archaeological sites, 9–10, 25, 106–7
migrations, Chácobo, 133–34
mines, mining, 208, 225*n23*
Ministry of Culture (Bolivia), 249–50
Miraflores, and Palmazú shrine, 53–54
Misionero, 184
missionaries, missions, 12, 130, 218; and Chácobo, 134–36; Protestant, 132, 133, 143*n16*; and Yucay crosses, 183, 185
mitimaes, terrace construction, 176–77
Mixtec, and ancient artifacts, 13–14
monoliths, at Khonkho Wankane, 215
Montezuma, avatars of, 89–90
monuments, 234; construction of, 15, 23, 27–28
moon, and *ch'ullpa* activities, 210–11, 222
Morales Ayma, Evo, 16, 29, 143*n16*, 202, 209, 210, 221, 249, 250
mortuary practices, Chácobo, 136, 138
mounds, 6, 15, 18; at Aguacatenango, 108; Yucatec Maya, *79f*, 80. *See also múul*
mountain gods. *See apu*
mountains, 22, 31*n11*, 101*n20*
mourning rituals, Chácobo, 125–26
muknal (burial place), 78, *79f*
multiculturalism, 11, 149
mummies, 22, 30; in Bolivia, 235, *236f*; as presolar beings, 16, 175; relocated, 244–45; Uyuni Salt Flat caves, *236f*, 236–37, 241, 253; at Yucay, 172–73
Museum of the Chullpas or Ancestral Mummies (Aguaquiza), 251
Museum of *Kawsay Wasy*, 241, 251, 253
Museu Paulista, 14
múul (mound), 75, 78, 79, *80f*, 83, 86, 90, 99–100*n7*, 101*n20*; builders and age of, 87–88; cultural heritage programs, 98–99; guardian spirits in, 80–82; roles of, 96–97; temporalization, 91–92; *yuuntsilo'ob* in, 84, 85
mythology: revisions of, 62–63; Yanesha, 41, 45–46, 51

NAGPRA. *See* Native American Graves Protection and Repatriation Act
Nahá, 105
Ñakaq, 174
National Institute of Culture (Peru), 176
nationalism, 26, 31*n12*, 203, 234
Native American Graves Protection and Repatriation Act (NAGPRA), 4
Navarro, Manuel, 45
Negro, Rio, 149
neo-Inca ceremonies, at Pisac, 186
neo-indianism, 250
neopatrimony, 10
neo-Protestant movements, 107
neo-shamans, 186, 194
New Age movement. *See* Andean New Age
Nimuendajú, Curt, 158
Ninabamba, 179
nocturnal activities, 210–11
nonhuman entities, 104, 115; in Chiapas, 114, 117; earthworks and, 155–56; lightning and, 120–21; ritual interaction with, 110, 119–20
Nor-Lípez province, 233, 238
Northern Potosí, 29, 221, 225*n32*; presolar ancestors, 204–5
Núcleo (*Núcleo Indigenal Ñuflo de Chávez*), 130, 131, 133, 141, 143*n14*
Núcleo indígena, 133
nukuch máako'ob/báalamo'ob, 80, 81, 84, 100*n15*
Nuñez del Prado, Juan, 188

obsidian, 21
OEFA. *See* Organismo de Evaluación y Fiscalización Ambiental
offerings, 43, 47, 82, 85, 119, 188, 245; at Charali, 246, 248; to mountain gods, 174, 176; New Age, 193–94; *Runa*, 195–96; at Tampak', 94, 95*f*
Office of Protected Natural Areas (Peru), 64
Ollantaytambo, 191, 196*n2*
Old World values, sacred places as, 7–8
Oracle of Delphi, 60
oral tradition, 153; Chácobo, 131, 132; Chiapas, 113–14; Manchineri, 154–55; nonhuman beings and, 119–20; on previous humanities, 109–10; Yanesha, 43, 52
Organismo de Evaluación y Fiscalización Ambiental (OEFA), 64
Oropesa, Marquis of, 174

Ortiz, Maro, 134
Ortiz, Rabi, 138
Oruro, 233, 234, 235
Otomi, 19
Oxapampa-Ashaninka-Yanesha Biosphere Reserve, 65–66

Pacaguara, 132, 133
pacha, 192–93, 216
Pachacuti Yamqi, Joan de Santa Cruz, 188, 189
pachakutí, 16, 193, 216, 221, 243
Pachetea River, 43
Paë, Capta, 133, 134
Paë Chavez (Paëcito), 131, 139
Paë Davalos, 131, 138
Paicoc Sisal, Maria, 174, 178
Pakacalle, 178
Palenque, 9–10, 101*n21*, 107, 113
Palmazú shrine, 15, 40, *42f*, *65f*; history of, 41–45; neglect and defilement of, 54–55, 57–58; origin myth of, 62–63; protection of, 65–66; restoration of, 53–54
palms, 6, 20, 140, 156; and earthworks, 154–55
Pampa Aullagas, as National Capital of Atlantis, 251, 252
Pan-Amerindian status, 11
Panoan speakers, 124, 141*n11*; afterlives, 139–40; in Amazonia, 132–33
Papuri River, 149
paqu, 176
Pará, 147, 148, 149
Parauá, 162
Pareni (Cerro de la Sal), 46
Paresi, 10
Parque Noel Kempff Mercado, 234
Pasión, 184
past, 92; ancestral, 115–16; relationships with, 76–77
pathology. *See* illnesses
patrimonialization, 4, 27, 28, 30, 39; Bolivia, 234–35; as Western concept, 60–61; Yanesha, 40–41
patrimony, 8, 10, 15, 31*n12*; Peruvian national, 64–65
patrimony of humanity, 60
Paucartambo River, 47, 48
Paumari, 139
Pazos Varela, J. F., 51

Pentecostals, Pentecostalism, 29, 204, 218, 222, 226–27n46; temporality of, 220–21
Perené Colony, 48–49, 52
Perené River, 47, 48–49
Peru, 16, 41, 52, 176; Cerro de la Sal and, 48–49; patrimony, 15, 31n12, 39; protected reserves in, 64–65. *See also* Pisac; Yanesha; Yukay
Peruvian Corporation Ltd., Perené River, 48–49
petrifications, 23, 31n11, 206, 208, 209, 216, 225n25, 227n48
petroglyphs, 10, 31n11
Phaqcha, 179
Phaqchayoq, 179
Pichis Trail, 52
Pilcobamba, 179
pilgrimages, pilgrims, 13, 194; Cerro de la Sal, 47, 48–49; to Juan Santos' tomb, 51–52, 62; Palmazú shrine, 42, 43
Pisac, 29; New Age followers at, 186–87, 189, 190–91, 192, 194, *195f*
pishtaku, 174, 196n5
Pitoqocha, 181
pixan (soul), 21, 86, 87
place names, history and, 208–9. *See also* toponyms
places, 27, 156; spiritually powerful, 151–52
plants, 6, 19, 20. *See also by type*
Plaza de Armas (Cuzco), 187
politics: Bolivian, 202–3, 249–50; Tapajós area, 161; Yanesha, 53
Porotoqolqa, 179
Posnansky, Arthur, 203
Posapno, 46. *See also* Cerro de la Sal
Posopno (Río de la Sal), 46
possums, as divine helpers, 15
potatoes, wild, 19
Potosí, 208, 234, 235
Potosí department, 233
pottery. *See* ceramics
power, 21, 215; seeking, 212–14
predation: New Age, 194–95; by *saqra*, 217–18
predecessors, 16, 80, 205
presolar beings: agency of, 214, 219, 221; geological formations and, 221–22
presolar era, 204, 209; Catholics in, 220–21; *ch'ullpa*, 204–5, 242–43; time in, 210–14
priest-leaders, Yanesha, 42–43

Programa Nacional de Pesquisas Arqueológicas da Bacia Amazônica (PRONAPABA), 150
prophecies: Maya, 89, 91; New Age, 192–93
proselytism, impacts of, 7–8
Prost, Gilbert (Papa Jicho), 133, 143n16
Prost, Marian, 133
protection: of geometric earthworks, 152–53; of Tampak', 93–94, 95–96
Protestants, missionaries, 132, 133, 143n16. *See also* Pentecostals
public heritage, 148
Pujllay, 234
puma heads, 179, 182
puna, 177; evil creatures in, 173–74
Punamarca, 179
Puraka, 206
purumpacha, 243, 244
Purus River region, 15–16, 163; geometric earthworks, 147–48, 150
P'uus, 89, 91
pyramids, 22, 23

q'ala warmi, 206, *207f*
Qallinch'aku, 212
Q'enqo, 189
Qhapaq Ñan, 234
Qhuchini, 206, 224–25n22
Qolqanpata, 179
Quechua, 13, 16, 29, 63; community rituals, 22–23
quechua, 173, 174, 177
Quechua speakers/language, 16–17, 216; in Bolivia, 204, 223n8, 233
Queñroĭ (Salt Person), 40, 47
Quillazú mission, Yanesha lands, 54–55
quinoa cultivation, 233
Qurikancha (Quricancha), 179, 189
Quriwayrachina, 174, 178
Quyllur Rit'i, 194

rainbows, Andean symbolism of, 181–82
ramon (*Brosimum alicastrum*), 20, 31n9
Ranzi, Alceu, 150
rap songs, Maya, 10
Rascar Capac, 173
Redfield, Robert, 98
reducciones, 107, 133; *ayllu* and, 184, 186, 196n2
relationships, with past, 76–77

remembrance, 12, 60, 119–20; of *saqra*, 217–18
repatriation, Museu Paulista, 14
resistance, 40; by Juan Santos Atahuallpa, 49–50
responsibilities, political and religious, 184–85
restructuring, in cosmology, 110–11
revolt/rebellion, Juan Santos Atahuallpa's, 49–50
Revolución India, La (Reynaga), 250
Riberalta, 132, 141*n1*
ribeirinhos, 158
ritual discourse, 81, 90
Ritual Museum (Incahuasi), 251
ritual paths, on Yucay terraces, 184
rituals, 15, 76, 100*n18*, 106, 142*n6*, 173, 189, 246, 251; breaching taboos in, 57–58; at Cerro de la Sal, 27, 47–48; *ch'ullpa*, 218–20; decolonization through, 202–3; failure in, 55–56; with nonhuman entities, 110, 119–20; Quechua community, 22–23; for *saqra*, 217–18; speeches, 85, 115–16; at Tampak', 94–95; *yuyay*, 213–14
ritual spaces, 150
ritual specialists, 10, 14, 85, 250; Yanesha, 47–48, 55–56
Roca family, 133
Ror. *See* Yompor Ror
Ross, Alexander, 52
ruins, 18, 111, 112; builders and age of, 87–88; and humans of the past, 89–90; Lacandon interpretations of, 10, 105–6; Maya, 74–76; origins of, 12–13, 22; as vestiges, 6–7. *See also múul*
runa, 188, 190, 198*n26*, 205; and *despacho*, 193, 194, 195–96
ruptures, 9, 75; in cosmology, 110–11; cultural heritage programs as, 98–99; in Maya history, 92, 97; presolar and solar eras, 204, 243; temporal, 24, 218–21; topography of, 208–9
rwiinas-type *múul*, 88, 96; ancient humans and, 89–91; cultural heritage programs, 98–99

sacred sites, 4, 11, 30*n3*, 106, 148; Amazonia, 149, 164; archaeological sites as, 245–48; as Old World value, 7–8
Sacred Valley, 16, 196*n2*; ecological levels, 173–75; Yucay in, 172–73

sacrifices, at Cheka Cheka, 246
Said, Edward, 5
Saint John the Baptist Day, giant anaconda dance, 164
Saitoco, 242, 246, 249
Sala, Gabriel, 48
Salar de Uyuni region, 17. *See also* Uyuni Salt Flat
salient places/spaces, 8, 104
Salinas (Bolivia), *237f*
Salinas family, 138
salt, 31*n11*, 47, 233
salt mines, mining, on Cerro de la Sal, 47, 58
Samaipata, 234
Samaúma, 158
Sammells, Clare A., 203
sanctuaries, *ceque* system, 179
San Juan necropolis, 241
Santarém: archaeological sites, 160–61; riverside villages in, 157–58
Santiago, 246; and Palmazú shrine, 53–54
Santos Ortiz. *See* Tsachopeñ
Saqraloma, 244
saqra, 209, 210, 216, 254*n6*; Pentecostals and, 219–21; as predators, 217–18; silence of, 214–15
Saqsabamba, 177
Saqsamuqu, 177
Saqsapata, 177
Saqsayhuaman, 189
scenography, mummies in, 22
Scotland, patrimony, 61
Selva Central region, 39
sensory experiences, 16, 18
Seven Wonders of the Ancient World, 60
shamans, shamanism, 43, 155, 176, 187; Chácobo, 127–28, 135
shape-shifting, 18
Shellmem, 51
shono, *137f*, 140; and *yoshini*, 136, 142*n7*
shrines, Palmazú, *42f–45*
Sidro, Don, 86
silence, 209; *saqra*, 214–15
SIL. *See* Summer Institute of Linguistics
Sinclair, Arthur, 52
Sisa, Bartolina, 250
Sivigngani, *237f*, 242, 248, 253
skeletal remains, 20, 22
skin, as boundary, 175, 180–81
sky world, in Yanesha cosmology, 41–42

snakes, 112
social memory, 104, 204; *ch'ullpa*, 242–43; geological formations and, 208–9
social organization, 110; Panoan speakers, 132–33
Sociedad Arqueologica de Bolivia, 203
soils. *See* dark earths/soils
solar era, 204, 243
"solar time," 29
Soqospukyu (San Miguel de Socospucyu), 181, 182
souls, 26; of buildings, 76; Chácobo, 134–36, 140–41; of dead, 85–86, 101*n21*, 116, 125; loss of, 59–60; and thunder, 126–27; in *Xabaya*, 128–29, 130–31, 138, 139. *See also lab*; *pixan*
sounds, soundscapes, 18, 82, 210; lithomorphs, 214–15
space(s), 5, 104, 108, 117; death and, 124–25; salient, 28, 104; as vertical category, 174, 176; *Xabaya* as, 130–32
spatial anchoring, 77
speeches, ritual, 85, 115–16
spirits, 15, 17, 28, 83–88, 140, 142*n9*, 143*n17*, 153, 163, 166; and earthworks, 153, 155–56; *yoshini*, 127–28. *See also nukuch máako'ob/báalamo'ob*; *yuuntsilo'ob*
spiritual guides (*guías espirituales*), 10
springs, *uq'a pukyu* in, 175
stelae, 19; petrified beings in, 15, 23, 96
stereotypes, Indigenized, 5–6
Stobart, Henry, 210, 214–15
stone alignments, 87; and Yucatec Maya, 77–78
stone gods: Palmazú shrine, *42f*, 45, 53–54, 57–58; Yanesha, 42–43
stones, 3, 19, 23, 88; historical ruptures and, 208–9; life and agency of, 20–22; lithomorphs, 205–6; power and agency of, 212–13, *213f*, 215, 217–18, 225*n30*, 225*n31*; as presolar beings, 211–12, 221–22; use in structures, 112–13
Sucre, 234, 235
Sucristu, 192
sumak kawsay, 11–12
Summer Institute of Linguistics (SIL), 132, 133, 143*n16*
sun, 223*n3*; and prehuman ancestors, 174–75, 243
Sunchupata, 179

sun gods, Yanesha, 42–43
Sun, Temple of (Quricancha), 179, 185, 189
supay, 244
superhuman power, 212
supernatural beings, 23; in Yanesha ritual, 56–57
suq'a, 181, 183; illnesses caused by, 175–76
suq'a machu, 181, 183, 194
Surumi, 208, 225*n24*
swamps, at Yucay, 181–82
swidden gardens, 6, 20; memories of, 156–57

Tahua, 246, 247
taia, giant, 153
Tamayo, Agusto, 44
Tampak', 74, 79, *94f*, 99, 100*n18*; community rituals at, 94–95; protection of, 93–94, 95–96
Tapajós region, 148, 149; dark earths and pottery, 158–59; land tenure in, 165–66; political dynamics of, 161–63
Tapaya (Alto Ivon), 129, 135–36
Tarabuco, 234
Tarma, Juan Santo's remains in, 52, 58–59
Tawantinsuyu, 189, 192; terraces in, 176–77
Taytacha Temblores (Lord of the Earthquakes), 187, 198*n24*
Teko, 10
Temple of the Condor (Machu Picchu), 192
Temple of Wiraqocha, 192
temples, 22, 43, 48, 62. *See also by name*
temporality, 77; religion and, 220–21
Tenam Puente, 108, 121; ceremonies in, 106, 120
Tequinho, *155f*
terraces, 16, 23; Inca construction of, 176–77; at Yucay, 172, 177–79, 181–82, 183–84
Terra Indígena, 149
Terra Indígena Cobra Grande, 163–64
terra preta do Indio, 19, 147. *See also* dark earths/soils
thunder, 142*n5*; and deceased's soul, 126–27
Tich'Muul pyramid, 79
tiempo de la religion, 219
Tikal, 3, 10
Tila, 107–8, 110, 114
Tila, Lord of, 117
time, 185, 223*n2*; ancestral, 115–16; death and, 124–25, 129–30; and *múul* mound, 91–92;

presolar, 210–14; rupture of, 218–21; as vertical category, 174, 176
Time of the Aymara (*Aymara timpu*), 205
Time of the Inca (*Inkas timpu*), 205
Titicaca, Lake, 235
Tiwanaku, 16, 202, 223*n*3, 234; political use of, 203, 250
toad, land (*Bufo spinulosus*), 180
toads: as boundary symbols, 180–81; giant stone, 211, *212f*
Tojolabal, 104, 106
tombs, 8, 15; boulders as, 21–22; *machu* in, 175, 180, 181, 186; Juan Santos Atahuallpa, 40, 41, 51–52, 59, 62; prehuman, 183, 185; Yucay, 172–73, 177
Toniná, ceremonies on, 106, 121
toponyms, Yucay landscape, 177–80, *178f*, 181–82
Toronó, 164
tourism, tourists, 3, 9, 29, 61, 66, 248, 250, 254*n*5; *ch'ullpas*, 251, 252–53; Maya region, 75, 113; at Pisac, 186–87; Uyuni Salt Flat, 232–33, 235–42, 249
transformation, manufacturing, 23
treasure, avoiding, 18
trees, at Yucay, 179–80. *See also by type*
Trio, 14
Tsachopeñ (Santos Ortiz), 43, 53, 62, 65, 66
Tseltal, 10, 15, 27, 84, 101*n*20, 104, 106, 107, 112, 115, 120; cosmological reconstruction, 110–11; and masters of the earth, 117–18, 122*n*6; oral traditions, 113–14
Tsotsil, 76, 104, 119; previous humanities, 109–10
Tulum, 15, 74, 89, 98
Tumiã Indigenous territory, 153
Tumi Chucua, 132, 143*n*11
Tunupa Mountain, 245, 251
Tupaj Amaru, 250
Tupaj Katarai, 250
Tupuna, 181
Turukuntur, 179
Tuxaua, João, 139

Uaupes River, 149
ukhupacha, 244
Uncía, 208
uncultivated zones, on Yucay terraces, 181
underworld, 216, 221; *ch'ullpa*, 209–10, 244; illnesses of, 22, 243; *múul* mound and, 82, 99–100*n*7; power and agency of, 213–14, 217, 222
UNESCO, 7, 151, 202, 234; biosphere reserves, 64–65; Convention on the Protection and Promotion of the Diversity of Cultural Expressions, 148–49
UN Declaration on the Rights of Indigenous Peoples, 149
United States, 4, 61
University of Cuzco, 187
Uray (Yucay), 183, 184
Uru-Chipaya, as descendants of *ch'ullpa*, 243, 249
Úuchben máako'ob (ancient people), in *rwiinas*-type *múul*, 90–91
Uyuni, 233, 235
Uyuni Salt Flat, 11, 22, 29, 232–33, 250, 252; heritage attractions, *239–40f*; mummies at, 236–38, 244–45; tourism, 235, 241–42

Valencia Espinoza, Abraham, 188
vestiges, 9, 13, 20, 74, 111; landscape of, 108–9; and legitimization, 75–76; as linkages, 24–25; ruins as, 6–7; Yucatec Maya and, 77–78
Viceministerio de Descolonización (Bolivia), 250; decolonization program, 202–3
villages, 113, 142–43*n*10; abandoned Amazonian, 124, 131, 139; abandoned Maya, 78, 83, 85, 86, 97; recently abandoned, 16, 28
Viracocha, Temple of, 179
Virgen de Natividad, and Aguacatenango, 110, 112
Virgen de la Natividad la Antigua, La. *See* La Virgen de la Natividad la Antigua
Virgin Mary, 15
Virgin of Surumi, 208
visions, on Yucay, 180
Vogt, Evon, 76

Waca Taquy Onccoy, 250
Wachaq, 178; swamp as, 181, 182
Wajãpi communities, 149
wak'a, 215, 216, 225*n*31, 250
wanka, 206
Wari', 126
wars, 212; interethnic, 206, 224*n*20
water sources, and rainbows, 181–82

Wayana, 10
Wayrapunk'u, 179, 191
weddings, at *chullpares*, 246, 248, 253
White Book of Ethnocide (Beghin), 131
White people, and Yanesha ritual sites, 57–60
Wichay (Yucay), 183, 184
Wilkabamba, 179
Willka, Zárate, 250
winds, 18; in *múul* mounds, 82; *yoshini* spirits as, 127, 136, 142n6; Yucatec spirits as, 92
Wiraqocha, 188
World Heritage Convention, 148
World Heritage Indigenous People's Forum, 148
World Heritage Sites, in Bolivia, 202, 234
worship houses (*puerahua*), Yanesha, 43, 48, 56, 62
wrestling, at Chácobo funerals, 126
Wispan Wakanqui, 179
witchcraft, executions for, 131, 138–39

Xaba, 129–30
Xabaya, xaba xobo, 28, 124, 141, 142n9; as land of the dead, 131–32; as physical place, 128–29, 130–32, 140; souls in, 127, 134–36, 138, 139
xla'kaaj, 78, 79f, 85, 97

Yachor Mamas, 40, 42, 43, 53, 54
Yaco River, 154
yanantin system, 191, 192, 193
Yanesha, 15, 23, 27, 39, 49, 66; and Cerro de la Sal, 45–48; gods, 41–43; historical memory, 61–62; landmark defilement and abandonment, 55–60; landmarks, 52–53, 64–65; land rights, 54–55; and Palmazú shrine, 41–45, 53–54; patrimonialization, 40–41; and Yompor Santo', 50–51
Yata River, 131, 134
Yato Queñfot (Posona'; Salt Man), 47, 58
yäxb'ä ch'eñ, 117
Yaxchilán, 101n21, 105, 120
Yine (Piro), 49
Yompor Ror, 41–42, 43, 46, 56, 62–63
Yompor Rret, 41
Yompor Santo' (Yanesha ancestor), 23, 48, 62
Yompor Yompere (Yompor Yompiri), 40, 42, 43, 53, 54, 58, 62–63, 64, 6*5f*
yoshini, 127–28, 134, 135, 136, 142n6
Yucatan Peninsula, 78; Maya ancestors in, 97–98
Yucatec Maya, 10, 15, 18, 21, 27, 74; ancient artifacts, 13–14; stone alignments, 77–78; *yuuntsilo'ob*, 84–85
Yucay, 16, 29, 172, 176, 196n2; caves as boundaries in, 174–75; crosses at, 183–85; *lucuma* trees at, 179–80; swamps at, 181–82; toads as boundary symbols, 180–81; toponyms, 177–80; vertical structure of, 173–74
Yungas (La Paz), 235
yuuntsilo'ob (spirit beings), 80, 94; characteristics of, 83–85, 86, 91t, 100n10; in *múul*, 81–82, 87, 90
yuyay, 213–14, 226n34

Zapatista Tseltal, 106
Zinacantán, 119
zombification, 15, 27, 40, 59–60, 98
zoomorphs, stone, 211–12. *See also* lithomorphoses

Contributors

CÉDRIC BECQUEY, UNAM/CEM

MARIE CHOSSON, INALCO/CESSMA

PABLO CRUZ, CONICET, Instituto Interdisciplinario Tilcara, FFyL-UBA

PHILIPPE ERIKSON, University Paris Nanterre, LESC/EREA

ANTOINETTE MOLINIÉ, Centre National de la Recherche Scientifique, LESC

FERNANDO SANTOS-GRANERO, Smithsonian Tropical Research Institute

EMILIE STOLL, Centre National de la Recherche Scientifique, Laboratoire Caribéen de Sciences Sociales LC2S

VALENTINA VAPNARSKY, Centre National de la Recherche Scientifique, LESC-EREA

PIRJO KRISTIINA VIRTANEN, University of Helsinki, EREA/LESC

LAURENCE CHARLIER ZEINEDDINE, University of Toulouse